Shojo Beat

Yona of the Dawn

27

Story & Art by

Mizuho Kusanagi

Yona of the Dawn
Volume 27

CONTENTS

Yona of the Dawn

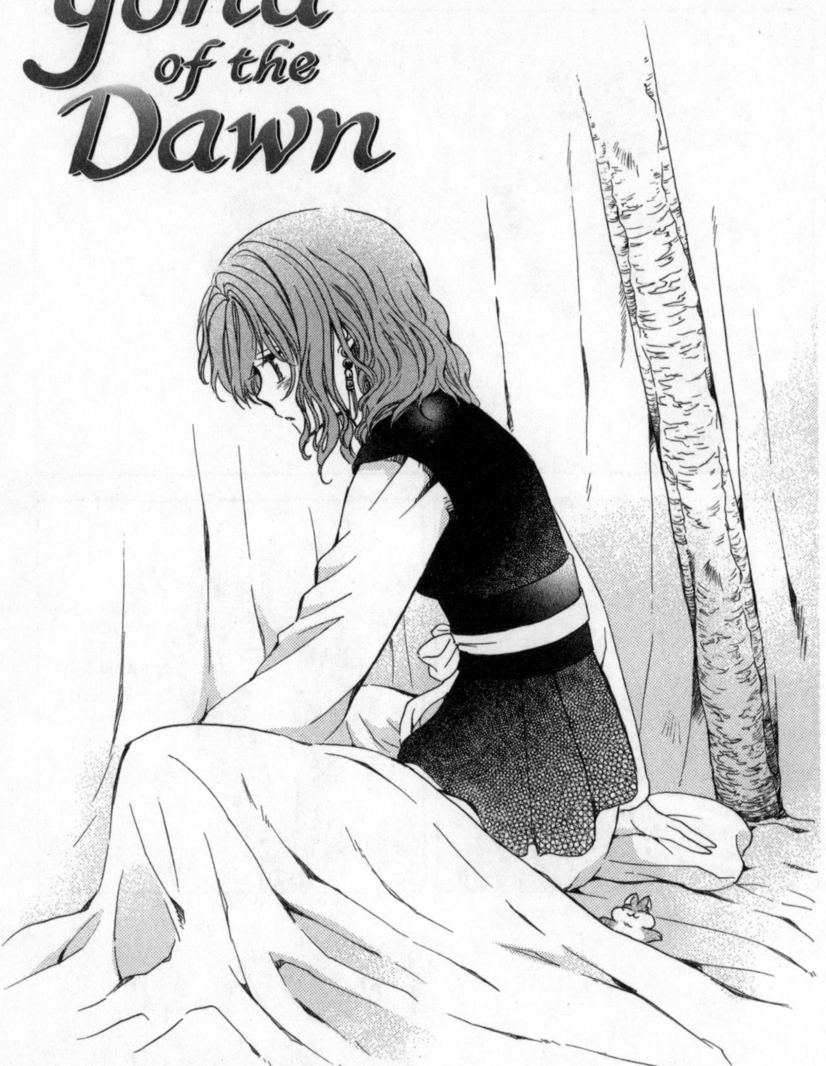

CHAPTER 153: A RARE SUNNY DAY

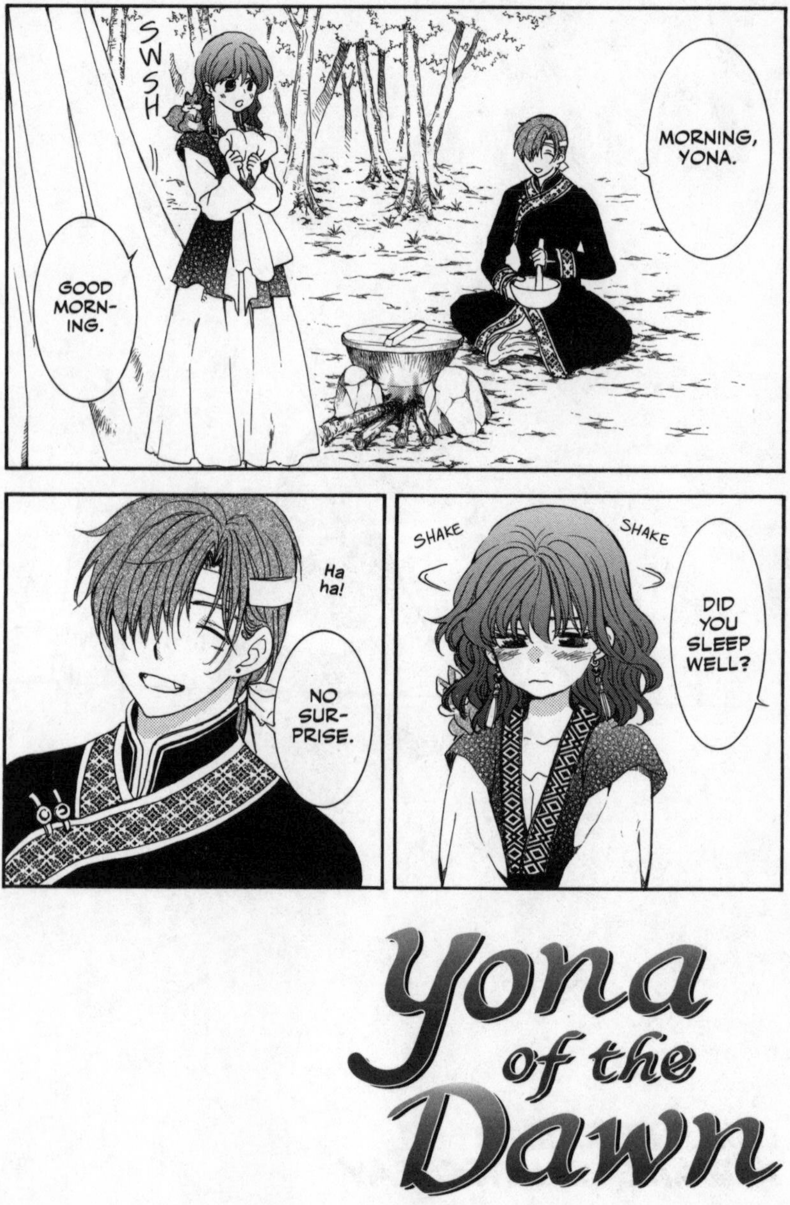
MORNING, YONA.
SWSH
GOOD MORN-ING.
SHAKE
SHAKE
DID YOU SLEEP WELL?
Ha ha!
NO SUR-PRISE.

Yona of the Dawn

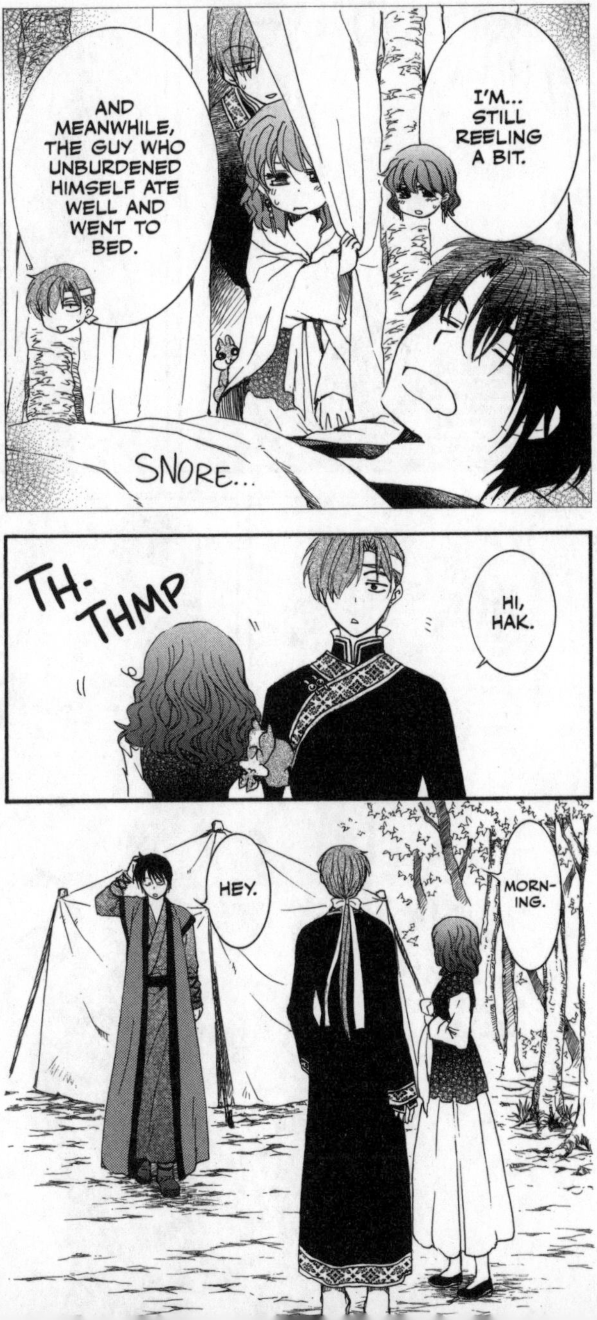
I'M... STILL REELING A BIT.
AND MEANWHILE, THE GUY WHO UNBURDENED HIMSELF ATE WELL AND WENT TO BED.
SNORE...
HI, HAK.
TH-THMP
MORN-ING.
HEY.

Thank you very much for picking up *Yona of the Dawn* volume 27!

After volume 26, a lot of people sent me comments.

Many readers congratulated Hak over chapter 152, but all he really did was confess his feelings out of frustration. Is that something to be congratulated for? Other than that, I'm glad some people correctly interpreted Gija and Jaeha's expressions.

In chapter 151, I had fun drawing Hak having frank, comfortable conversations with his childhood friends from Fuuga. He has female friends, he jokes around and he laughs out loud. I want him to continue being someone who cherishes all sorts of things.

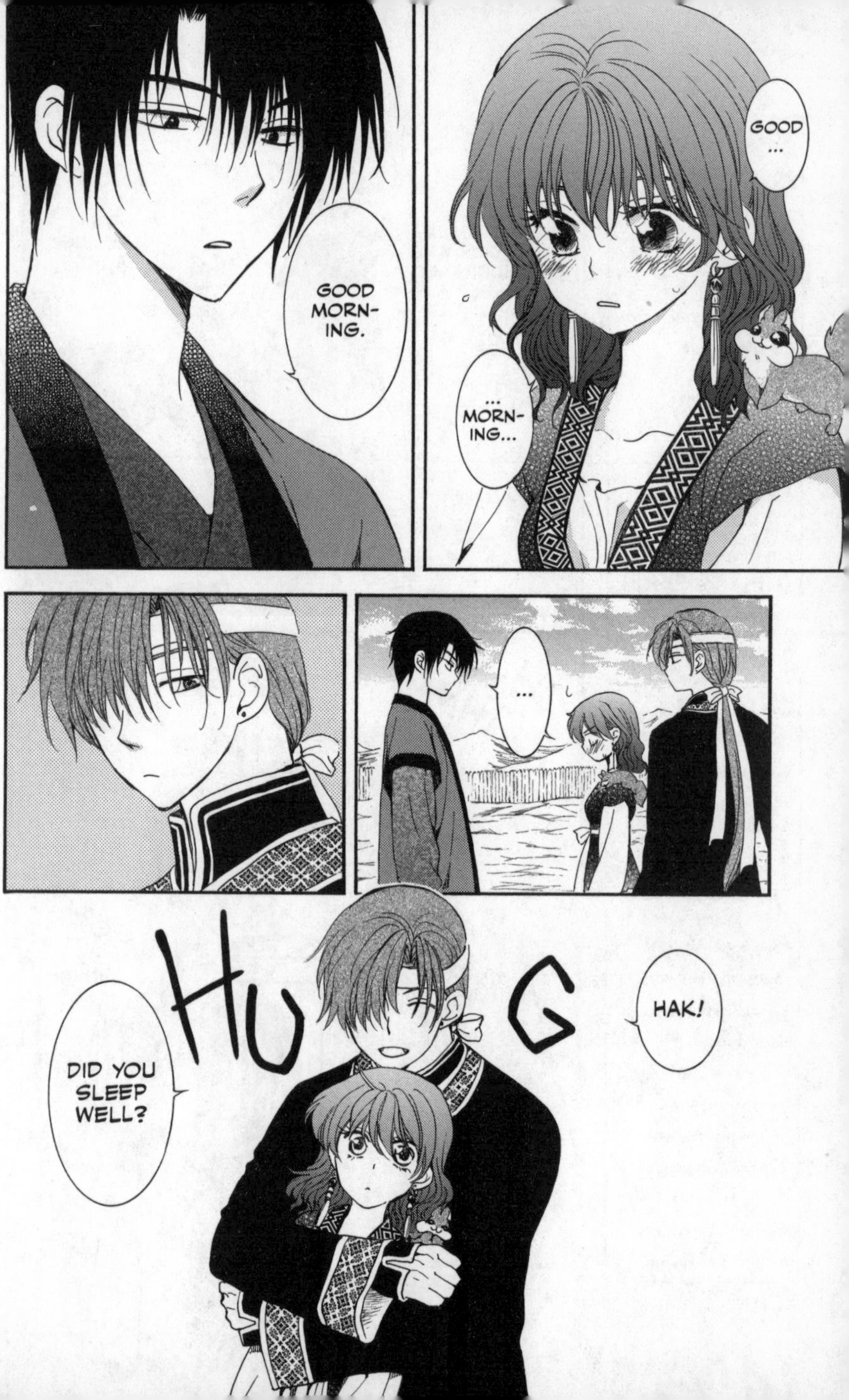
GOOD ...
... MORN-ING...
GOOD MORN-ING.
...
HAK!
HUG
DID YOU SLEEP WELL?

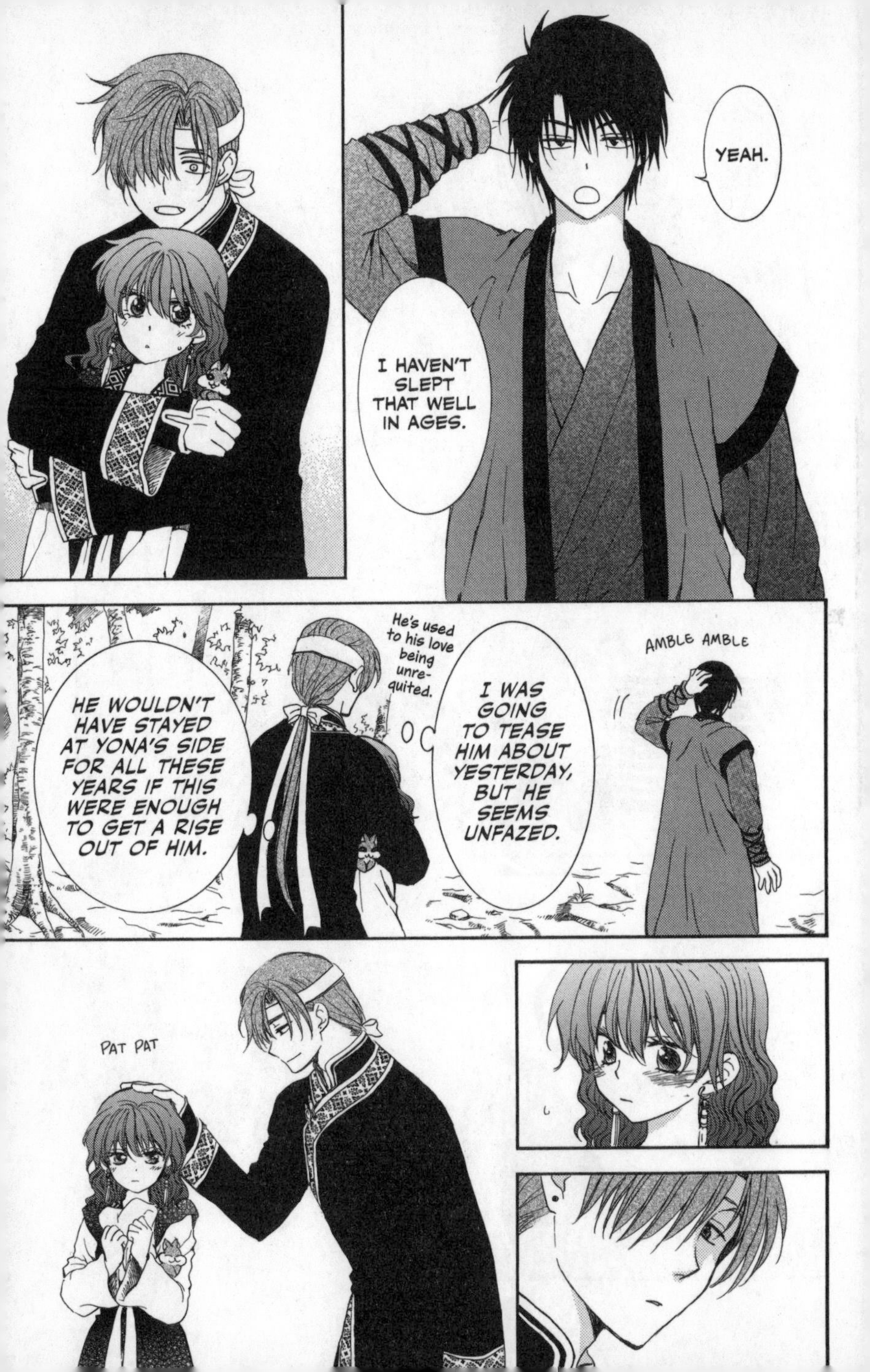
YEAH.
I HAVEN'T SLEPT THAT WELL IN AGES.
AMBLE AMBLE
I WAS GOING TO TEASE HIM ABOUT YESTERDAY, BUT HE SEEMS UNFAZED.
He's used to his love being unre-quited.
HE WOULDN'T HAVE STAYED AT YONA'S SIDE FOR ALL THESE YEARS IF THIS WERE ENOUGH TO GET A RISE OUT OF HIM.
PAT PAT

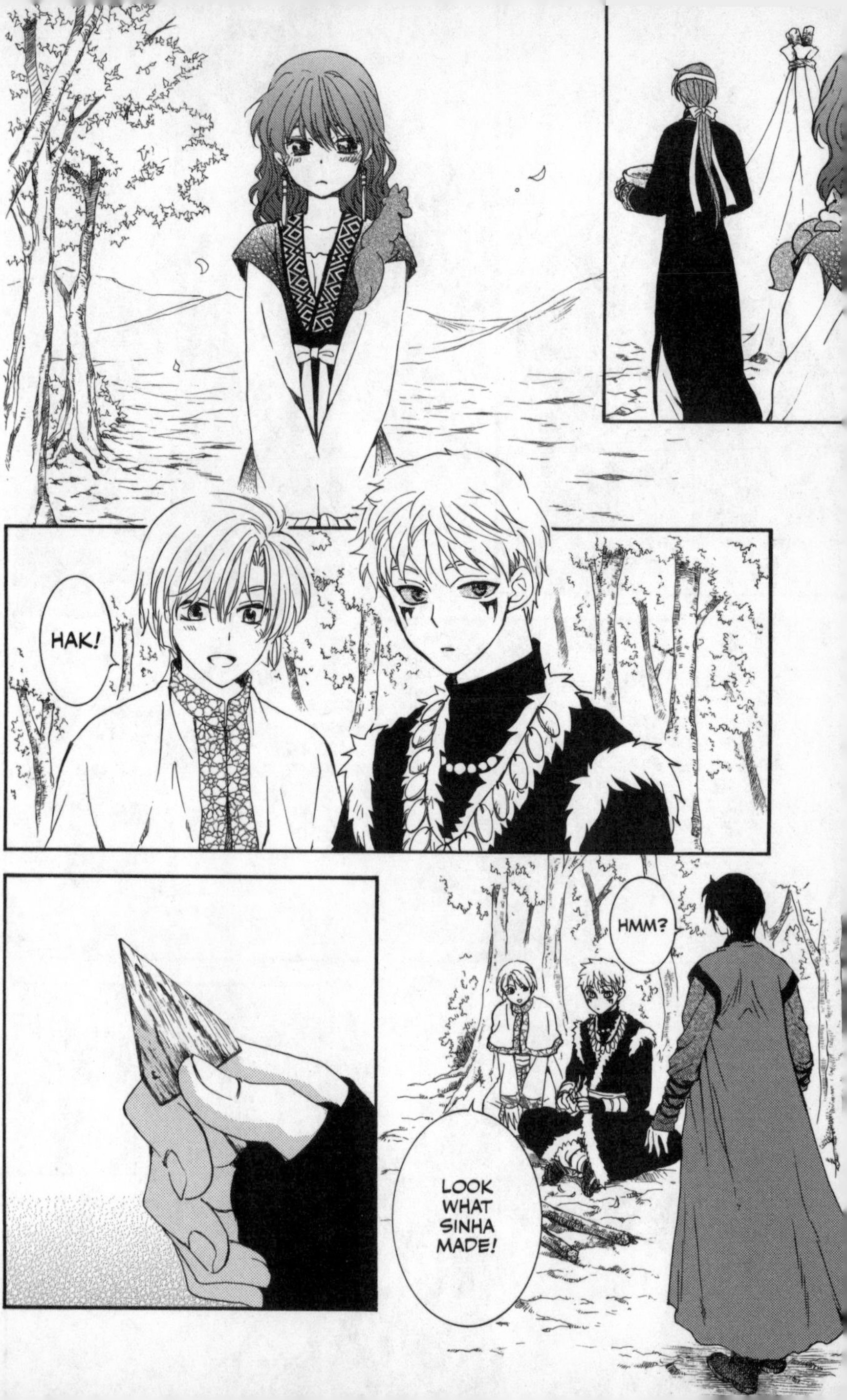
HAK!
HMM?
LOOK WHAT SINHA MADE!

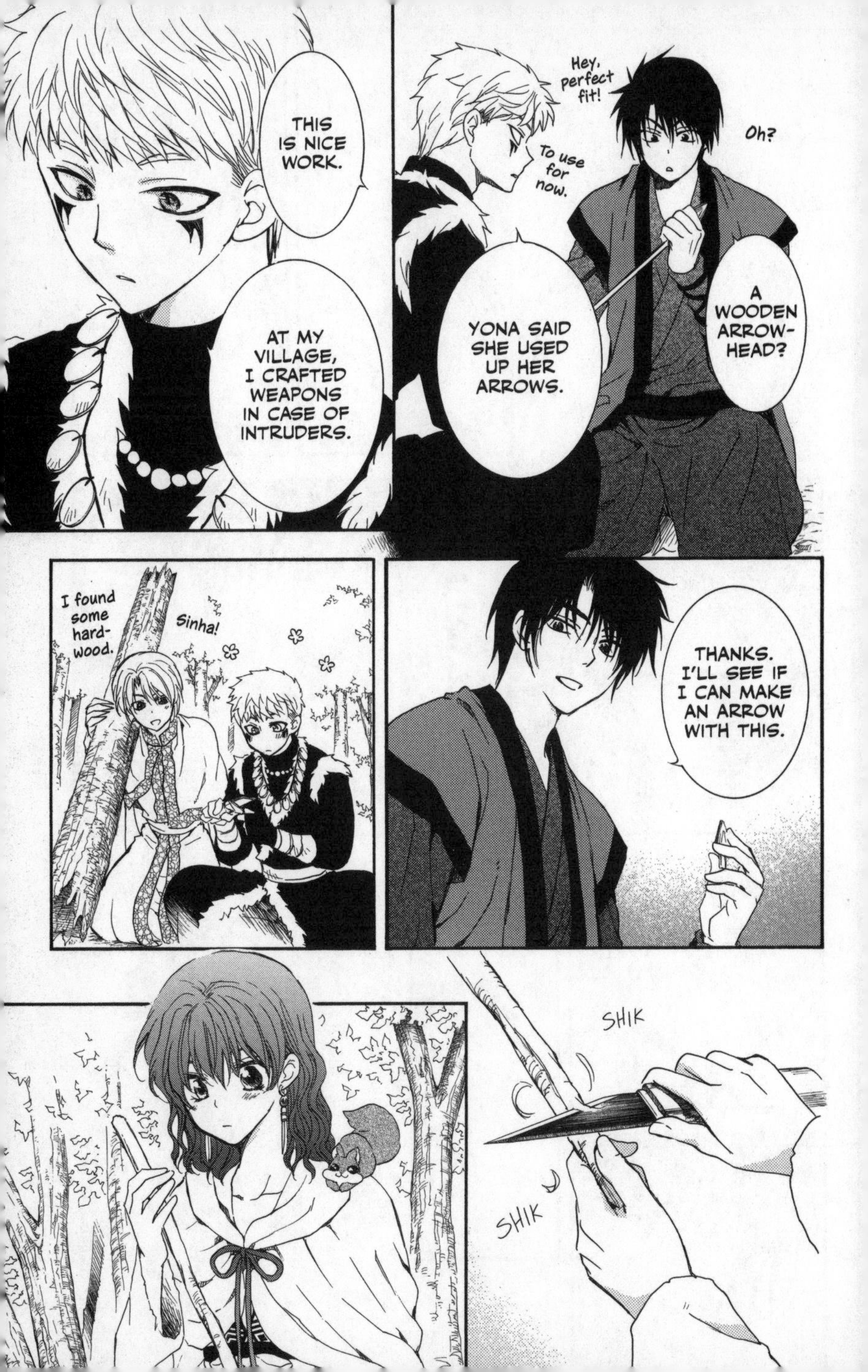
Oh?
A WOODEN ARROW-HEAD?
YONA SAID SHE USED UP HER ARROWS.
To use for now.
Hey, perfect fit!
THIS IS NICE WORK.
AT MY VILLAGE, I CRAFTED WEAPONS IN CASE OF INTRUDERS.
THANKS. I'LL SEE IF I CAN MAKE AN ARROW WITH THIS.
Sinha!
I found some hard-wood.
SHIK
SHIK

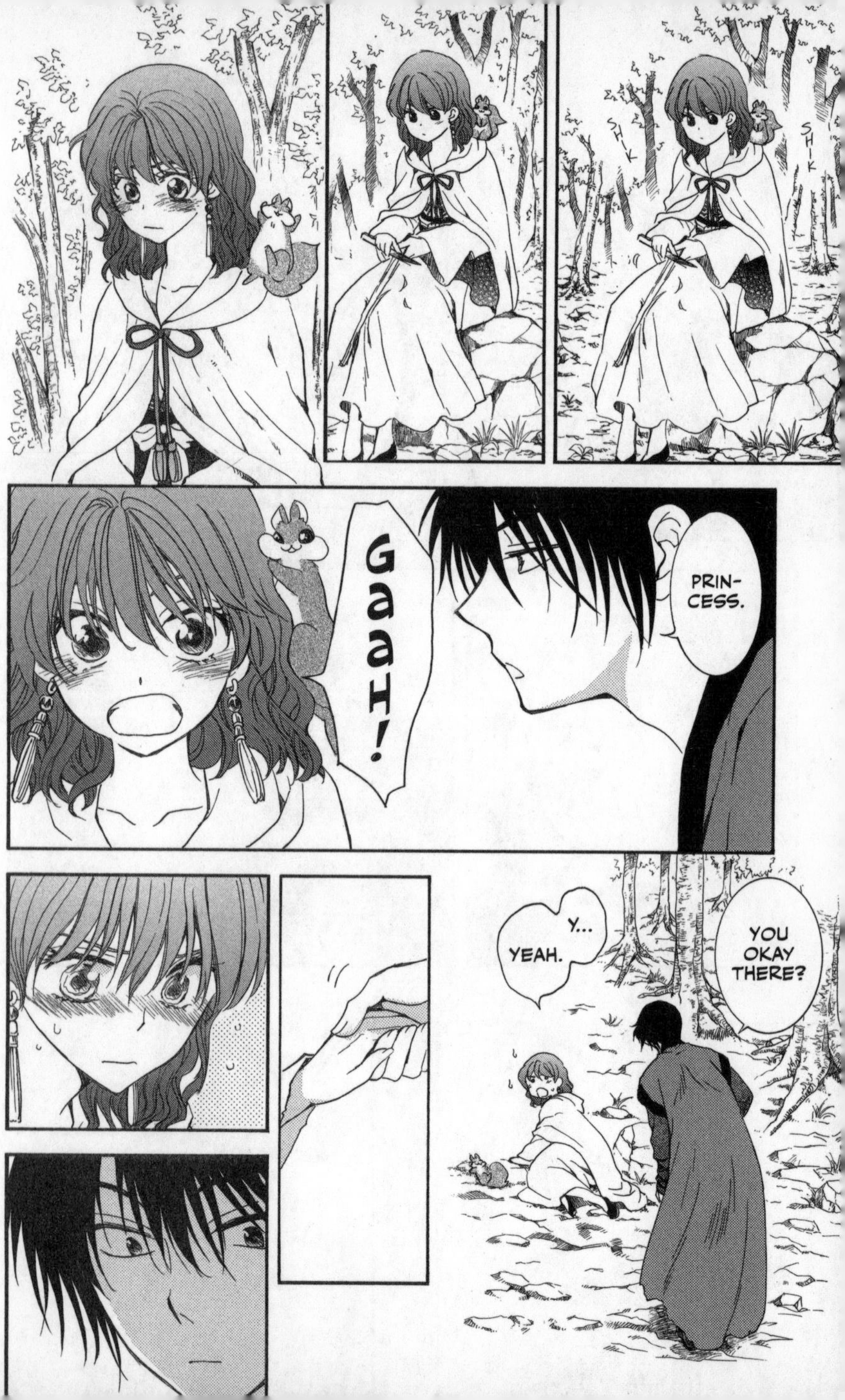
SHIK
SHIK
PRIN-CESS.
GAAH!
YOU OKAY THERE?
Y... YEAH.

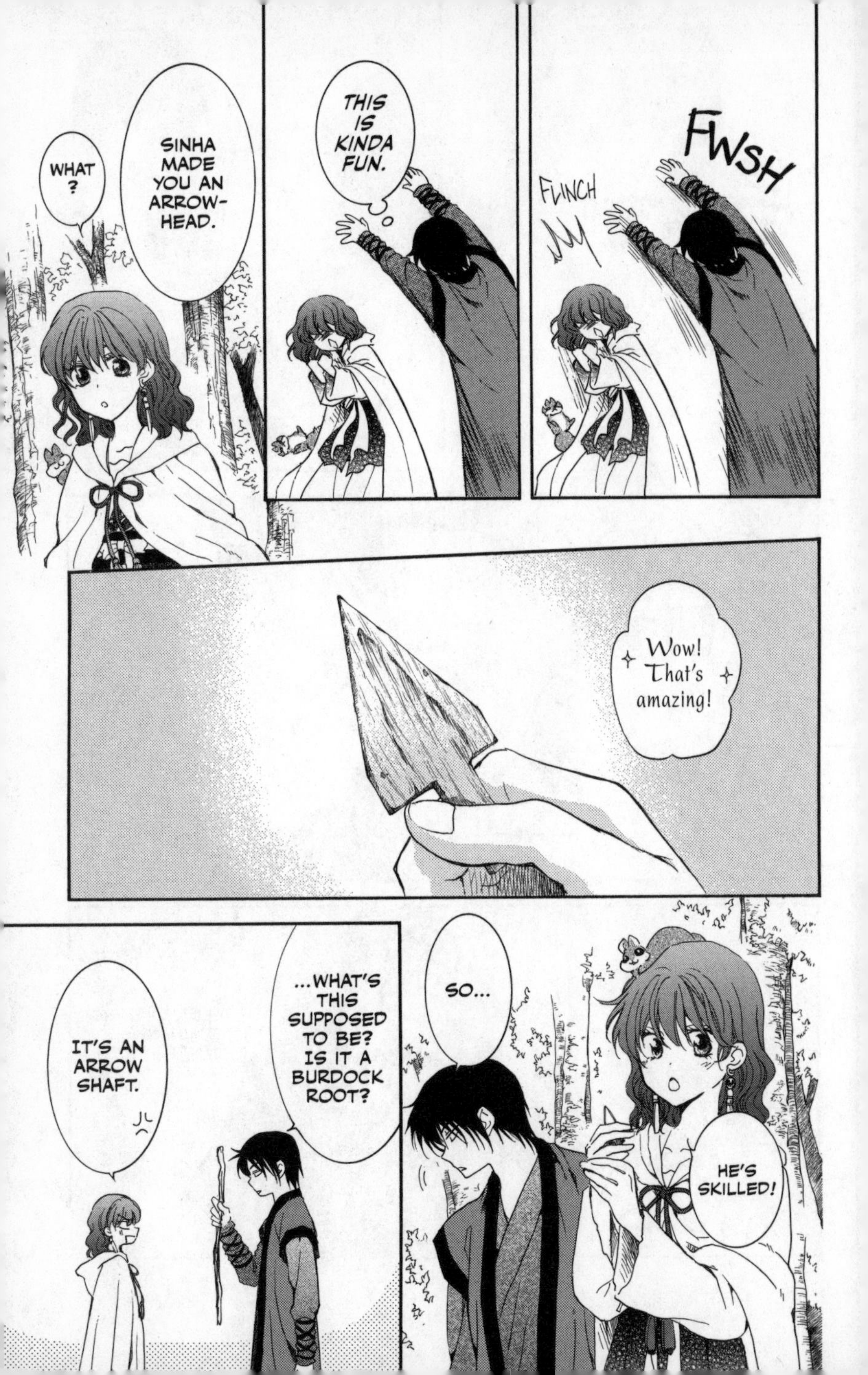
FWSH
FLINCH
THIS IS KINDA FUN.
SINHA MADE YOU AN ARROW-HEAD.
WHAT?
Wow! That's amazing!
HE'S SKILLED!
SO...
...WHAT'S THIS SUPPOSED TO BE? IS IT A BURDOCK ROOT?
IT'S AN ARROW SHAFT.

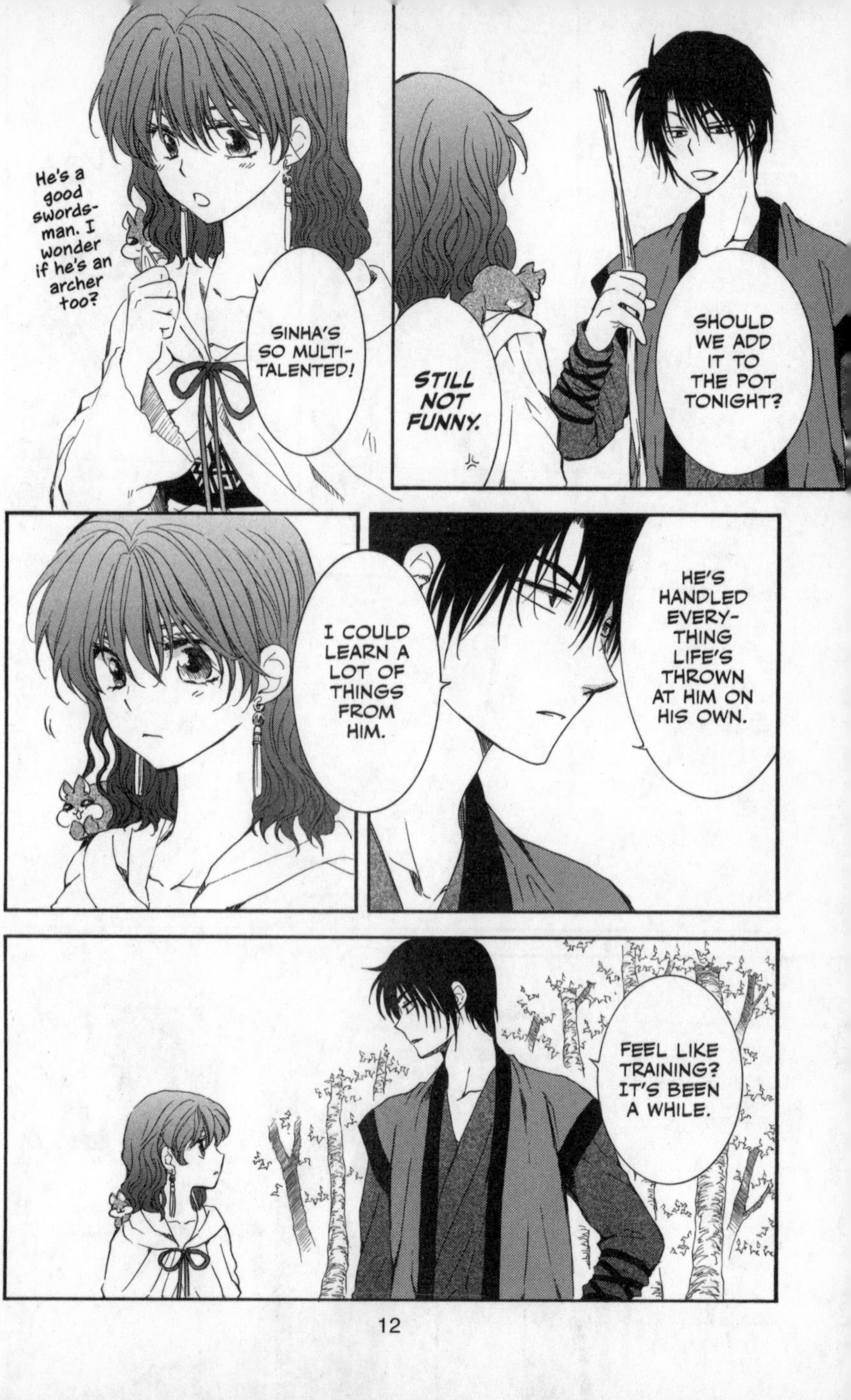
SHOULD WE ADD IT TO THE POT TONIGHT?
STILL NOT FUNNY.
SINHA'S SO MULTI-TALENTED!
He's a good swordsman. I wonder if he's an archer too?
HE'S HANDLED EVERYTHING LIFE'S THROWN AT HIM ON HIS OWN.
I COULD LEARN A LOT OF THINGS FROM HIM.
FEEL LIKE TRAINING? IT'S BEEN A WHILE.

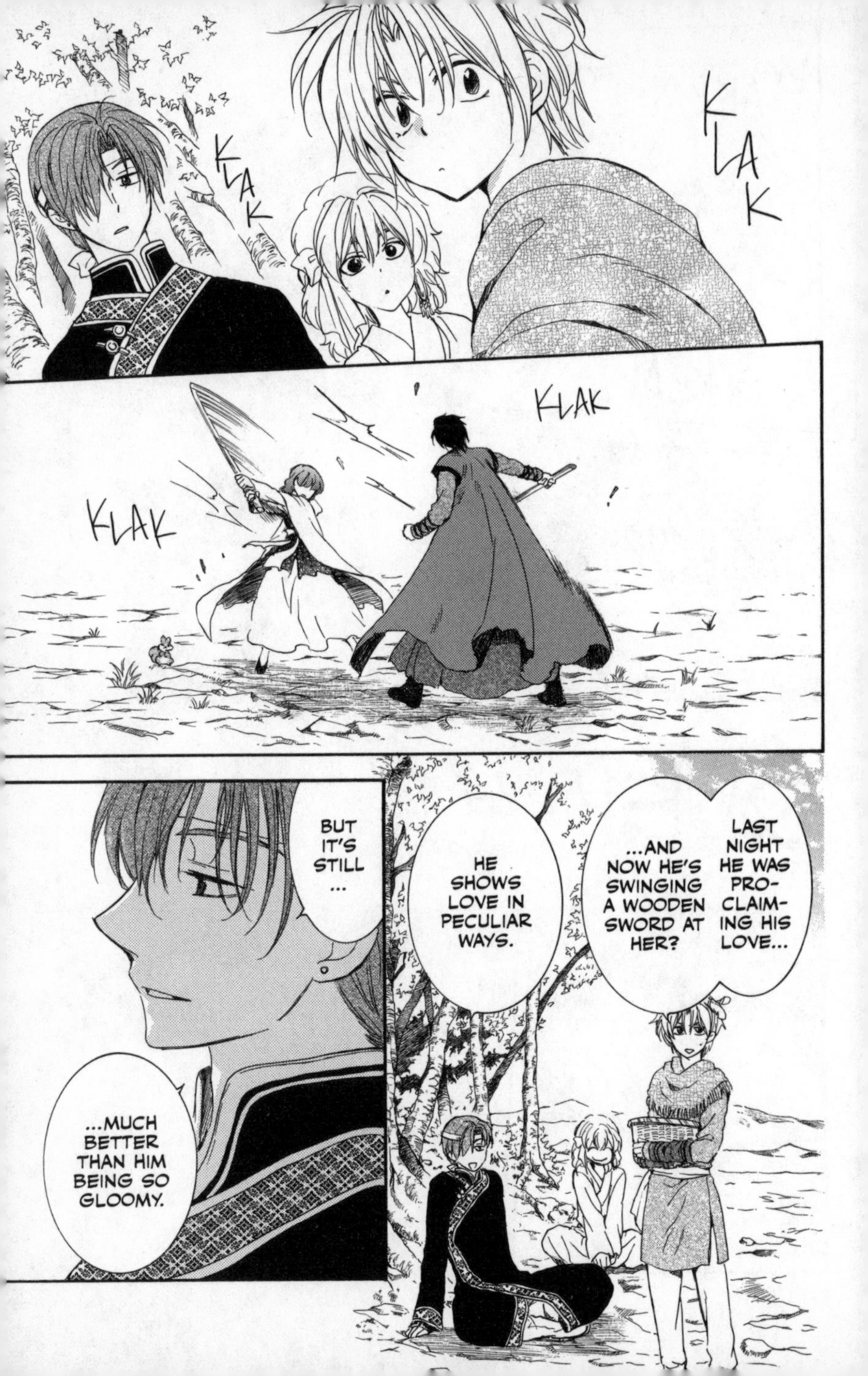
KLAK
KLAK
KLAK
KLAK
LAST NIGHT HE WAS PRO-CLAIM-ING HIS LOVE...
...AND NOW HE'S SWINGING A WOODEN SWORD AT HER?
HE SHOWS LOVE IN PECULIAR WAYS.
BUT IT'S STILL ...
...MUCH BETTER THAN HIM BEING SO GLOOMY.

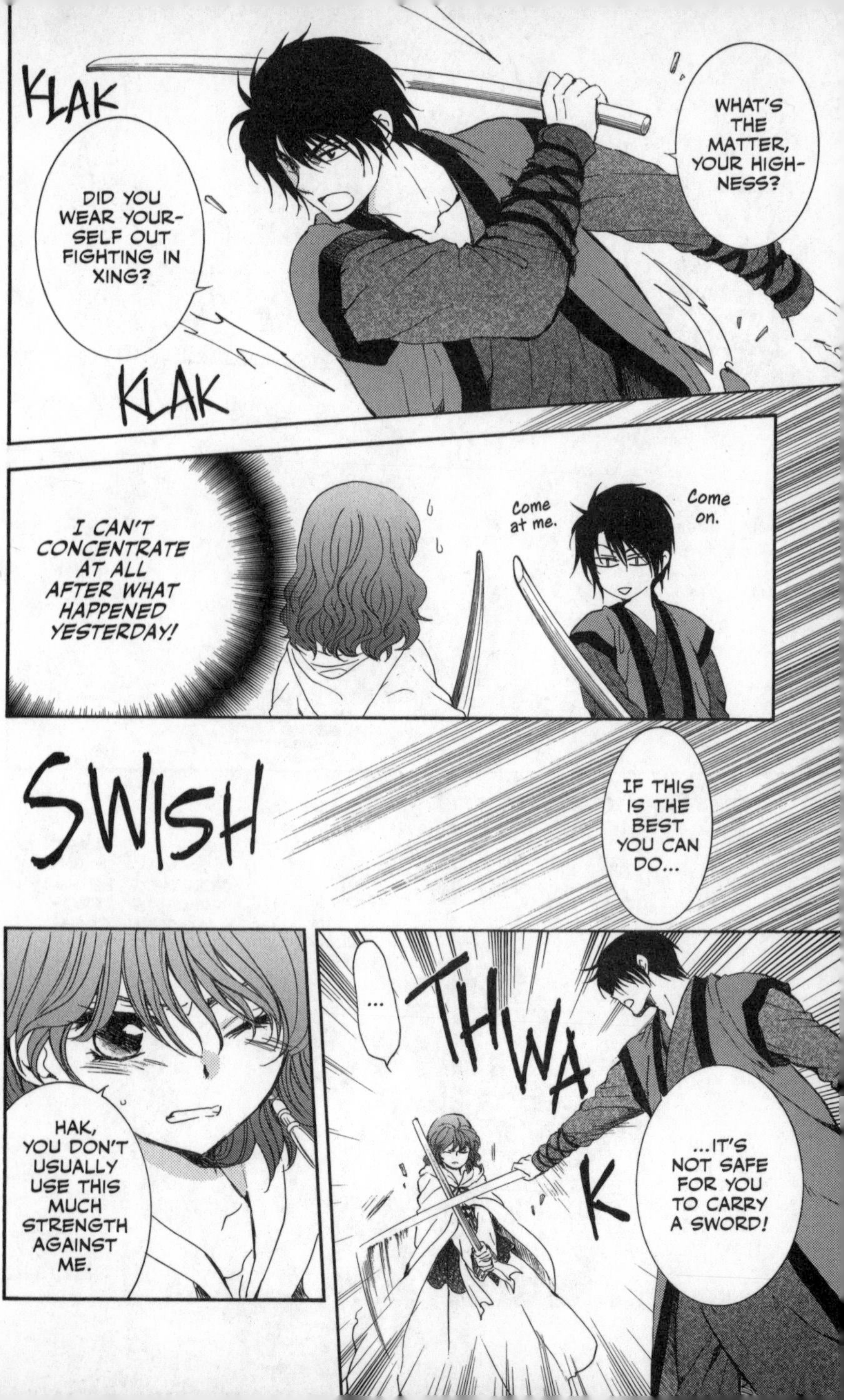
WHAT'S THE MATTER, YOUR HIGHNESS?
KLAK
DID YOU WEAR YOURSELF OUT FIGHTING IN XING?
KLAK
Come on.
Come at me.
I CAN'T CONCENTRATE AT ALL AFTER WHAT HAPPENED YESTERDAY!
IF THIS IS THE BEST YOU CAN DO...
SWISH
...
THWAK
...IT'S NOT SAFE FOR YOU TO CARRY A SWORD!
HAK, YOU DON'T USUALLY USE THIS MUCH STRENGTH AGAINST ME.

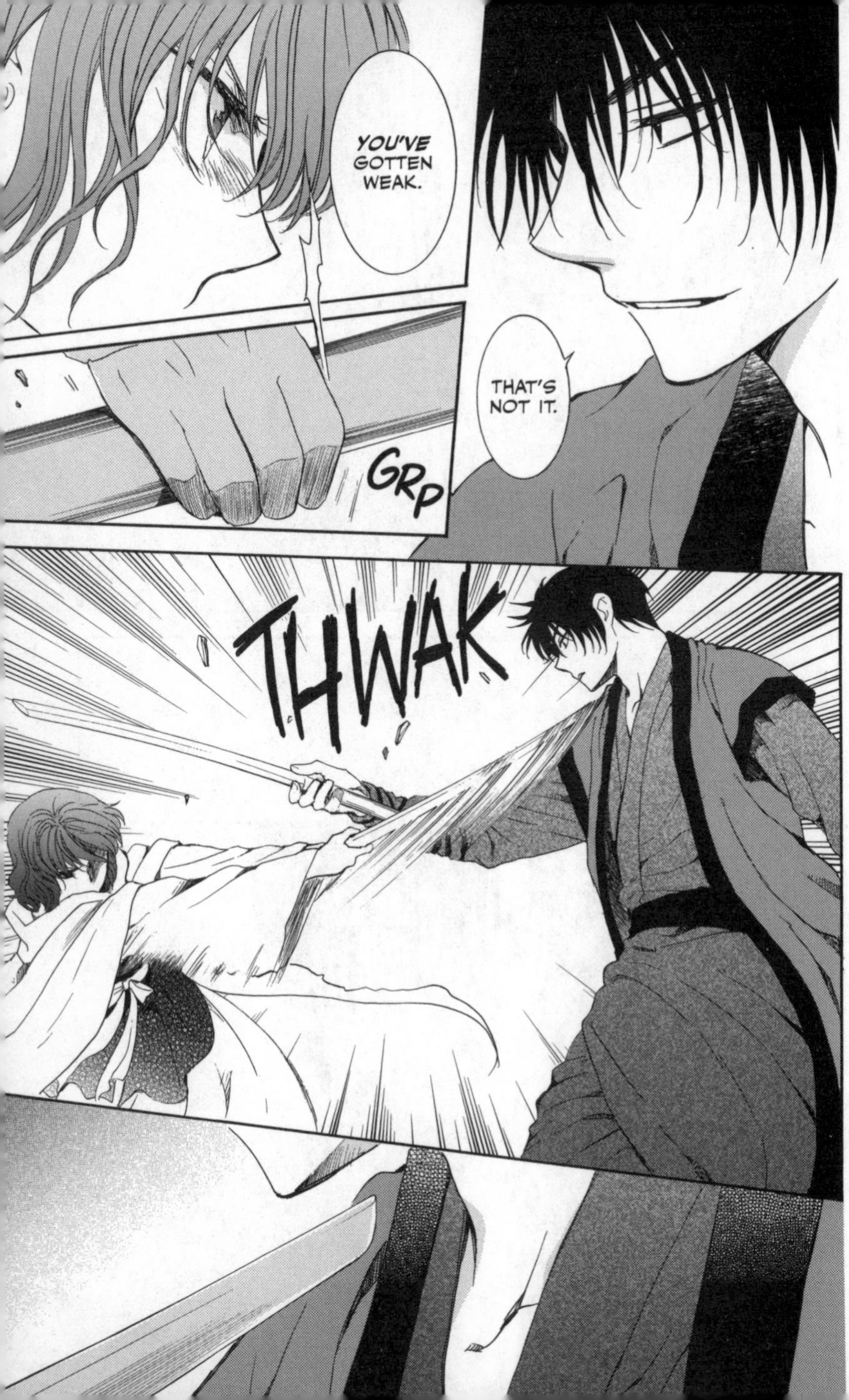

YOU'VE GOTTEN WEAK.
THAT'S NOT IT.
GRP
THWAK

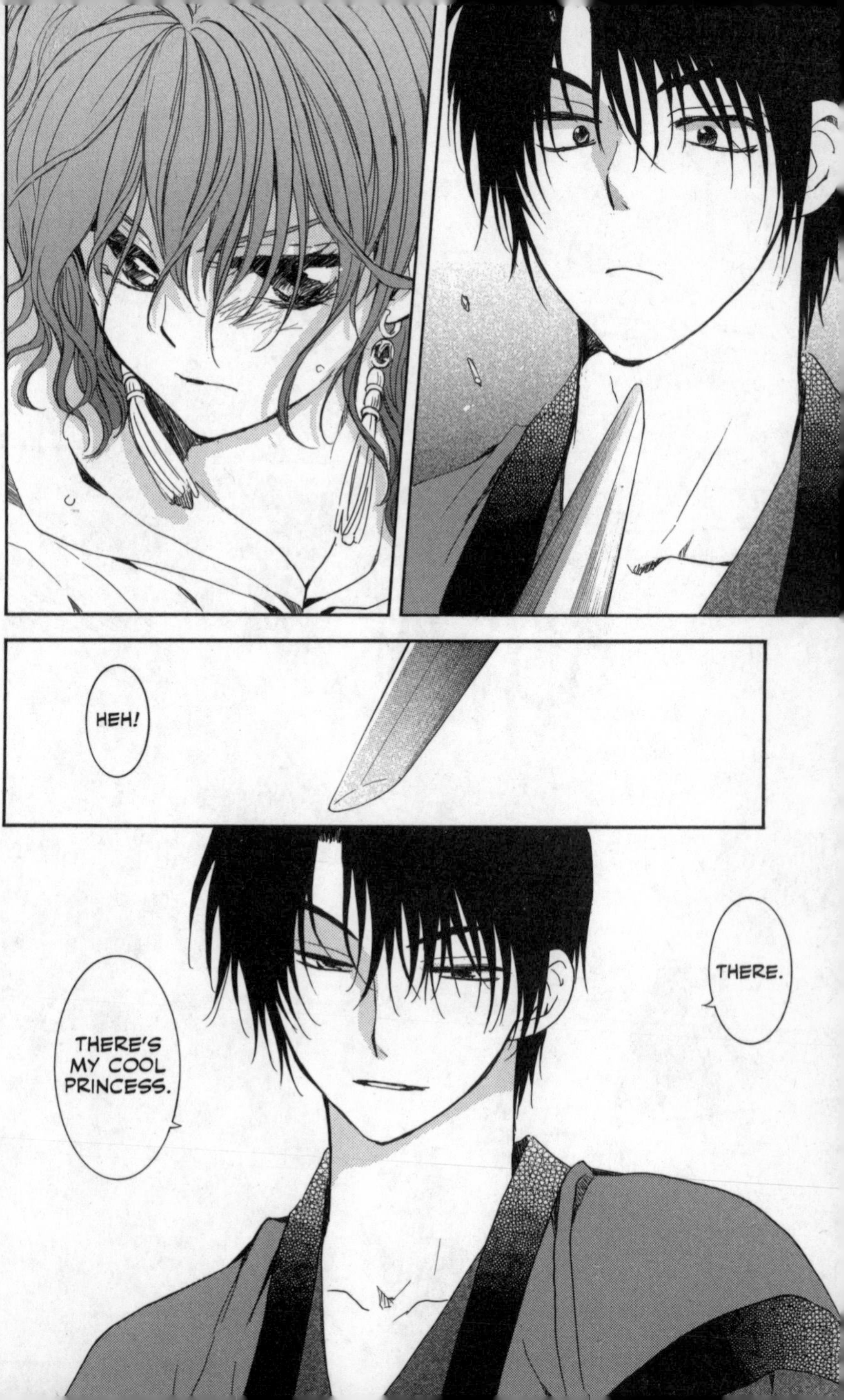
HEH!
THERE.
THERE'S MY COOL PRINCESS.

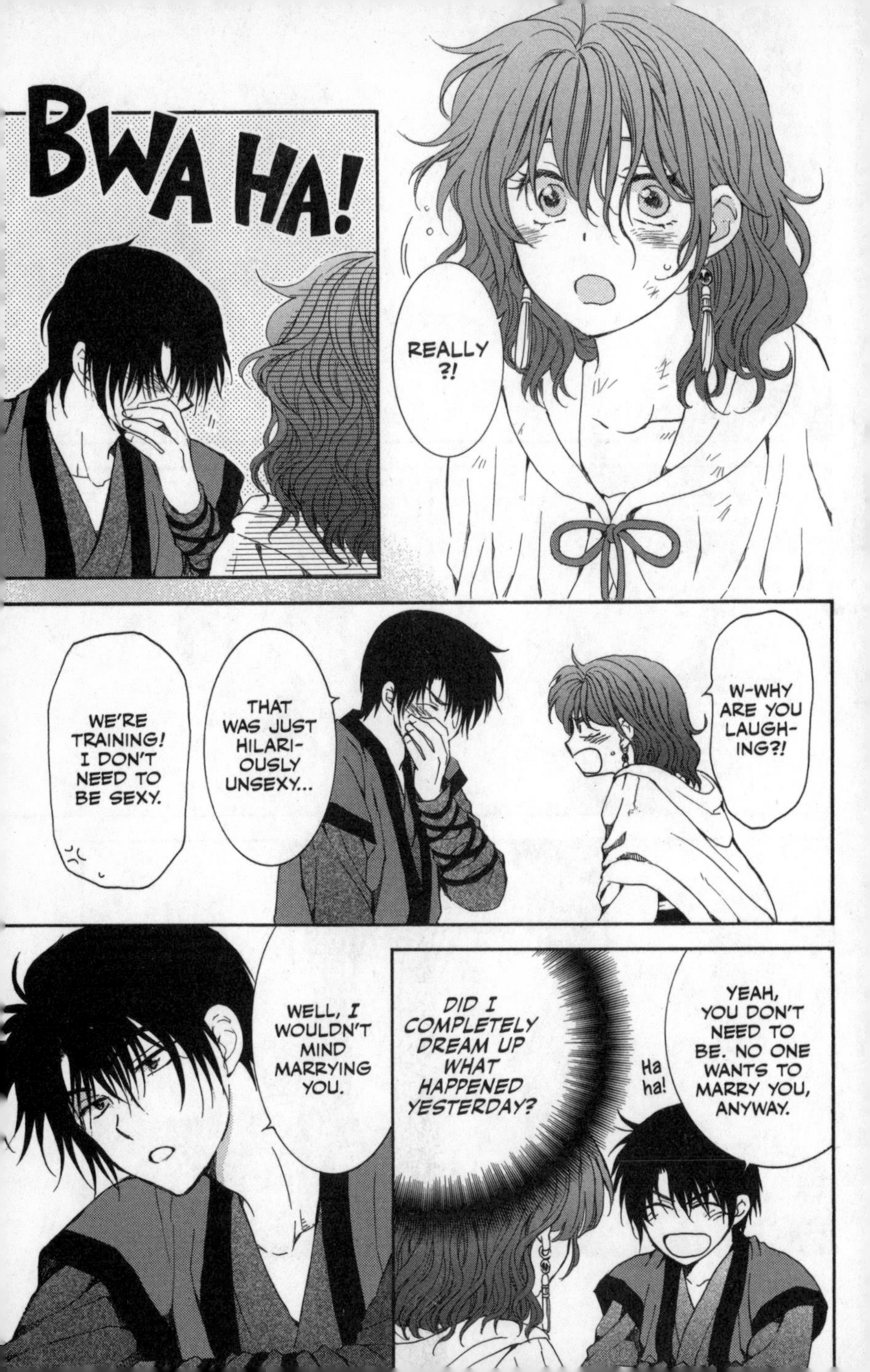
REALLY ?!
BWA HA!
W-WHY ARE YOU LAUGHING?!
THAT WAS JUST HILARIOUSLY UNSEXY...
WE'RE TRAINING! I DON'T NEED TO BE SEXY.
YEAH, YOU DON'T NEED TO BE. NO ONE WANTS TO MARRY YOU, ANYWAY.
Ha ha!
DID I COMPLETELY DREAM UP WHAT HAPPENED YESTERDAY?
WELL, I WOULDN'T MIND MARRYING YOU.

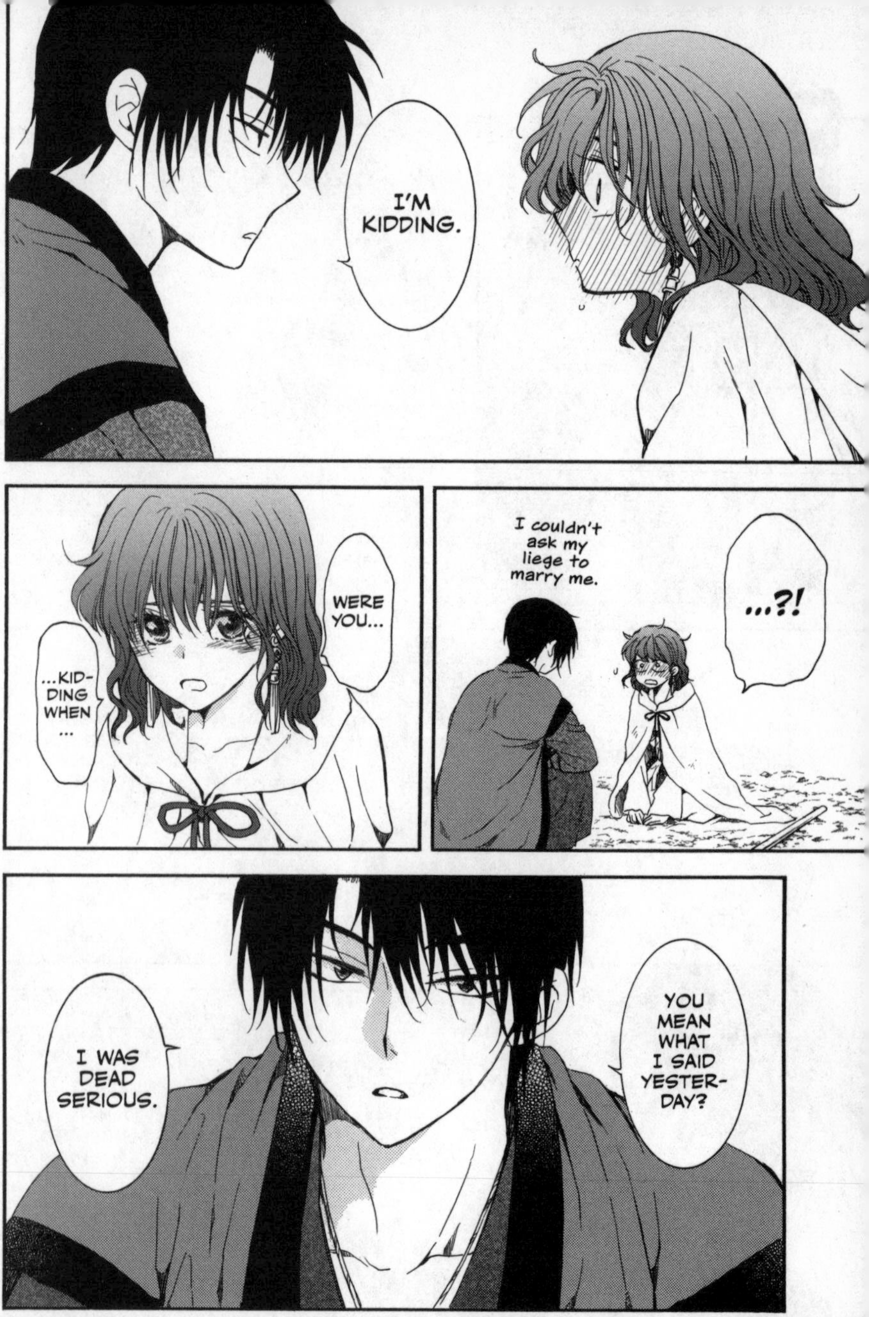
I'M KIDDING.
...?!
I couldn't ask my liege to marry me.
WERE YOU...
...KID-DING WHEN ...
YOU MEAN WHAT I SAID YESTER-DAY?
I WAS DEAD SERIOUS.

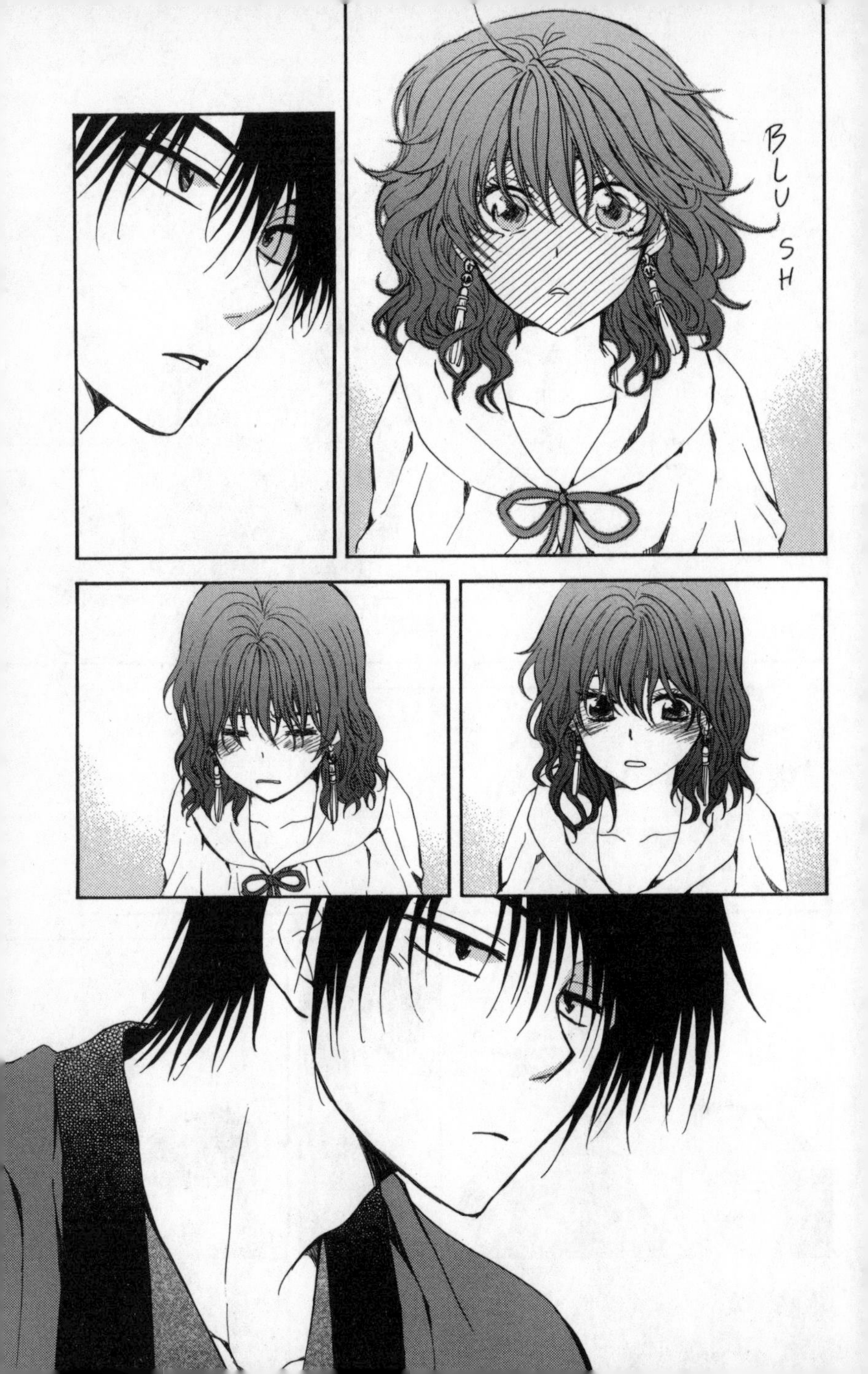
BLUSH

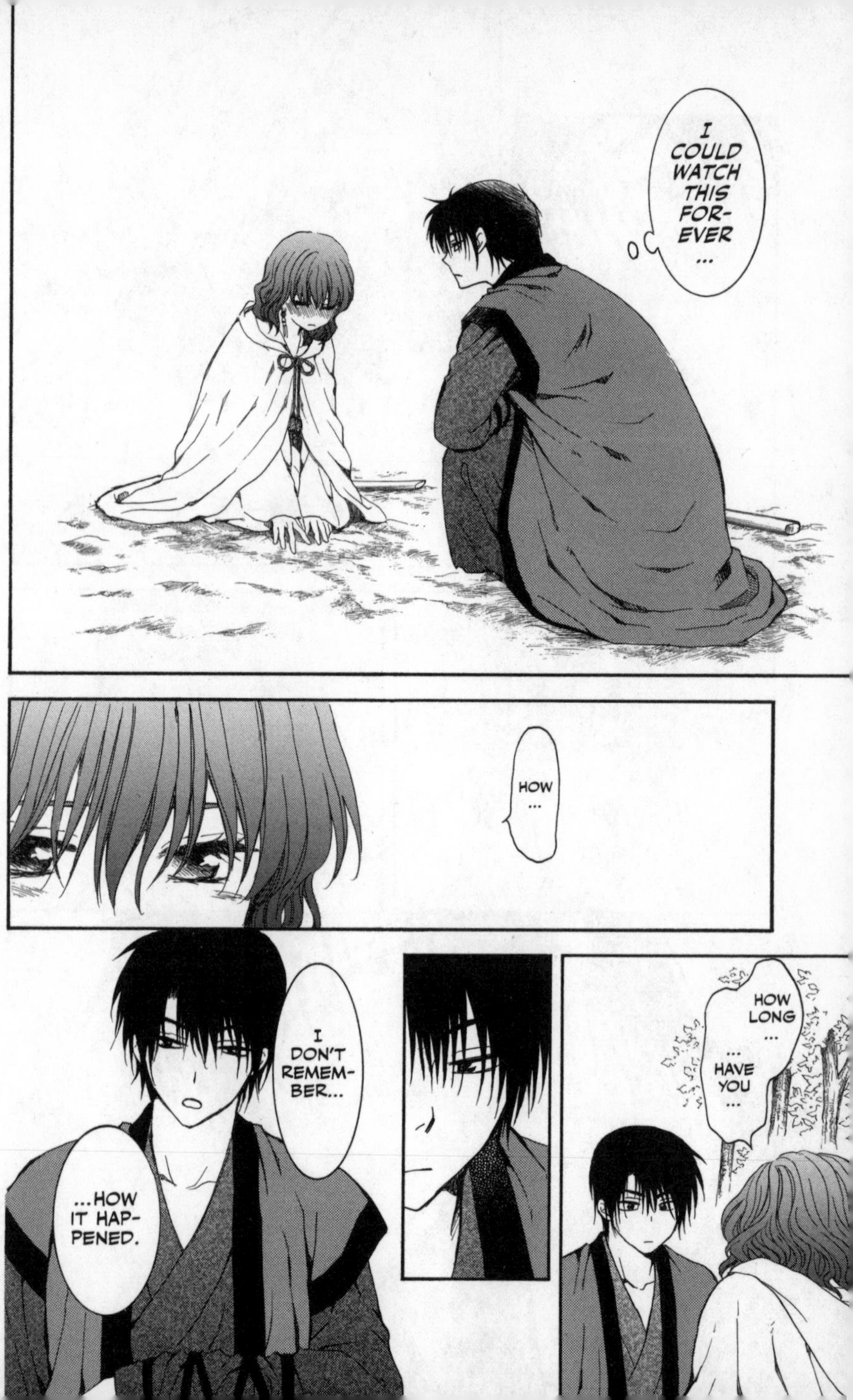
I COULD WATCH THIS FOREVER...
HOW...
HOW LONG... ...HAVE YOU...
I DON'T REMEMBER...
...HOW IT HAPPENED.

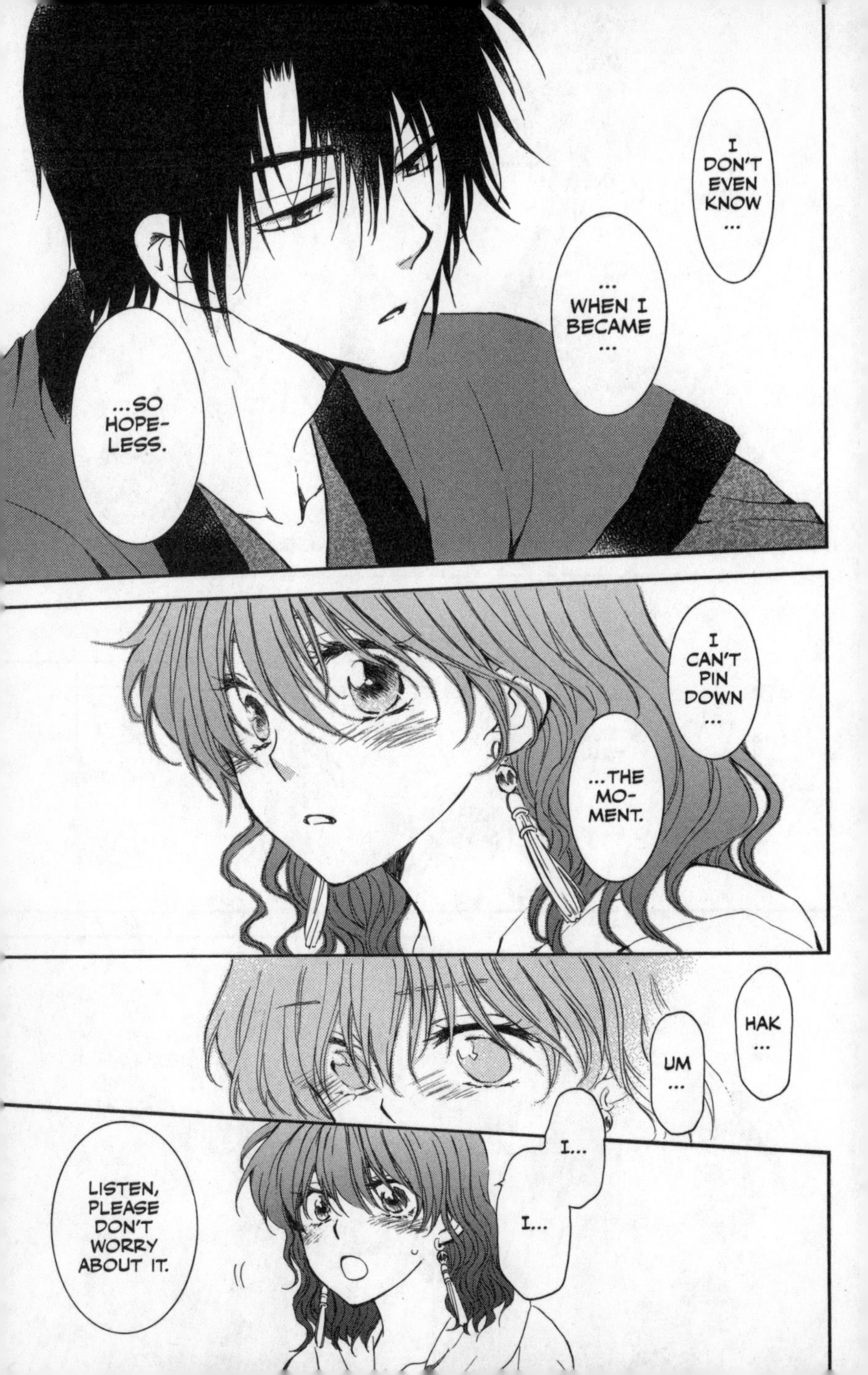

I DON'T EVEN KNOW ...
... WHEN I BECAME ...
...SO HOPE-LESS.
I CAN'T PIN DOWN ...
...THE MO-MENT.
HAK ...
UM ...
I...
I...
LISTEN, PLEASE DON'T WORRY ABOUT IT.

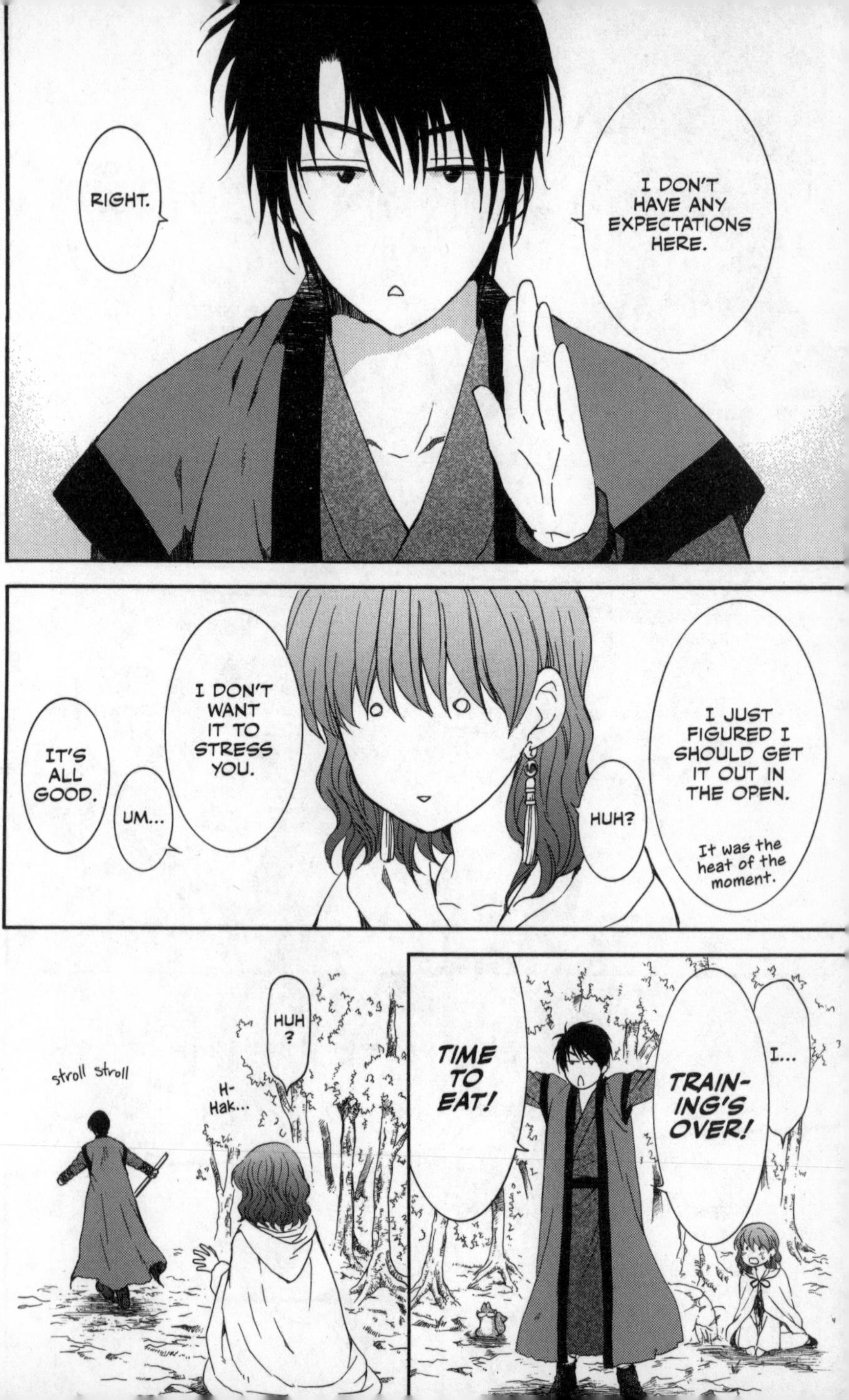
I DON'T HAVE ANY EXPECTATIONS HERE.
RIGHT.
I JUST FIGURED I SHOULD GET IT OUT IN THE OPEN.
It was the heat of the moment.
HUH?
I DON'T WANT IT TO STRESS YOU.
UM...
IT'S ALL GOOD.
I...
TRAIN-ING'S OVER!
TIME TO EAT!
HUH ?
H-Hak...
stroll stroll

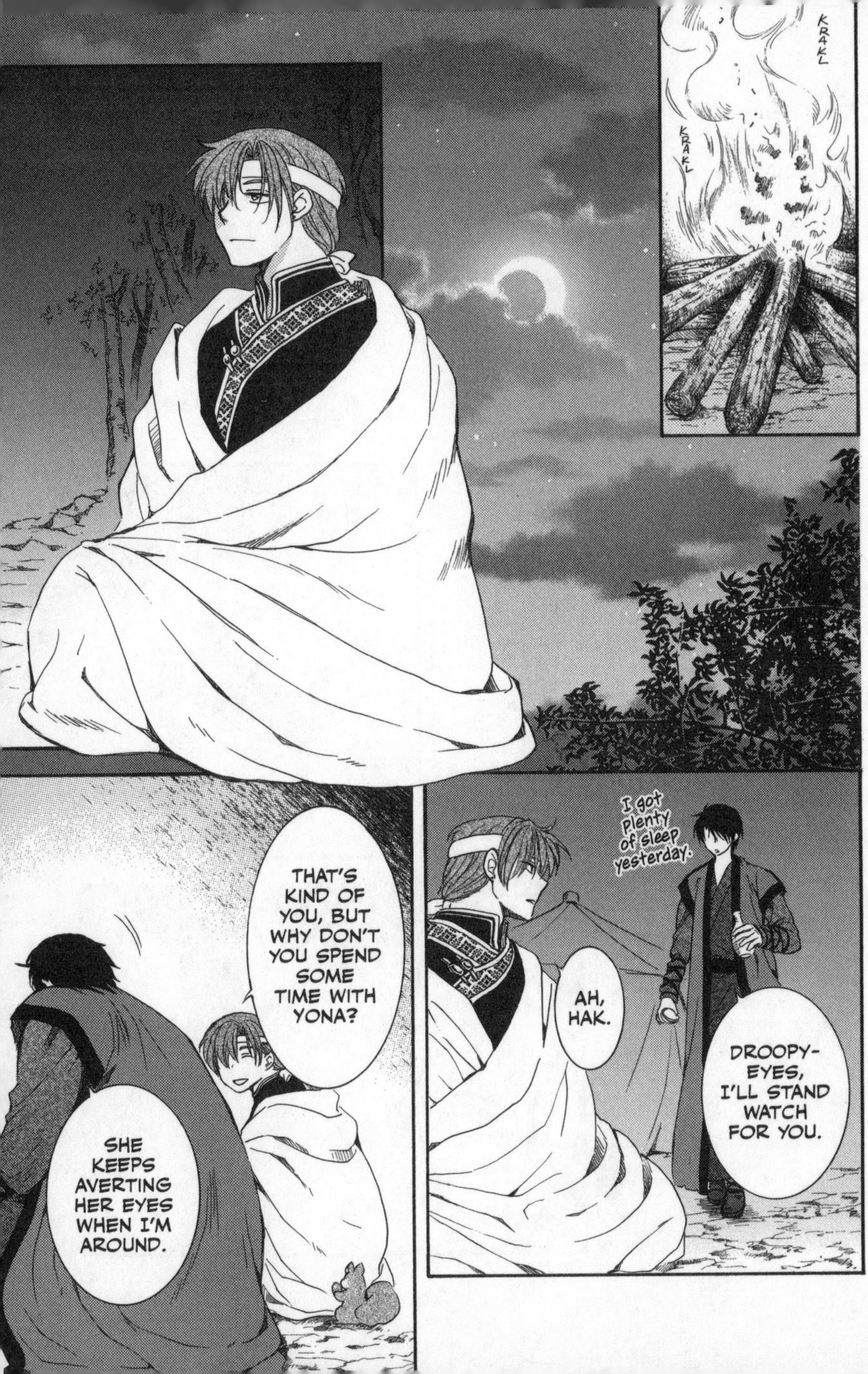
KRAKL
KRAKL
AH, HAK.
DROOPY-EYES, I'LL STAND WATCH FOR YOU.
I got plenty of sleep yesterday.
THAT'S KIND OF YOU, BUT WHY DON'T YOU SPEND SOME TIME WITH YONA?
SHE KEEPS AVERTING HER EYES WHEN I'M AROUND.

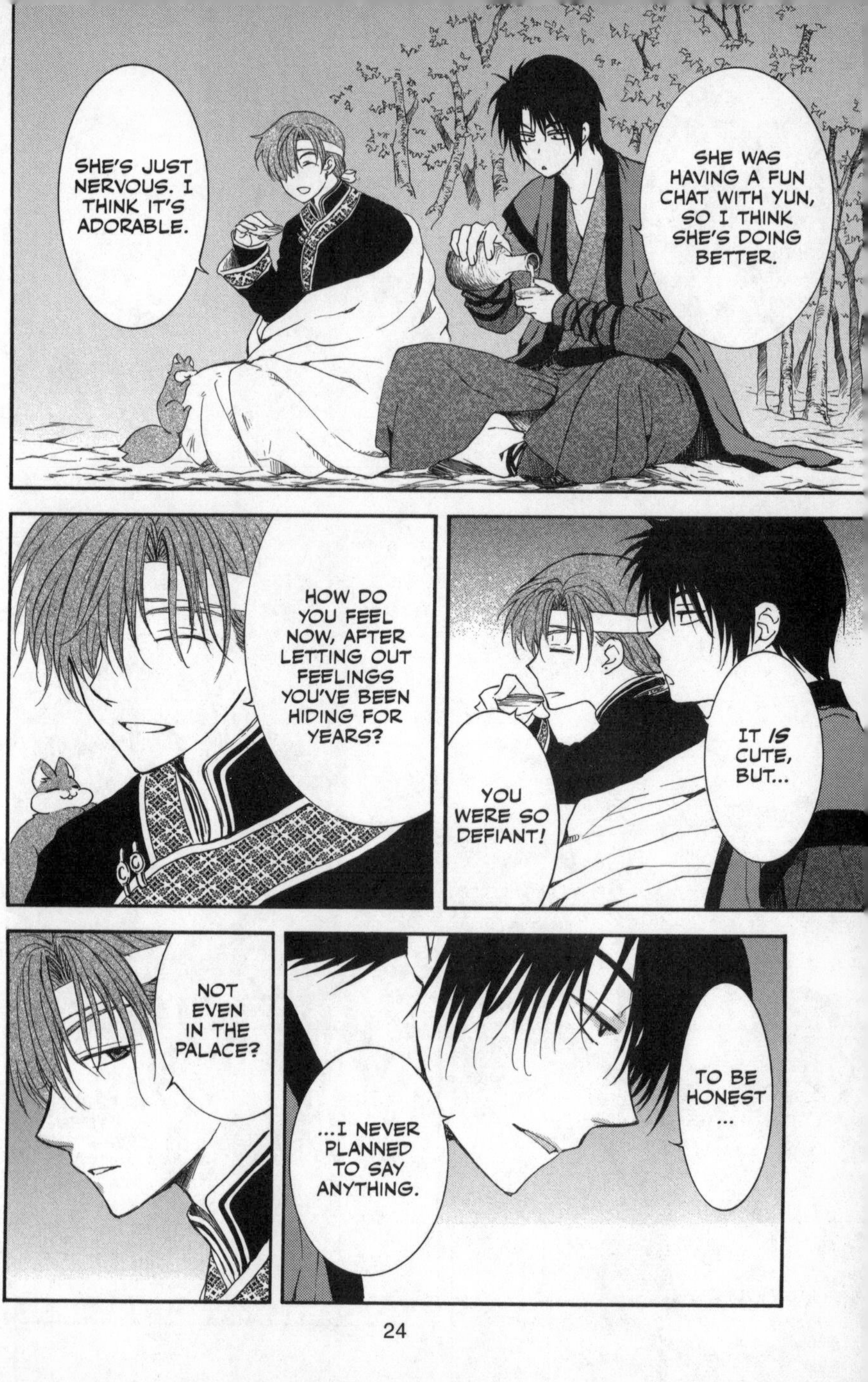
SHE WAS HAVING A FUN CHAT WITH YUN, SO I THINK SHE'S DOING BETTER.
SHE'S JUST NERVOUS. I THINK IT'S ADORABLE.
IT *IS* CUTE, BUT...
YOU WERE SO DEFIANT!
HOW DO YOU FEEL NOW, AFTER LETTING OUT FEELINGS YOU'VE BEEN HIDING FOR YEARS?
TO BE HONEST ...
...I NEVER PLANNED TO SAY ANYTHING.
NOT EVEN IN THE PALACE?

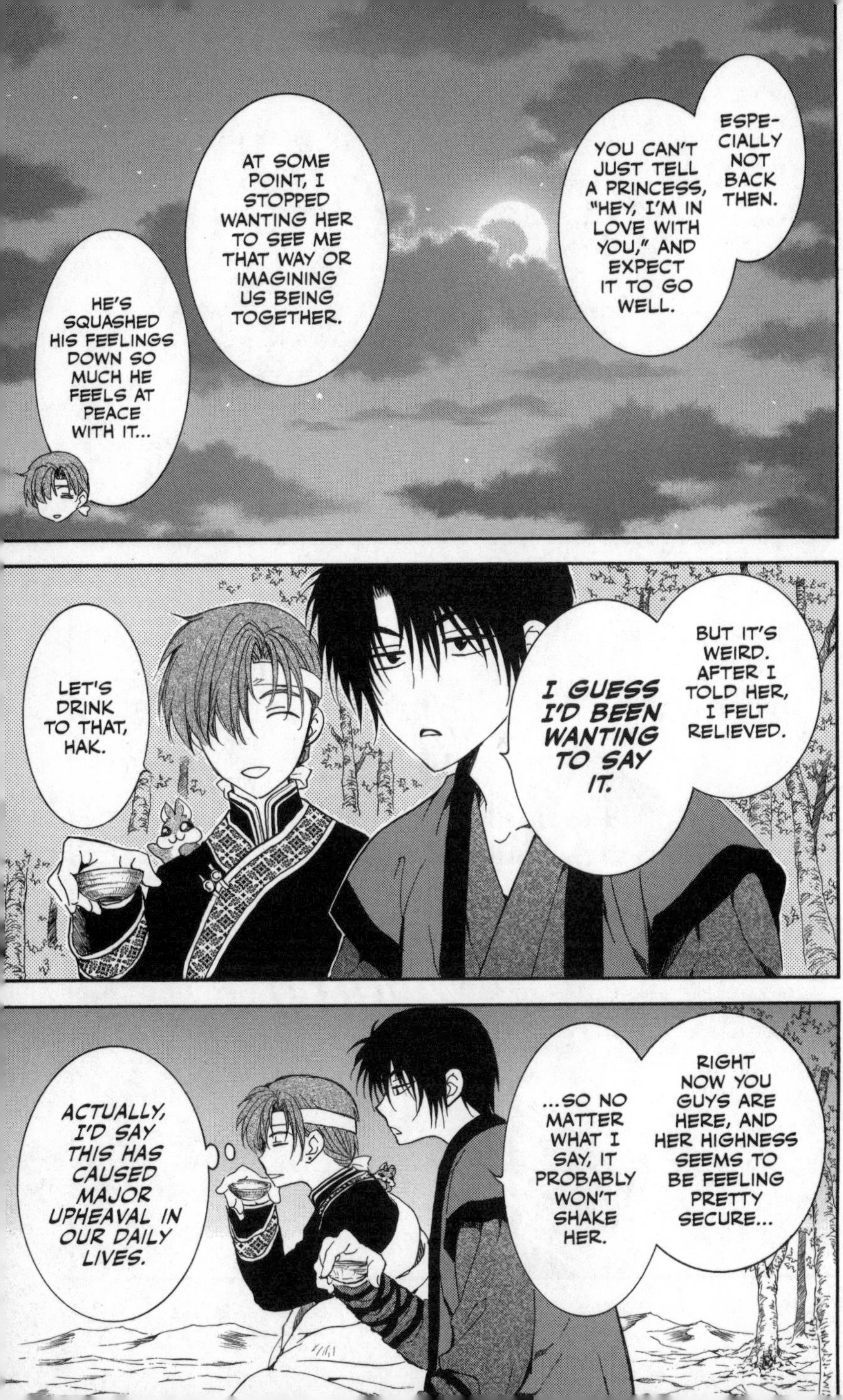
YOU CAN'T JUST TELL A PRINCESS, "HEY, I'M IN LOVE WITH YOU," AND EXPECT IT TO GO WELL.
ESPE-CIALLY NOT BACK THEN.
AT SOME POINT, I STOPPED WANTING HER TO SEE ME THAT WAY OR IMAGINING US BEING TOGETHER.
HE'S SQUASHED HIS FEELINGS DOWN SO MUCH HE FEELS AT PEACE WITH IT...
BUT IT'S WEIRD. AFTER I TOLD HER, I FELT RELIEVED.
I GUESS I'D BEEN WANTING TO SAY IT.
LET'S DRINK TO THAT, HAK.
RIGHT NOW YOU GUYS ARE HERE, AND HER HIGHNESS SEEMS TO BE FEELING PRETTY SECURE...
...SO NO MATTER WHAT I SAY, IT PROBABLY WON'T SHAKE HER.
ACTUALLY, I'D SAY THIS HAS CAUSED MAJOR UPHEAVAL IN OUR DAILY LIVES.

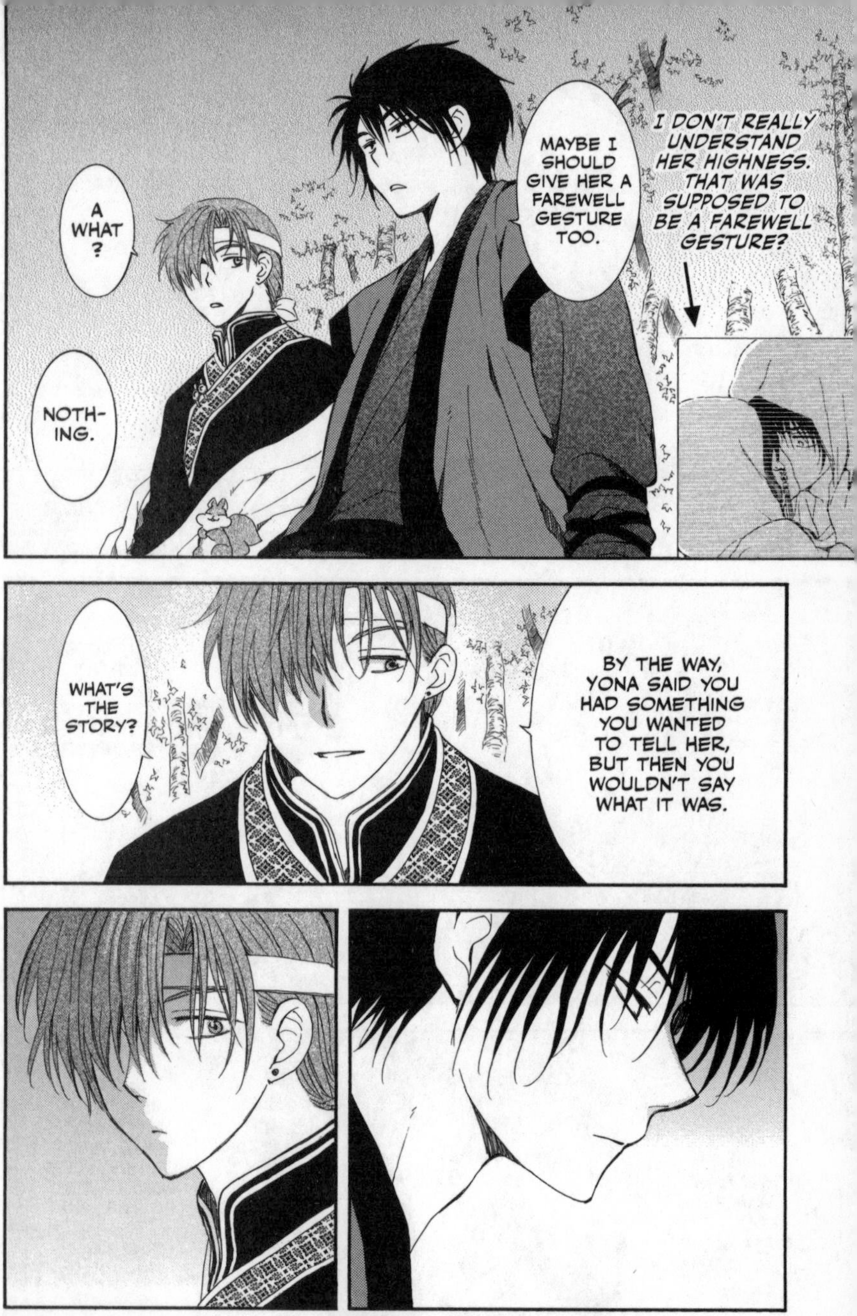
I DON'T REALLY UNDERSTAND HER HIGHNESS. THAT WAS SUPPOSED TO BE A FAREWELL GESTURE?
MAYBE I SHOULD GIVE HER A FAREWELL GESTURE TOO.
A WHAT?
NOTH-ING.
BY THE WAY, YONA SAID YOU HAD SOMETHING YOU WANTED TO TELL HER, BUT THEN YOU WOULDN'T SAY WHAT IT WAS.
WHAT'S THE STORY?

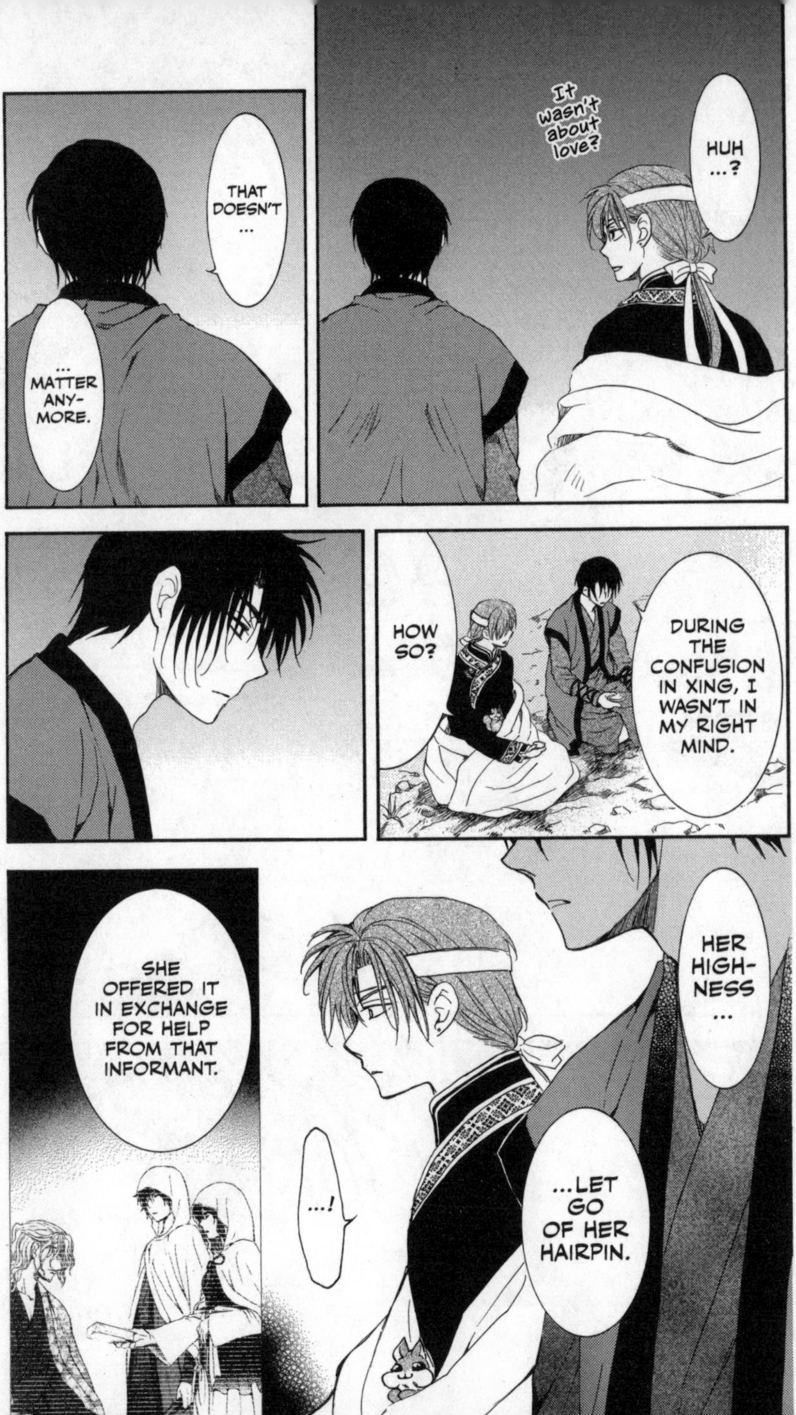
HUH ...?
It wasn't about love?
THAT DOESN'T ...
... MATTER ANY-MORE.
DURING THE CONFUSION IN XING, I WASN'T IN MY RIGHT MIND.
HOW SO?
HER HIGH-NESS ...
...LET GO OF HER HAIRPIN.
...!
SHE OFFERED IT IN EXCHANGE FOR HELP FROM THAT INFORMANT.

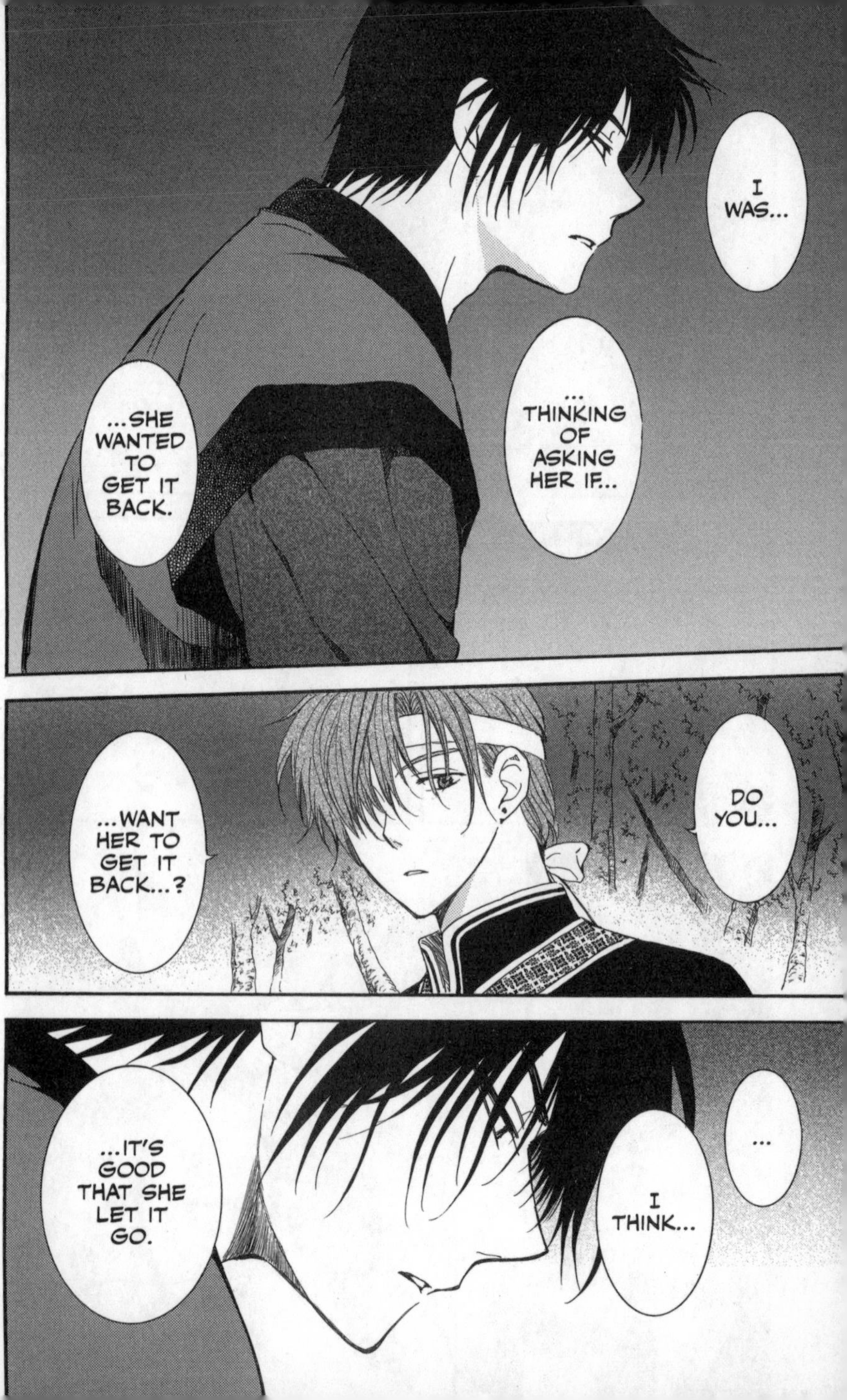
I WAS...
...THINKING OF ASKING HER IF...
...SHE WANTED TO GET IT BACK.
DO YOU...
...WANT HER TO GET IT BACK...?
...
I THINK...
...IT'S GOOD THAT SHE LET IT GO.

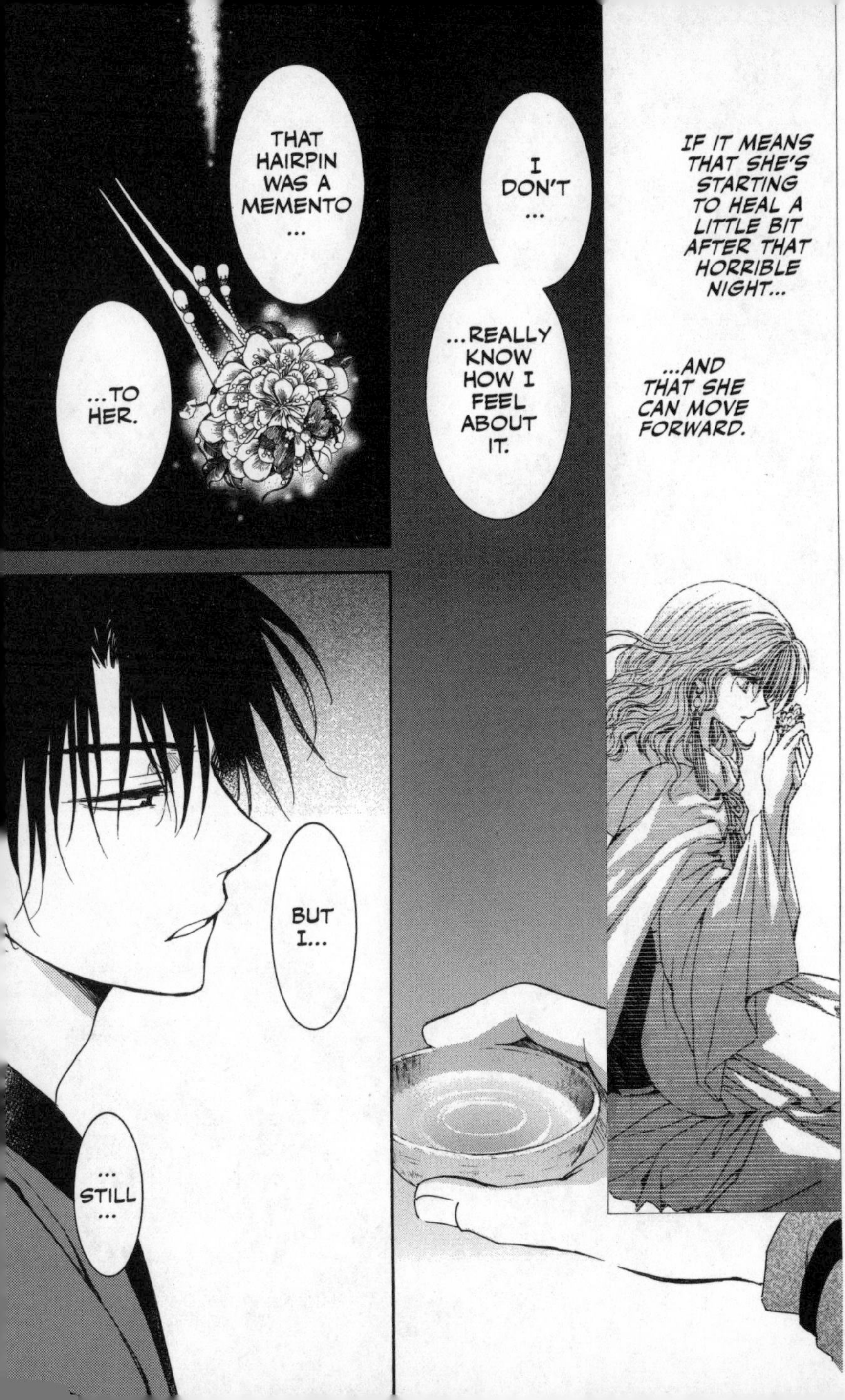
IF IT MEANS THAT SHE'S STARTING TO HEAL A LITTLE BIT AFTER THAT HORRIBLE NIGHT...
...AND THAT SHE CAN MOVE FORWARD.
I DON'T ...
...REALLY KNOW HOW I FEEL ABOUT IT.
THAT HAIRPIN WAS A MEMENTO ...
...TO HER.
BUT I...
... STILL ...

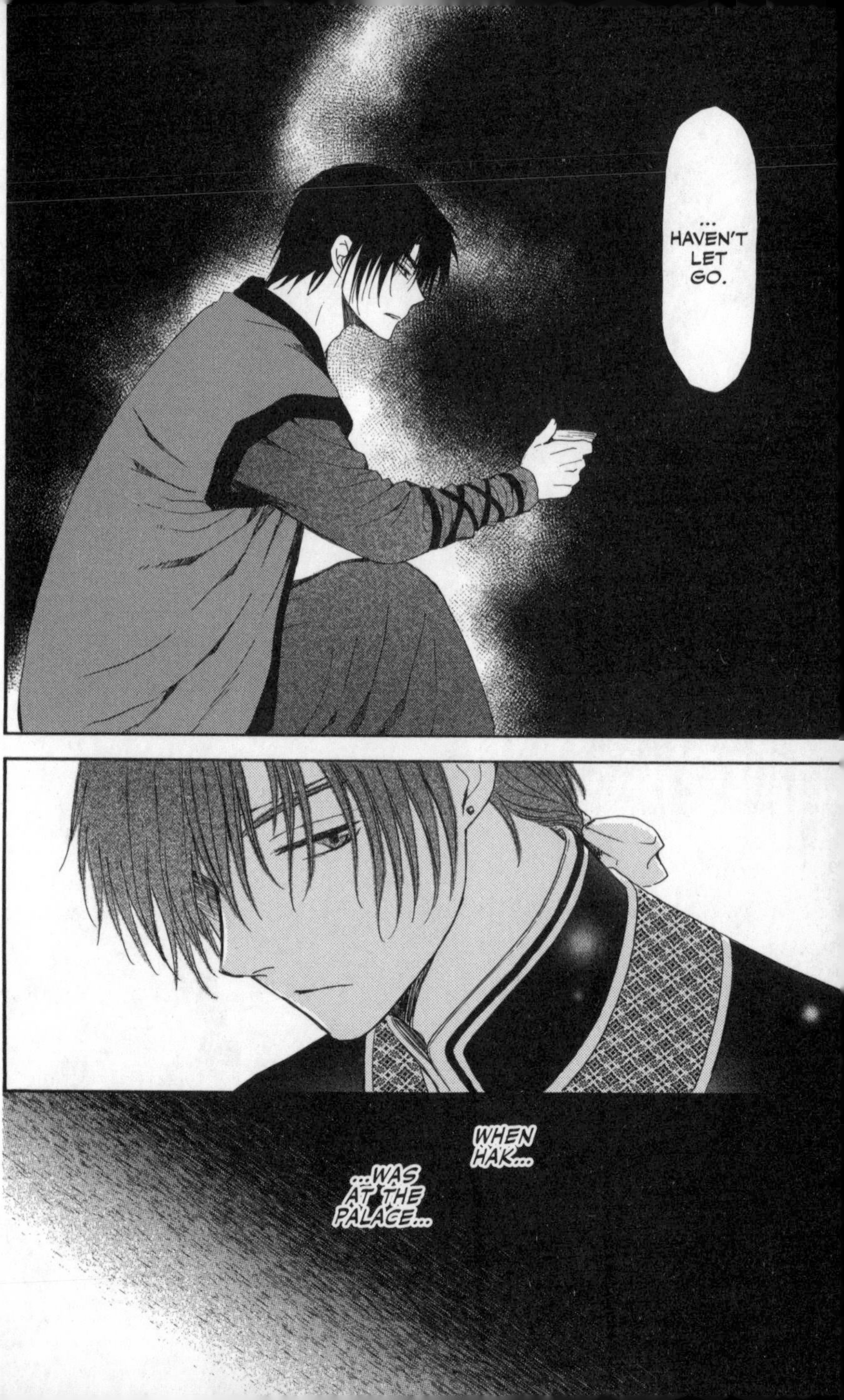
... HAVEN'T LET GO.
WHEN HAK...
...WAS AT THE PALACE...

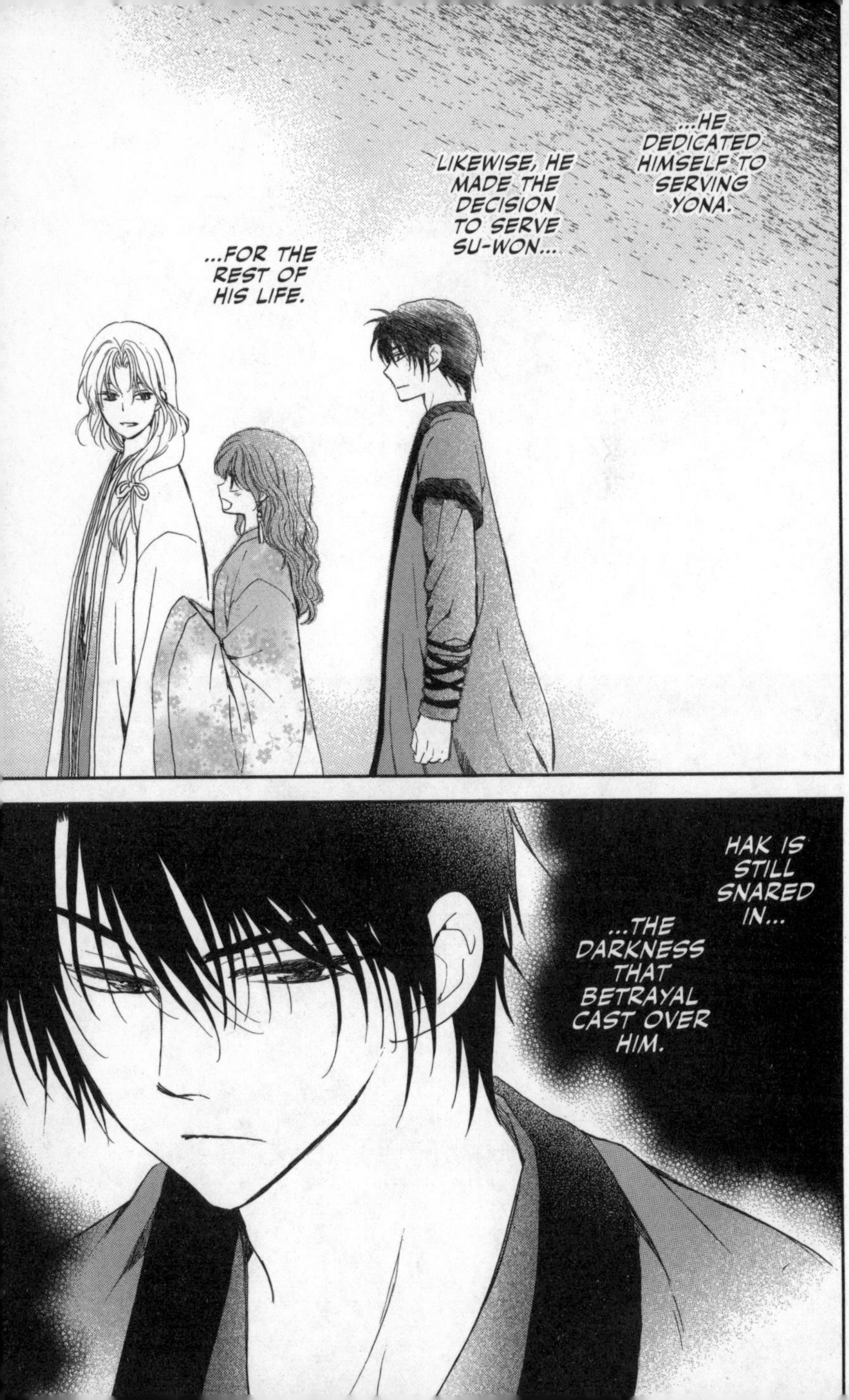
...HE DEDICATED HIMSELF TO SERVING YONA.
LIKEWISE, HE MADE THE DECISION TO SERVE SU-WON...
...FOR THE REST OF HIS LIFE.
HAK IS STILL SNARED IN...
...THE DARKNESS THAT BETRAYAL CAST OVER HIM.

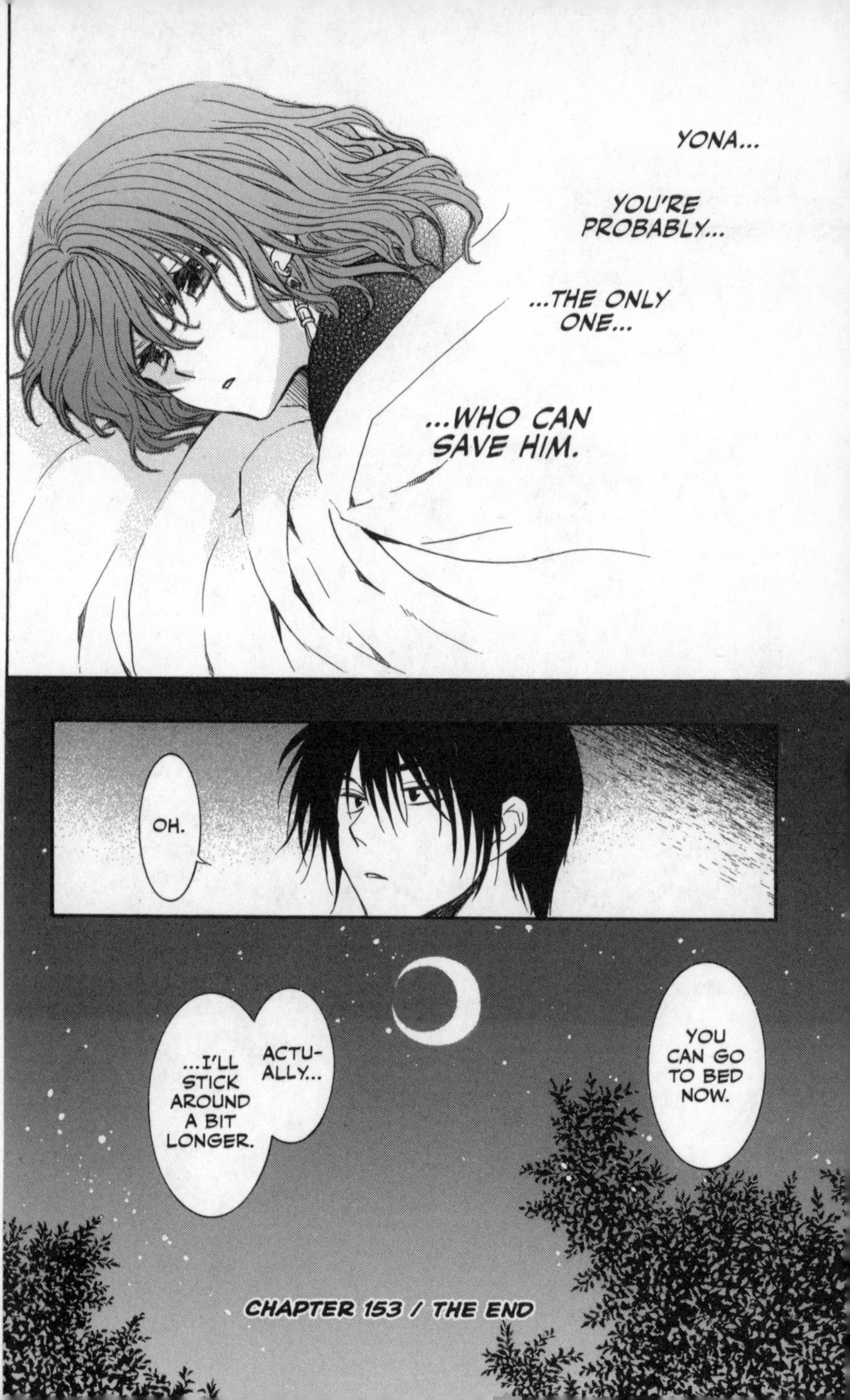
YONA...
YOU'RE PROBABLY...
...THE ONLY ONE...
...WHO CAN SAVE HIM.
OH.
YOU CAN GO TO BED NOW.
ACTU-ALLY...
...I'LL STICK AROUND A BIT LONGER.
CHAPTER 153 / THE END

Spending some time at an inn.

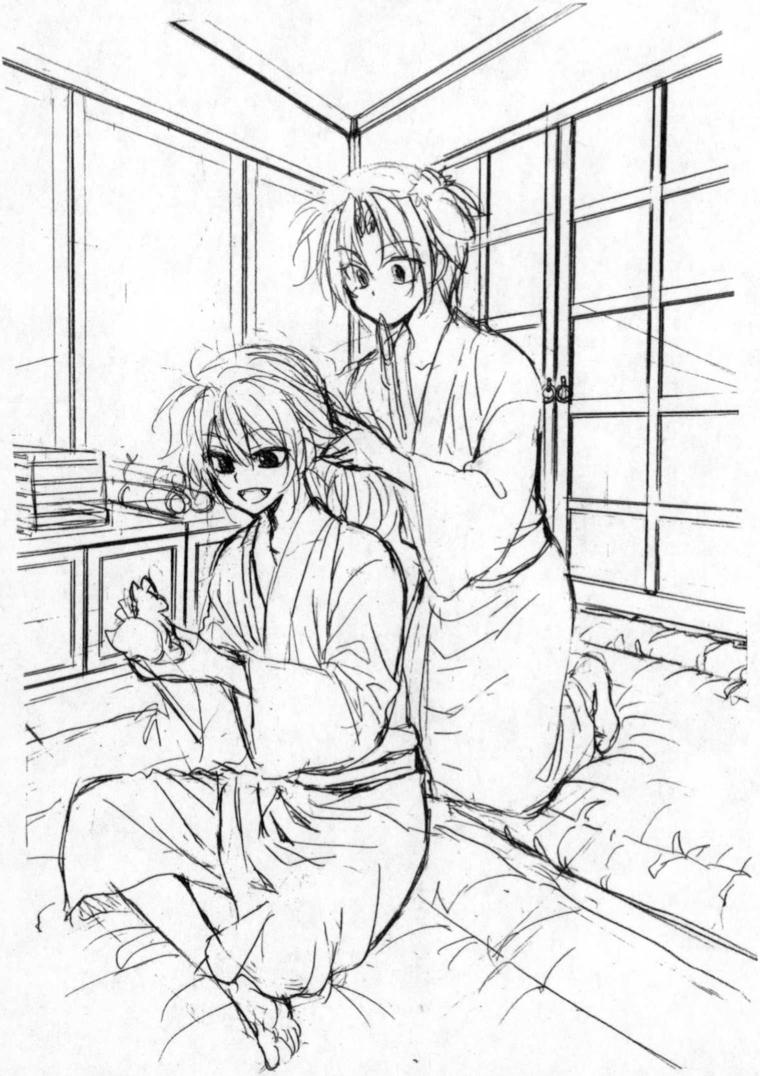

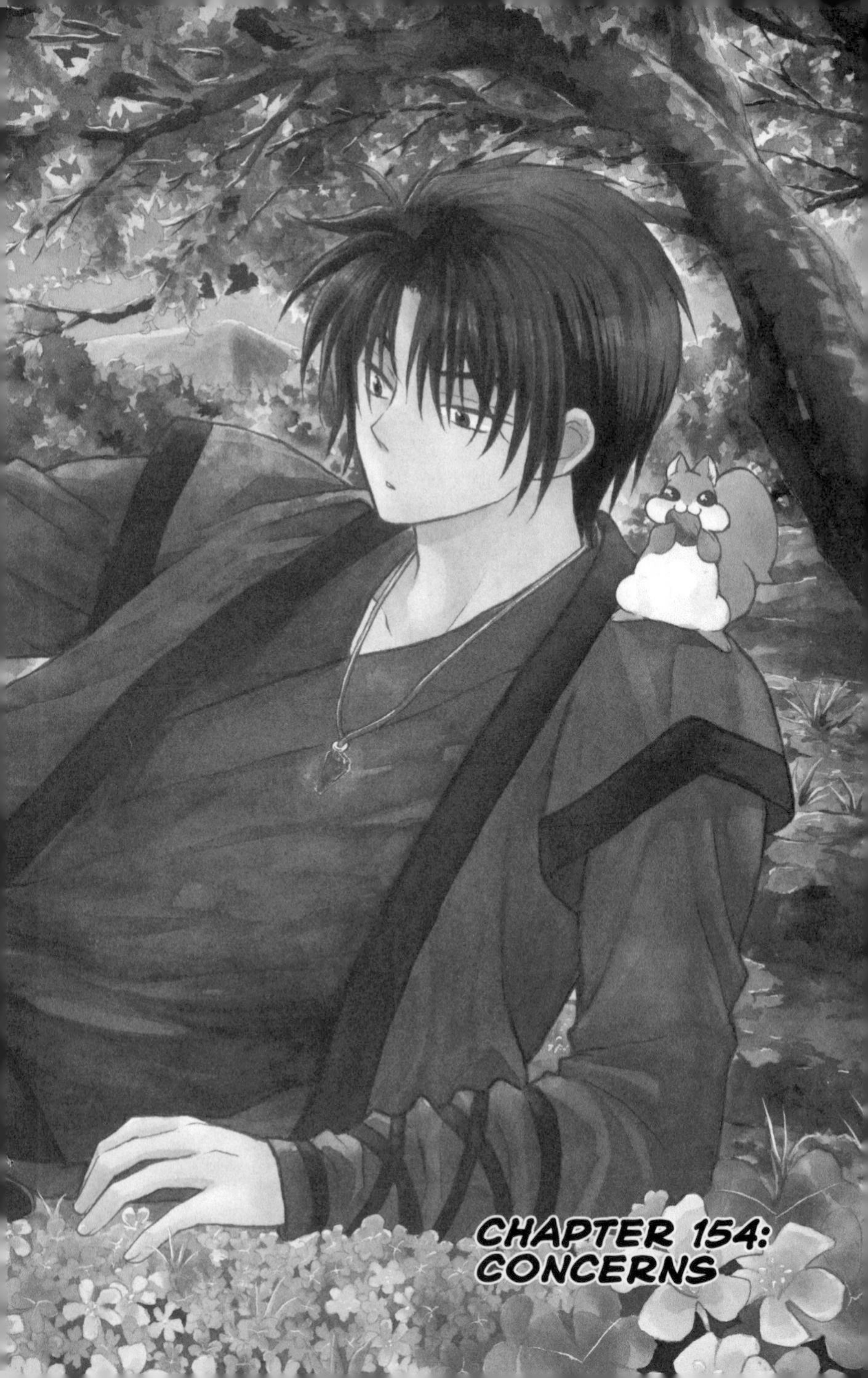
CHAPTER 154:
CONCERNS

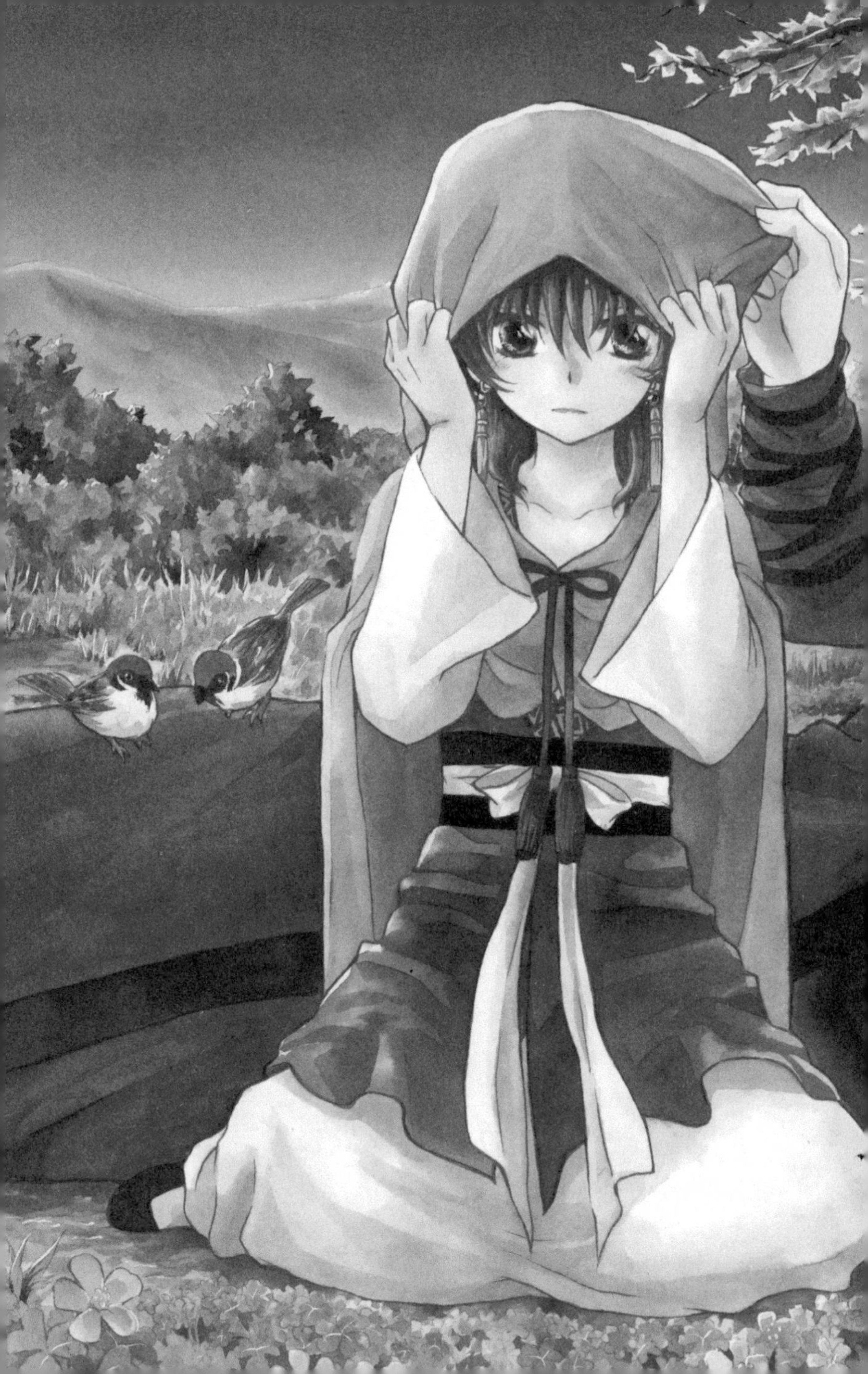

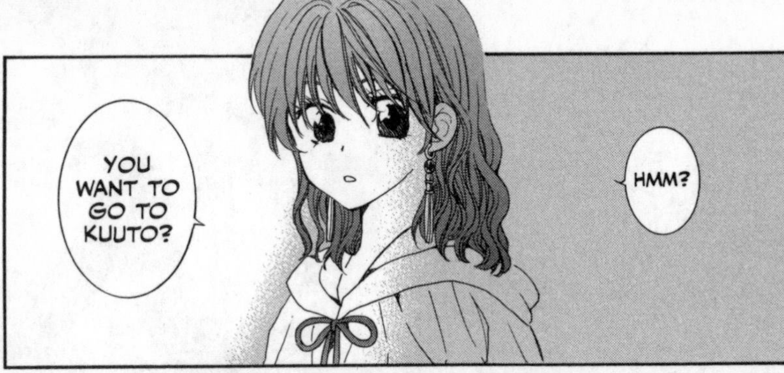
HMM?
YOU WANT TO GO TO KUUTO?

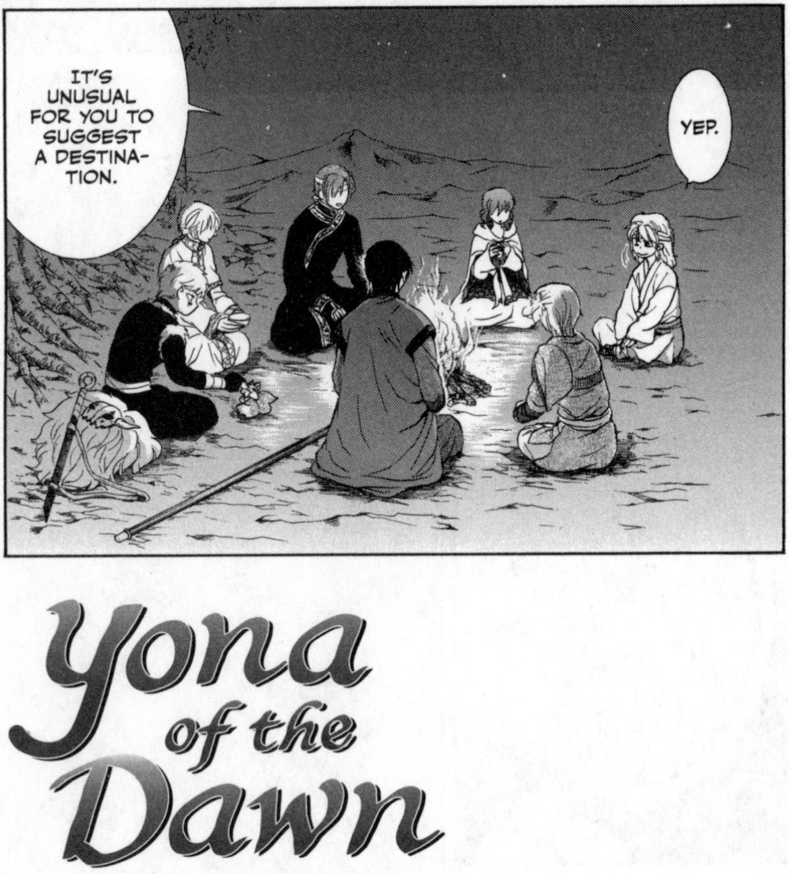
YEP.
IT'S UNUSUAL FOR YOU TO SUGGEST A DESTINATION.

Yona of the Dawn

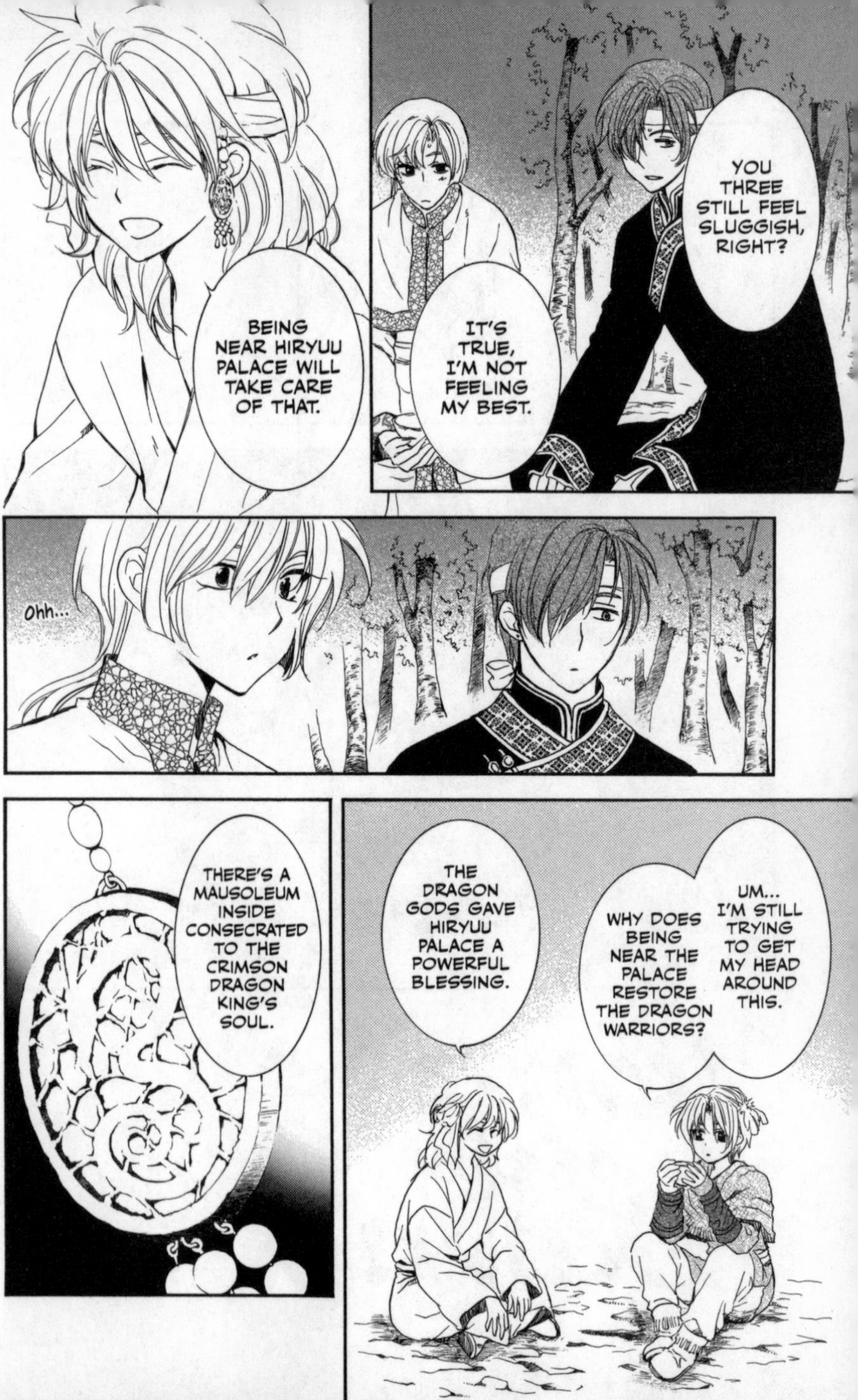
YOU THREE STILL FEEL SLUGGISH, RIGHT?
IT'S TRUE, I'M NOT FEELING MY BEST.
BEING NEAR HIRYUU PALACE WILL TAKE CARE OF THAT.
Ohh...
UM... I'M STILL TRYING TO GET MY HEAD AROUND THIS.
WHY DOES BEING NEAR THE PALACE RESTORE THE DRAGON WARRIORS?
THE DRAGON GODS GAVE HIRYUU PALACE A POWERFUL BLESSING.
THERE'S A MAUSOLEUM INSIDE CONSECRATED TO THE CRIMSON DRAGON KING'S SOUL.

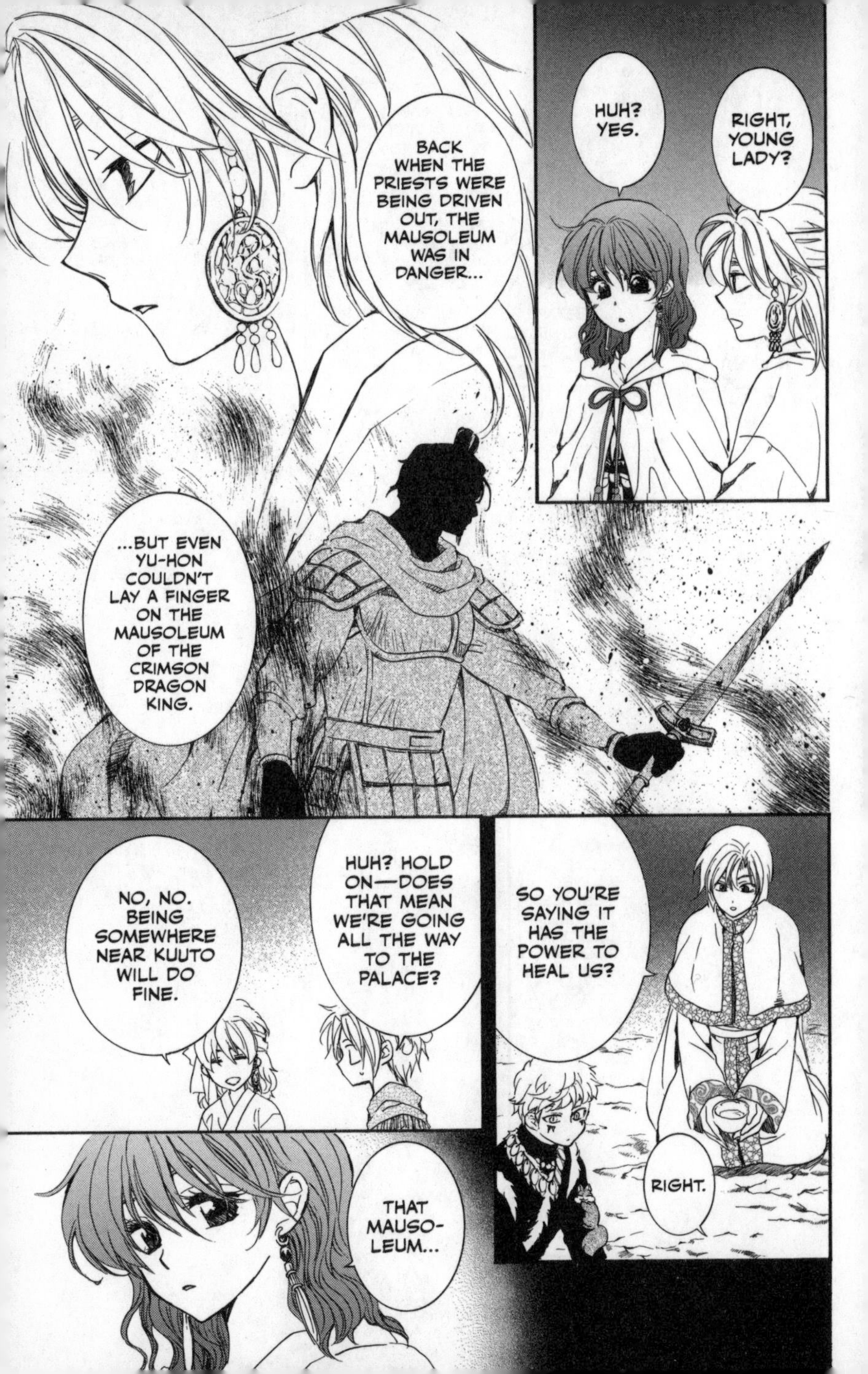
RIGHT, YOUNG LADY?
HUH? YES.
BACK WHEN THE PRIESTS WERE BEING DRIVEN OUT, THE MAUSOLEUM WAS IN DANGER...
...BUT EVEN YU-HON COULDN'T LAY A FINGER ON THE MAUSOLEUM OF THE CRIMSON DRAGON KING.
SO YOU'RE SAYING IT HAS THE POWER TO HEAL US?
RIGHT.
HUH? HOLD ON—DOES THAT MEAN WE'RE GOING ALL THE WAY TO THE PALACE?
NO, NO. BEING SOMEWHERE NEAR KUUTO WILL DO FINE.
THAT MAUSO-LEUM...

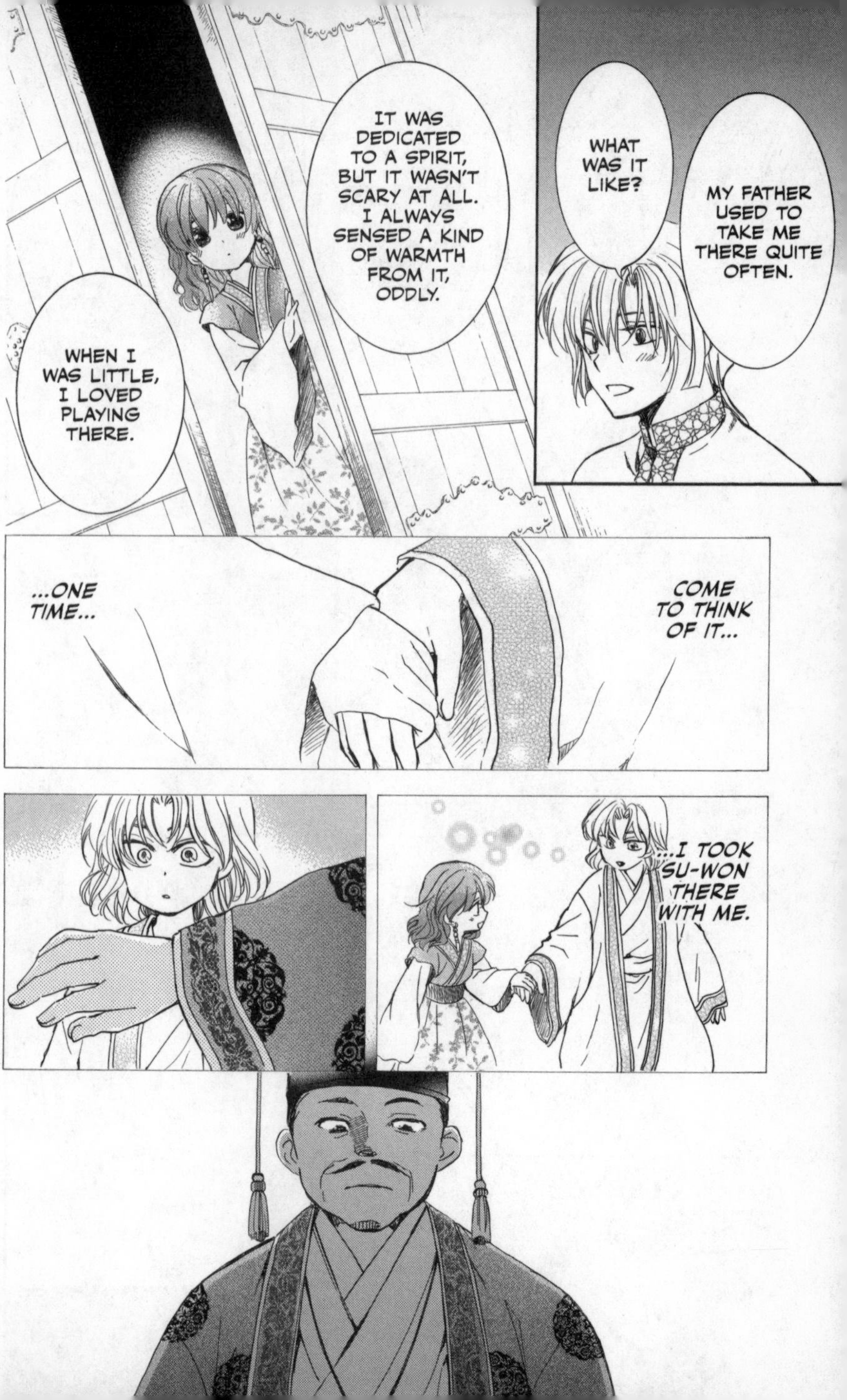
MY FATHER USED TO TAKE ME THERE QUITE OFTEN.
WHAT WAS IT LIKE?
IT WAS DEDICATED TO A SPIRIT, BUT IT WASN'T SCARY AT ALL. I ALWAYS SENSED A KIND OF WARMTH FROM IT, ODDLY.
WHEN I WAS LITTLE, I LOVED PLAYING THERE.
COME TO THINK OF IT...
...ONE TIME...
...I TOOK SU-WON THERE WITH ME.

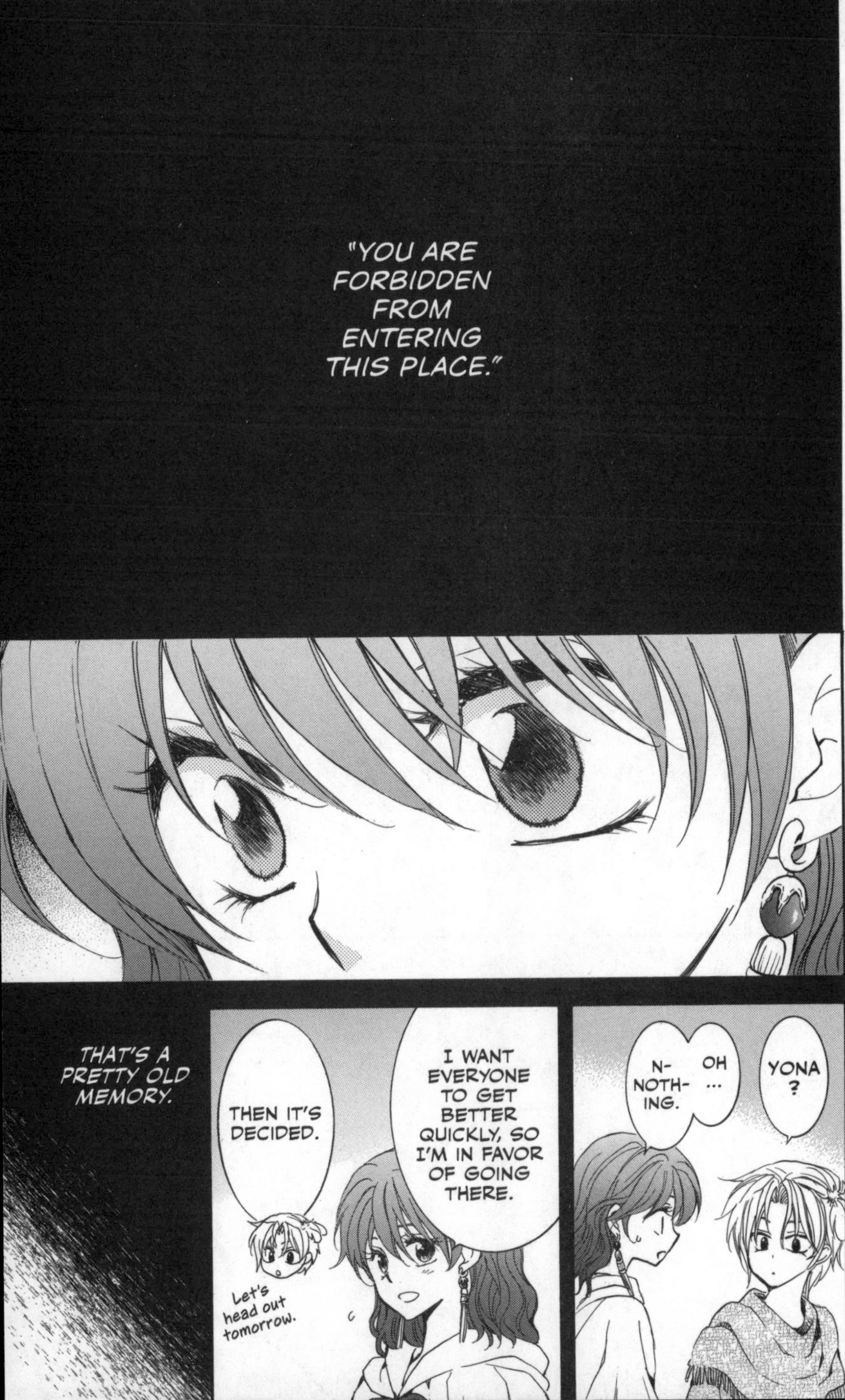
"YOU ARE FORBIDDEN FROM ENTERING THIS PLACE."
YONA?
OH...
N-NOTHING.
I WANT EVERYONE TO GET BETTER QUICKLY, SO I'M IN FAVOR OF GOING THERE.
THEN IT'S DECIDED.
Let's head out tomorrow.
THAT'S A PRETTY OLD MEMORY.

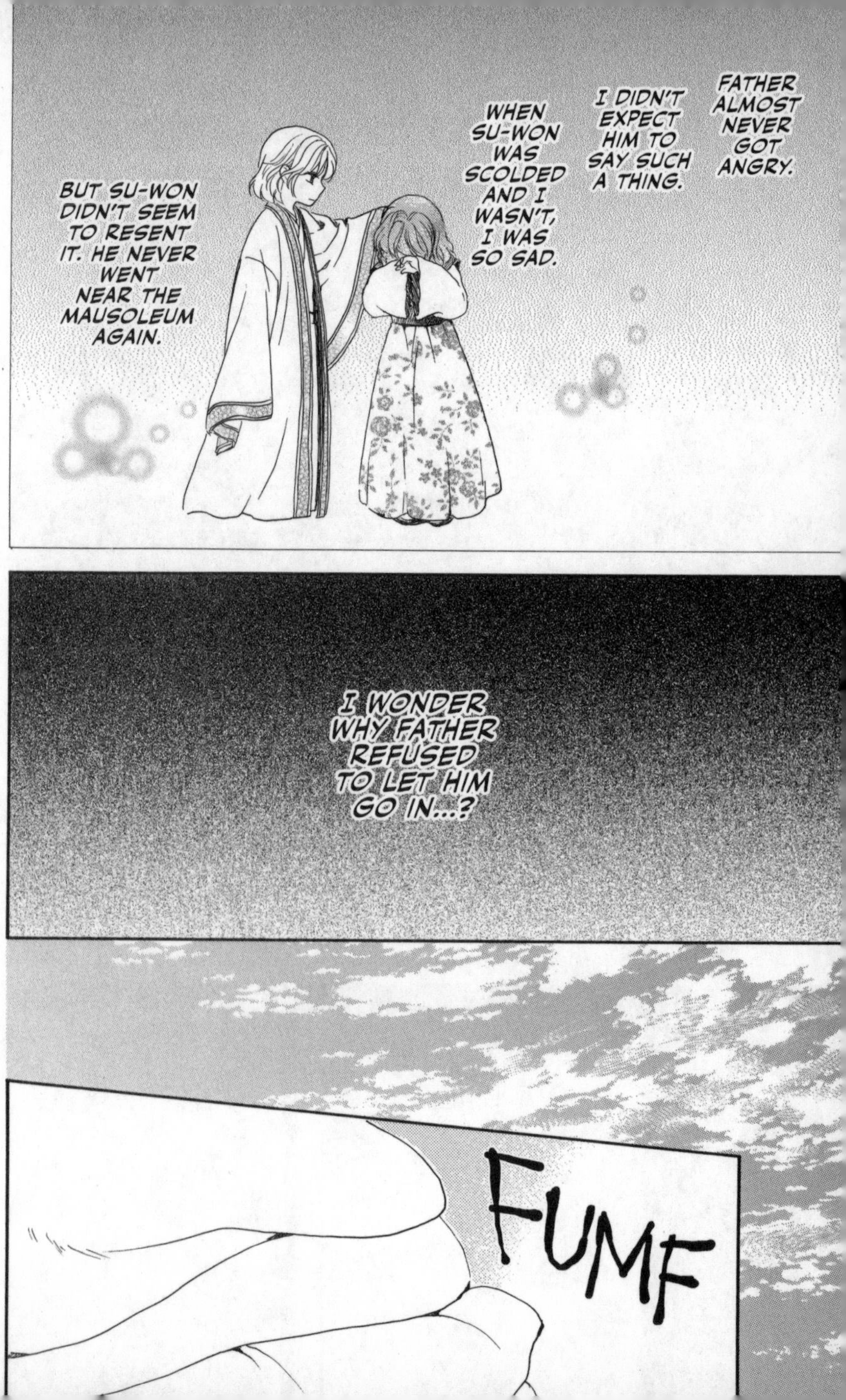
FATHER ALMOST NEVER GOT ANGRY.
I DIDN'T EXPECT HIM TO SAY SUCH A THING.
WHEN SU-WON WAS SCOLDED AND I WASN'T, I WAS SO SAD.
BUT SU-WON DIDN'T SEEM TO RESENT IT. HE NEVER WENT NEAR THE MAUSOLEUM AGAIN.
I WONDER WHY FATHER REFUSED TO LET HIM GO IN...?
FUMF

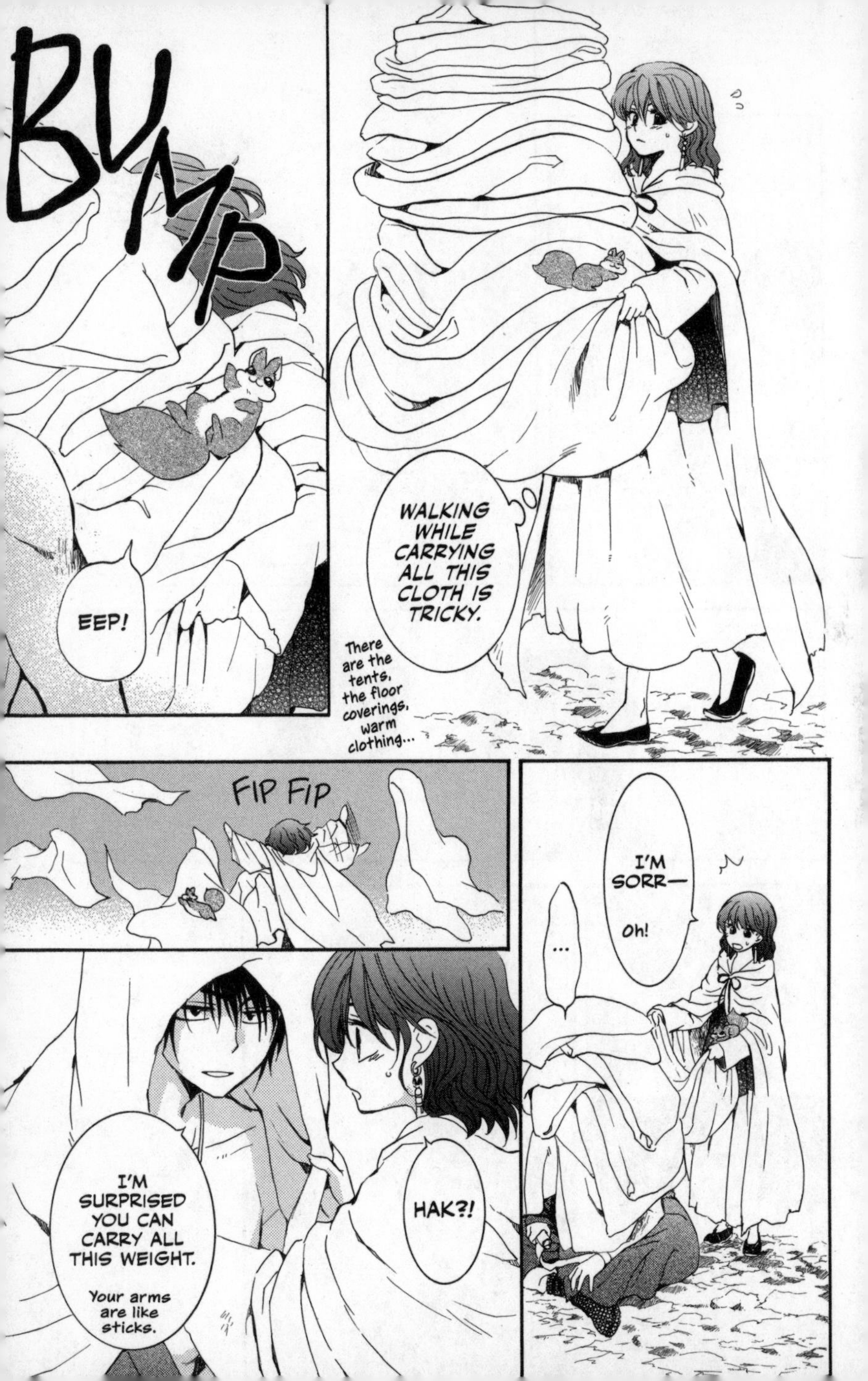
WALKING WHILE CARRYING ALL THIS CLOTH IS TRICKY.
There are the tents, the floor coverings, warm clothing...
BUMP
EEP!
I'M SORR—
Oh!
...
FIP FIP
HAK?!
I'M SURPRISED YOU CAN CARRY ALL THIS WEIGHT.
Your arms are like sticks.

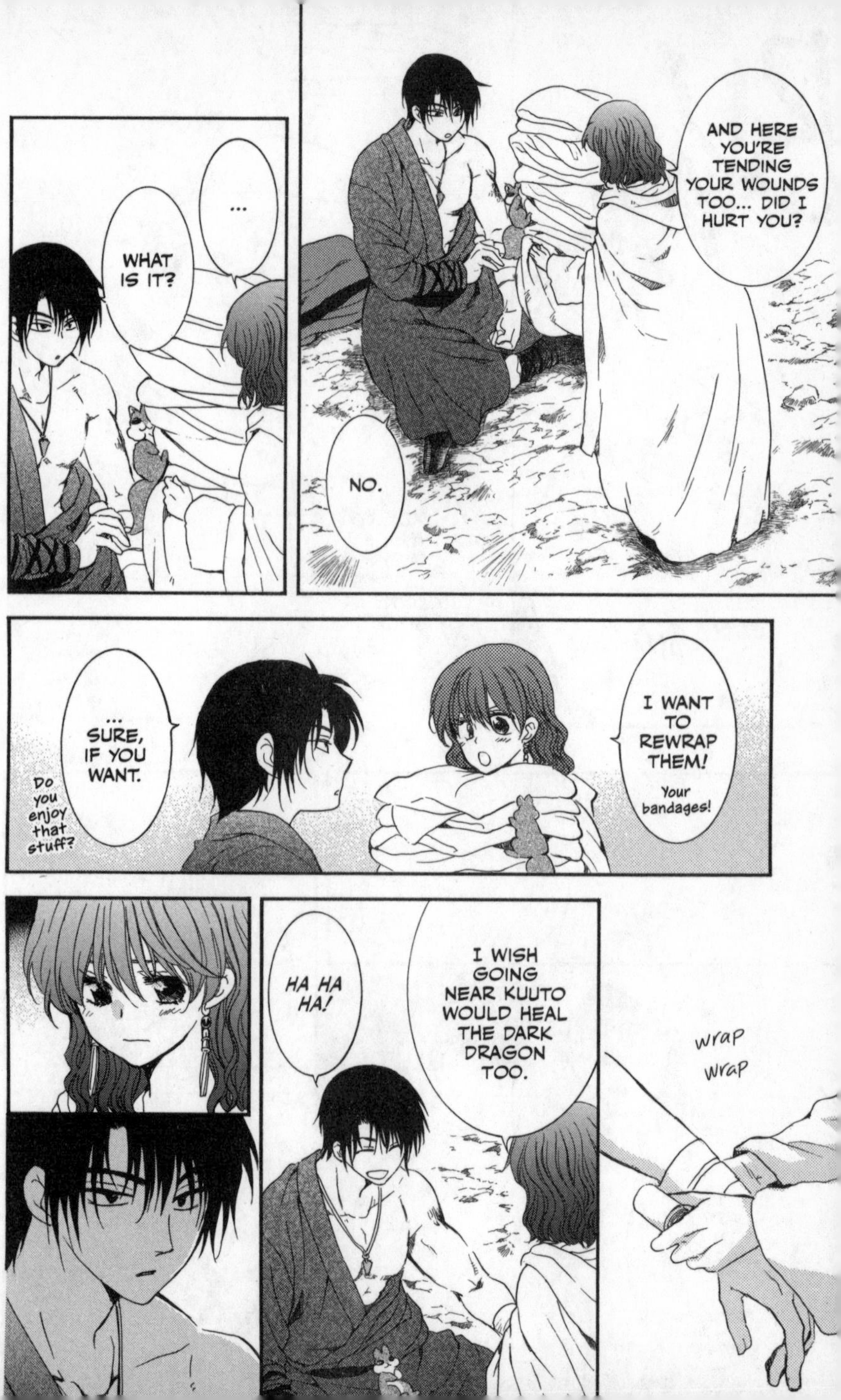
AND HERE YOU'RE TENDING YOUR WOUNDS TOO... DID I HURT YOU?
NO.
...
WHAT IS IT?
I WANT TO REWRAP THEM!
Your bandages!
... SURE, IF YOU WANT.
Do you enjoy that stuff?
wrap
wrap
I WISH GOING NEAR KUUTO WOULD HEAL THE DARK DRAGON TOO.
HA HA HA!

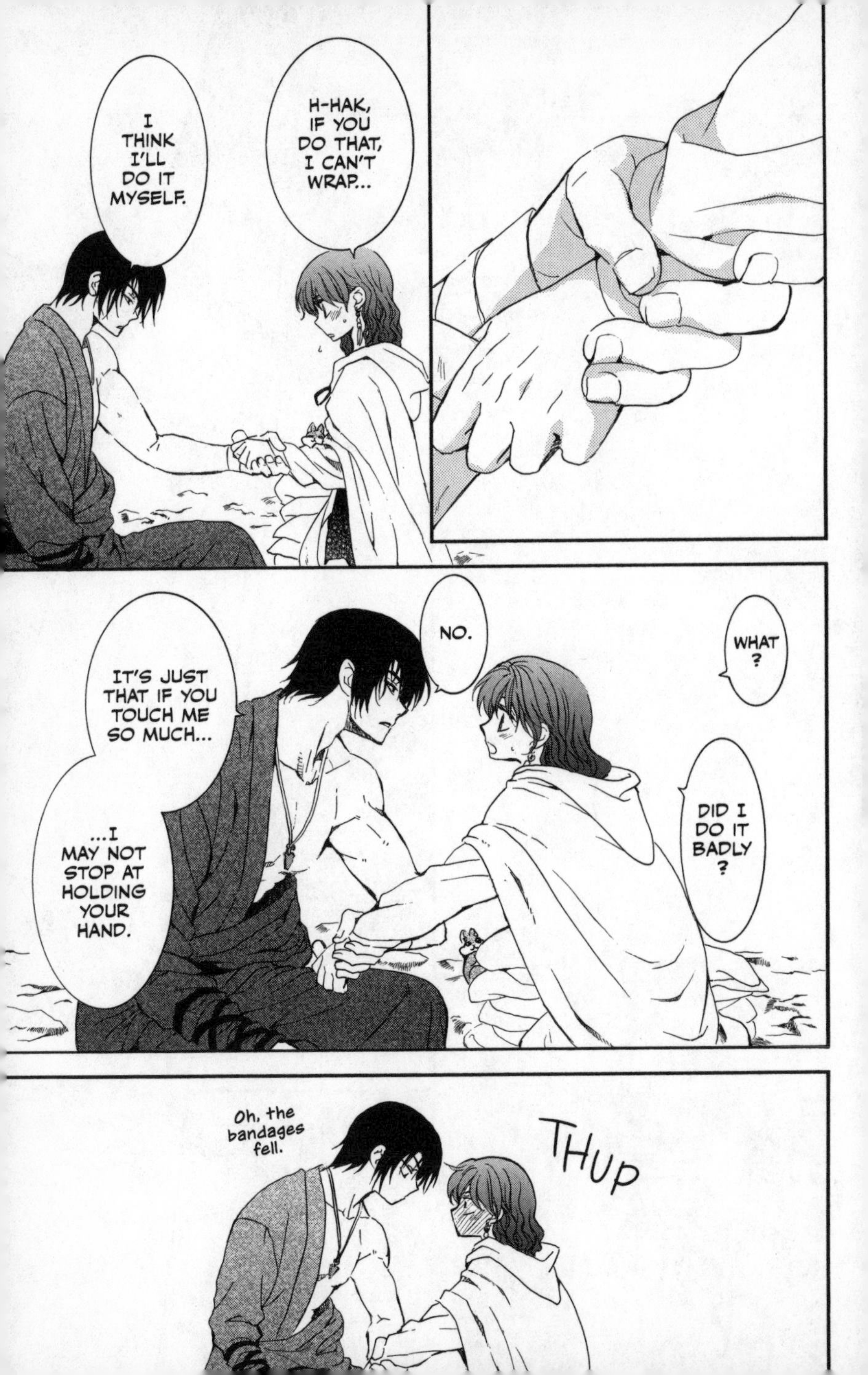
H-HAK, IF YOU DO THAT, I CAN'T WRAP...
I THINK I'LL DO IT MYSELF.
WHAT?
DID I DO IT BADLY?
NO.
IT'S JUST THAT IF YOU TOUCH ME SO MUCH...
...I MAY NOT STOP AT HOLDING YOUR HAND.
THUP
Oh, the bandages fell.

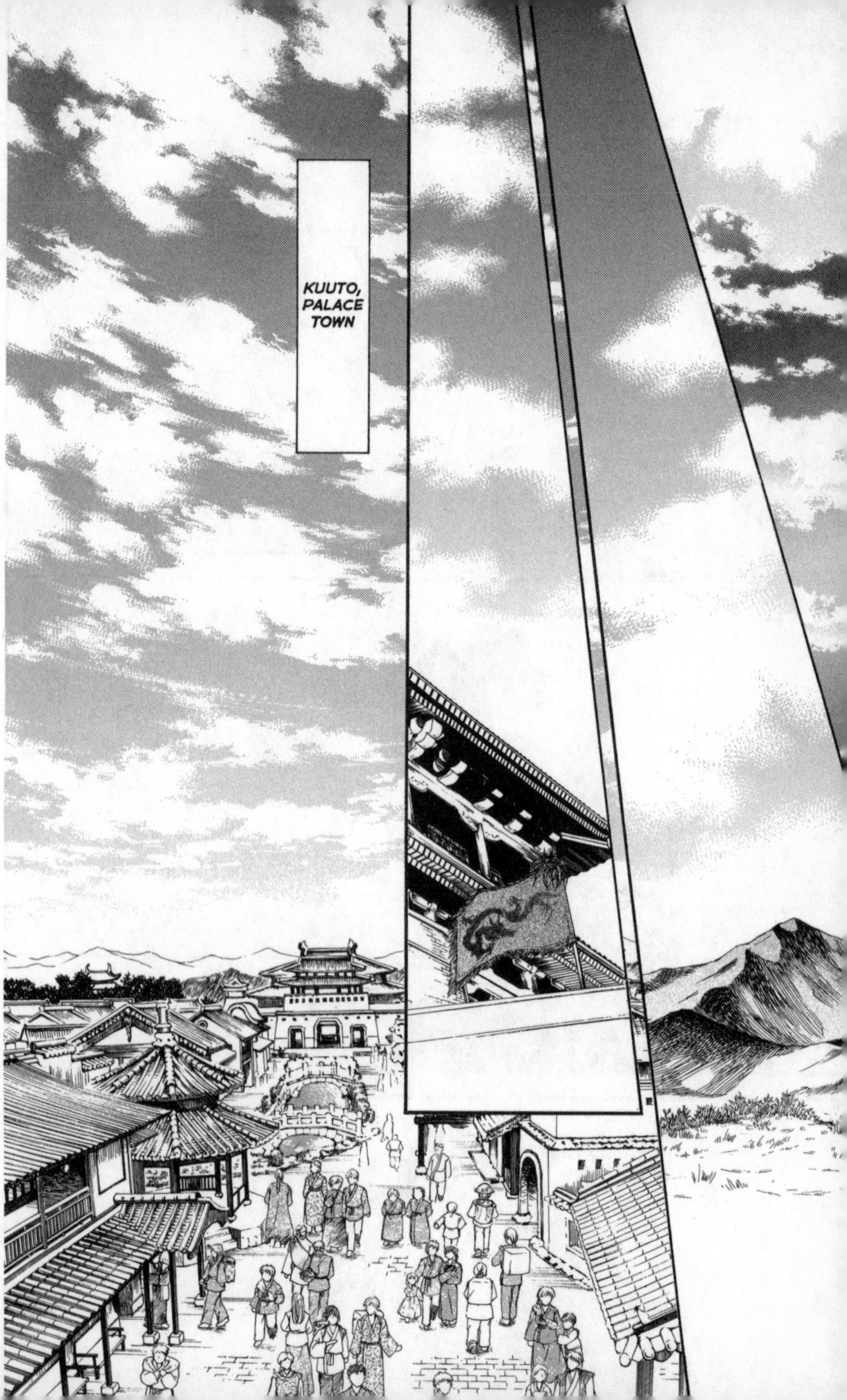
KUUTO, PALACE TOWN

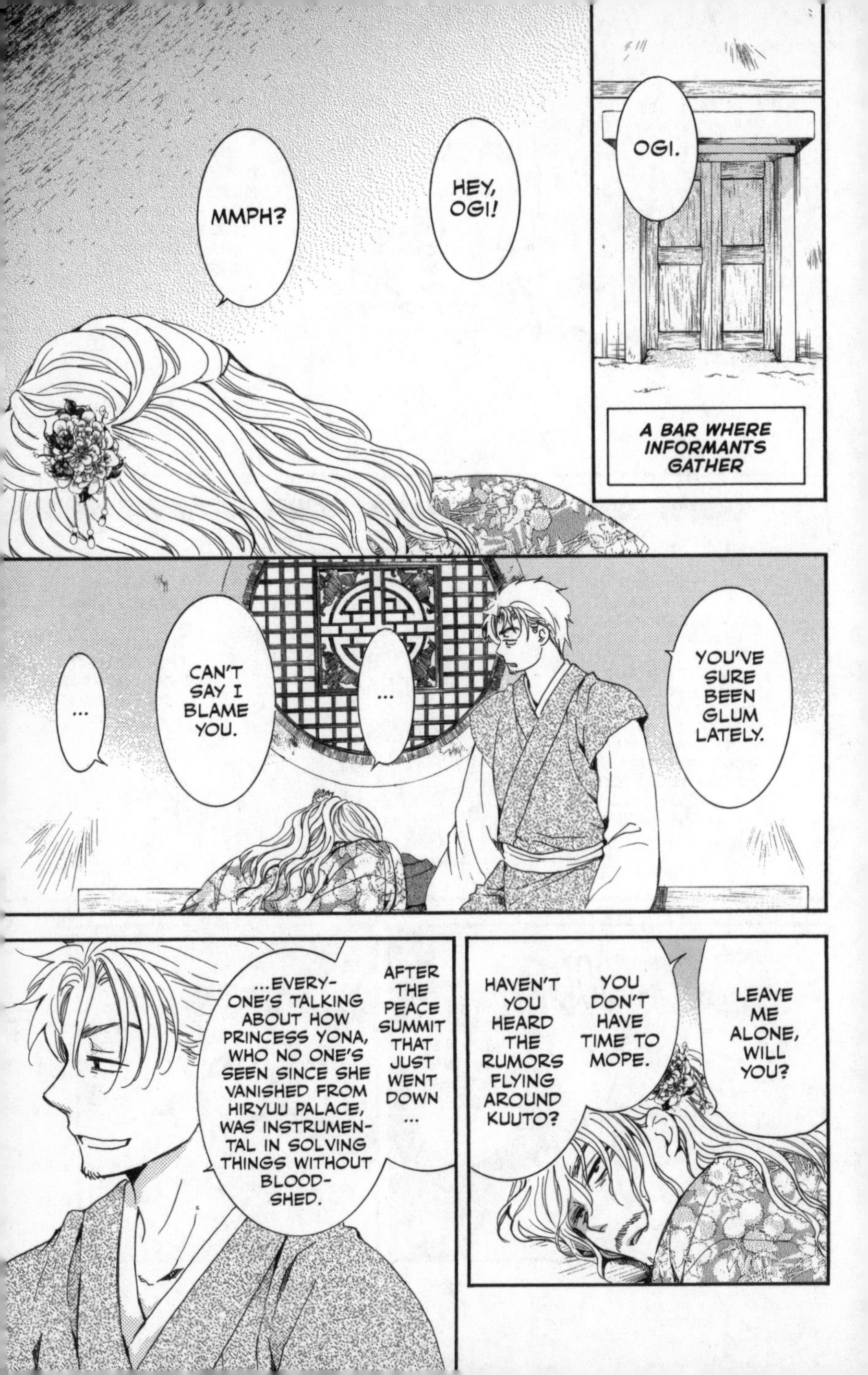
OGI.
A BAR WHERE INFORMANTS GATHER
HEY, OGI!
MMPH?
YOU'VE SURE BEEN GLUM LATELY.
...
CAN'T SAY I BLAME YOU.
...
LEAVE ME ALONE, WILL YOU?
YOU DON'T HAVE TIME TO MOPE.
HAVEN'T YOU HEARD THE RUMORS FLYING AROUND KUUTO?
AFTER THE PEACE SUMMIT THAT JUST WENT DOWN...
...EVERYONE'S TALKING ABOUT HOW PRINCESS YONA, WHO NO ONE'S SEEN SINCE SHE VANISHED FROM HIRYUU PALACE, WAS INSTRUMENTAL IN SOLVING THINGS WITHOUT BLOODSHED.

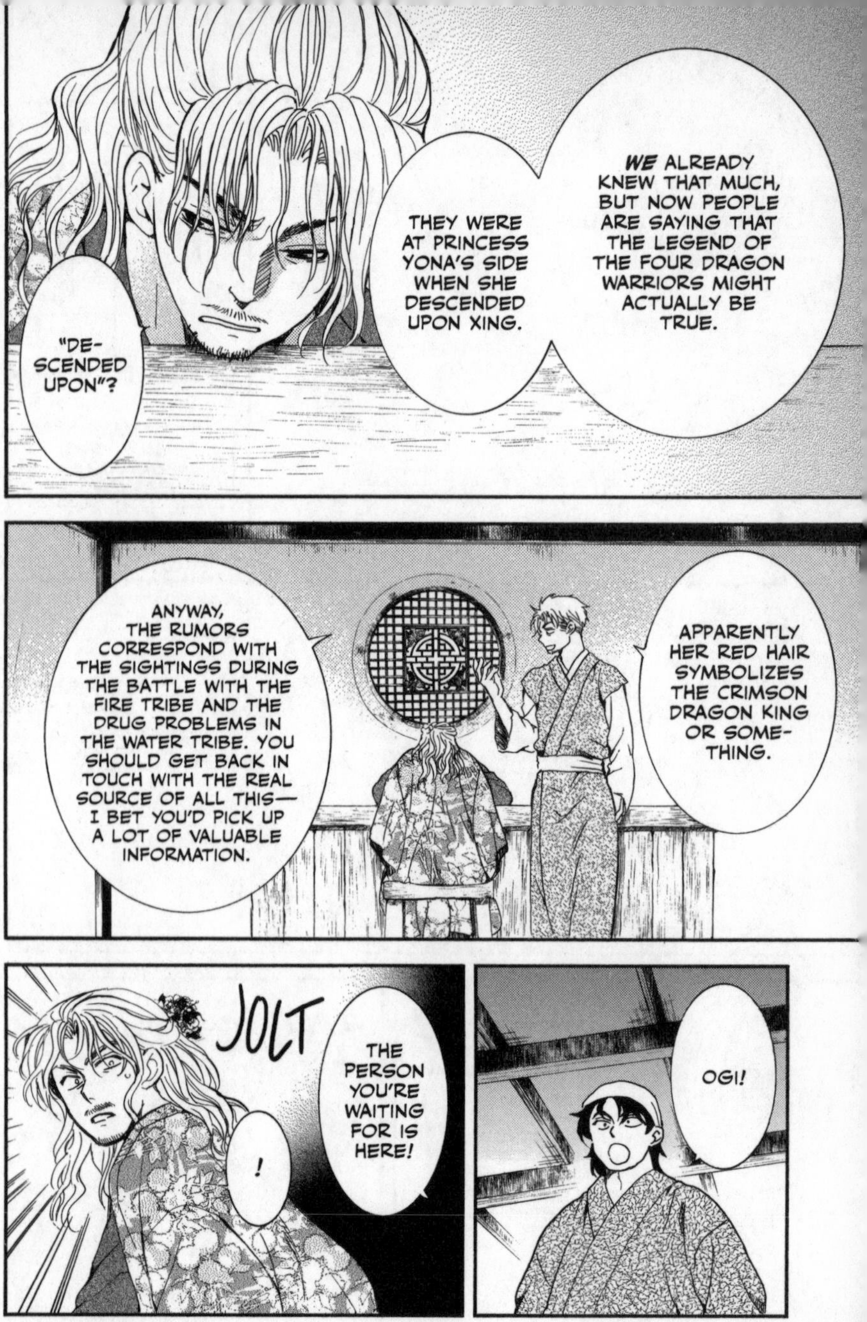
WE ALREADY KNEW THAT MUCH, BUT NOW PEOPLE ARE SAYING THAT THE LEGEND OF THE FOUR DRAGON WARRIORS MIGHT ACTUALLY BE TRUE.
THEY WERE AT PRINCESS YONA'S SIDE WHEN SHE DESCENDED UPON XING.
"DE-SCENDED UPON"?
APPARENTLY HER RED HAIR SYMBOLIZES THE CRIMSON DRAGON KING OR SOME-THING.
ANYWAY, THE RUMORS CORRESPOND WITH THE SIGHTINGS DURING THE BATTLE WITH THE FIRE TRIBE AND THE DRUG PROBLEMS IN THE WATER TRIBE. YOU SHOULD GET BACK IN TOUCH WITH THE REAL SOURCE OF ALL THIS— I BET YOU'D PICK UP A LOT OF VALUABLE INFORMATION.
OGI!
THE PERSON YOU'RE WAITING FOR IS HERE!
JOLT
!

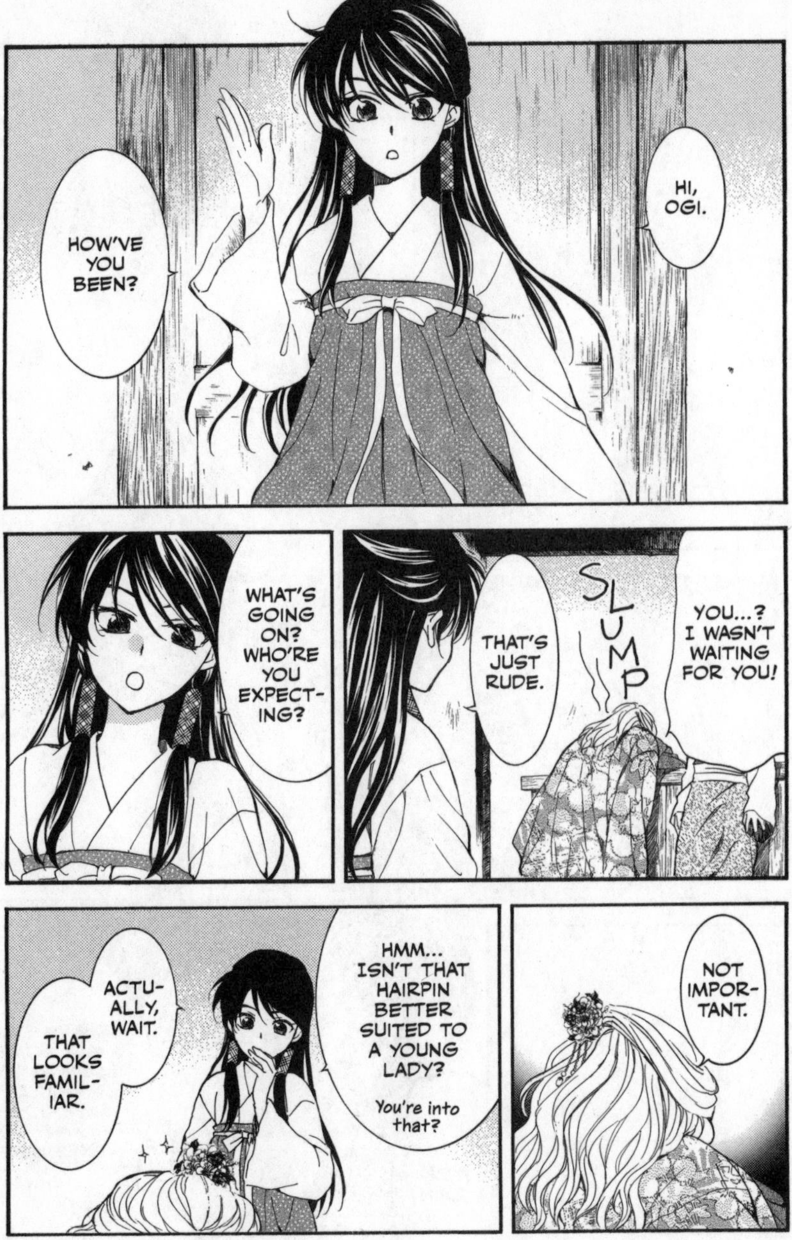
HI, OGI.
HOW'VE YOU BEEN?
YOU...? I WASN'T WAITING FOR YOU!
SLUMP
THAT'S JUST RUDE.
WHAT'S GOING ON? WHO'RE YOU EXPECTING?
NOT IMPORTANT.
HMM... ISN'T THAT HAIRPIN BETTER SUITED TO A YOUNG LADY?
You're into that?
ACTUALLY, WAIT.
THAT LOOKS FAMILIAR.

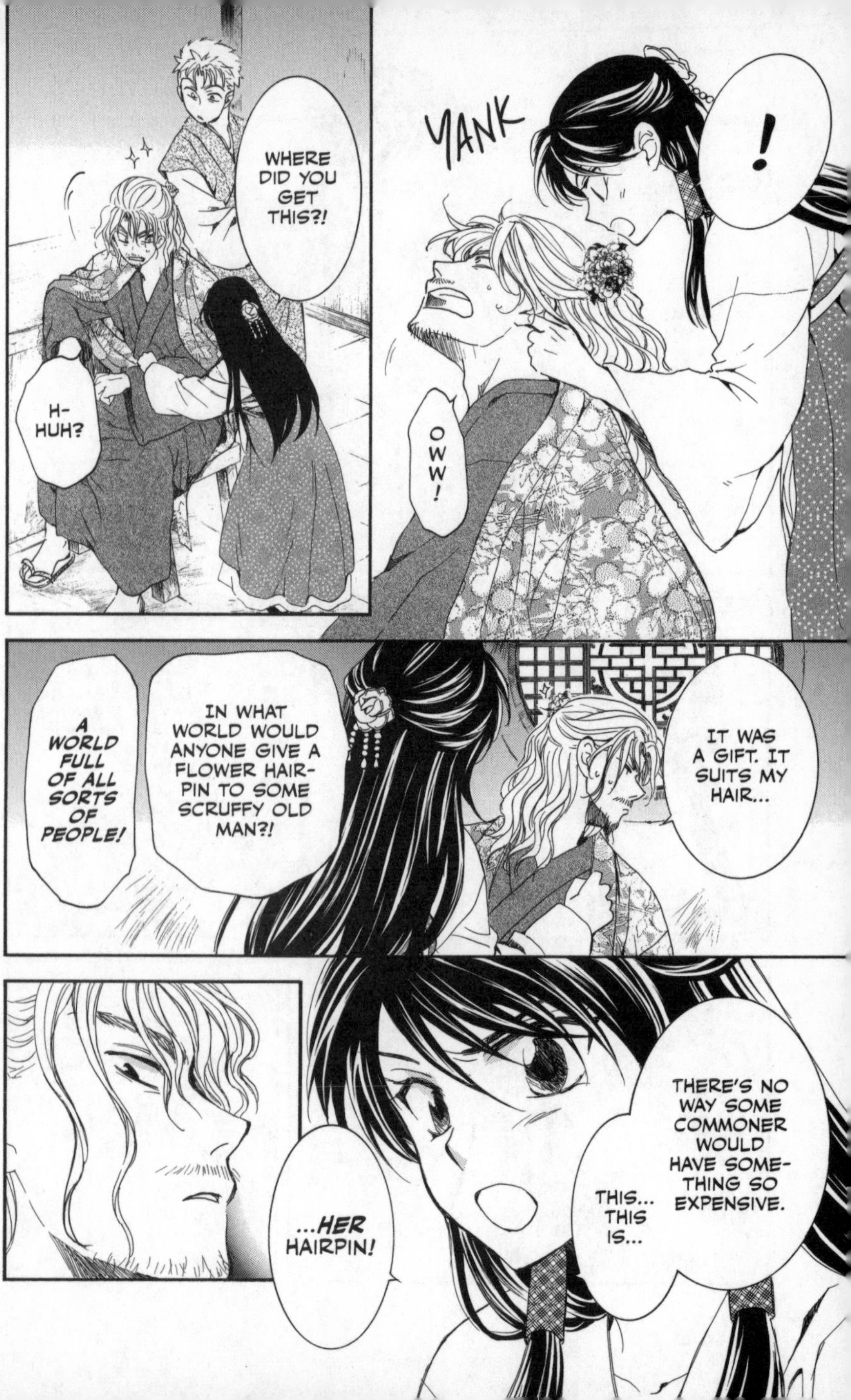
!
YANK
OWW!
WHERE DID YOU GET THIS?!
H-HUH?
IT WAS A GIFT. IT SUITS MY HAIR...
IN WHAT WORLD WOULD ANYONE GIVE A FLOWER HAIR-PIN TO SOME SCRUFFY OLD MAN?!
A WORLD FULL OF ALL SORTS OF PEOPLE!
THERE'S NO WAY SOME COMMONER WOULD HAVE SOME-THING SO EXPENSIVE.
THIS... THIS IS...
...HER HAIRPIN!

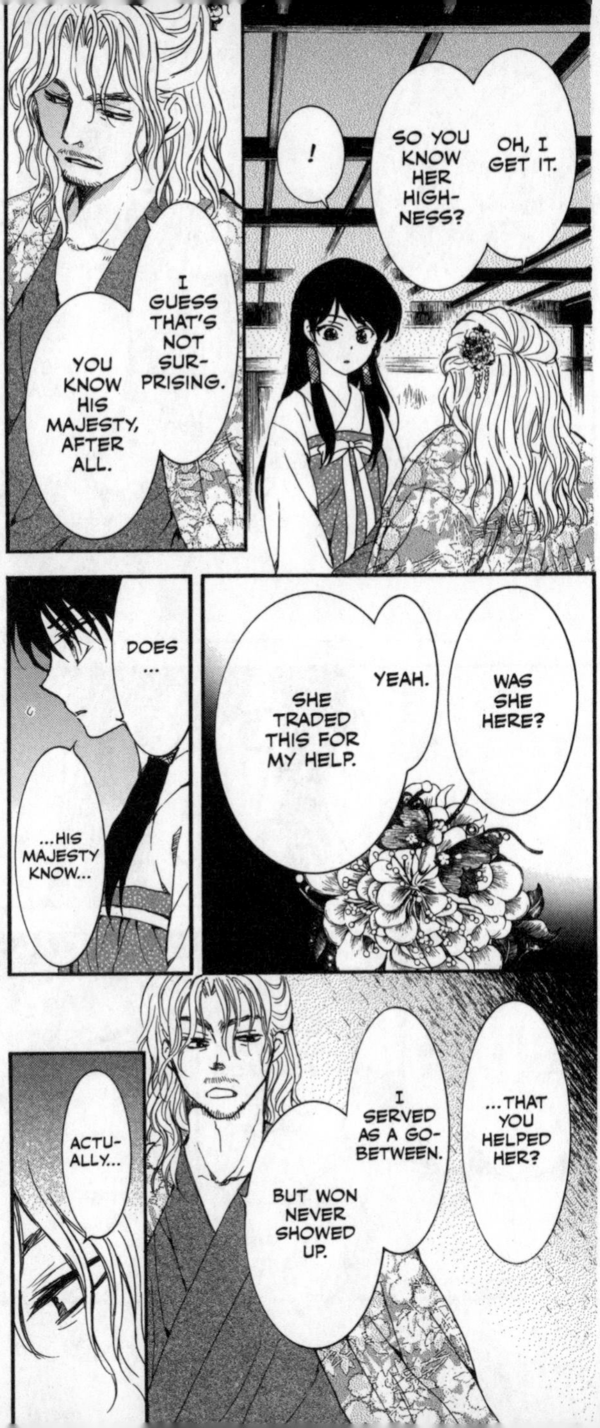
OH, I GET IT.
SO YOU KNOW HER HIGH-NESS?
!
I GUESS THAT'S NOT SUR-PRISING.
YOU KNOW HIS MAJESTY, AFTER ALL.
WAS SHE HERE?
YEAH.
SHE TRADED THIS FOR MY HELP.
DOES...
...HIS MAJESTY KNOW...
...THAT YOU HELPED HER?
I SERVED AS A GO-BETWEEN.
BUT WON NEVER SHOWED UP.
ACTU-ALLY...

Issue 18 of *Hana to Yume*, which goes on sale 8/20/2018, comes with a Yona drama CD! It contains chapters 151-153, as well as the bonus chapter "Take Care, Part 3."

Some people hoped there'd be a CD covering the Xing arc, but it wasn't possible. It would be much too long and the cast would be too large. ♪

With *Yona of the Dawn*, a bit more than 1-3 chapters is the perfect amount (I feel) to put on a CD.

Hak's short-tempered confession, Yona's squirming, the dialogue between Yun and the Dragon Warriors... The cast performed it all so adorably!

The issue will be on sale from 8/20 to 9/4. It might sell out, so make sure you go to the bookstore quickly.

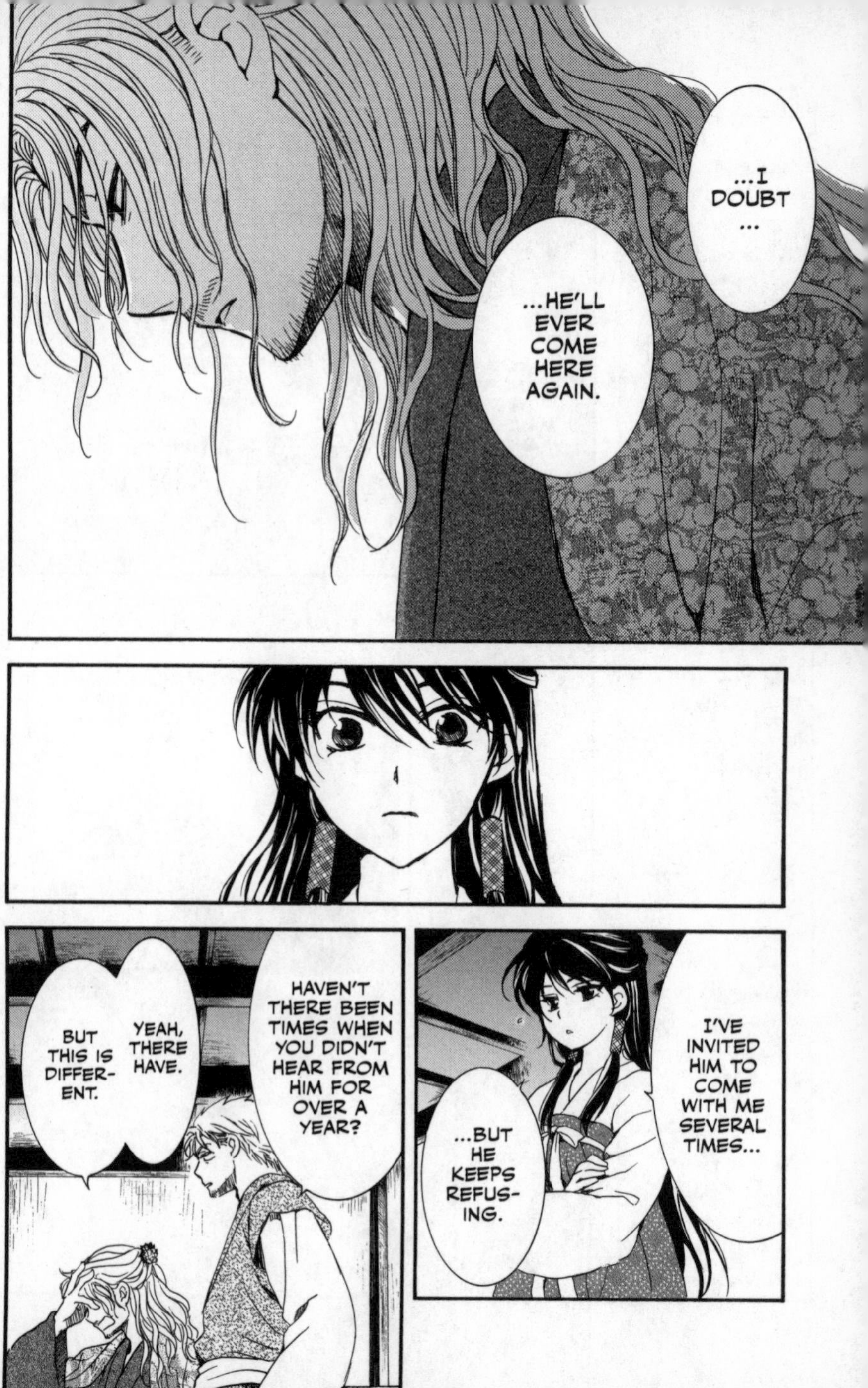
...I DOUBT ...
...HE'LL EVER COME HERE AGAIN.
I'VE INVITED HIM TO COME WITH ME SEVERAL TIMES...
...BUT HE KEEPS REFUSING.
HAVEN'T THERE BEEN TIMES WHEN YOU DIDN'T HEAR FROM HIM FOR OVER A YEAR?
YEAH, THERE HAVE.
BUT THIS IS DIFFERENT.

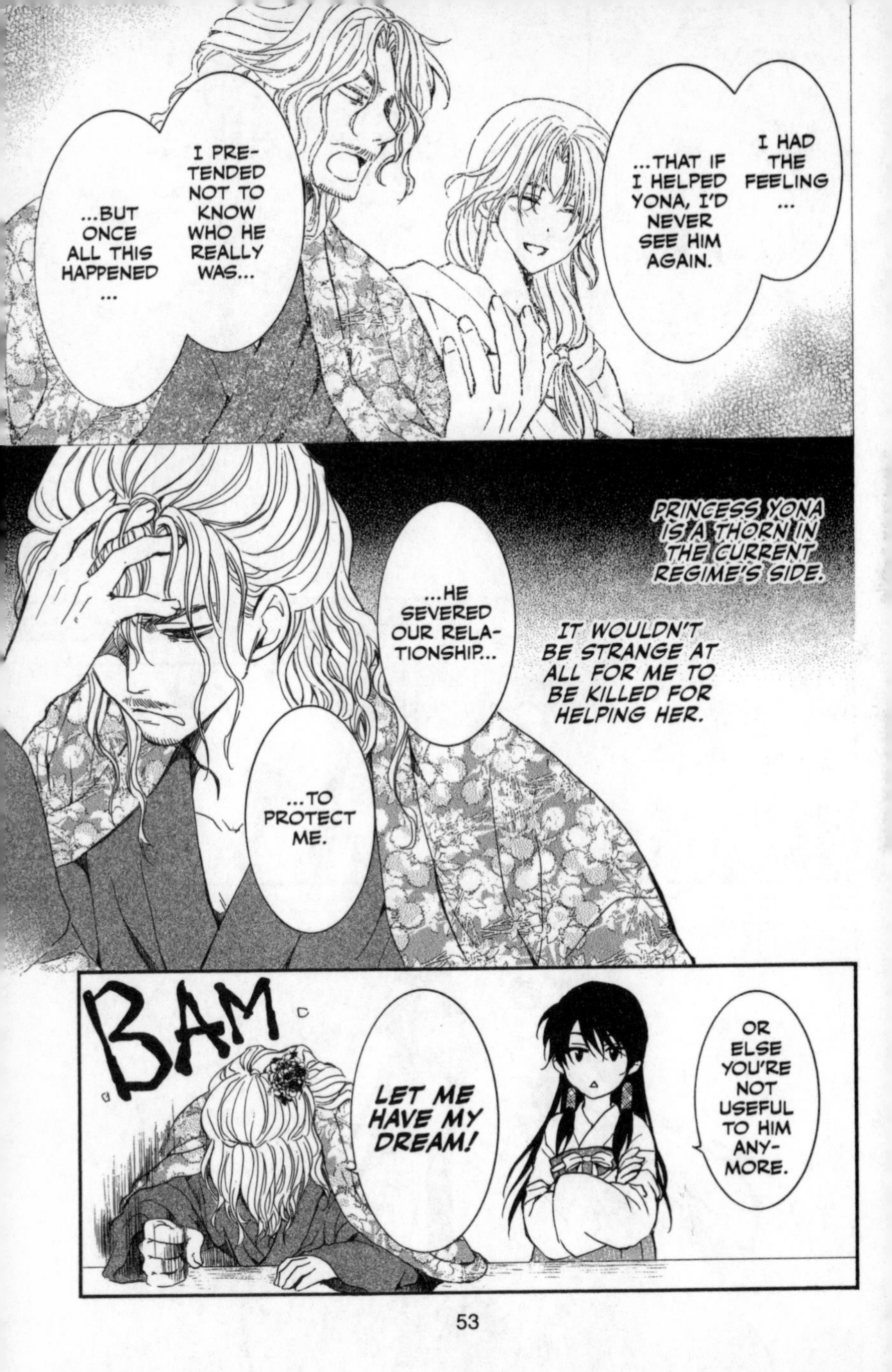
I HAD THE FEELING ...
...THAT IF I HELPED YONA, I'D NEVER SEE HIM AGAIN.
I PRETENDED NOT TO KNOW WHO HE REALLY WAS...
...BUT ONCE ALL THIS HAPPENED ...
PRINCESS YONA IS A THORN IN THE CURRENT REGIME'S SIDE.
IT WOULDN'T BE STRANGE AT ALL FOR ME TO BE KILLED FOR HELPING HER.
...HE SEVERED OUR RELATIONSHIP...
...TO PROTECT ME.
OR ELSE YOU'RE NOT USEFUL TO HIM ANYMORE.
LET ME HAVE MY DREAM!
BAM

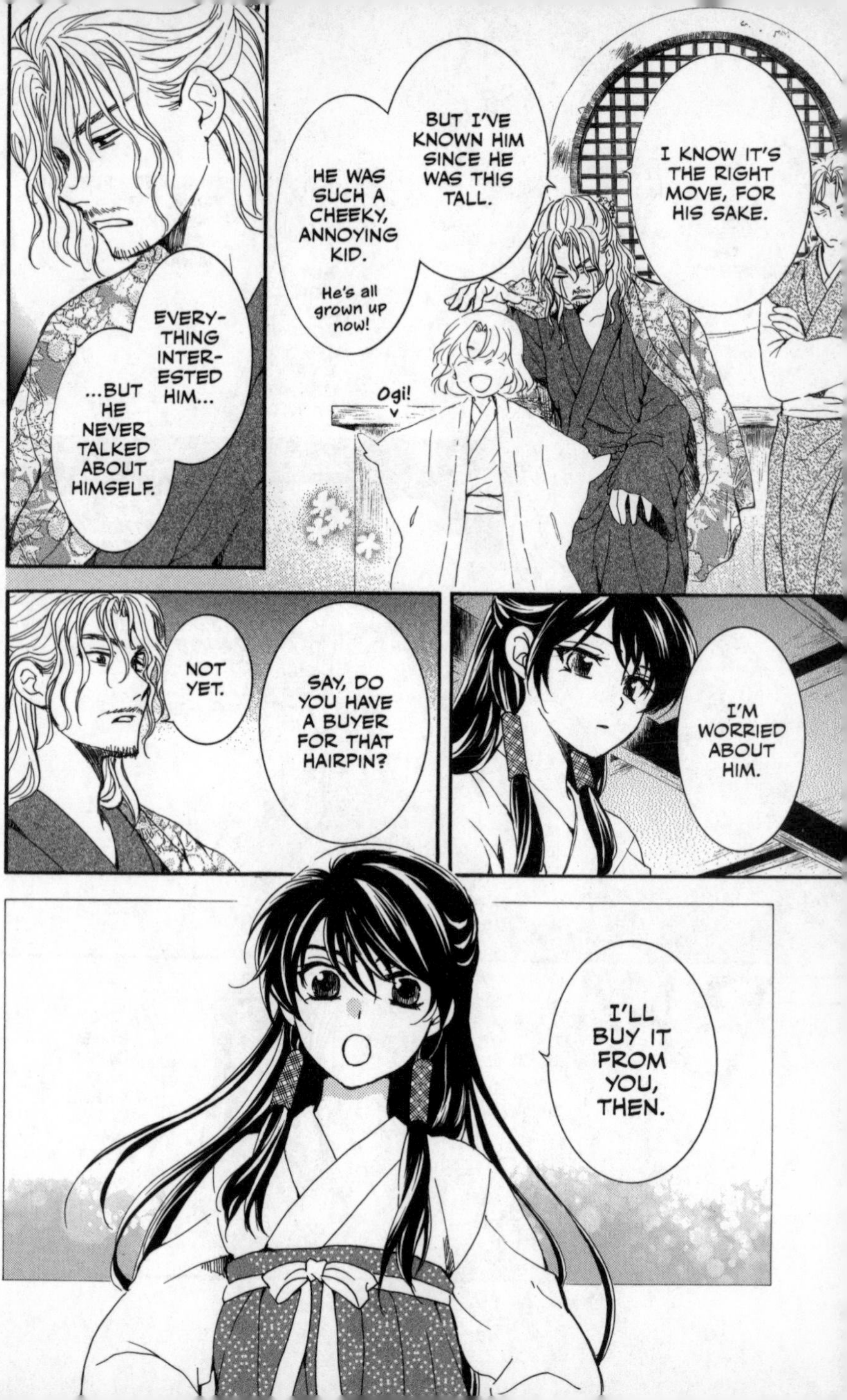
I KNOW IT'S THE RIGHT MOVE, FOR HIS SAKE.
BUT I'VE KNOWN HIM SINCE HE WAS THIS TALL.
HE WAS SUCH A CHEEKY, ANNOYING KID.
He's all grown up now!
Ogi!
EVERYTHING INTERESTED HIM...
...BUT HE NEVER TALKED ABOUT HIMSELF.
I'M WORRIED ABOUT HIM.
SAY, DO YOU HAVE A BUYER FOR THAT HAIRPIN?
NOT YET.
I'LL BUY IT FROM YOU, THEN.

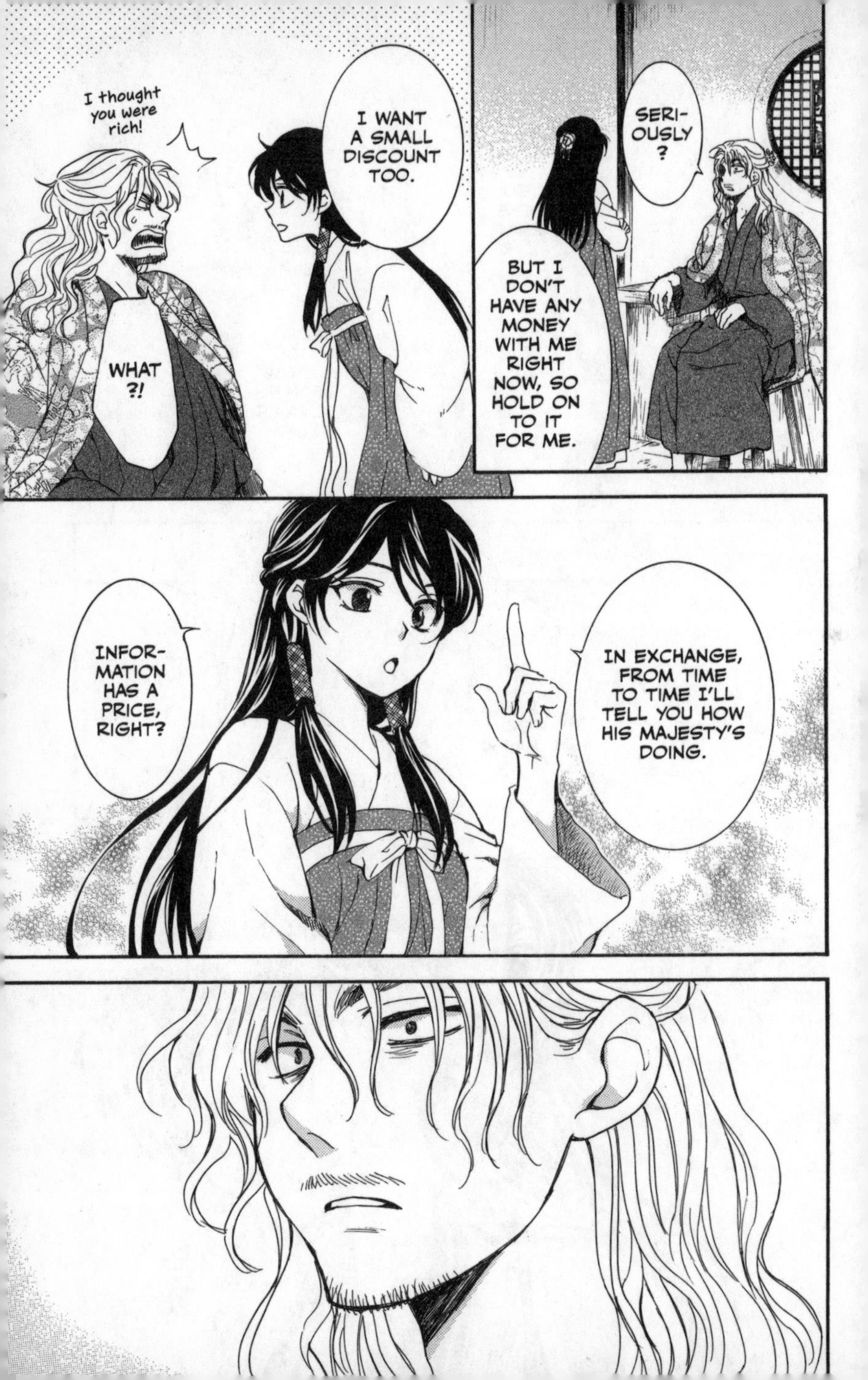
SERIOUSLY?
BUT I DON'T HAVE ANY MONEY WITH ME RIGHT NOW, SO HOLD ON TO IT FOR ME.
I WANT A SMALL DISCOUNT TOO.
I thought you were rich!
WHAT?!
IN EXCHANGE, FROM TIME TO TIME I'LL TELL YOU HOW HIS MAJESTY'S DOING.
INFORMATION HAS A PRICE, RIGHT?

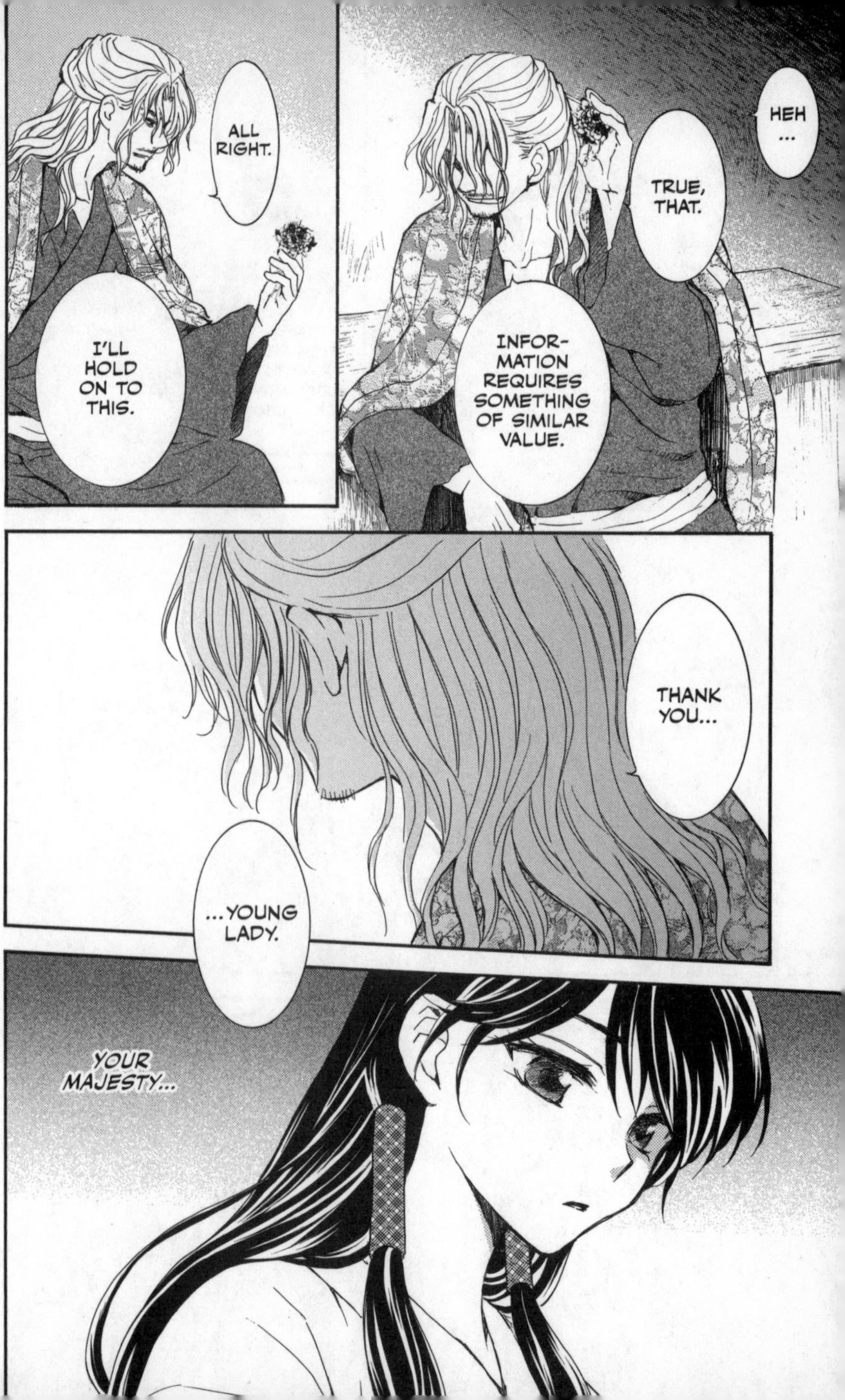
HEH ...
TRUE, THAT.
INFOR-MATION REQUIRES SOMETHING OF SIMILAR VALUE.
ALL RIGHT.
I'LL HOLD ON TO THIS.
THANK YOU...
...YOUNG LADY.
YOUR MAJESTY...

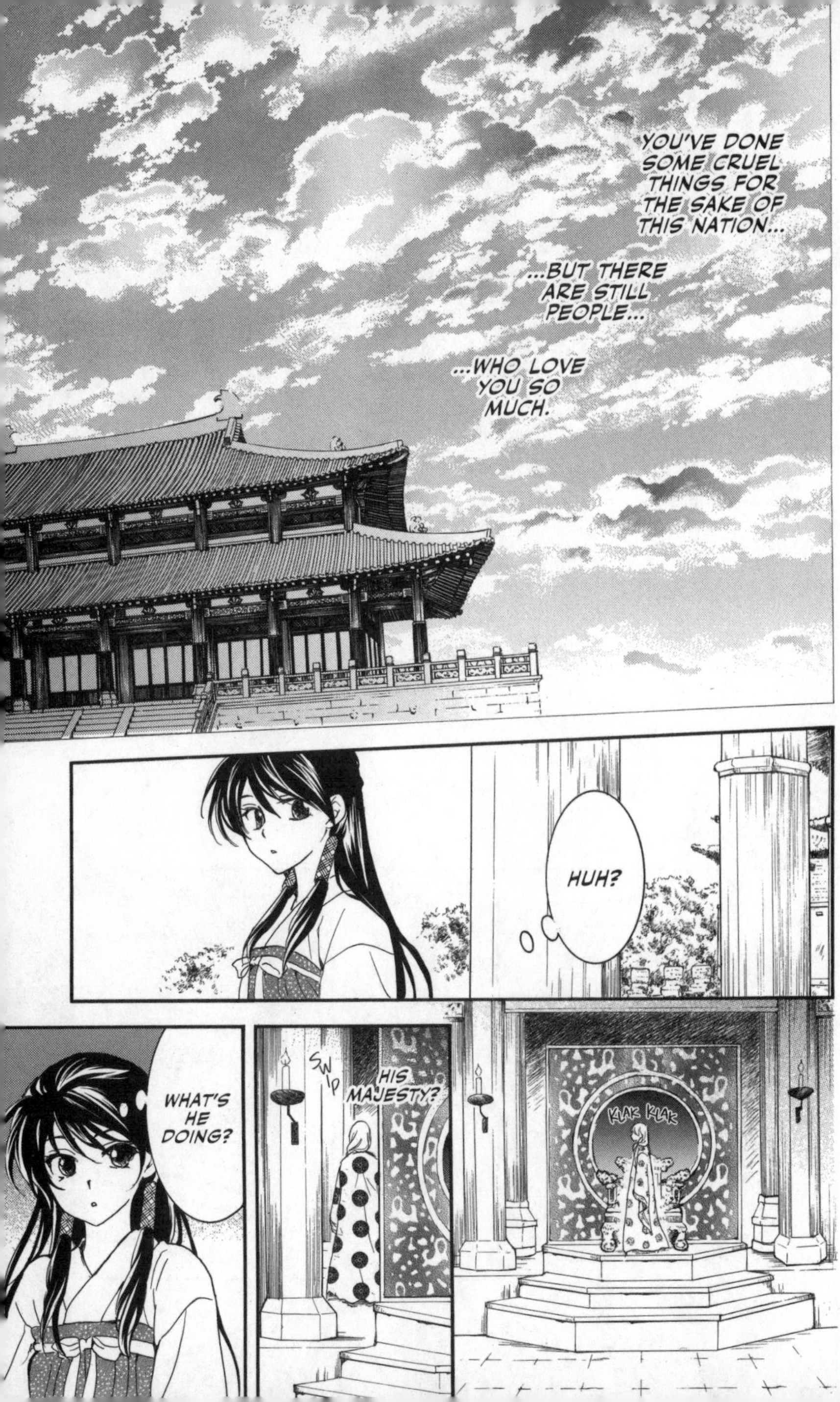
YOU'VE DONE SOME CRUEL THINGS FOR THE SAKE OF THIS NATION...
...BUT THERE ARE STILL PEOPLE...
...WHO LOVE YOU SO MUCH.
HUH?
KLAK KLAK
SWIP
HIS MAJESTY?
WHAT'S HE DOING?

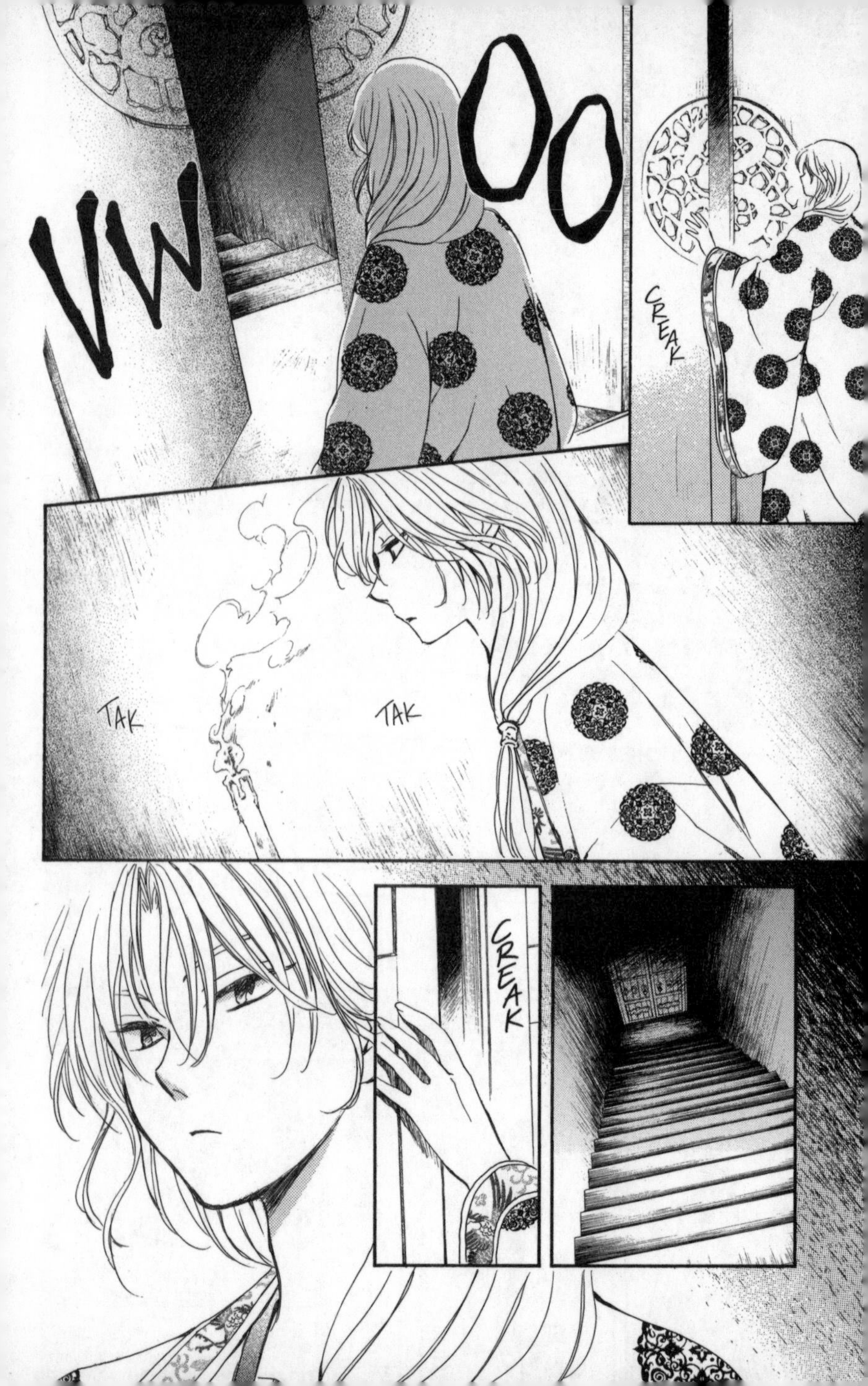
CREAK
VVOO
TAK
TAK
CREAK

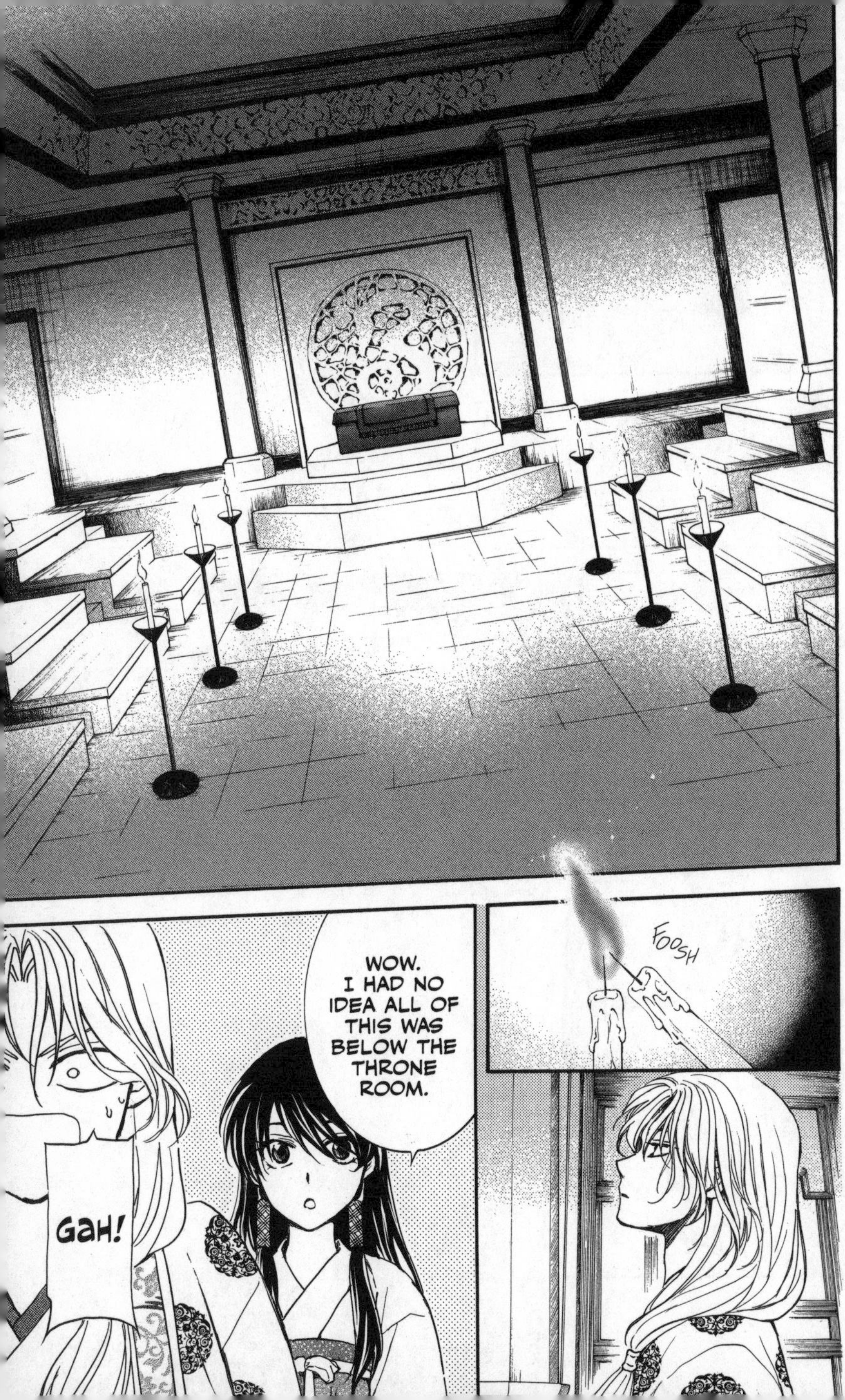
FOOSH
WOW. I HAD NO IDEA ALL OF THIS WAS BELOW THE THRONE ROOM.
GAH!

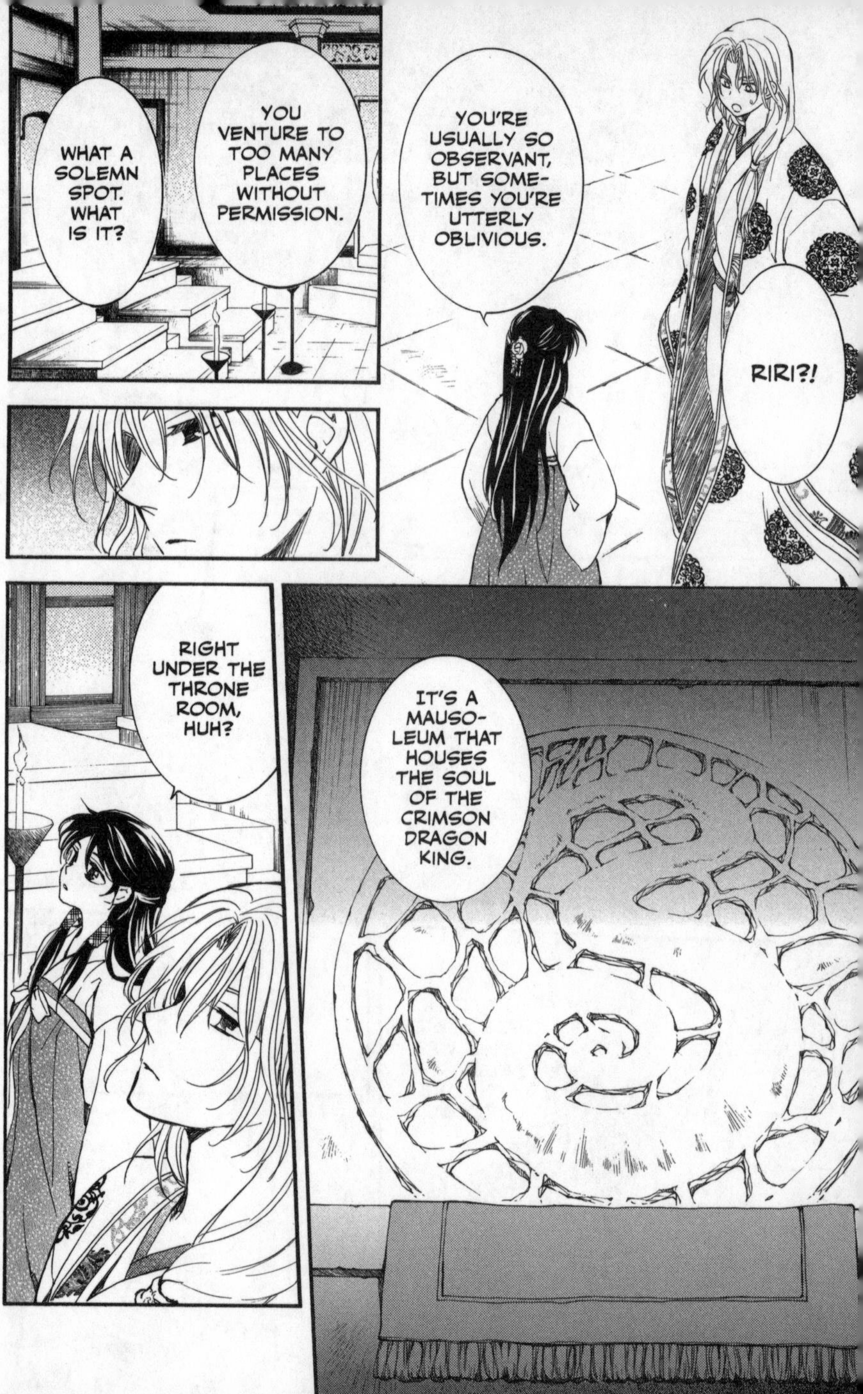
RIRI?!
YOU'RE USUALLY SO OBSERVANT, BUT SOME-TIMES YOU'RE UTTERLY OBLIVIOUS.
YOU VENTURE TO TOO MANY PLACES WITHOUT PERMISSION.
WHAT A SOLEMN SPOT. WHAT IS IT?
IT'S A MAUSO-LEUM THAT HOUSES THE SOUL OF THE CRIMSON DRAGON KING.
RIGHT UNDER THE THRONE ROOM, HUH?

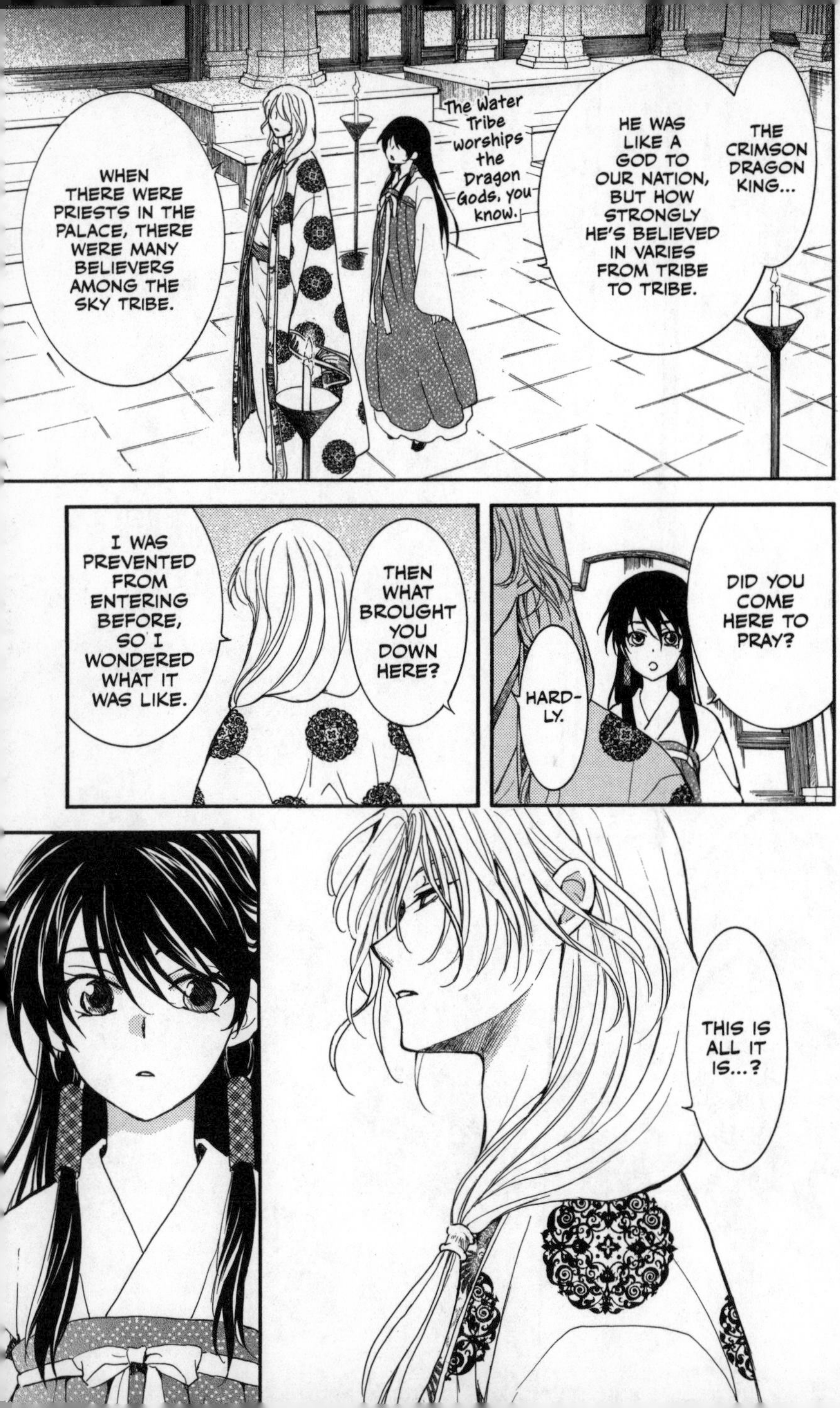
THE CRIMSON DRAGON KING...
HE WAS LIKE A GOD TO OUR NATION, BUT HOW STRONGLY HE'S BELIEVED IN VARIES FROM TRIBE TO TRIBE.
The Water Tribe worships the Dragon Gods, you know.
WHEN THERE WERE PRIESTS IN THE PALACE, THERE WERE MANY BELIEVERS AMONG THE SKY TRIBE.
DID YOU COME HERE TO PRAY?
HARD-LY.
THEN WHAT BROUGHT YOU DOWN HERE?
I WAS PREVENTED FROM ENTERING BEFORE, SO I WONDERED WHAT IT WAS LIKE.
THIS IS ALL IT IS...?

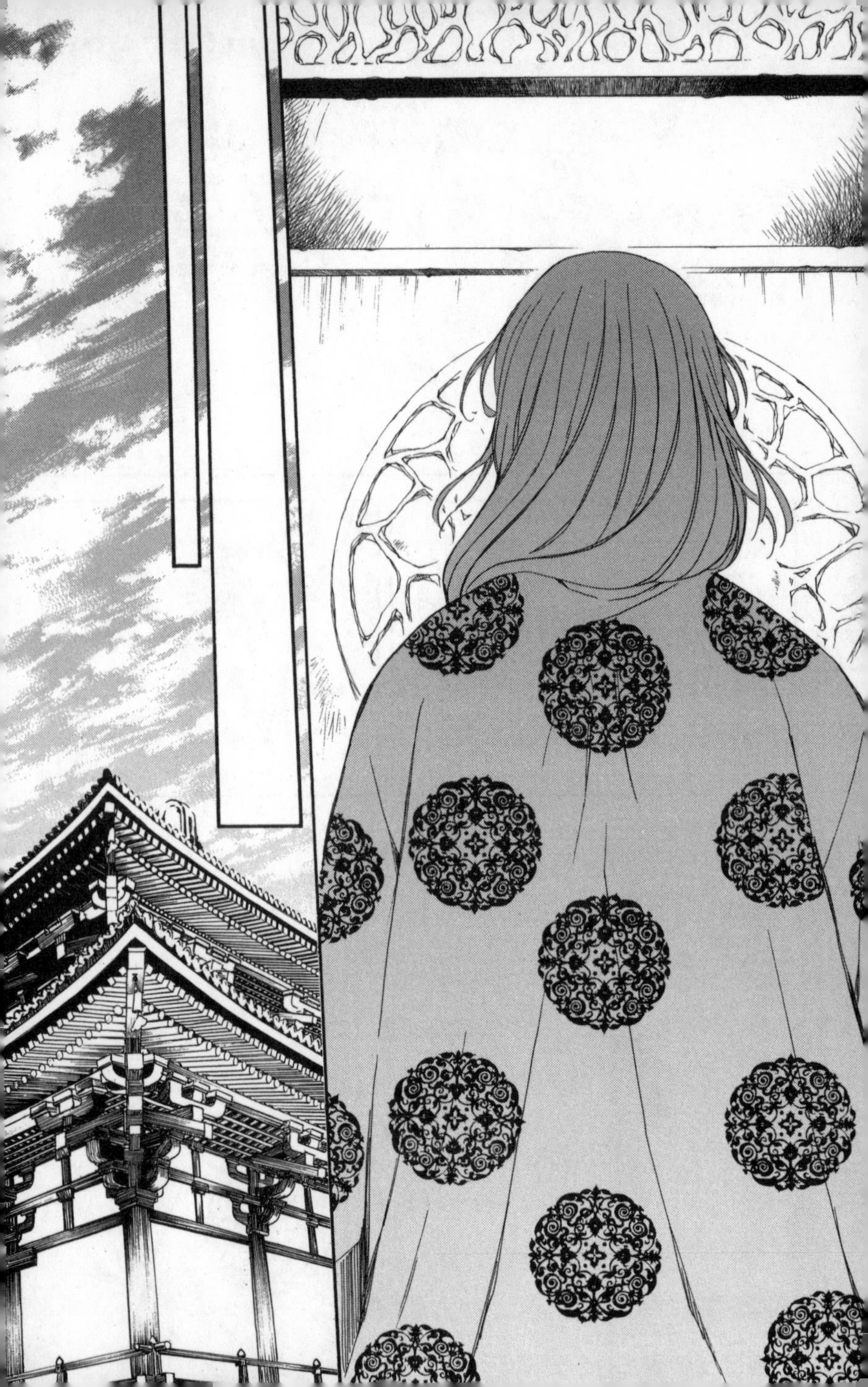

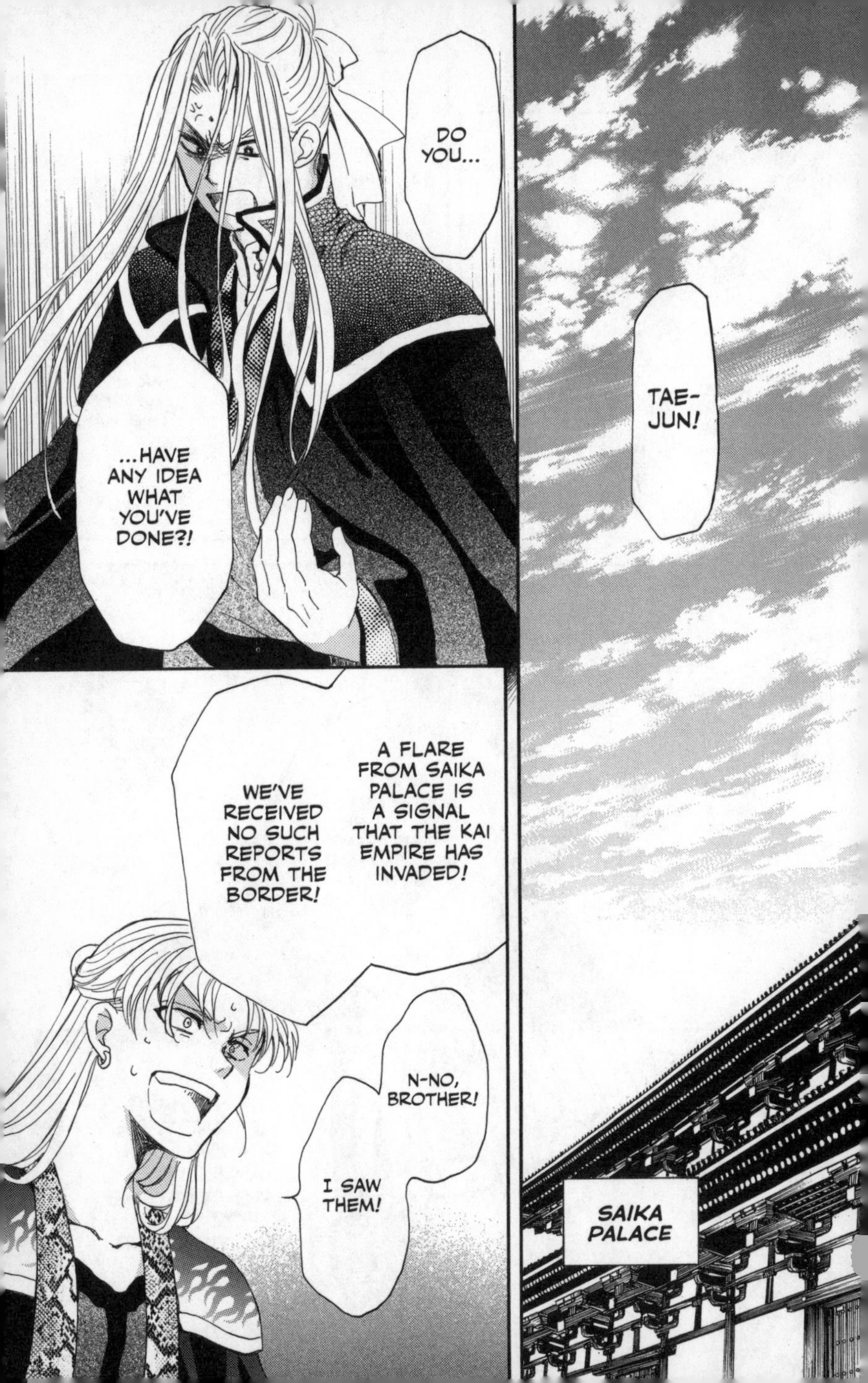
TAE-JUN!
SAIKA PALACE
DO YOU...
...HAVE ANY IDEA WHAT YOU'VE DONE?!
A FLARE FROM SAIKA PALACE IS A SIGNAL THAT THE KAI EMPIRE HAS INVADED!
WE'VE RECEIVED NO SUCH REPORTS FROM THE BORDER!
N-NO, BROTHER!
I SAW THEM!

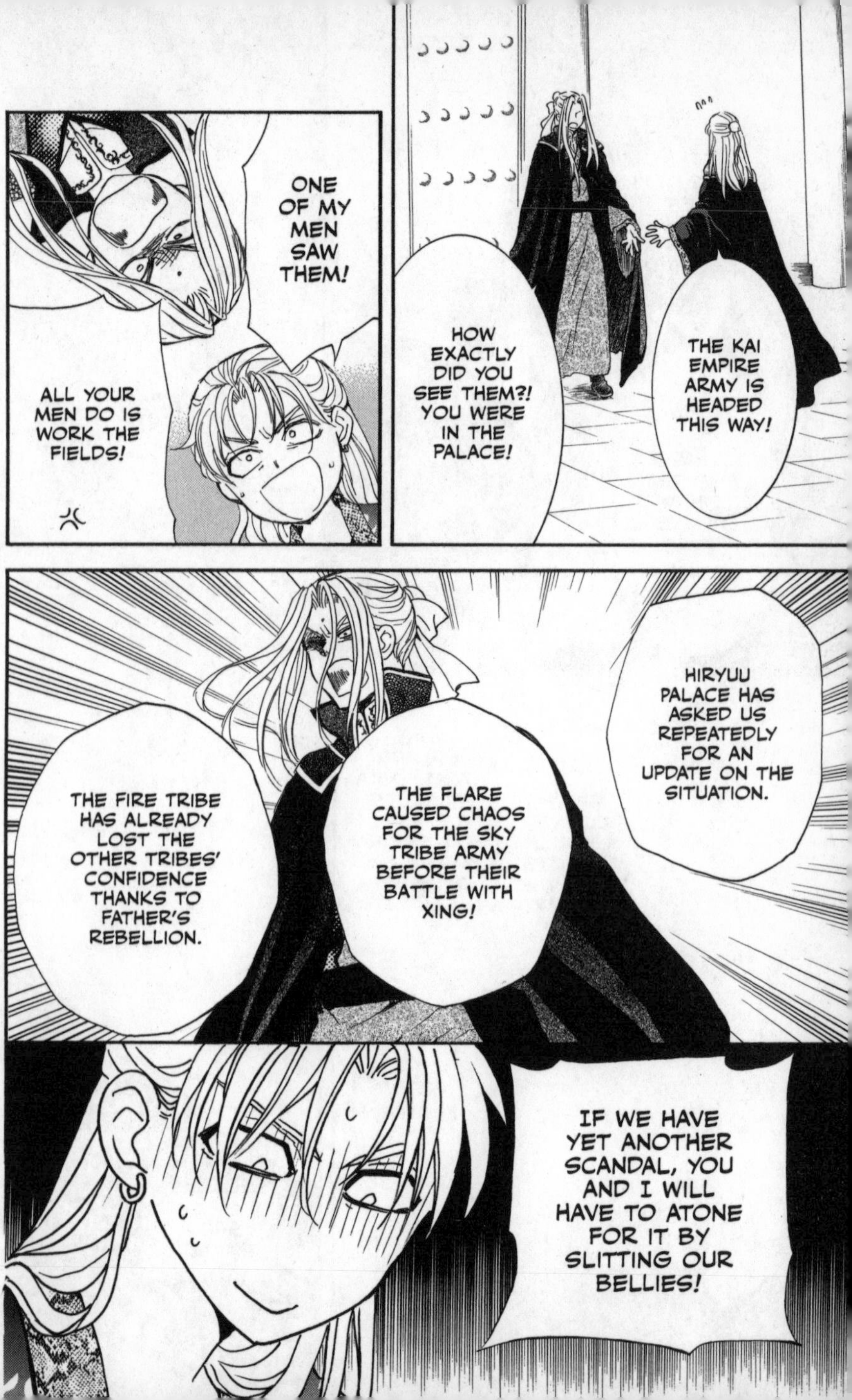
THE KAI EMPIRE ARMY IS HEADED THIS WAY!
HOW EXACTLY DID YOU SEE THEM?! YOU WERE IN THE PALACE!
ONE OF MY MEN SAW THEM!
ALL YOUR MEN DO IS WORK THE FIELDS!
HIRYUU PALACE HAS ASKED US REPEATEDLY FOR AN UPDATE ON THE SITUATION.
THE FLARE CAUSED CHAOS FOR THE SKY TRIBE ARMY BEFORE THEIR BATTLE WITH XING!
THE FIRE TRIBE HAS ALREADY LOST THE OTHER TRIBES' CONFIDENCE THANKS TO FATHER'S REBELLION.
IF WE HAVE YET ANOTHER SCANDAL, YOU AND I WILL HAVE TO ATONE FOR IT BY SLITTING OUR BELLIES!

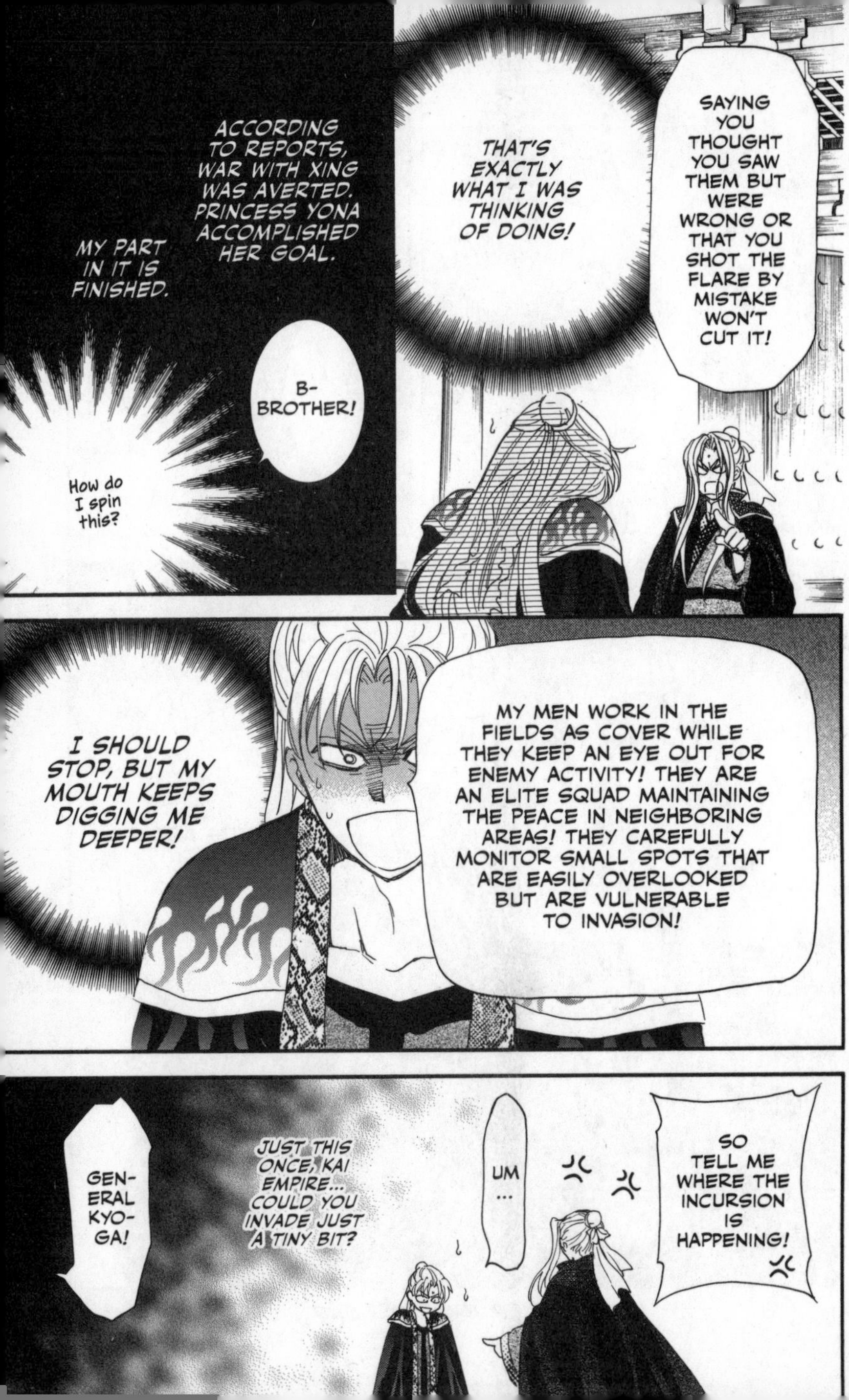
SAYING YOU THOUGHT YOU SAW THEM BUT WERE WRONG OR THAT YOU SHOT THE FLARE BY MISTAKE WON'T CUT IT!
THAT'S EXACTLY WHAT I WAS THINKING OF DOING!
ACCORDING TO REPORTS, WAR WITH XING WAS AVERTED. PRINCESS YONA ACCOMPLISHED HER GOAL.
MY PART IN IT IS FINISHED.
B-BROTHER!
How do I spin this?
MY MEN WORK IN THE FIELDS AS COVER WHILE THEY KEEP AN EYE OUT FOR ENEMY ACTIVITY! THEY ARE AN ELITE SQUAD MAINTAINING THE PEACE IN NEIGHBORING AREAS! THEY CAREFULLY MONITOR SMALL SPOTS THAT ARE EASILY OVERLOOKED BUT ARE VULNERABLE TO INVASION!
I SHOULD STOP, BUT MY MOUTH KEEPS DIGGING ME DEEPER!
SO TELL ME WHERE THE INCURSION IS HAPPENING!
UM...
JUST THIS ONCE, KAI EMPIRE... COULD YOU INVADE JUST A TINY BIT?
GEN-ERAL KYO-GA!

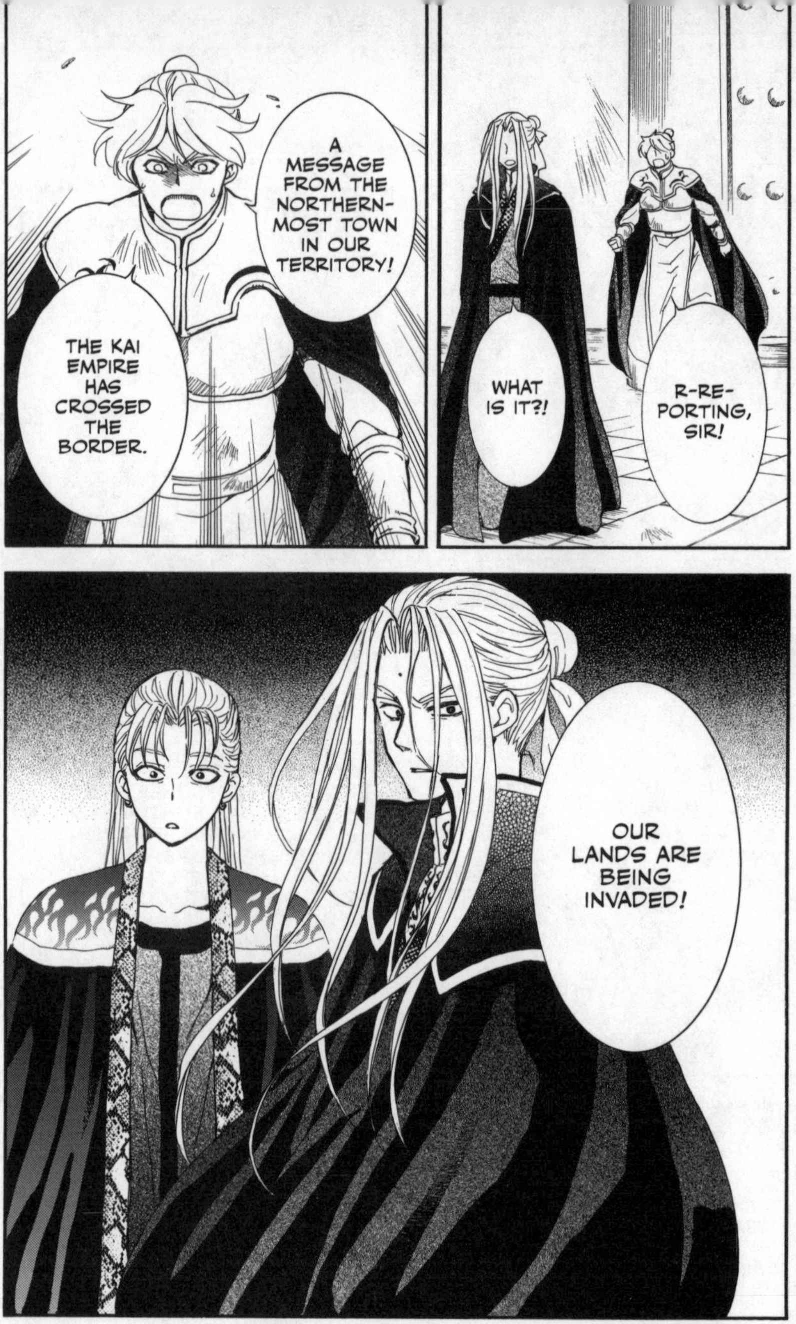
R-RE-PORTING, SIR!
WHAT IS IT?!
A MESSAGE FROM THE NORTHERN-MOST TOWN IN OUR TERRITORY!
THE KAI EMPIRE HAS CROSSED THE BORDER.
OUR LANDS ARE BEING INVADED!

CHAPTER 154 / THE END

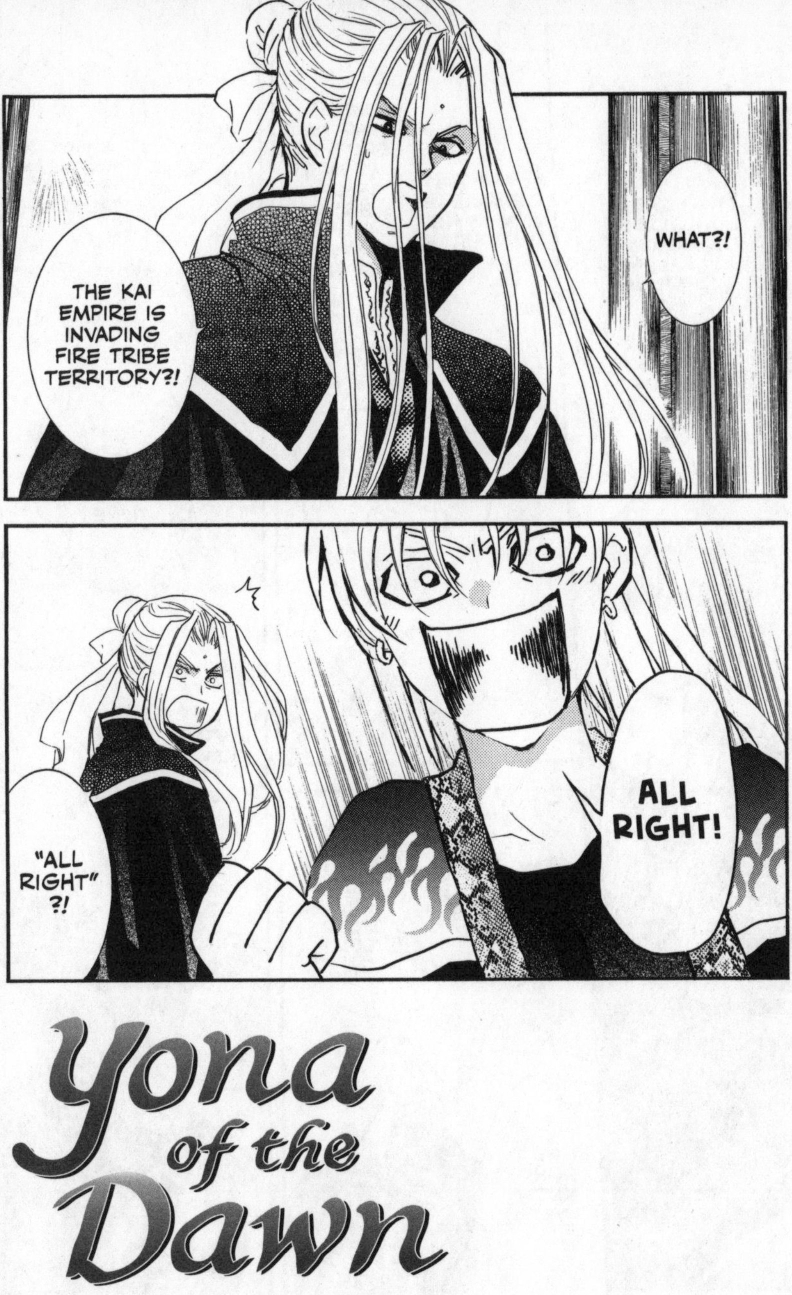
WHAT?!
THE KAI EMPIRE IS INVADING FIRE TRIBE TERRITORY?!
ALL RIGHT!
"ALL RIGHT" ?!

Yona of the Dawn

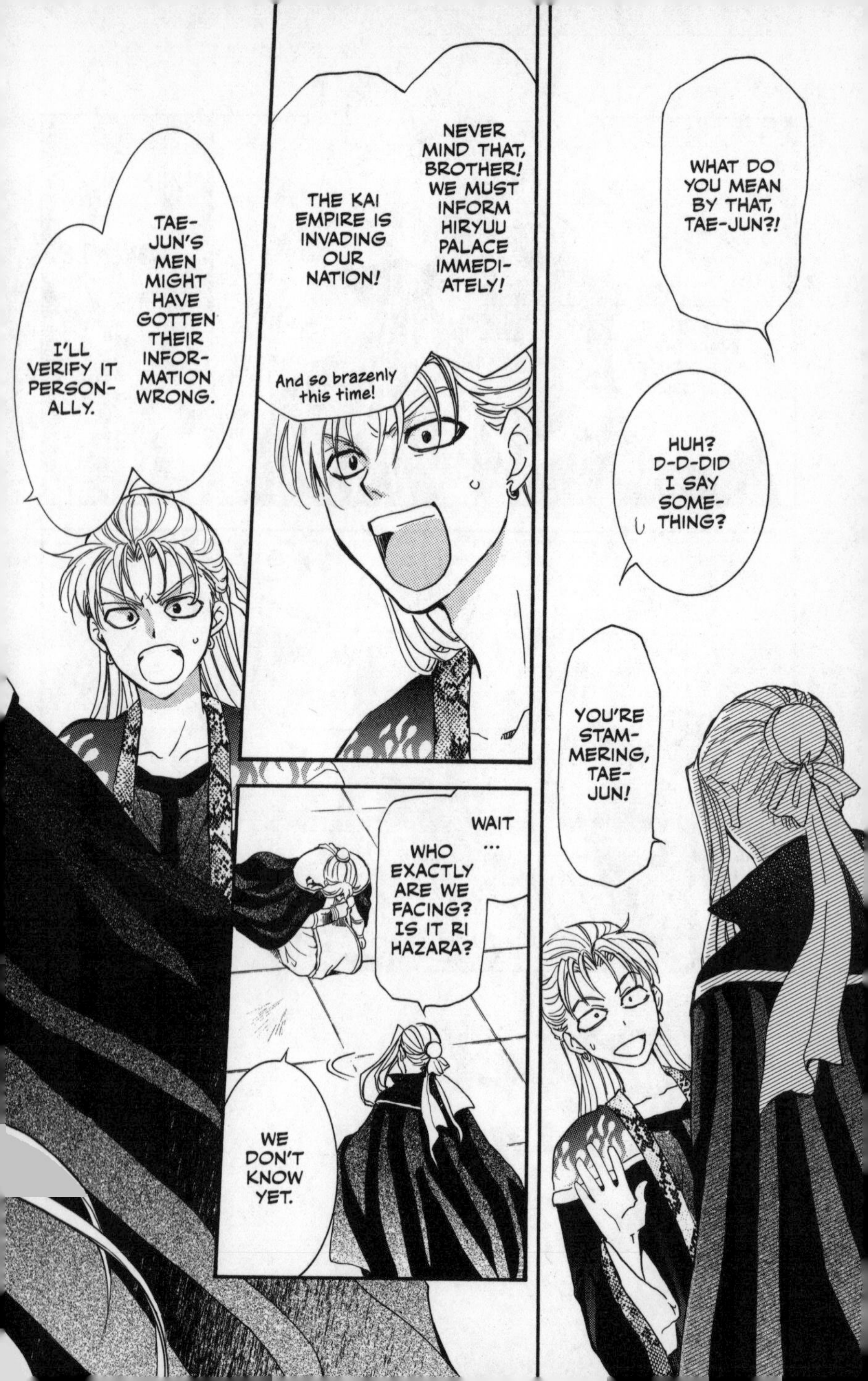
WHAT DO YOU MEAN BY THAT, TAE-JUN?!
HUH? D-D-DID I SAY SOME-THING?
YOU'RE STAM-MERING, TAE-JUN!
NEVER MIND THAT, BROTHER! WE MUST INFORM HIRYUU PALACE IMMEDI-ATELY!
THE KAI EMPIRE IS INVADING OUR NATION!
And so brazenly this time!
WAIT ...
WHO EXACTLY ARE WE FACING? IS IT RI HAZARA?
WE DON'T KNOW YET.
TAE-JUN'S MEN MIGHT HAVE GOTTEN THEIR INFOR-MATION WRONG.
I'LL VERIFY IT PERSON-ALLY.

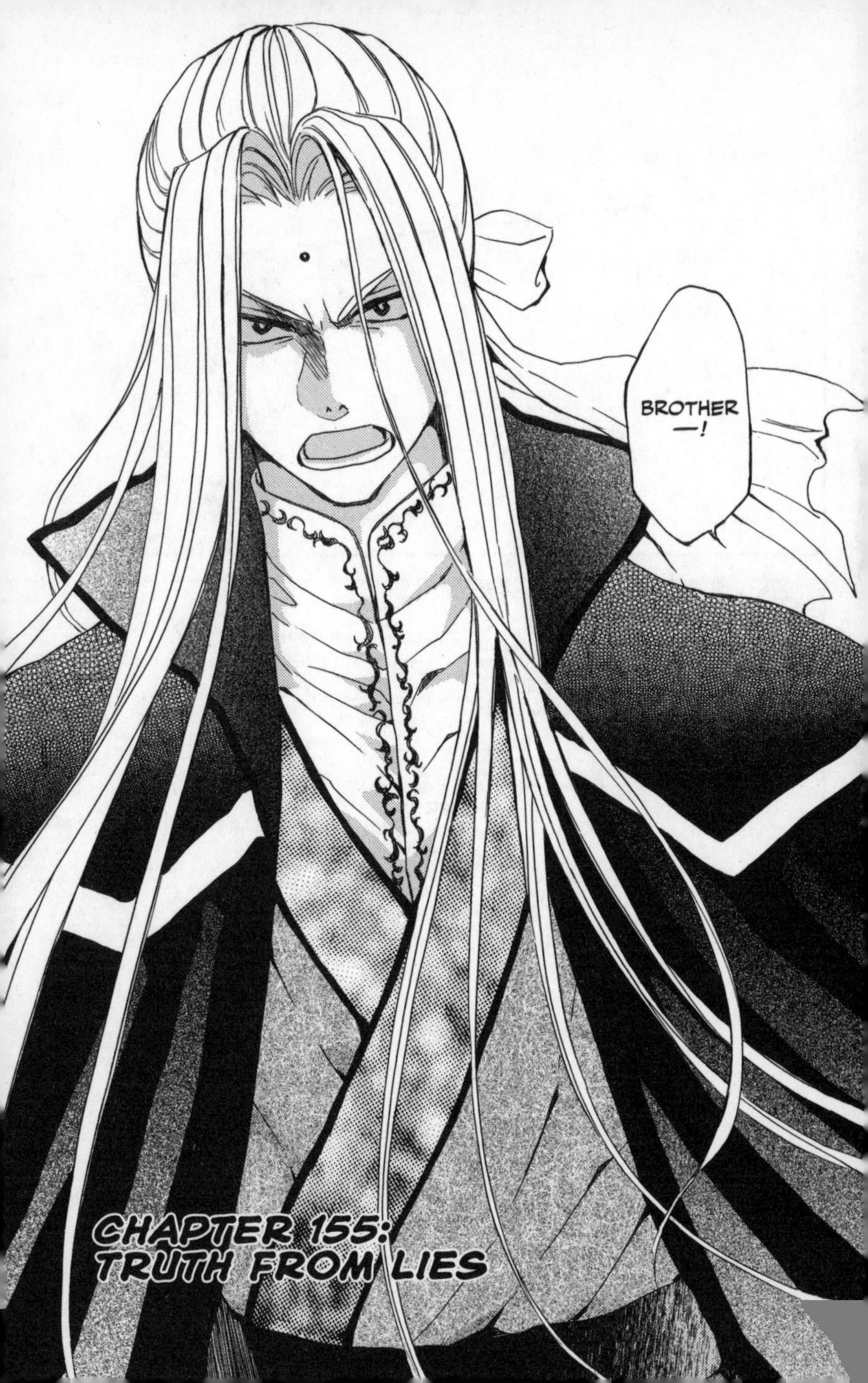
BROTHER—!
CHAPTER 155:
TRUTH FROM LIES

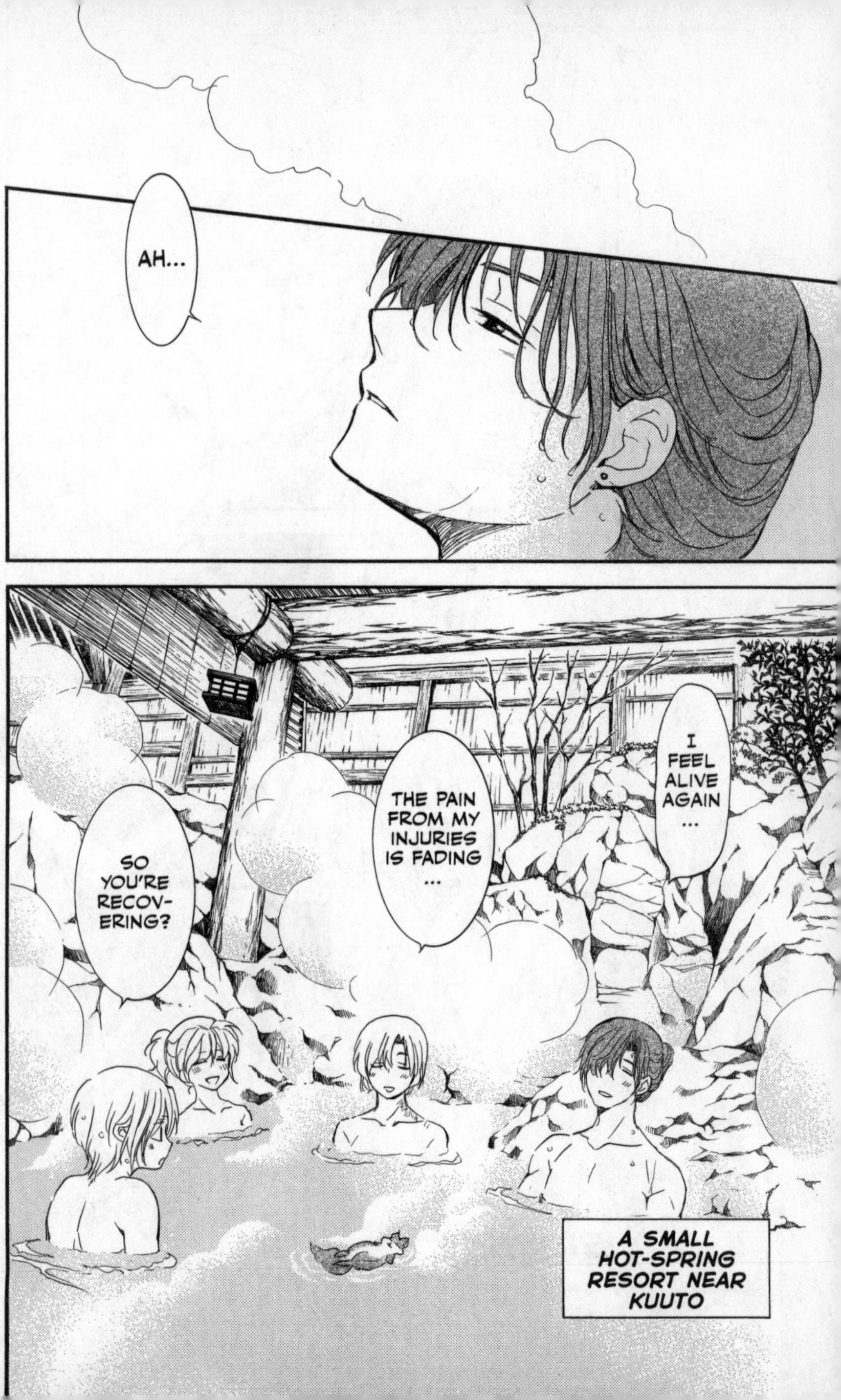
AH...
I FEEL ALIVE AGAIN...
THE PAIN FROM MY INJURIES IS FADING...
SO YOU'RE RECOV-ERING?
A SMALL HOT-SPRING RESORT NEAR KUUTO

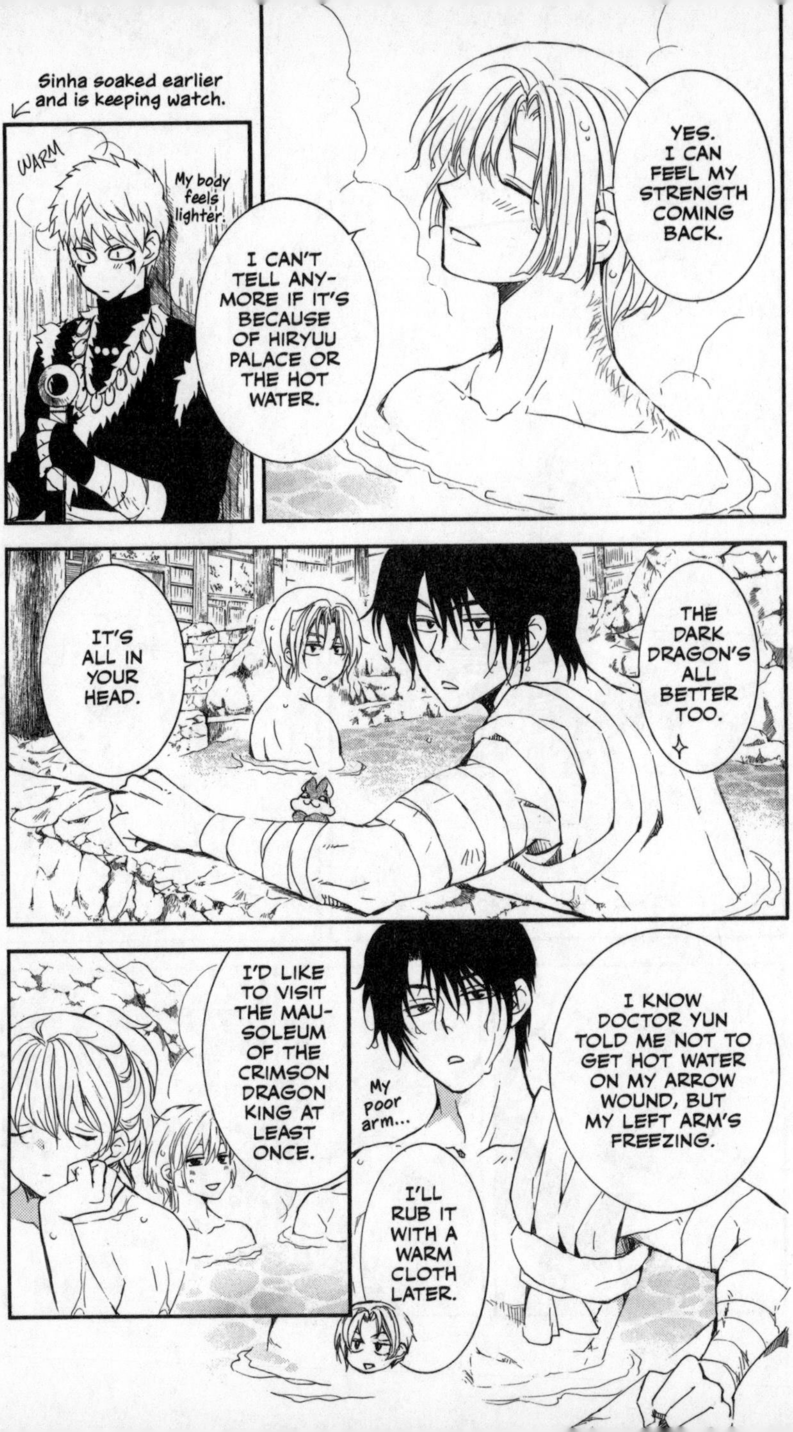
YES. I CAN FEEL MY STRENGTH COMING BACK.
I CAN'T TELL ANYMORE IF IT'S BECAUSE OF HIRYUU PALACE OR THE HOT WATER.
Sinha soaked earlier and is keeping watch.
WARM
My body feels lighter.
THE DARK DRAGON'S ALL BETTER TOO.
IT'S ALL IN YOUR HEAD.
I KNOW DOCTOR YUN TOLD ME NOT TO GET HOT WATER ON MY ARROW WOUND, BUT MY LEFT ARM'S FREEZING.
My poor arm...
I'LL RUB IT WITH A WARM CLOTH LATER.
I'D LIKE TO VISIT THE MAUSOLEUM OF THE CRIMSON DRAGON KING AT LEAST ONCE.

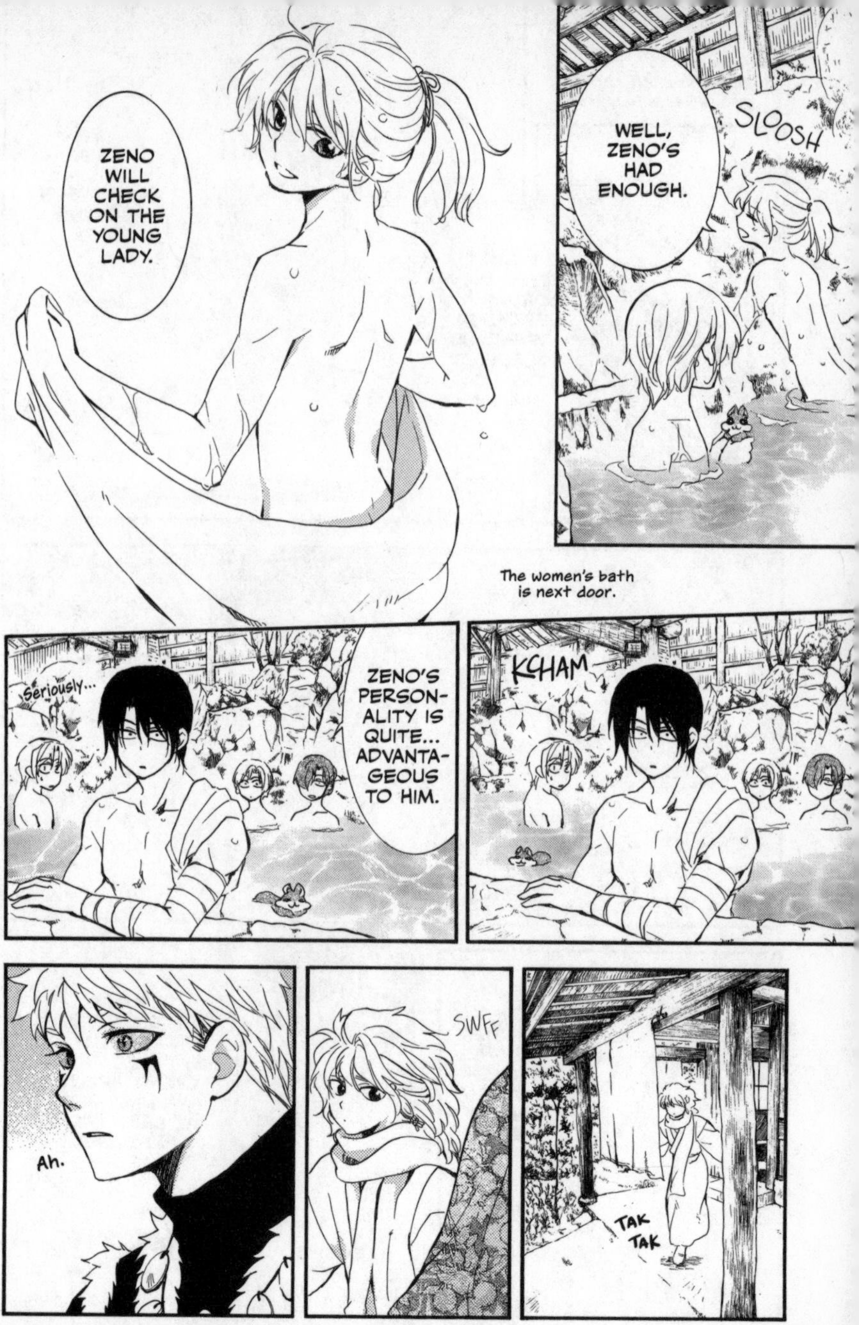
WELL, ZENO'S HAD ENOUGH.
SLOOSH
ZENO WILL CHECK ON THE YOUNG LADY.
The women's bath is next door.
KCHAM
ZENO'S PERSONALITY IS QUITE... ADVANTAGEOUS TO HIM.
Seriously...
TAK TAK
SWFF
Ah.

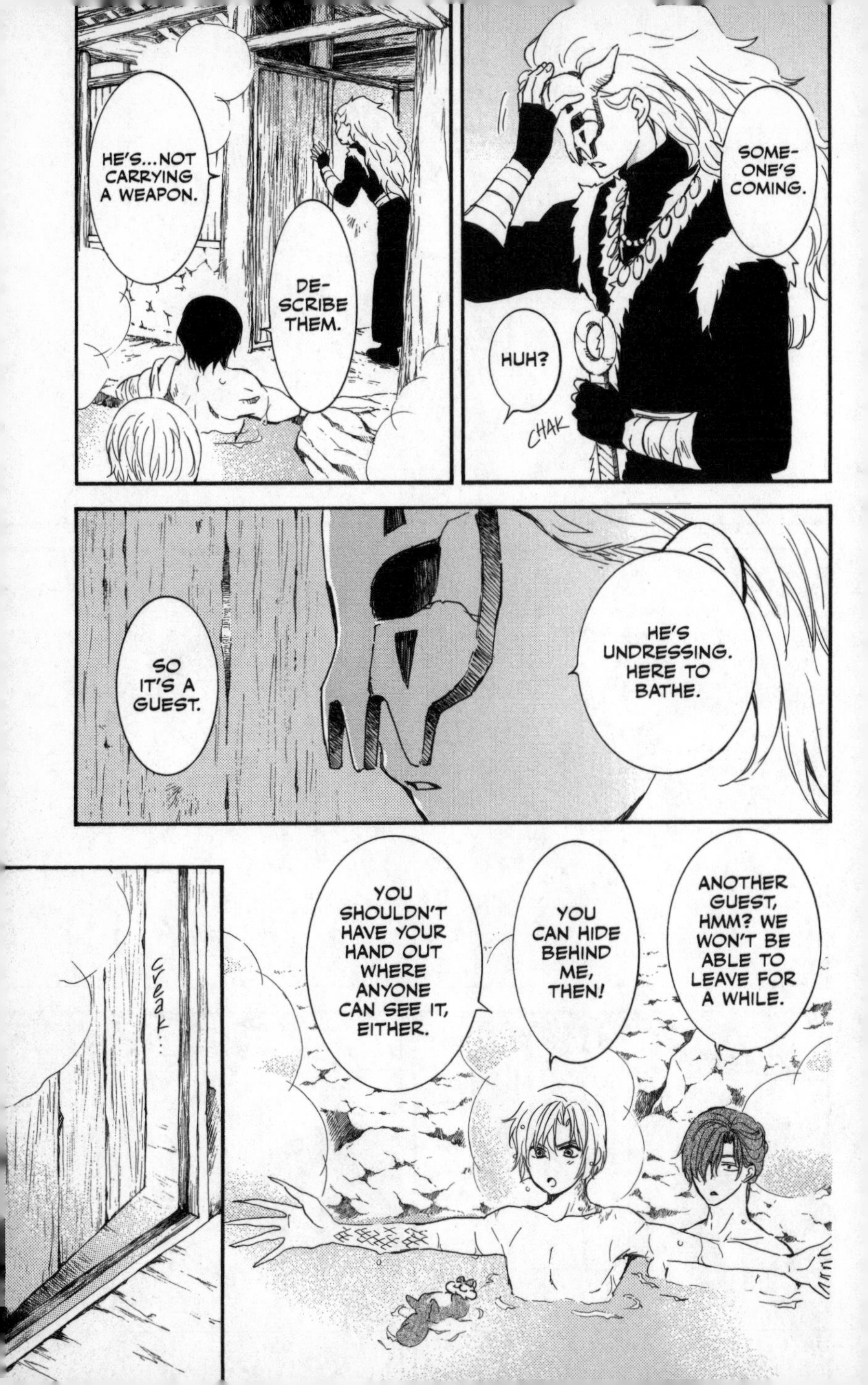
SOME-ONE'S COMING.
HUH?
CHAK
DE-SCRIBE THEM.
HE'S...NOT CARRYING A WEAPON.
HE'S UNDRESSING. HERE TO BATHE.
SO IT'S A GUEST.
ANOTHER GUEST, HMM? WE WON'T BE ABLE TO LEAVE FOR A WHILE.
YOU CAN HIDE BEHIND ME, THEN!
YOU SHOULDN'T HAVE YOUR HAND OUT WHERE ANYONE CAN SEE IT, EITHER.
Creak...

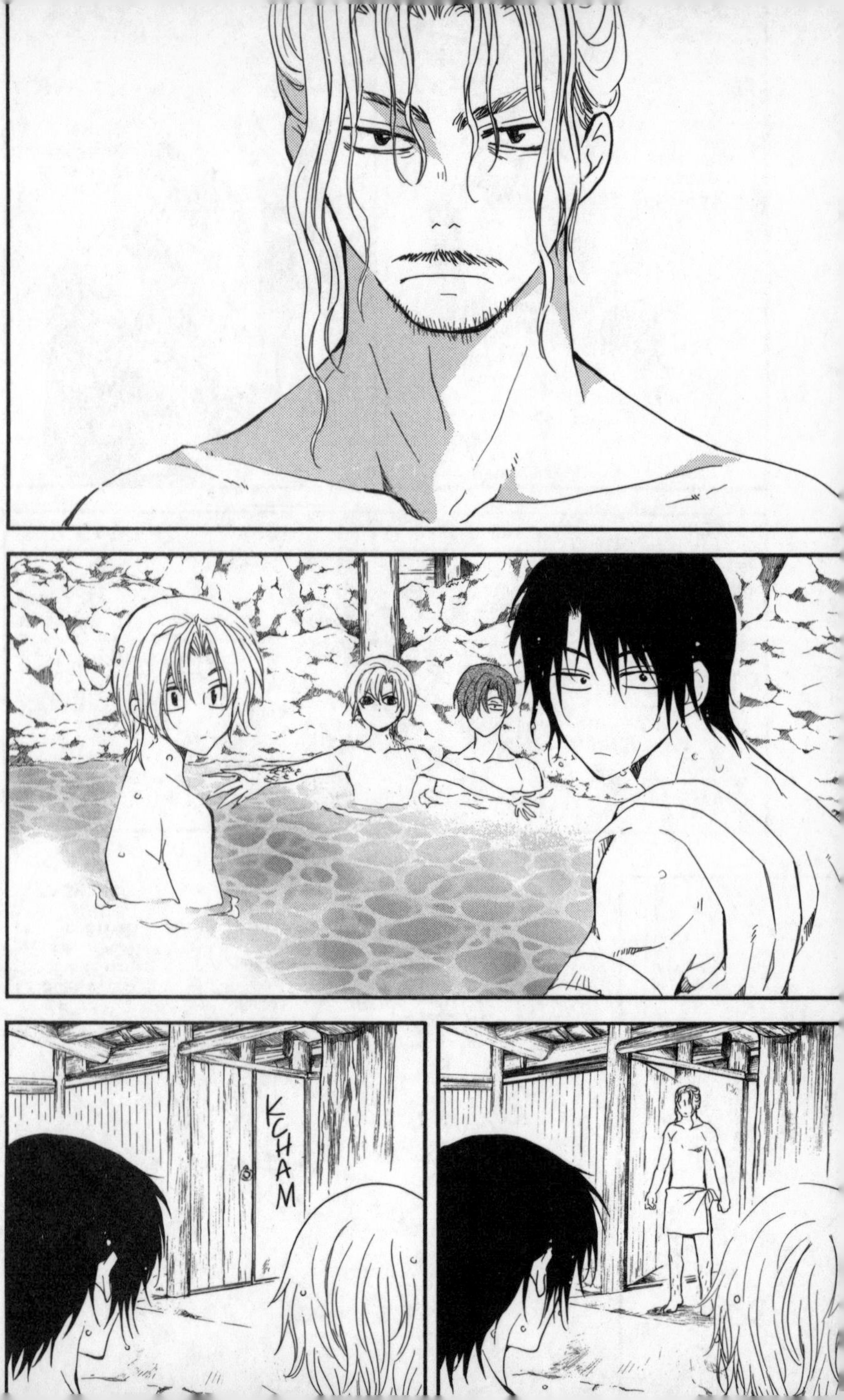
KCHAM

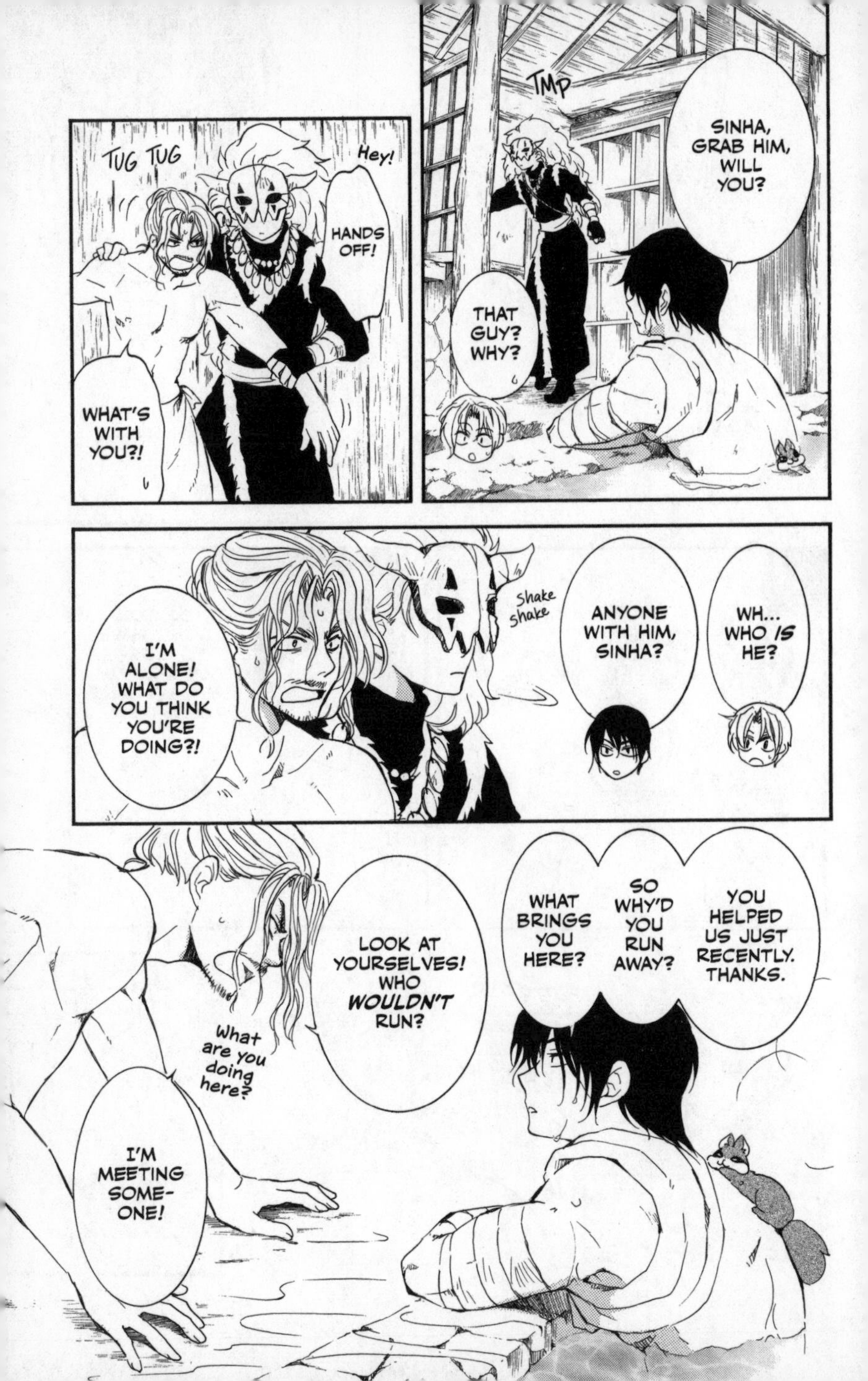
TMP
SINHA, GRAB HIM, WILL YOU?
THAT GUY? WHY?
Hey!
HANDS OFF!
TUG TUG
WHAT'S WITH YOU?!
WH... WHO *IS* HE?
ANYONE WITH HIM, SINHA?
Shake shake
I'M ALONE! WHAT DO YOU THINK YOU'RE DOING?!
YOU HELPED US JUST RECENTLY. THANKS.
SO WHY'D YOU RUN AWAY?
WHAT BRINGS YOU HERE?
LOOK AT YOURSELVES! WHO *WOULDN'T* RUN?
What are you doing here?
I'M MEETING SOME-ONE!

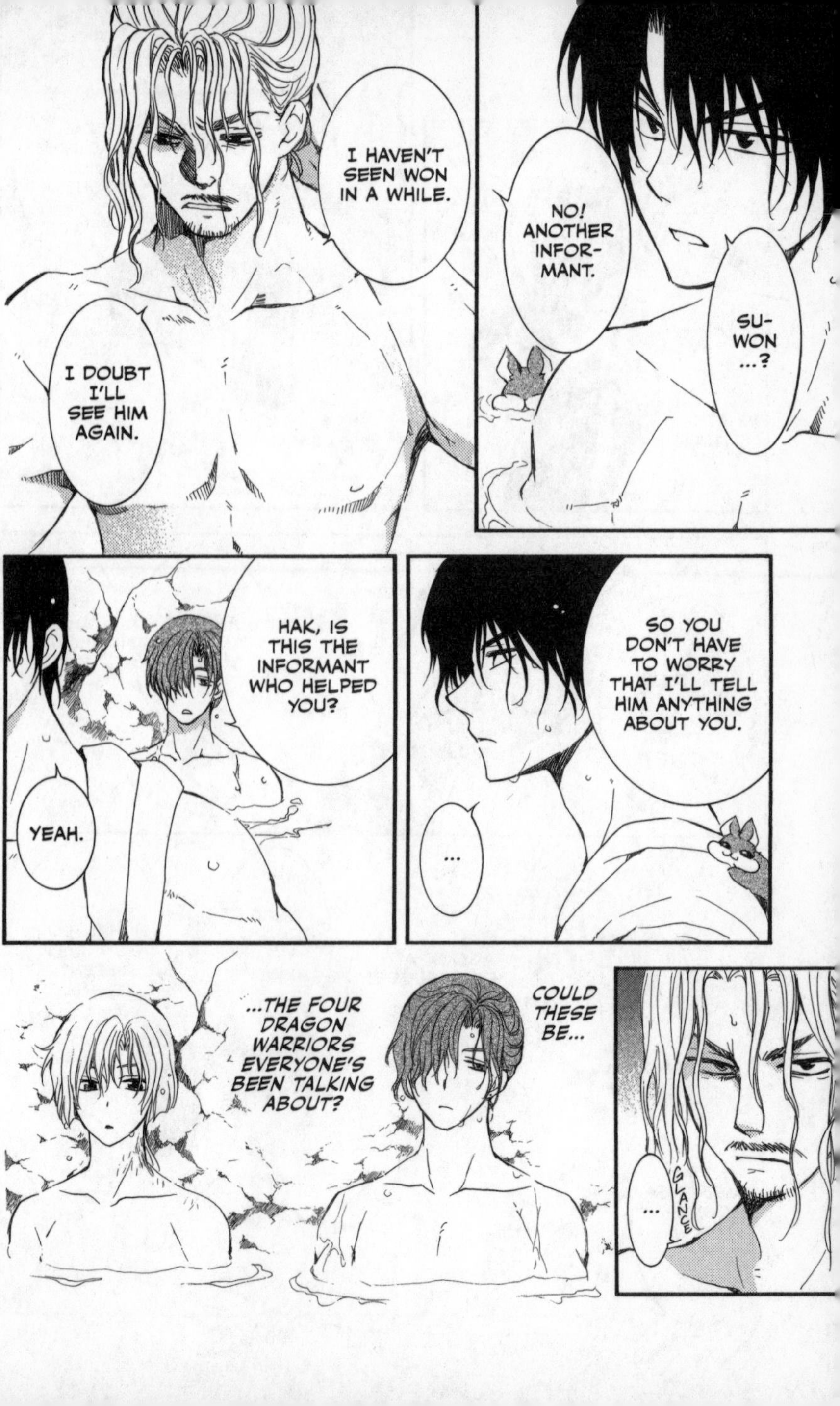
SU-WON ...?
NO! ANOTHER INFORMANT.
I HAVEN'T SEEN WON IN A WHILE.
I DOUBT I'LL SEE HIM AGAIN.
SO YOU DON'T HAVE TO WORRY THAT I'LL TELL HIM ANYTHING ABOUT YOU.
...
HAK, IS THIS THE INFORMANT WHO HELPED YOU?
YEAH.
GLANCE
...
COULD THESE BE...
...THE FOUR DRAGON WARRIORS EVERYONE'S BEEN TALKING ABOUT?

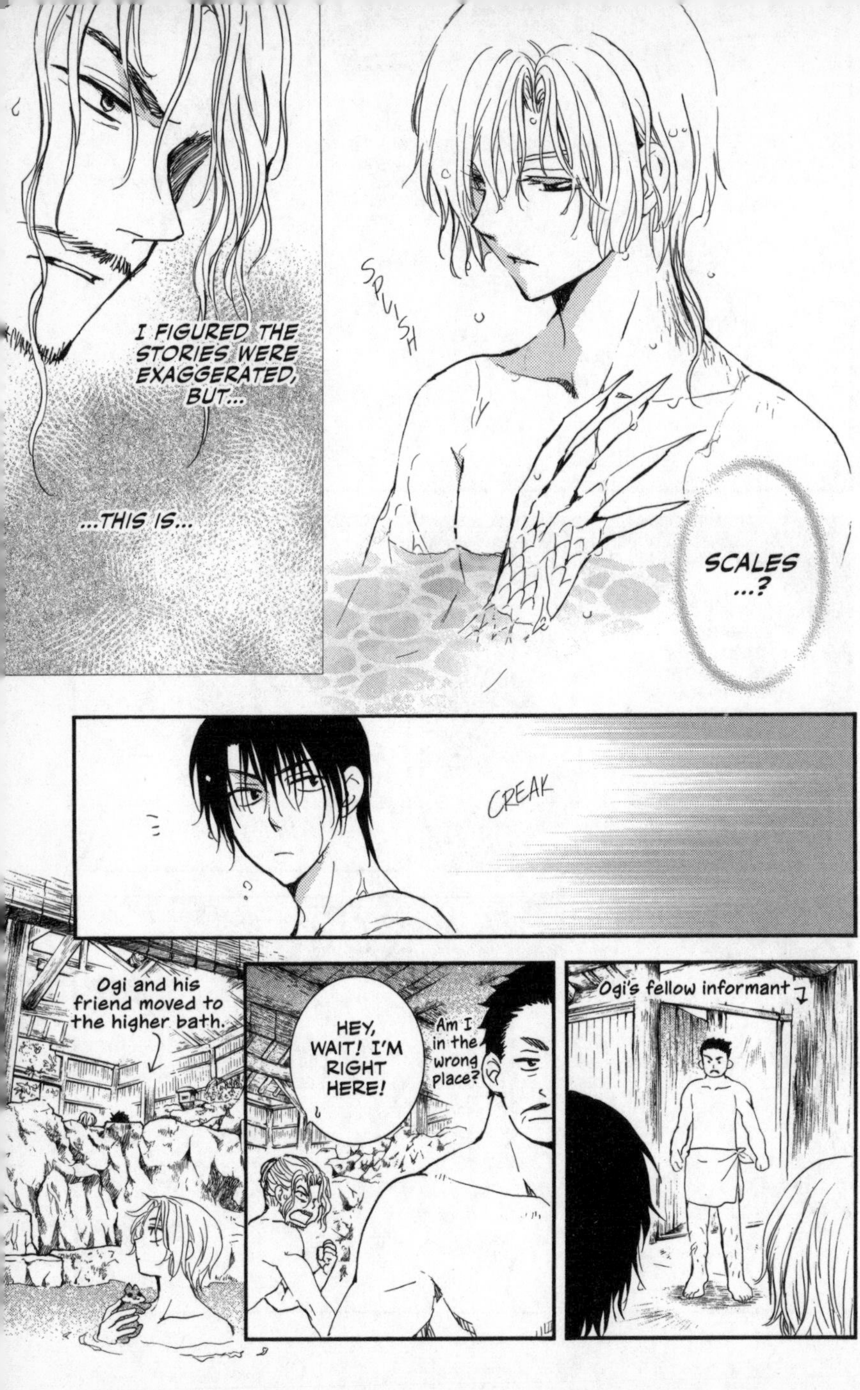
SPLISH
SCALES ...?
I FIGURED THE STORIES WERE EXAGGERATED, BUT...
...THIS IS...
CREAK
Ogi's fellow informant
Am I in the wrong place?
HEY, WAIT! I'M RIGHT HERE!
Ogi and his friend moved to the higher bath.

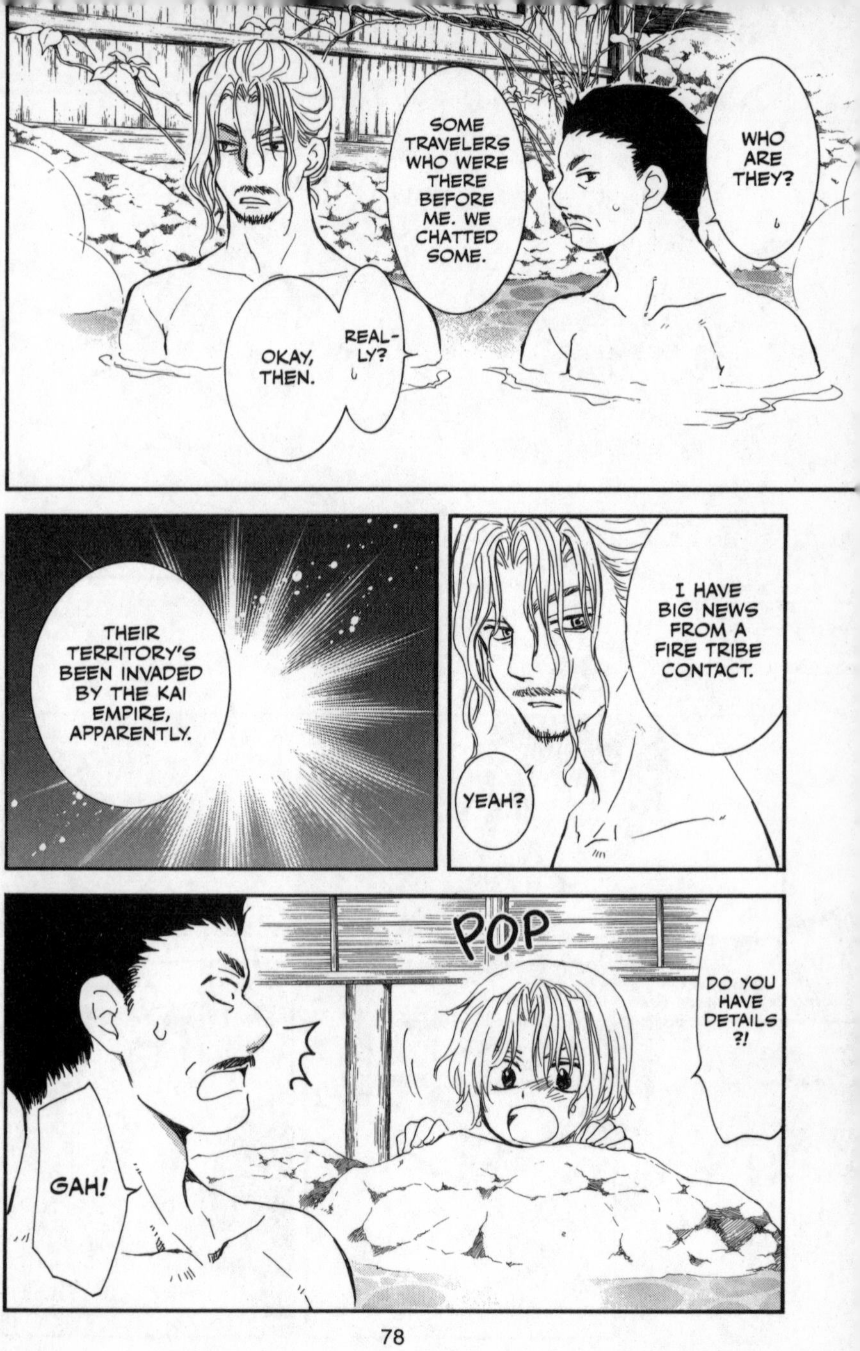

WHO ARE THEY?
SOME TRAVELERS WHO WERE THERE BEFORE ME. WE CHATTED SOME.
REAL-LY?
OKAY, THEN.
I HAVE BIG NEWS FROM A FIRE TRIBE CONTACT.
YEAH?
THEIR TERRITORY'S BEEN INVADED BY THE KAI EMPIRE, APPARENTLY.
DO YOU HAVE DETAILS ?!
POP
GAH!

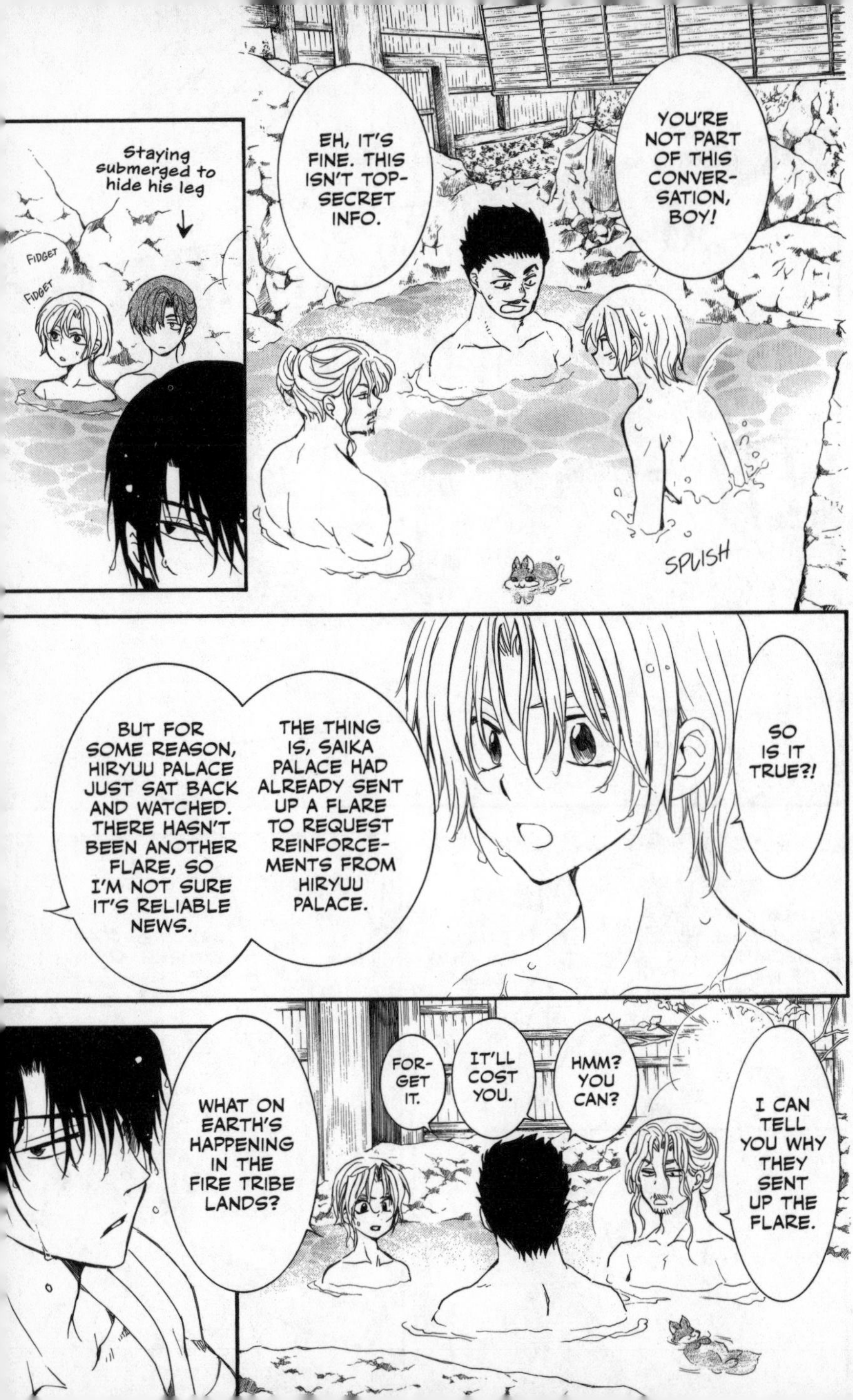
YOU'RE NOT PART OF THIS CONVERSATION, BOY!
EH, IT'S FINE. THIS ISN'T TOP-SECRET INFO.
SPLISH
Staying submerged to hide his leg
FIDGET
FIDGET
SO IS IT TRUE?!
THE THING IS, SAIKA PALACE HAD ALREADY SENT UP A FLARE TO REQUEST REINFORCEMENTS FROM HIRYUU PALACE.
BUT FOR SOME REASON, HIRYUU PALACE JUST SAT BACK AND WATCHED. THERE HASN'T BEEN ANOTHER FLARE, SO I'M NOT SURE IT'S RELIABLE NEWS.
I CAN TELL YOU WHY THEY SENT UP THE FLARE.
HMM? YOU CAN?
IT'LL COST YOU.
FORGET IT.
WHAT ON EARTH'S HAPPENING IN THE FIRE TRIBE LANDS?

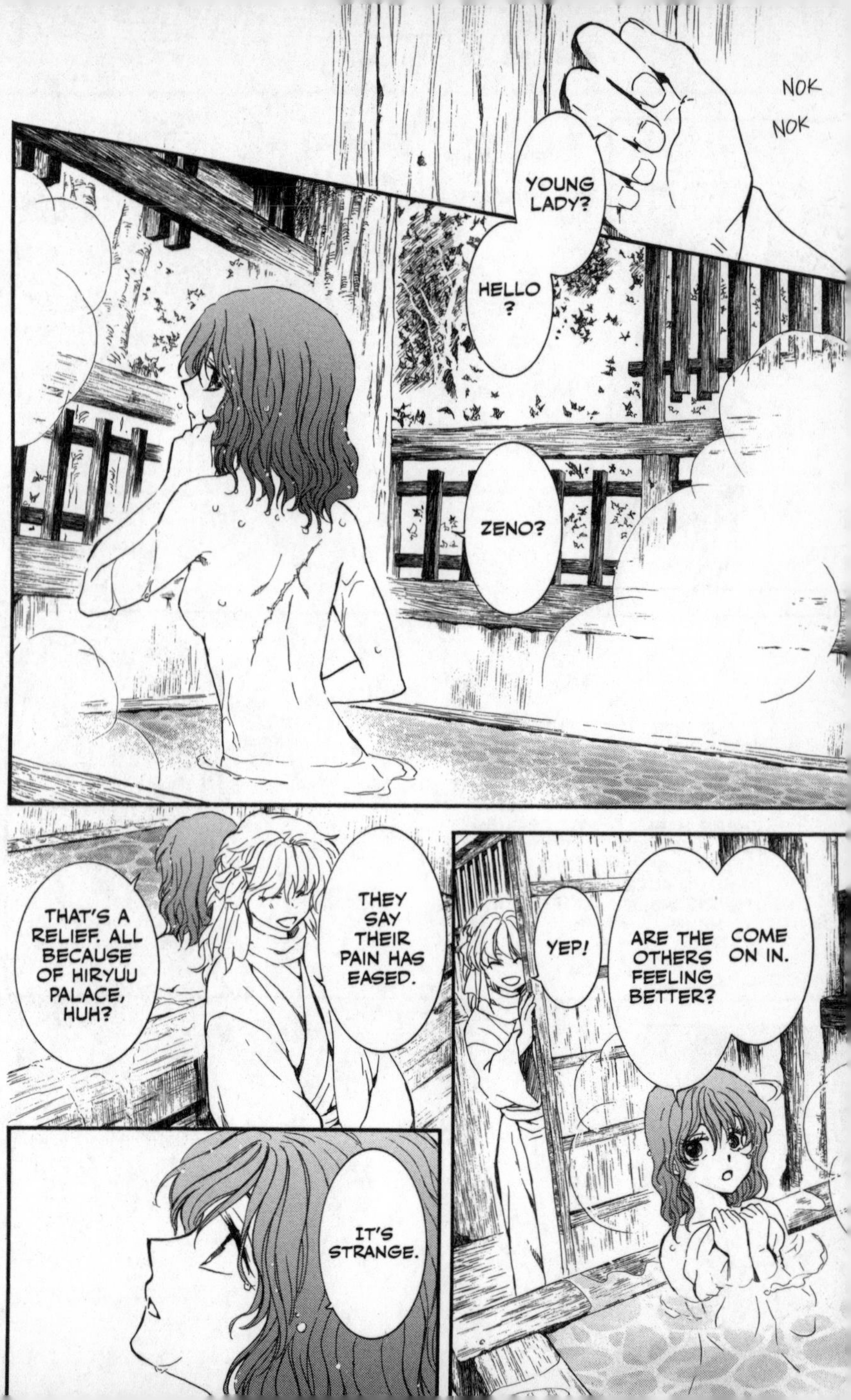
NOK
NOK
YOUNG LADY?
HELLO?
ZENO?
COME ON IN.
ARE THE OTHERS FEELING BETTER?
YEP!
THEY SAY THEIR PAIN HAS EASED.
THAT'S A RELIEF. ALL BECAUSE OF HIRYUU PALACE, HUH?
IT'S STRANGE.

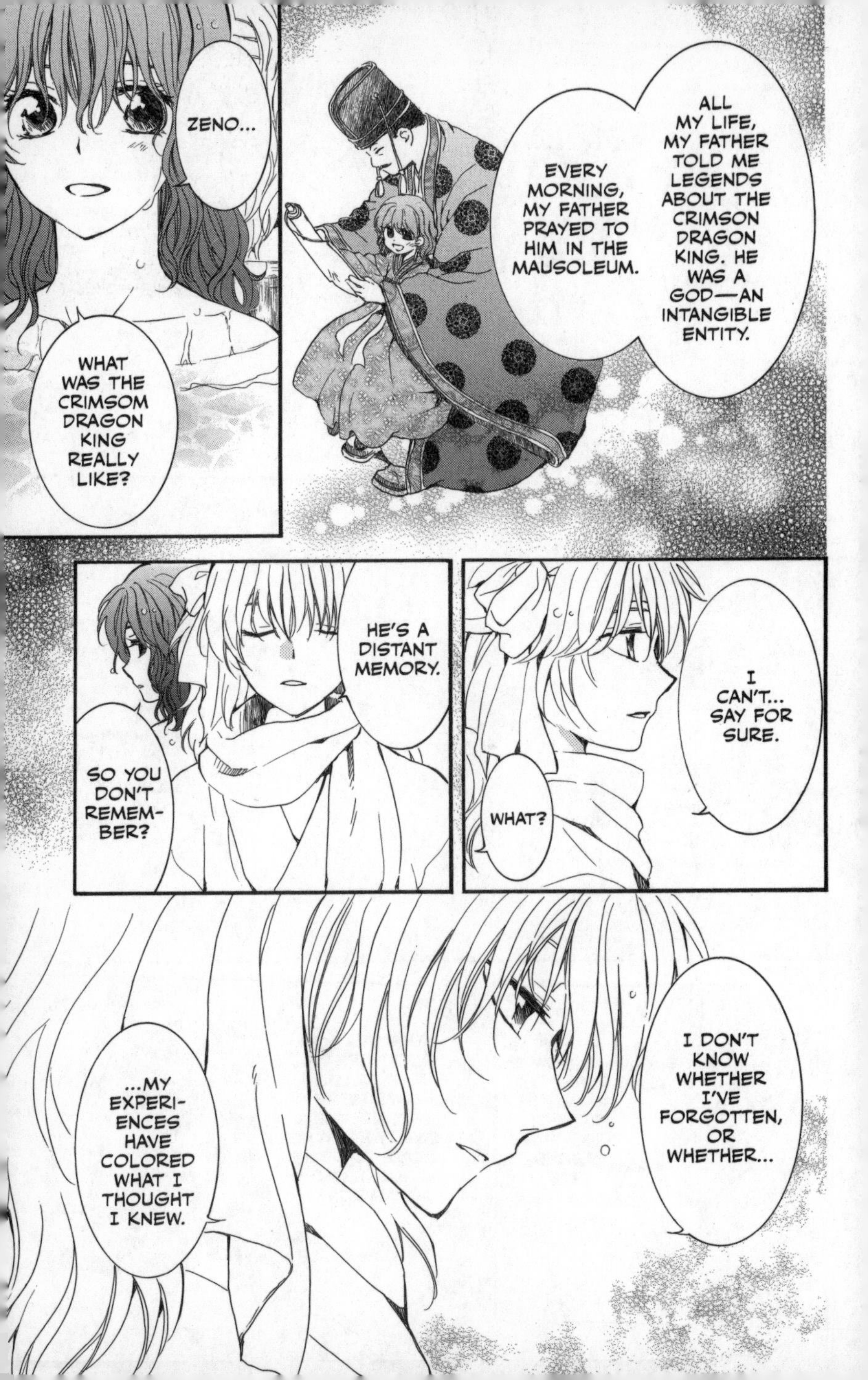
ALL MY LIFE, MY FATHER TOLD ME LEGENDS ABOUT THE CRIMSON DRAGON KING. HE WAS A GOD—AN INTANGIBLE ENTITY.
EVERY MORNING, MY FATHER PRAYED TO HIM IN THE MAUSOLEUM.
ZENO...
WHAT WAS THE CRIMSOM DRAGON KING REALLY LIKE?
I CAN'T... SAY FOR SURE.
WHAT?
HE'S A DISTANT MEMORY.
SO YOU DON'T REMEMBER?
I DON'T KNOW WHETHER I'VE FORGOTTEN, OR WHETHER...
...MY EXPERIENCES HAVE COLORED WHAT I THOUGHT I KNEW.

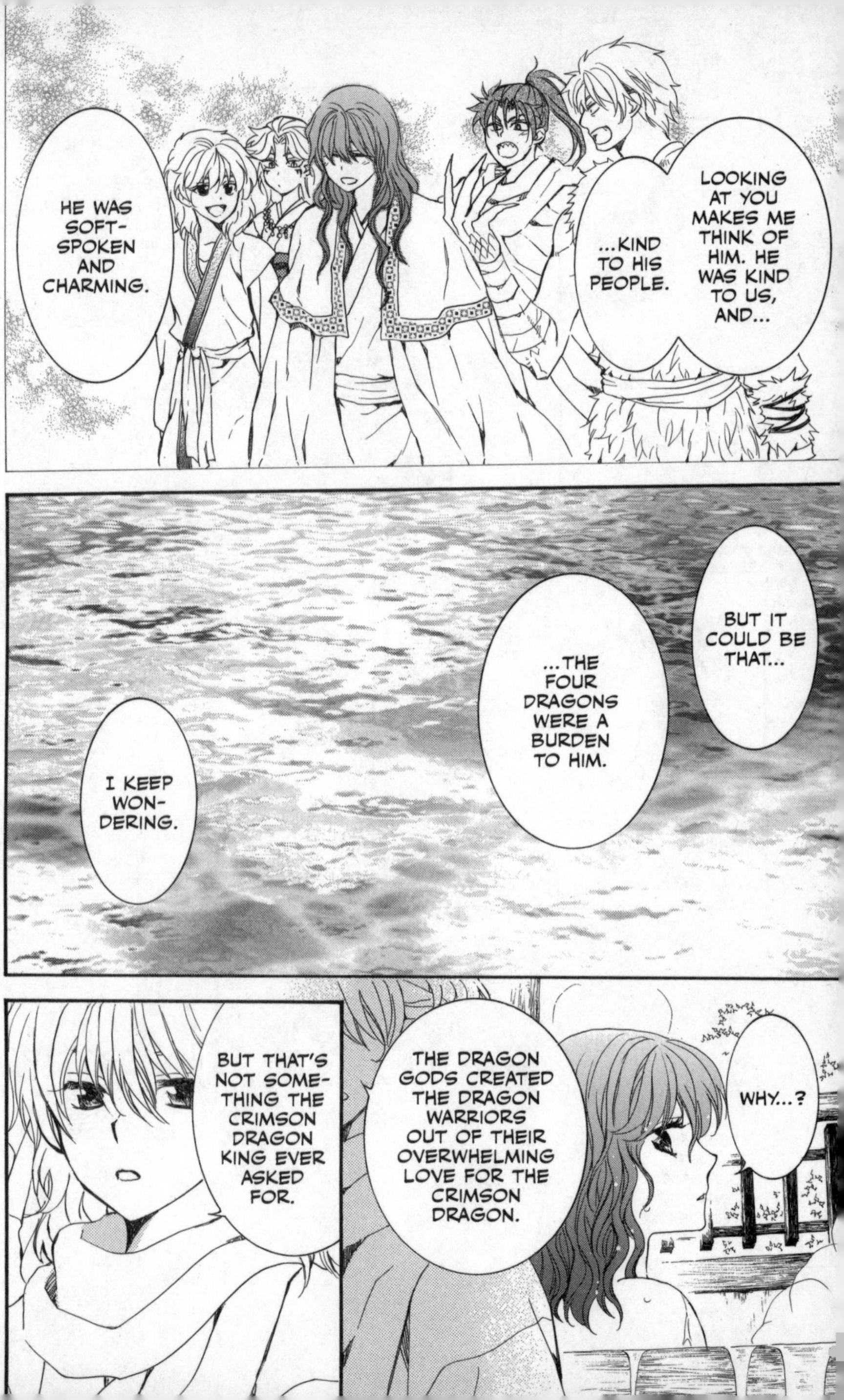
LOOKING AT YOU MAKES ME THINK OF HIM. HE WAS KIND TO US, AND...
...KIND TO HIS PEOPLE.
HE WAS SOFT-SPOKEN AND CHARMING.
BUT IT COULD BE THAT...
...THE FOUR DRAGONS WERE A BURDEN TO HIM.
I KEEP WONDERING.
WHY...?
THE DRAGON GODS CREATED THE DRAGON WARRIORS OUT OF THEIR OVERWHELMING LOVE FOR THE CRIMSON DRAGON.
BUT THAT'S NOT SOMETHING THE CRIMSON DRAGON KING EVER ASKED FOR.

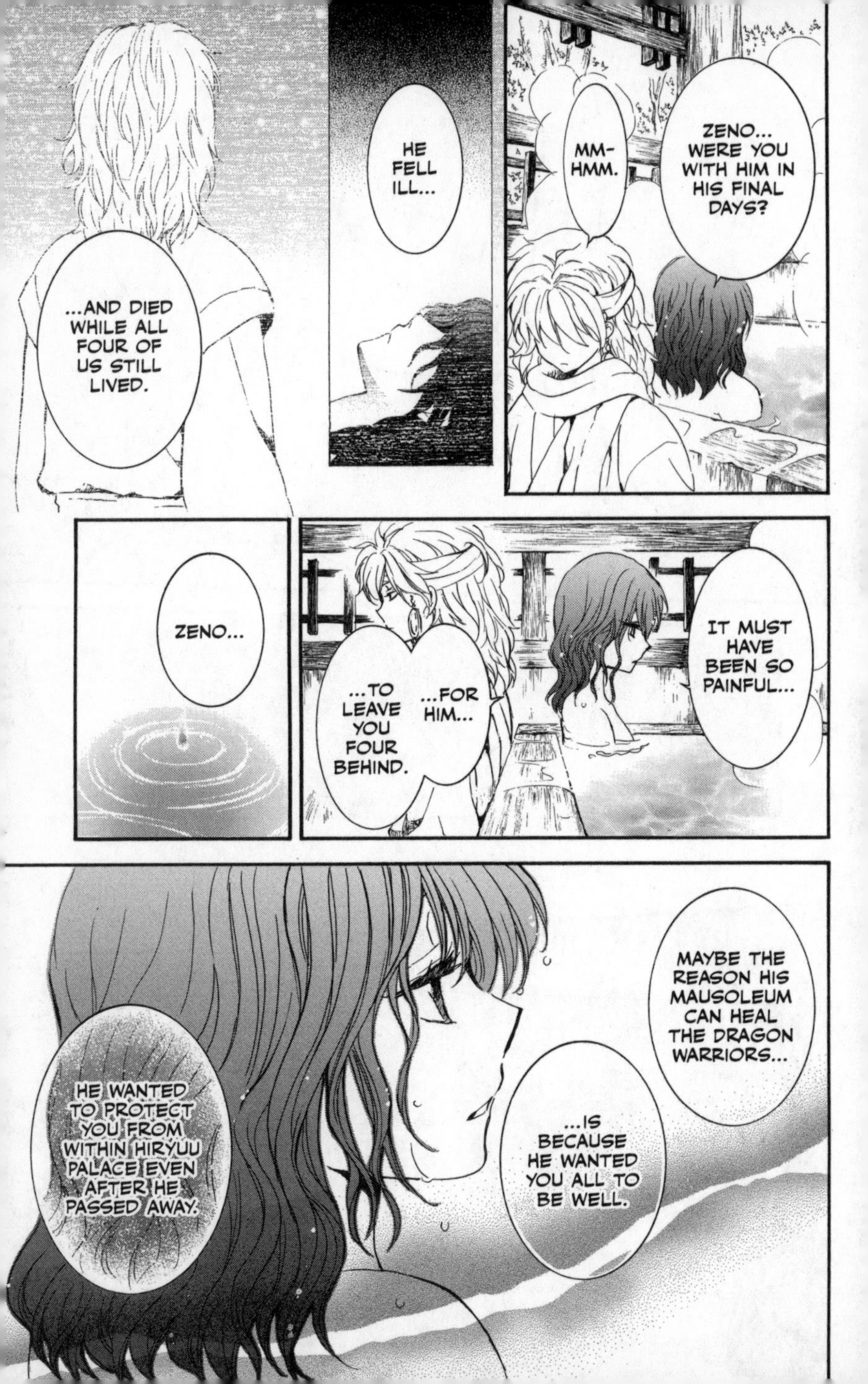
ZENO... WERE YOU WITH HIM IN HIS FINAL DAYS?
MM-HMM.
HE FELL ILL...
...AND DIED WHILE ALL FOUR OF US STILL LIVED.
IT MUST HAVE BEEN SO PAINFUL...
...FOR HIM...
...TO LEAVE YOU FOUR BEHIND.
ZENO...
MAYBE THE REASON HIS MAUSOLEUM CAN HEAL THE DRAGON WARRIORS...
...IS BECAUSE HE WANTED YOU ALL TO BE WELL.
HE WANTED TO PROTECT YOU FROM WITHIN HIRYUU PALACE EVEN AFTER HE PASSED AWAY.

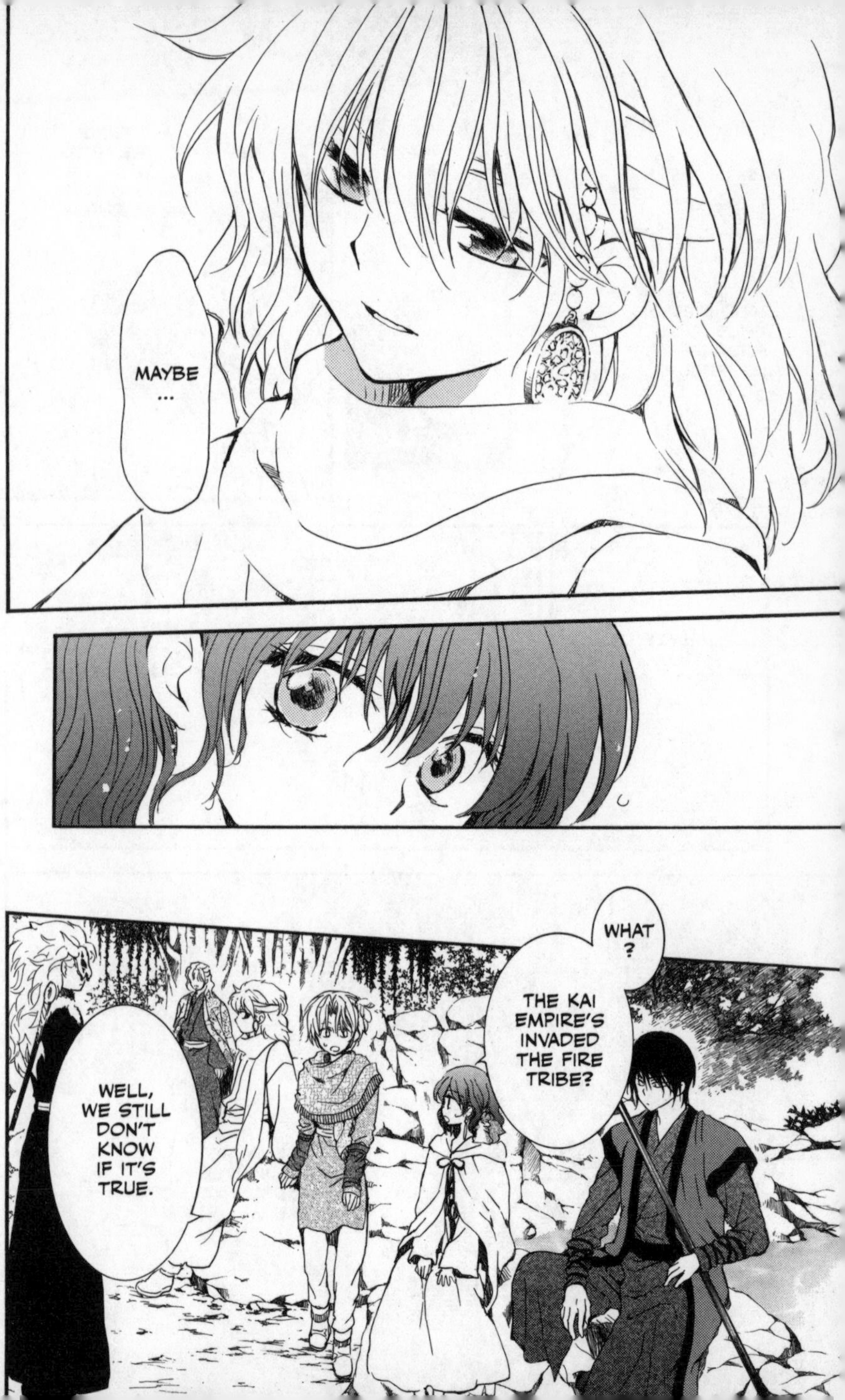
MAYBE ...
WHAT?
THE KAI EMPIRE'S INVADED THE FIRE TRIBE?
WELL, WE STILL DON'T KNOW IF IT'S TRUE.

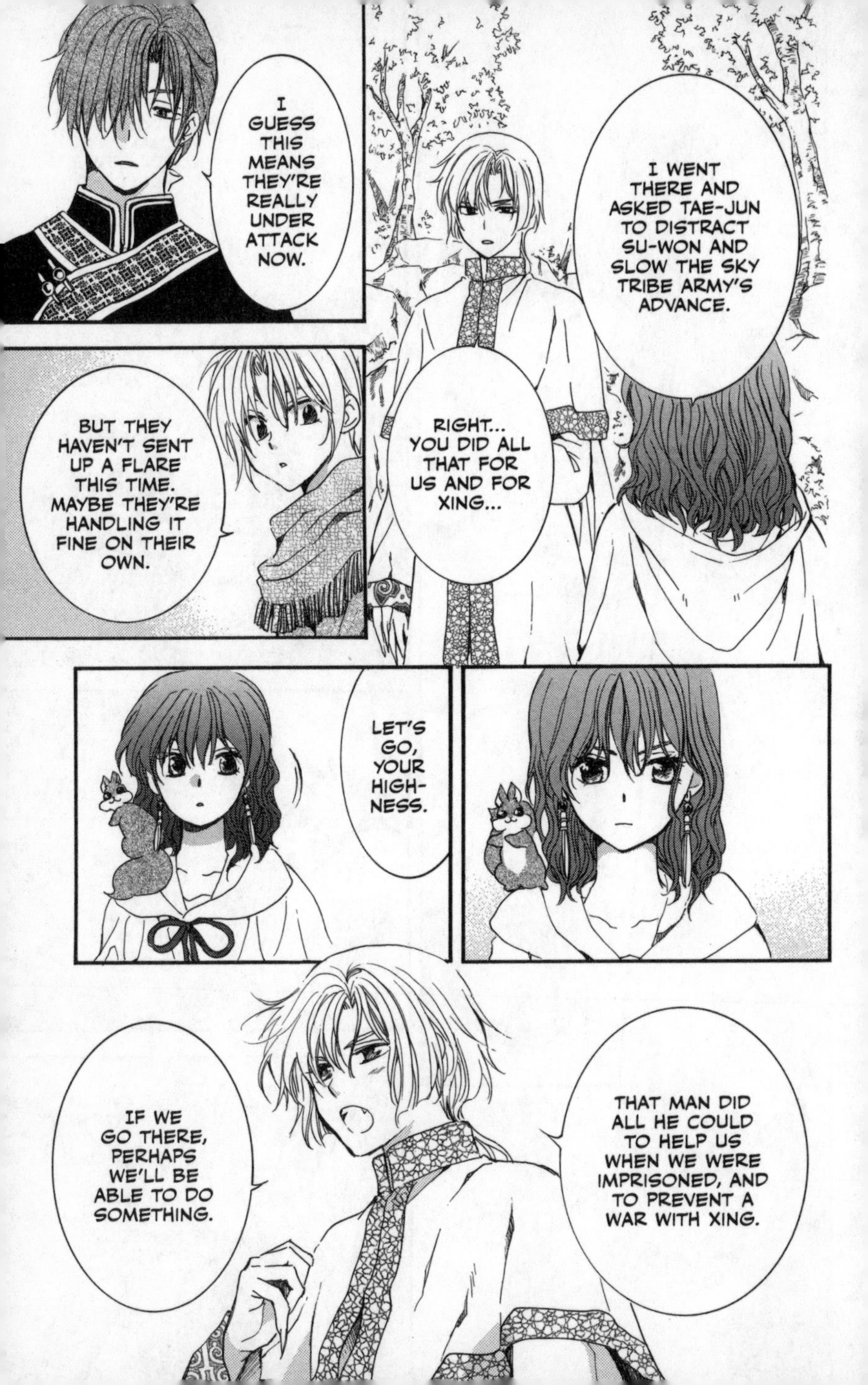
I WENT THERE AND ASKED TAE-JUN TO DISTRACT SU-WON AND SLOW THE SKY TRIBE ARMY'S ADVANCE.
RIGHT... YOU DID ALL THAT FOR US AND FOR XING...
I GUESS THIS MEANS THEY'RE REALLY UNDER ATTACK NOW.
BUT THEY HAVEN'T SENT UP A FLARE THIS TIME. MAYBE THEY'RE HANDLING IT FINE ON THEIR OWN.
LET'S GO, YOUR HIGH-NESS.
THAT MAN DID ALL HE COULD TO HELP US WHEN WE WERE IMPRISONED, AND TO PREVENT A WAR WITH XING.
IF WE GO THERE, PERHAPS WE'LL BE ABLE TO DO SOMETHING.

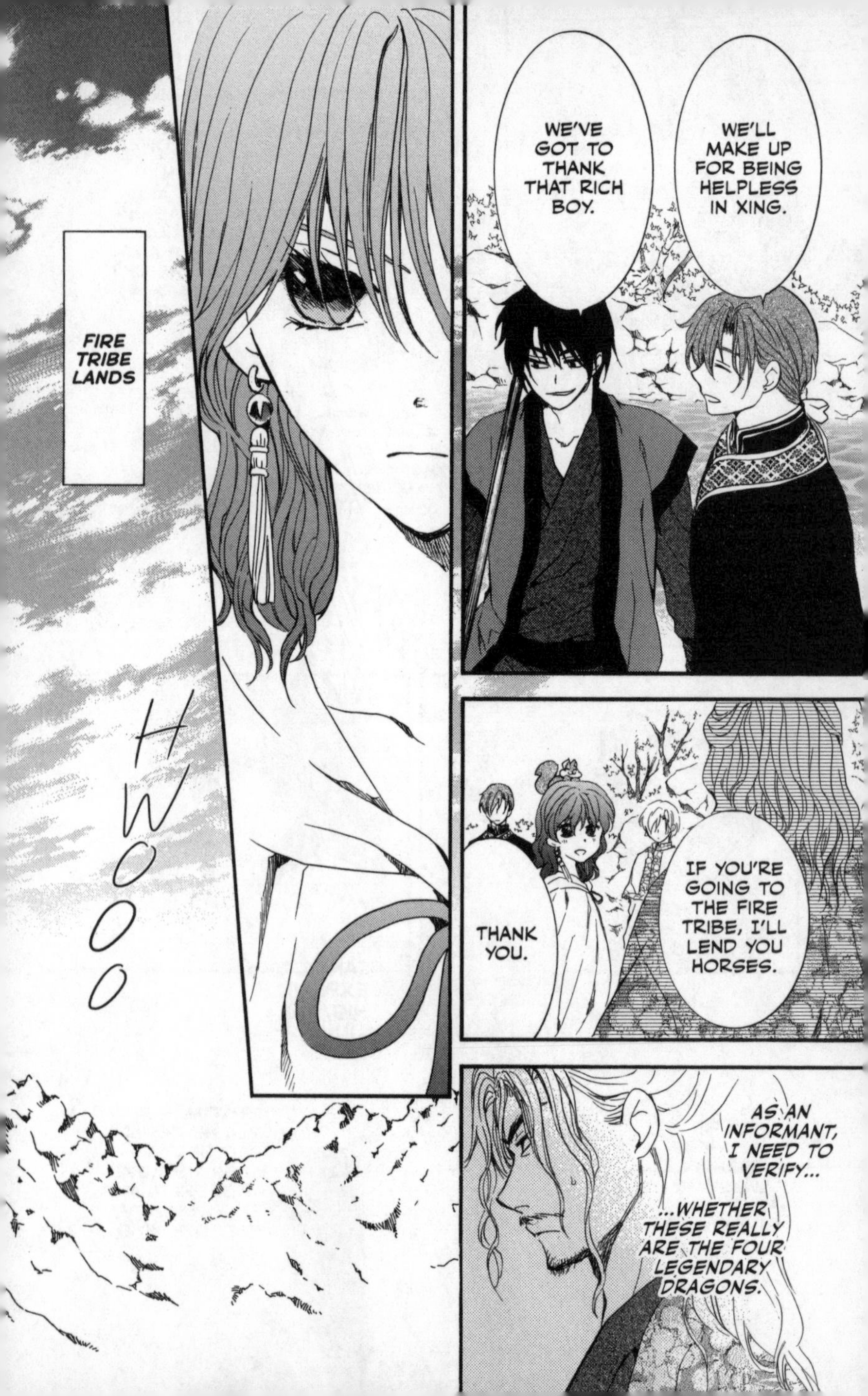
WE'LL MAKE UP FOR BEING HELPLESS IN XING.
WE'VE GOT TO THANK THAT RICH BOY.
IF YOU'RE GOING TO THE FIRE TRIBE, I'LL LEND YOU HORSES.
THANK YOU.
AS AN INFORMANT, I NEED TO VERIFY...
...WHETHER THESE REALLY ARE THE FOUR LEGENDARY DRAGONS.
FIRE TRIBE LANDS
HWOOOO

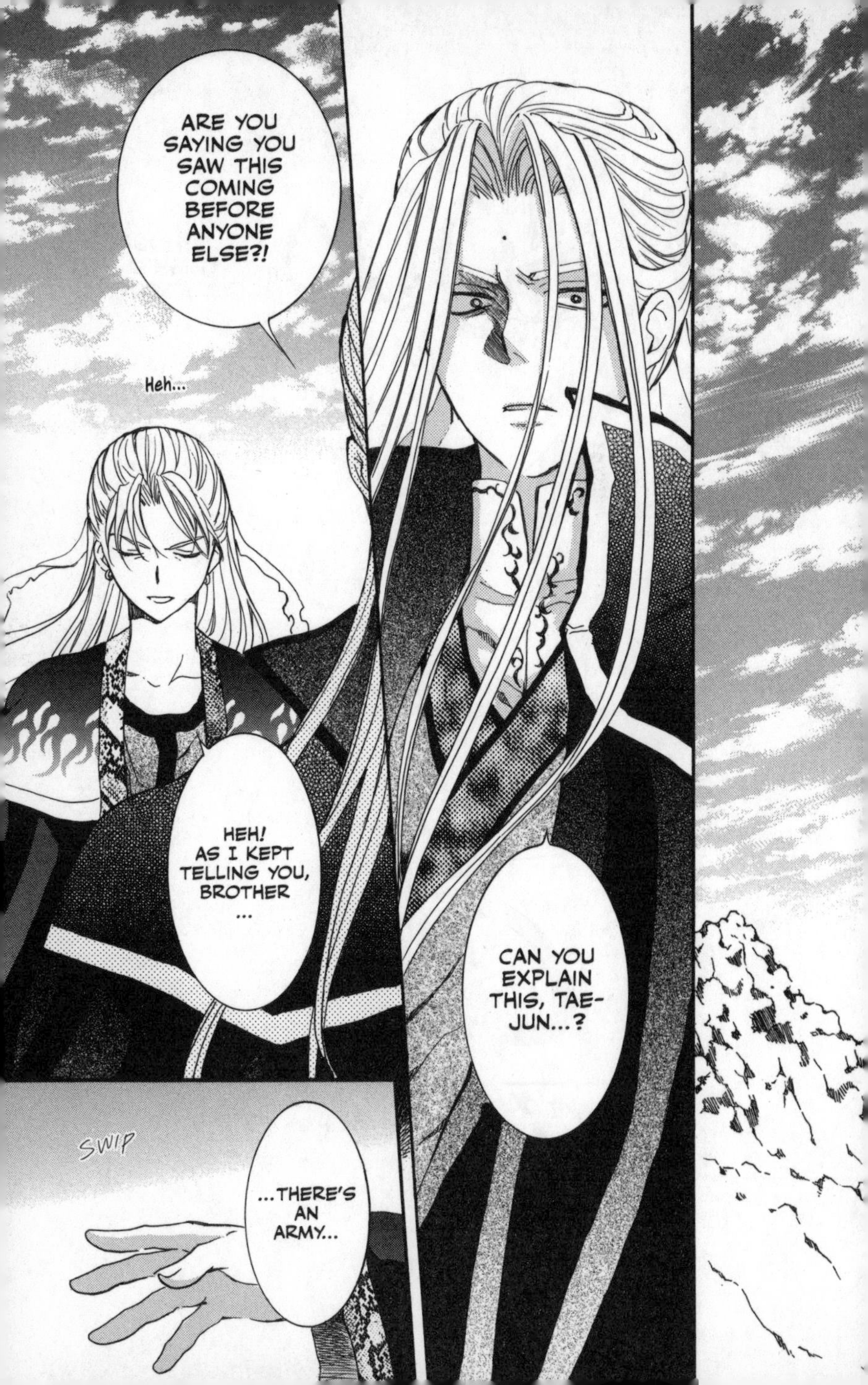
CAN YOU EXPLAIN THIS, TAE-JUN...?
ARE YOU SAYING YOU SAW THIS COMING BEFORE ANYONE ELSE?!
Heh...
HEH! AS I KEPT TELLING YOU, BROTHER ...
...THERE'S AN ARMY...
SWIP

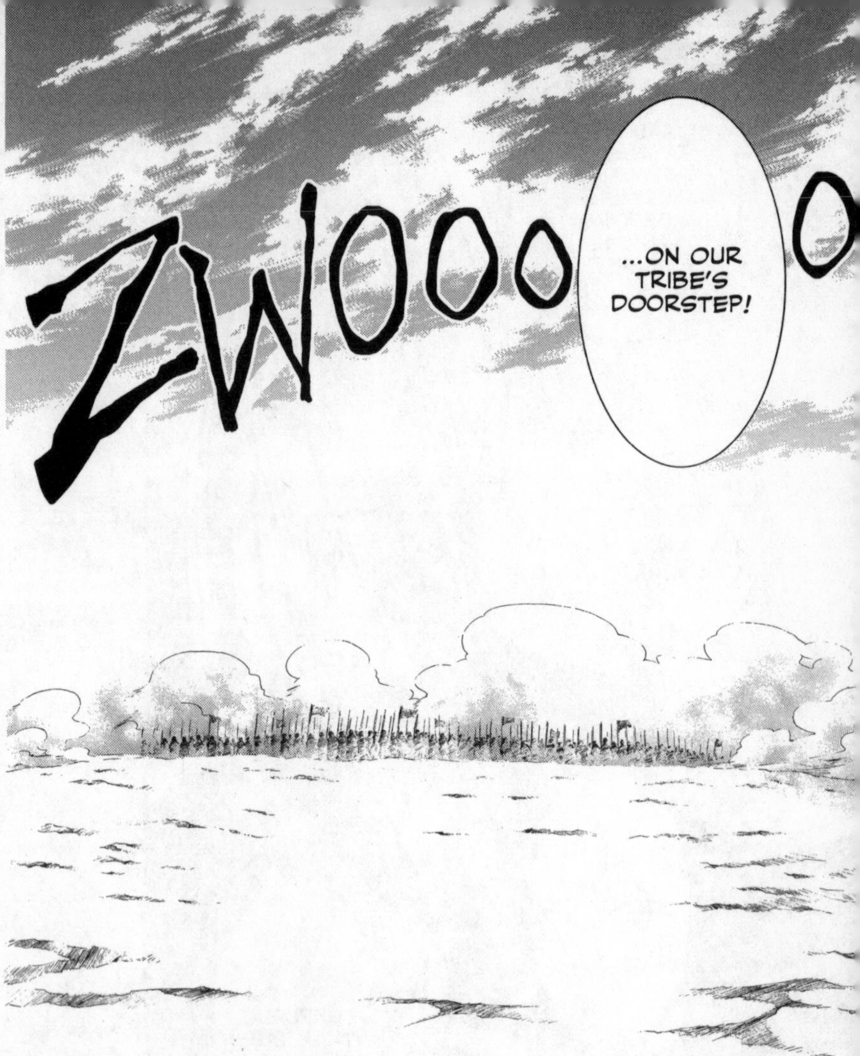
ZWOOOO
...ON OUR TRIBE'S DOORSTEP!

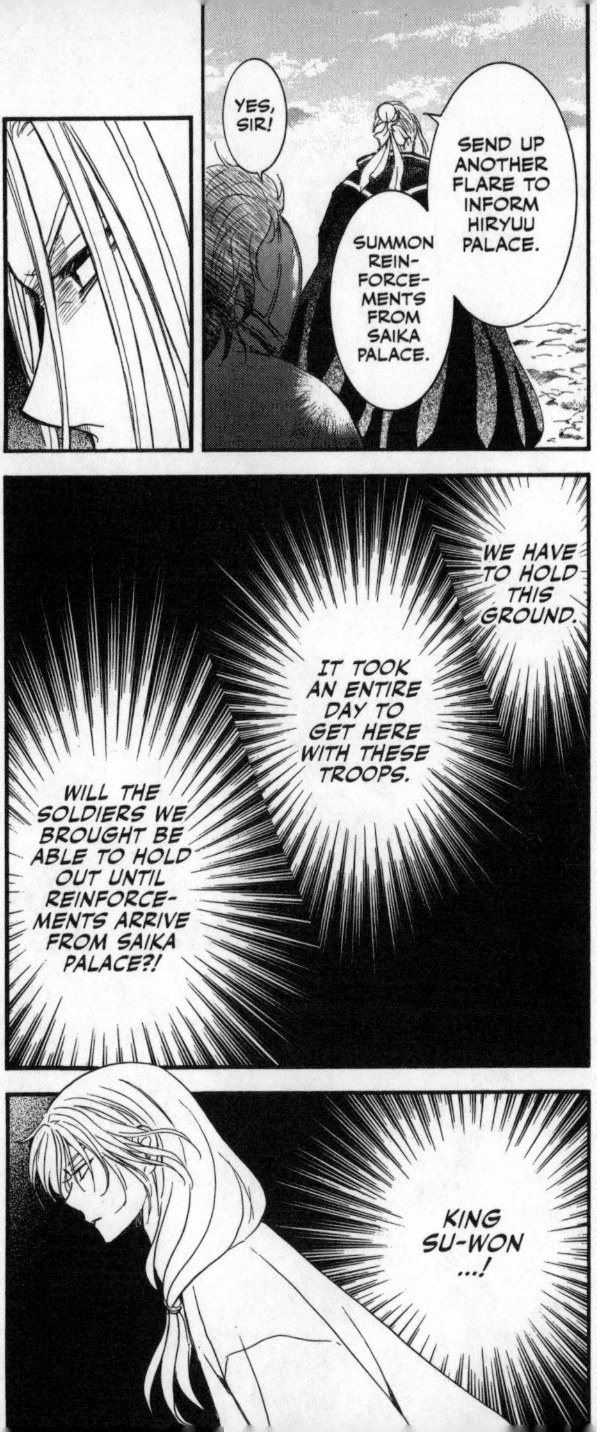
SEND UP ANOTHER FLARE TO INFORM HIRYUU PALACE.
SUMMON REIN-FORCE-MENTS FROM SAIKA PALACE.
YES, SIR!
WE HAVE TO HOLD THIS GROUND.
IT TOOK AN ENTIRE DAY TO GET HERE WITH THESE TROOPS.
WILL THE SOLDIERS WE BROUGHT BE ABLE TO HOLD OUT UNTIL REINFORCE-MENTS ARRIVE FROM SAIKA PALACE?!
KING SU-WON ...!

I'm creating a Yona fanbook to go on sale when Yona volume 28 does (sometime in the fall).

I'm worried about how much work it takes to make a fanbook. I'm so busy with the series and colored bonus material that I haven't started on it. I've gotten some time off, but I've been using it to do coloring work... I want more time to do my storyboards and drawings.

At any rate, the Hana to Yume bonus material will most likely be some sketches I put a lot of effort into, so pick it up if you want those! See you later!

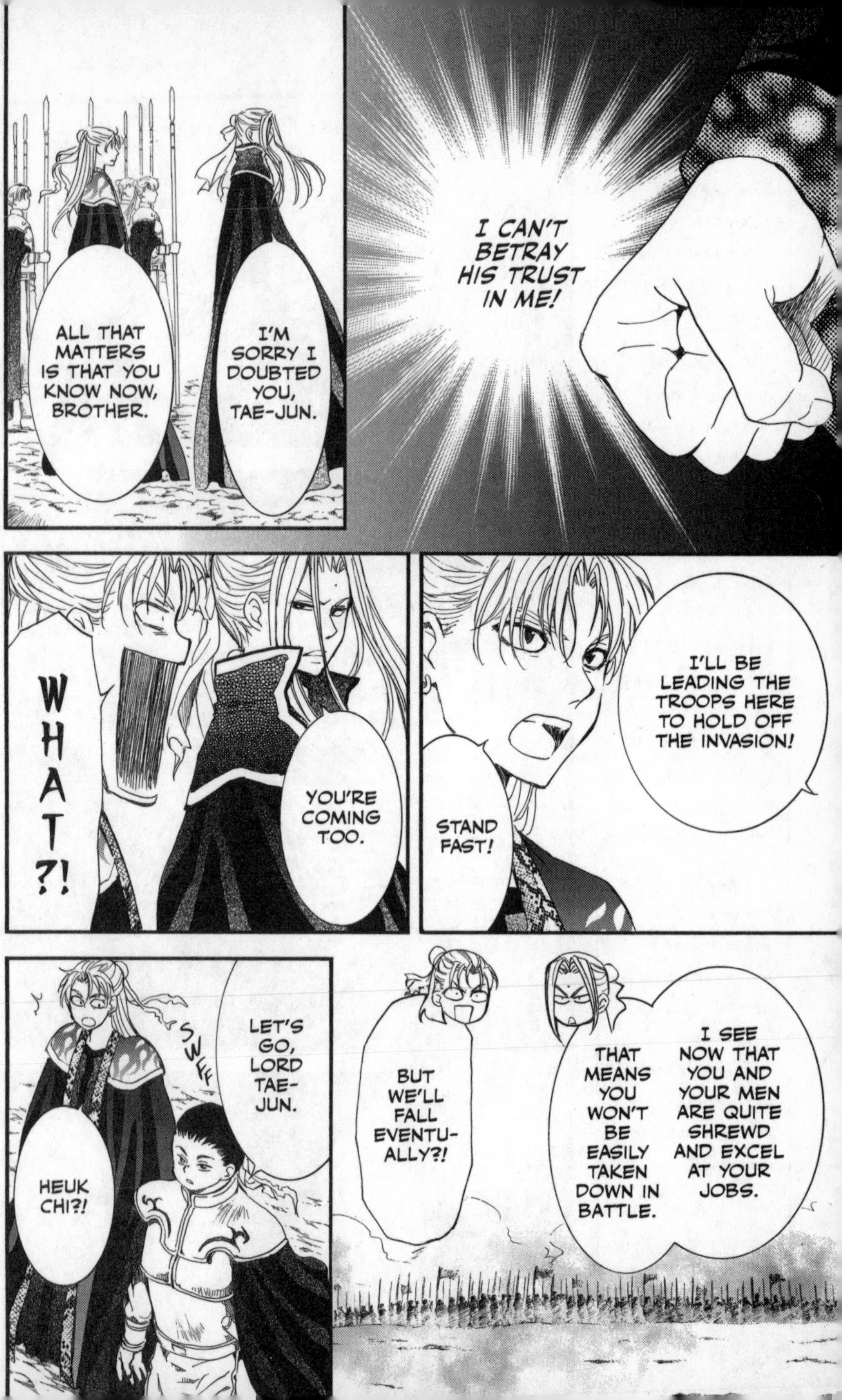
I CAN'T BETRAY HIS TRUST IN ME!
I'M SORRY I DOUBTED YOU, TAE-JUN.
ALL THAT MATTERS IS THAT YOU KNOW NOW, BROTHER.
I'LL BE LEADING THE TROOPS HERE TO HOLD OFF THE INVASION!
STAND FAST!
YOU'RE COMING TOO.
WHAT?!
I SEE NOW THAT YOU AND YOUR MEN ARE QUITE SHREWD AND EXCEL AT YOUR JOBS.
THAT MEANS YOU WON'T BE EASILY TAKEN DOWN IN BATTLE.
BUT WE'LL FALL EVENTU-ALLY?!
LET'S GO, LORD TAE-JUN.
SWFF
HEUK CHI?!

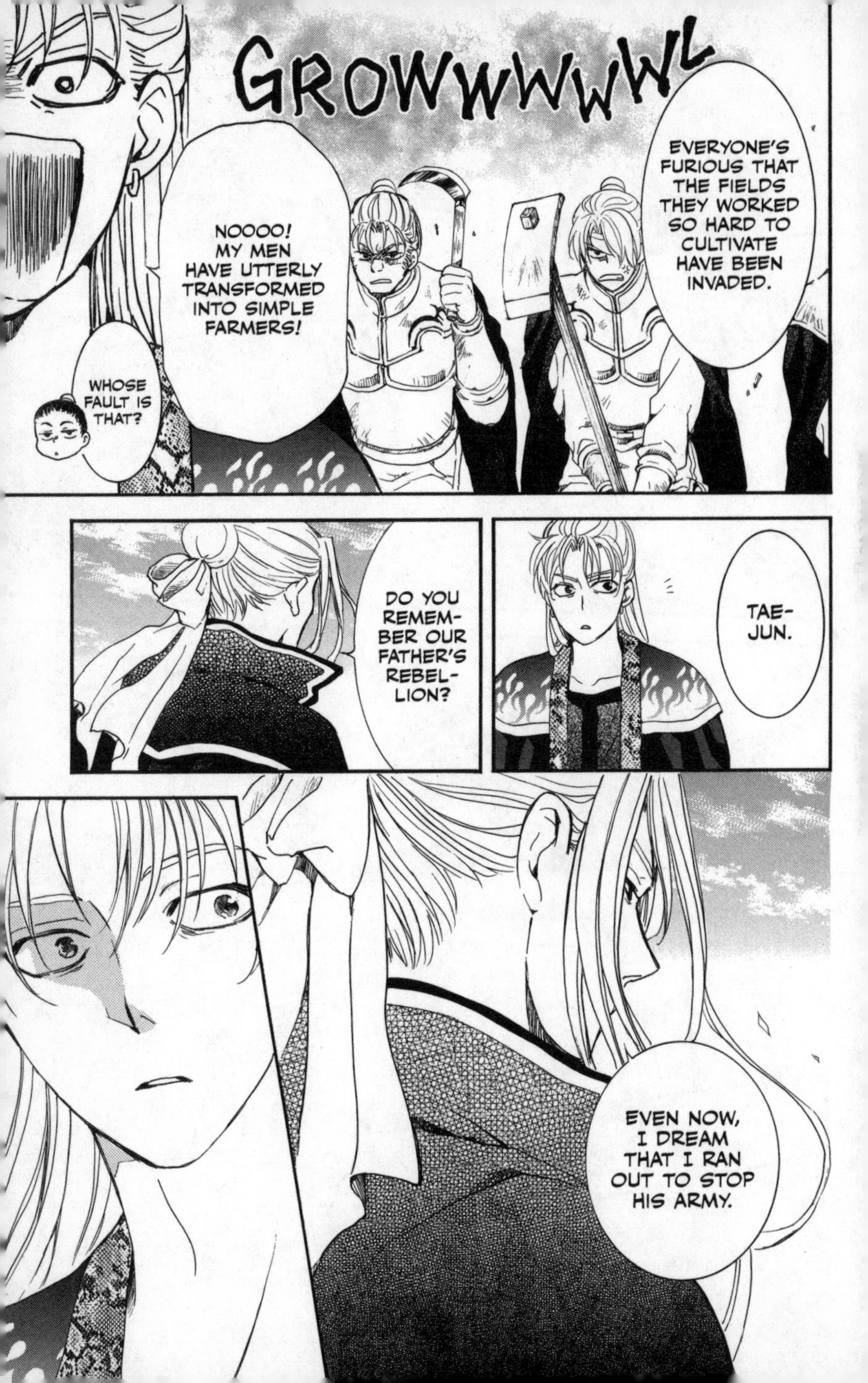
GROWWWWWL
EVERYONE'S FURIOUS THAT THE FIELDS THEY WORKED SO HARD TO CULTIVATE HAVE BEEN INVADED.
NOOOO! MY MEN HAVE UTTERLY TRANSFORMED INTO SIMPLE FARMERS!
WHOSE FAULT IS THAT?
TAE-JUN.
DO YOU REMEM-BER OUR FATHER'S REBEL-LION?
EVEN NOW, I DREAM THAT I RAN OUT TO STOP HIS ARMY.

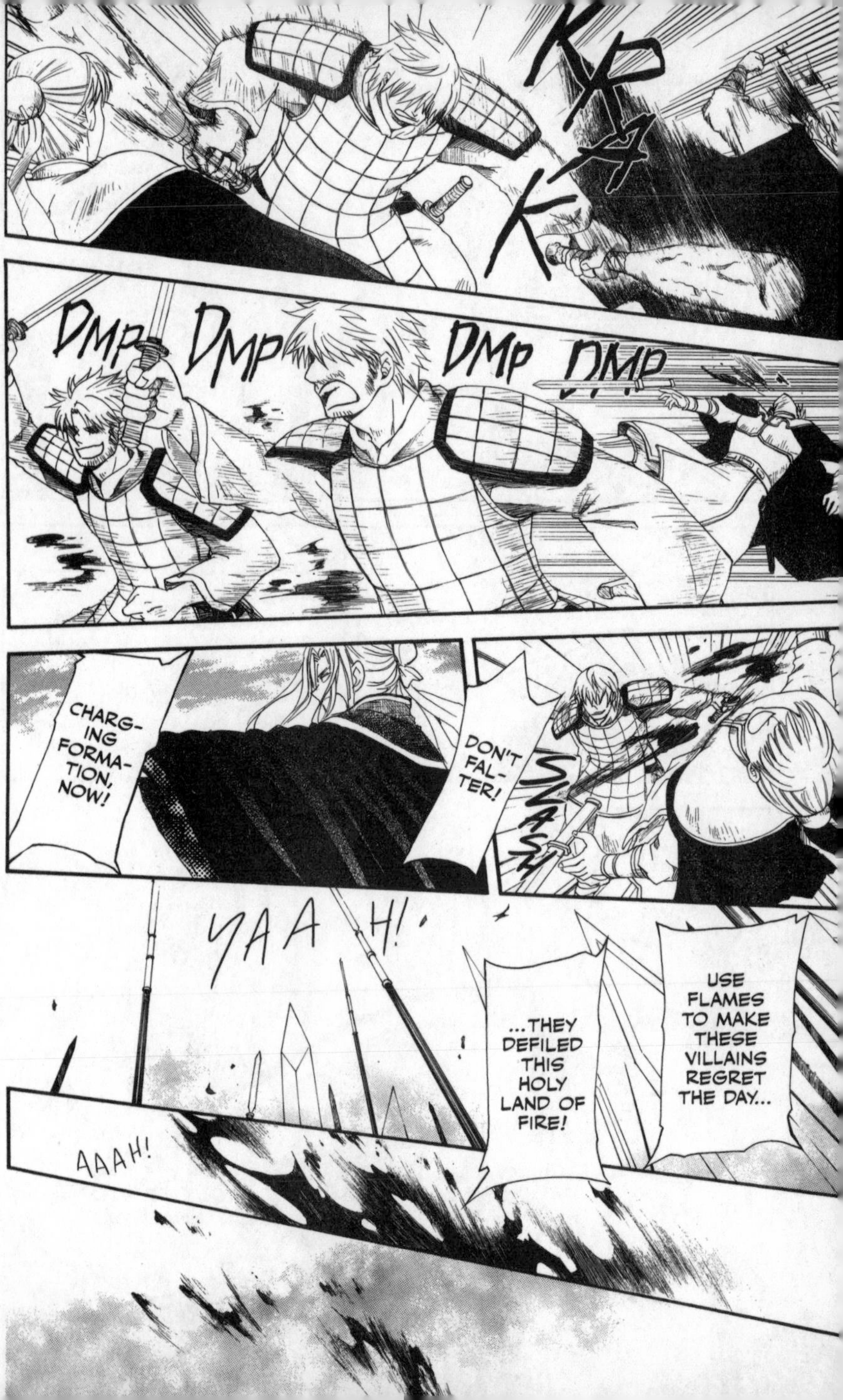
KRAK
DMP DMP DMP DMP
DON'T FALTER!
SLASH
CHARGING FORMATION, NOW!
USE FLAMES TO MAKE THESE VILLAINS REGRET THE DAY...
...THEY DEFILED THIS HOLY LAND OF FIRE!
YAAAH!
AAAH!

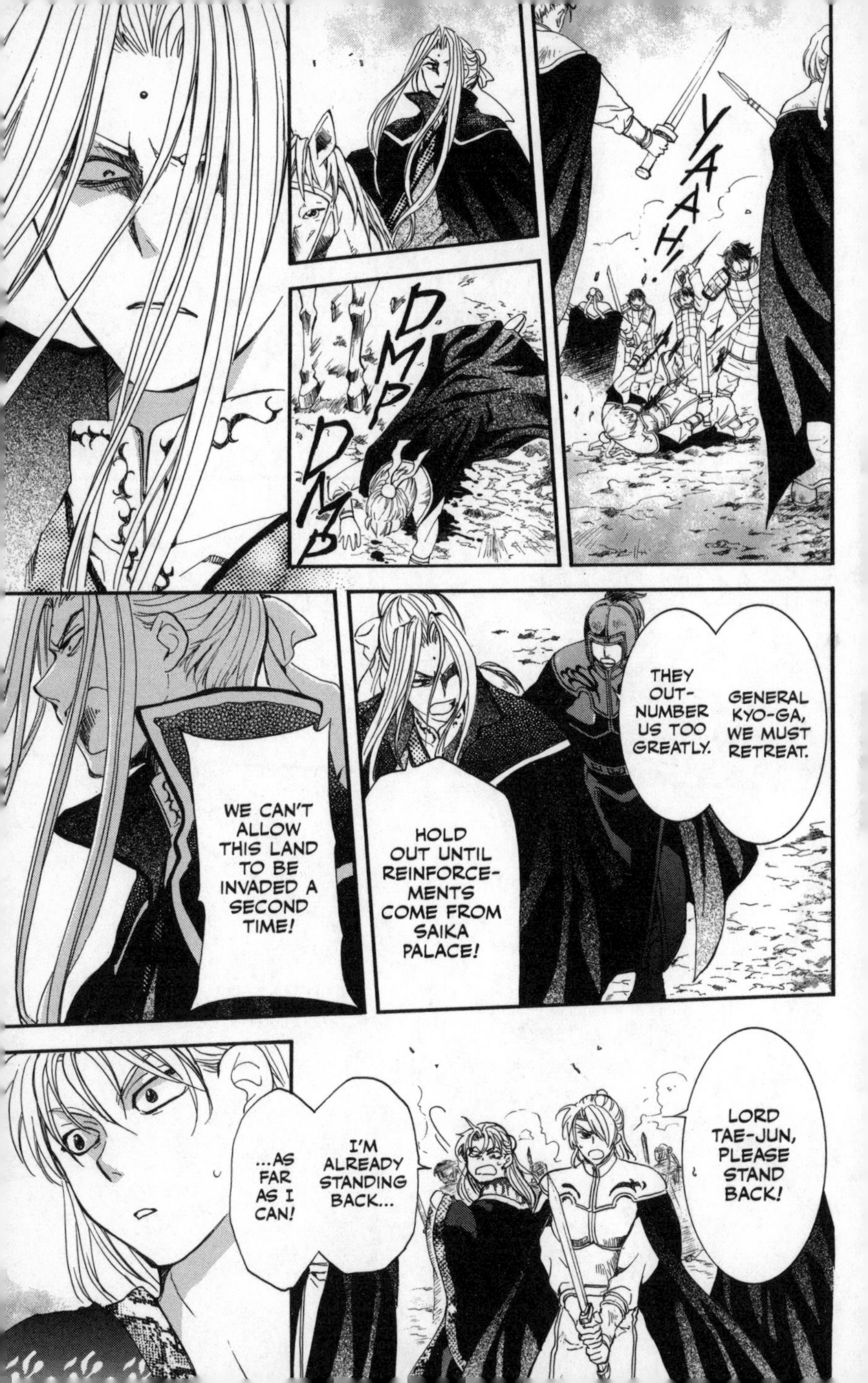
YAAH!
DMP
DMP
GENERAL KYO-GA, WE MUST RETREAT.
THEY OUT-NUMBER US TOO GREATLY.
HOLD OUT UNTIL REINFORCE-MENTS COME FROM SAIKA PALACE!
WE CAN'T ALLOW THIS LAND TO BE INVADED A SECOND TIME!
LORD TAE-JUN, PLEASE STAND BACK!
I'M ALREADY STANDING BACK...
...AS FAR AS I CAN!

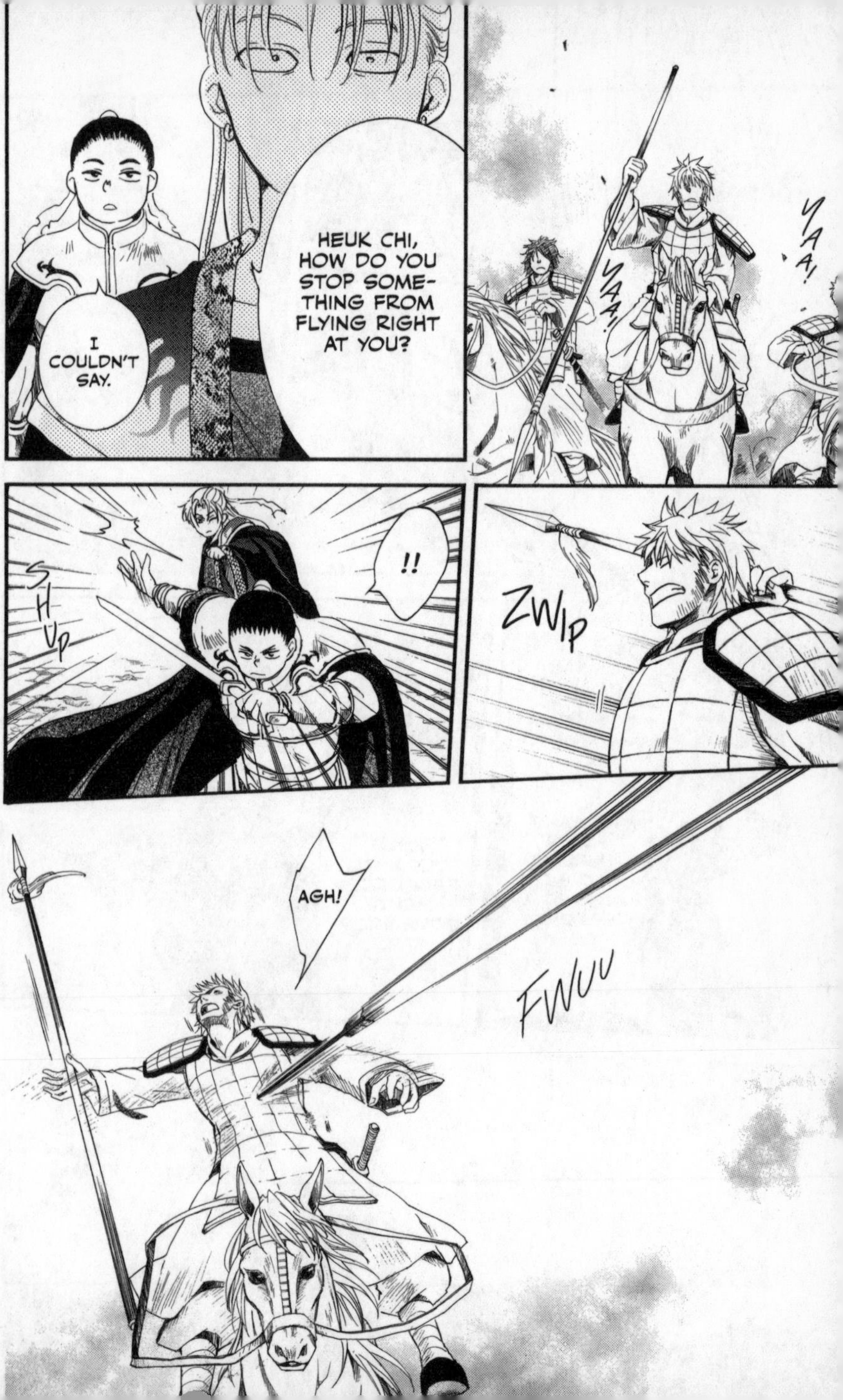
YAAA!
YAAA!
HEUK CHI, HOW DO YOU STOP SOMETHING FROM FLYING RIGHT AT YOU?
I COULDN'T SAY.
ZWIP
!!
SHUP
AGH!
FWUU

HUH
?

THUD

GUH!

AN
ARROW
...?

95

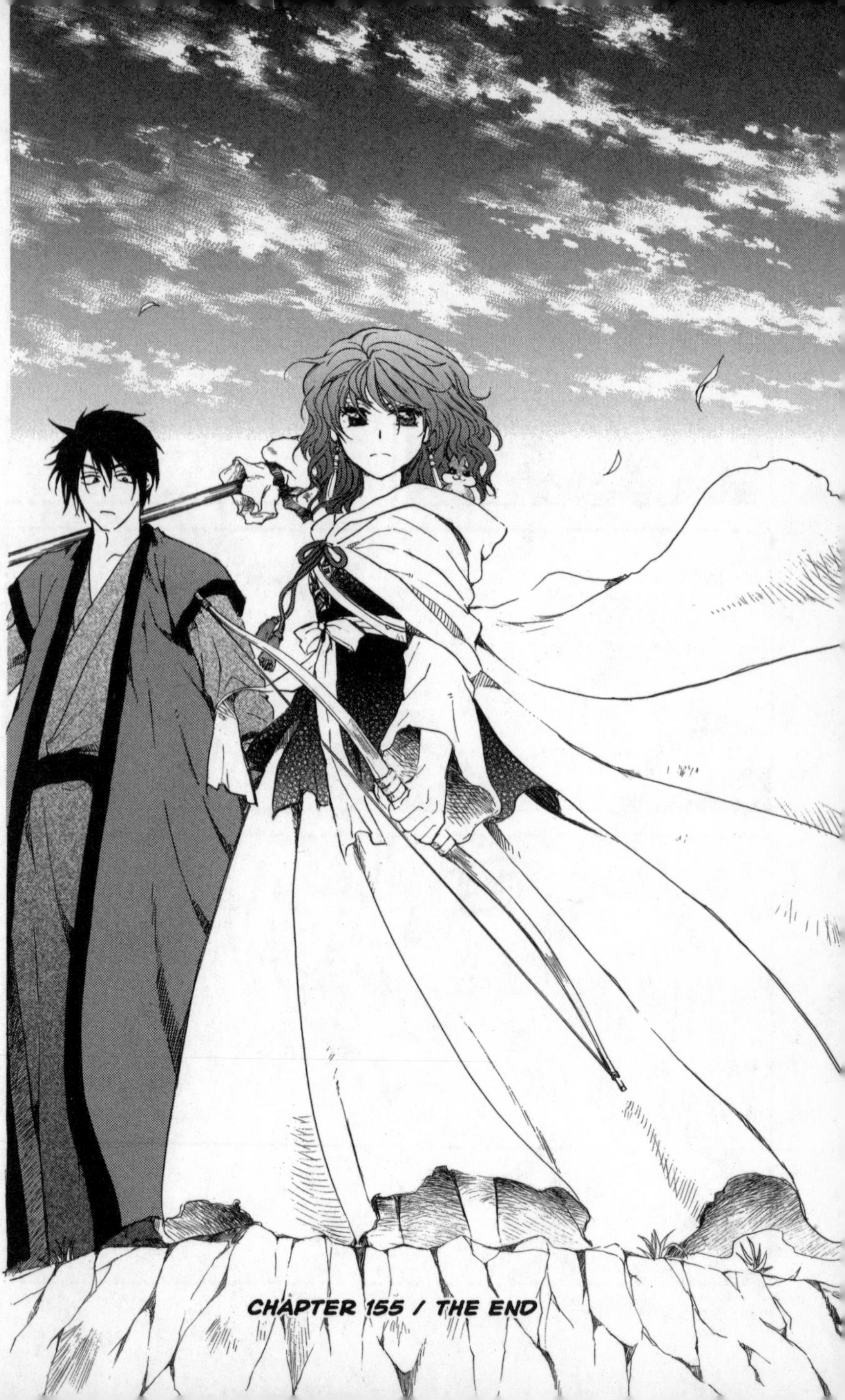
CHAPTER 155 / THE END

CHAPTER 156: THERE'S NO WAY I'M LOSING IT

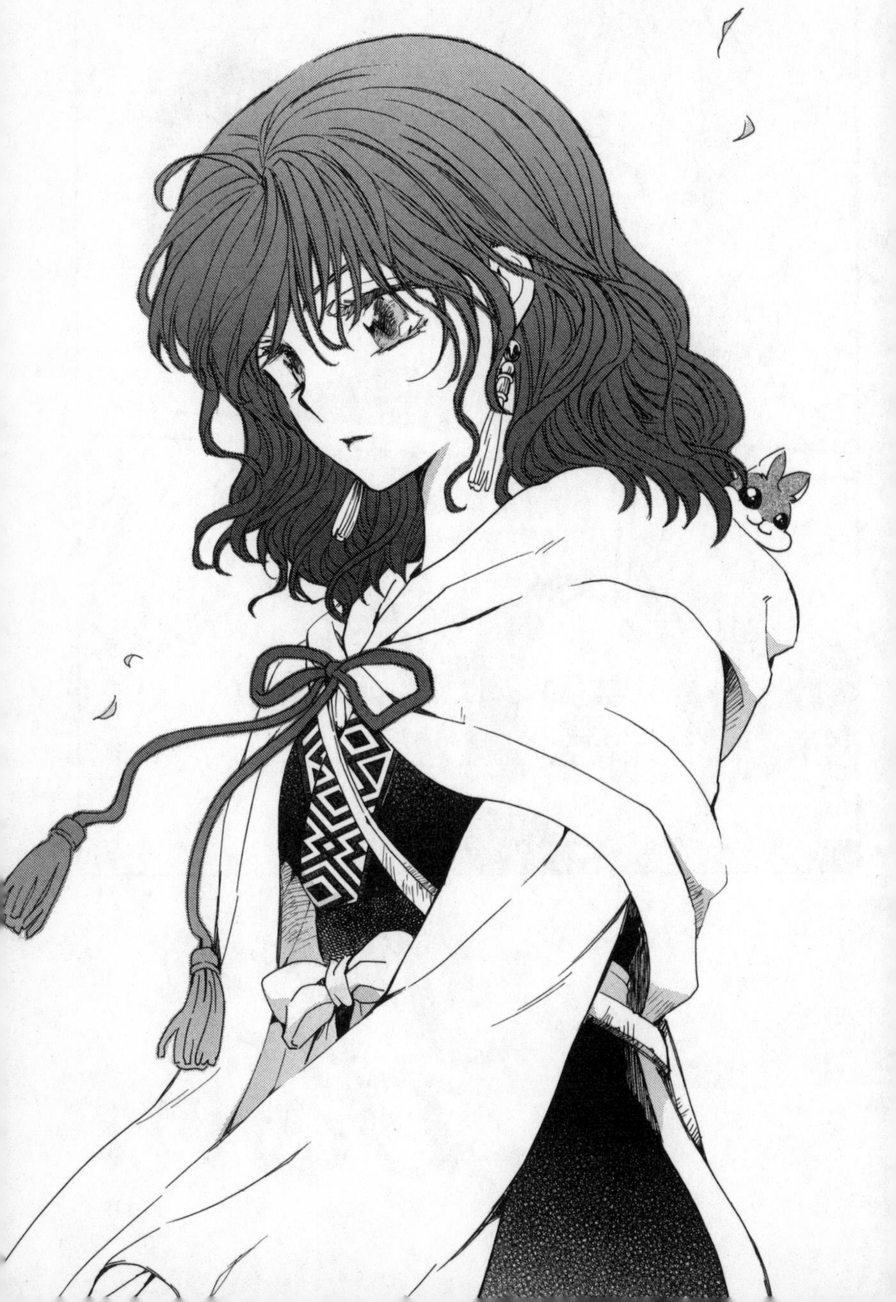

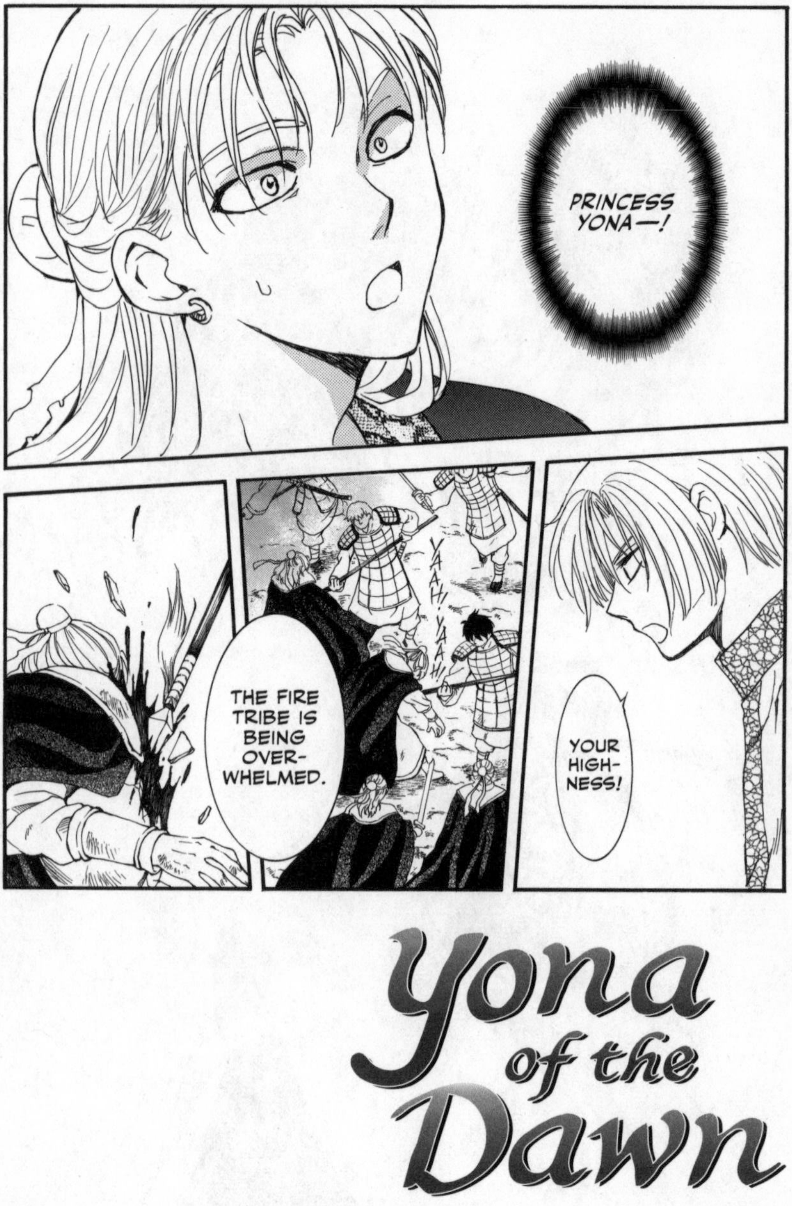
PRINCESS YONA—!
YOUR HIGH-NESS!
YAAH! YAAH!
THE FIRE TRIBE IS BEING OVER-WHELMED.

Yona of the Dawn

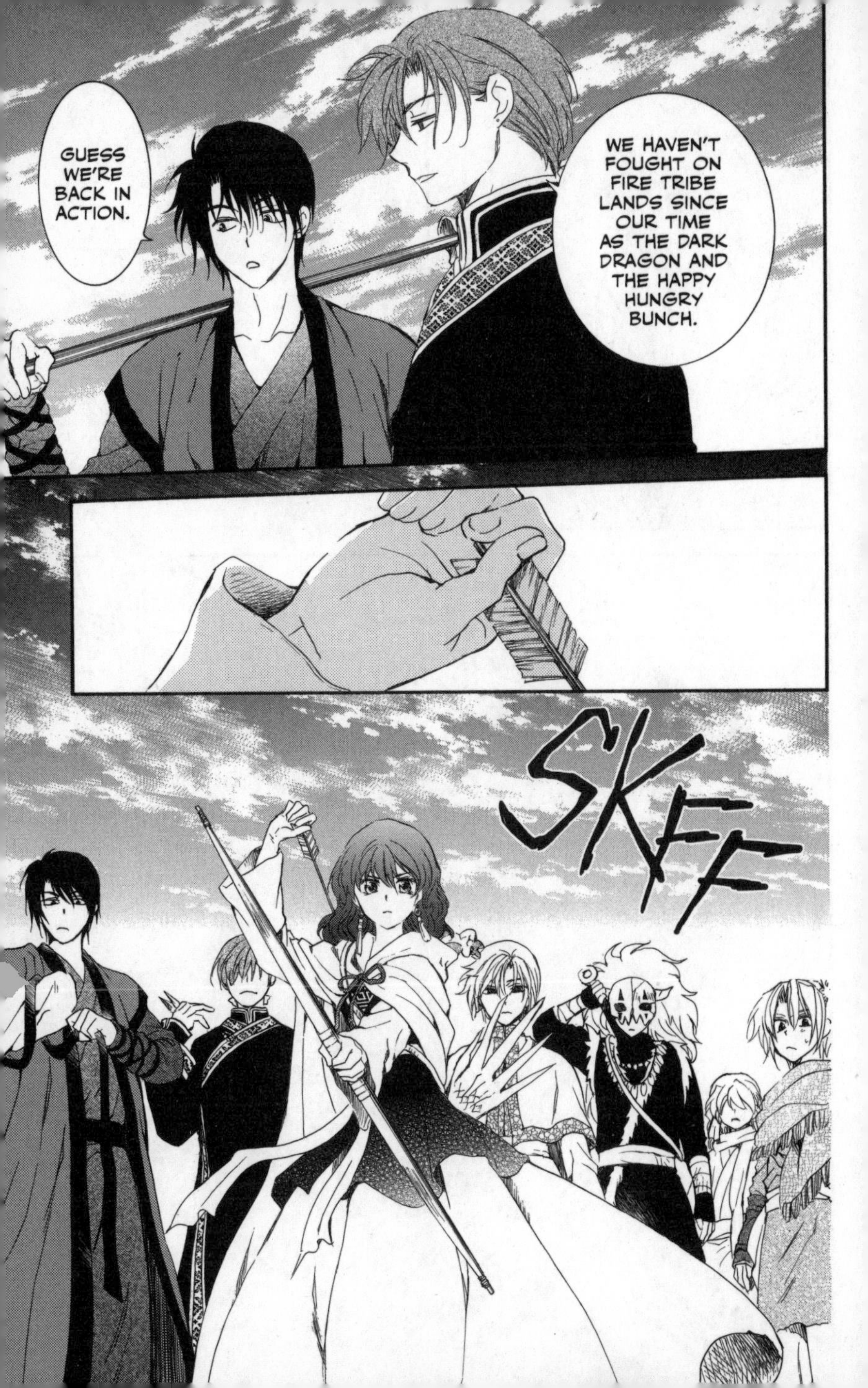
WE HAVEN'T FOUGHT ON FIRE TRIBE LANDS SINCE OUR TIME AS THE DARK DRAGON AND THE HAPPY HUNGRY BUNCH.
GUESS WE'RE BACK IN ACTION.
SKFF

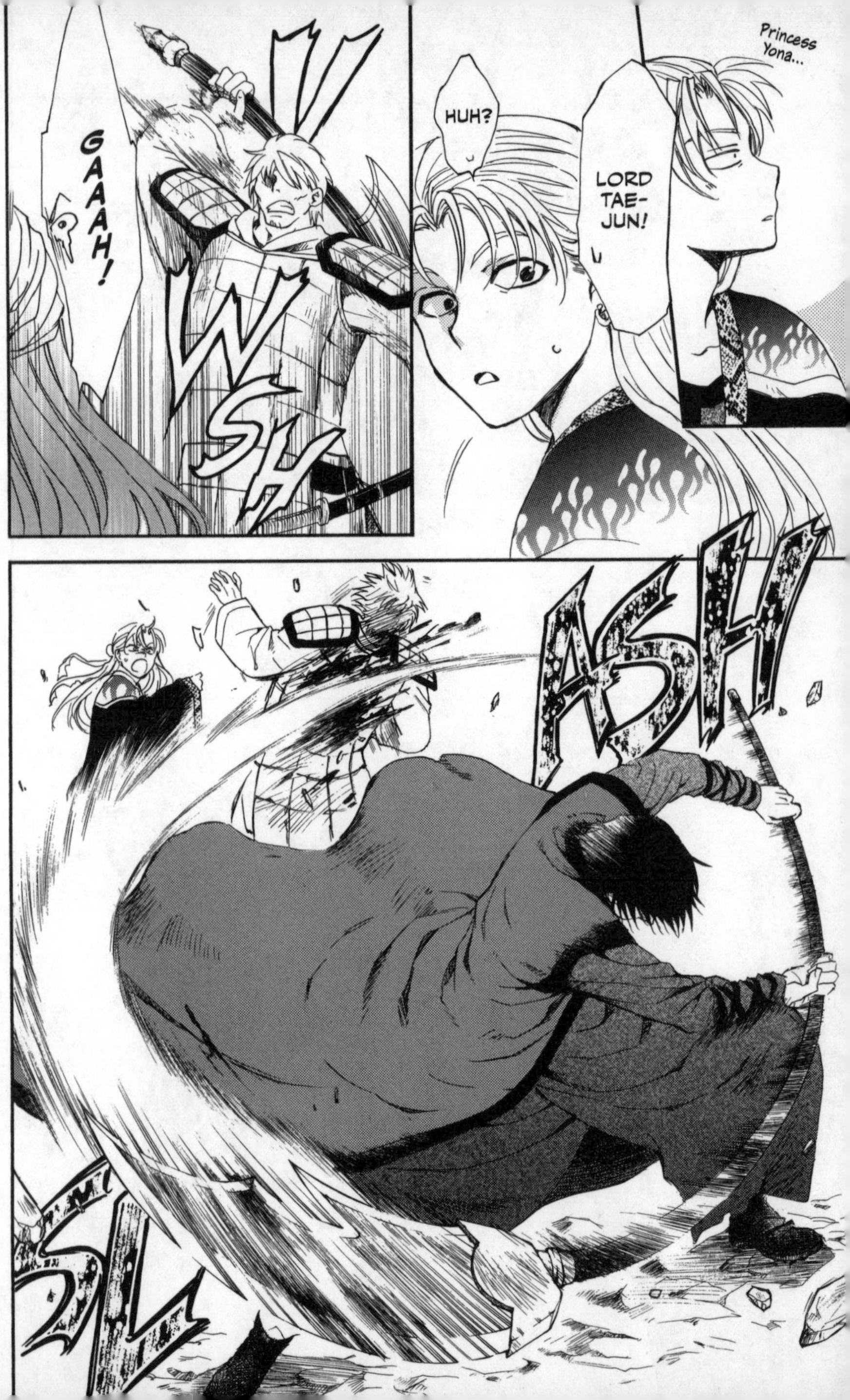
Princess Yona...
LORD TAE-JUN!
HUH?
GAAAH!
WSH
ASH!

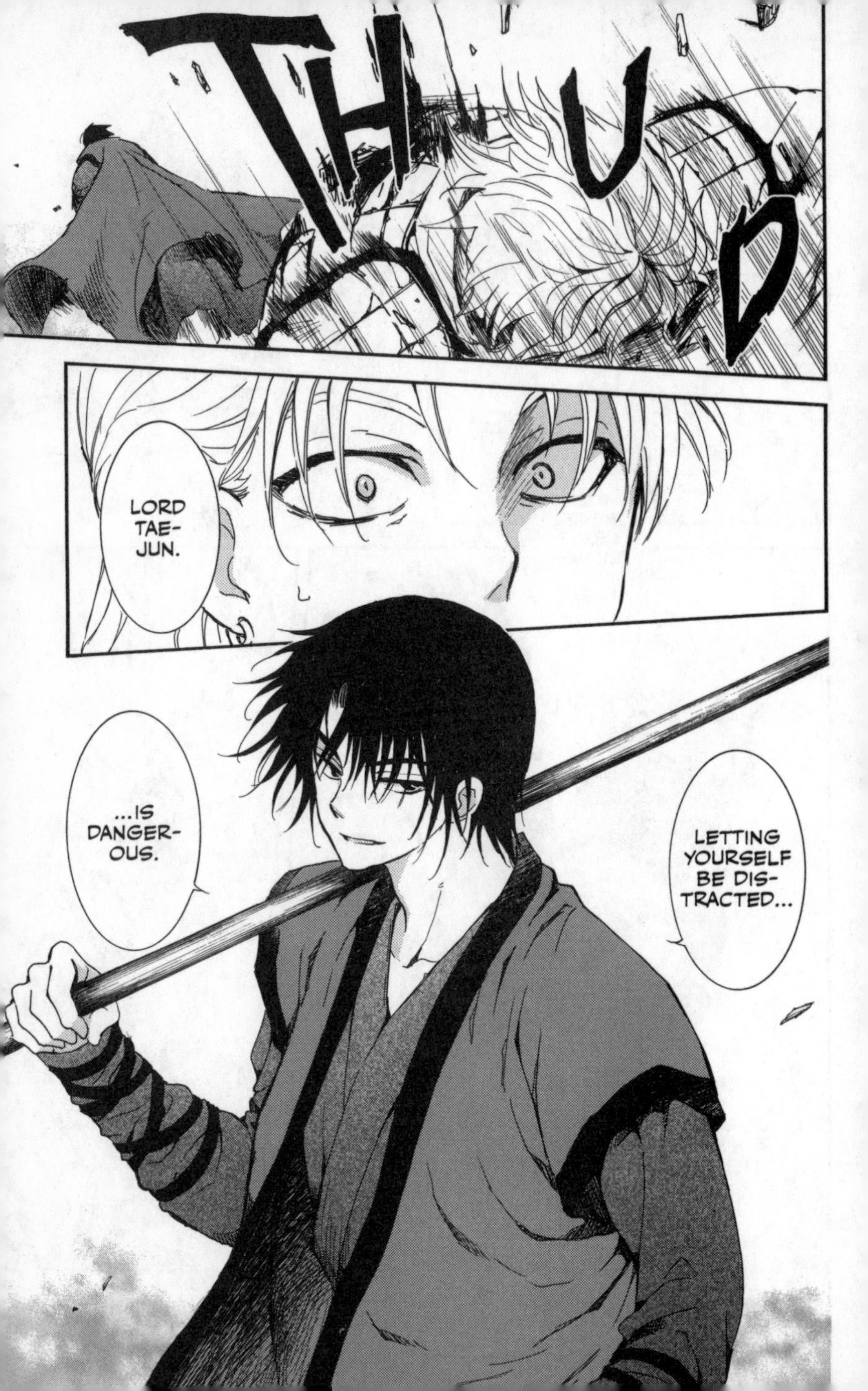
THUD
LORD TAE-JUN.
LETTING YOURSELF BE DIS-TRACTED...
...IS DANGER-OUS.

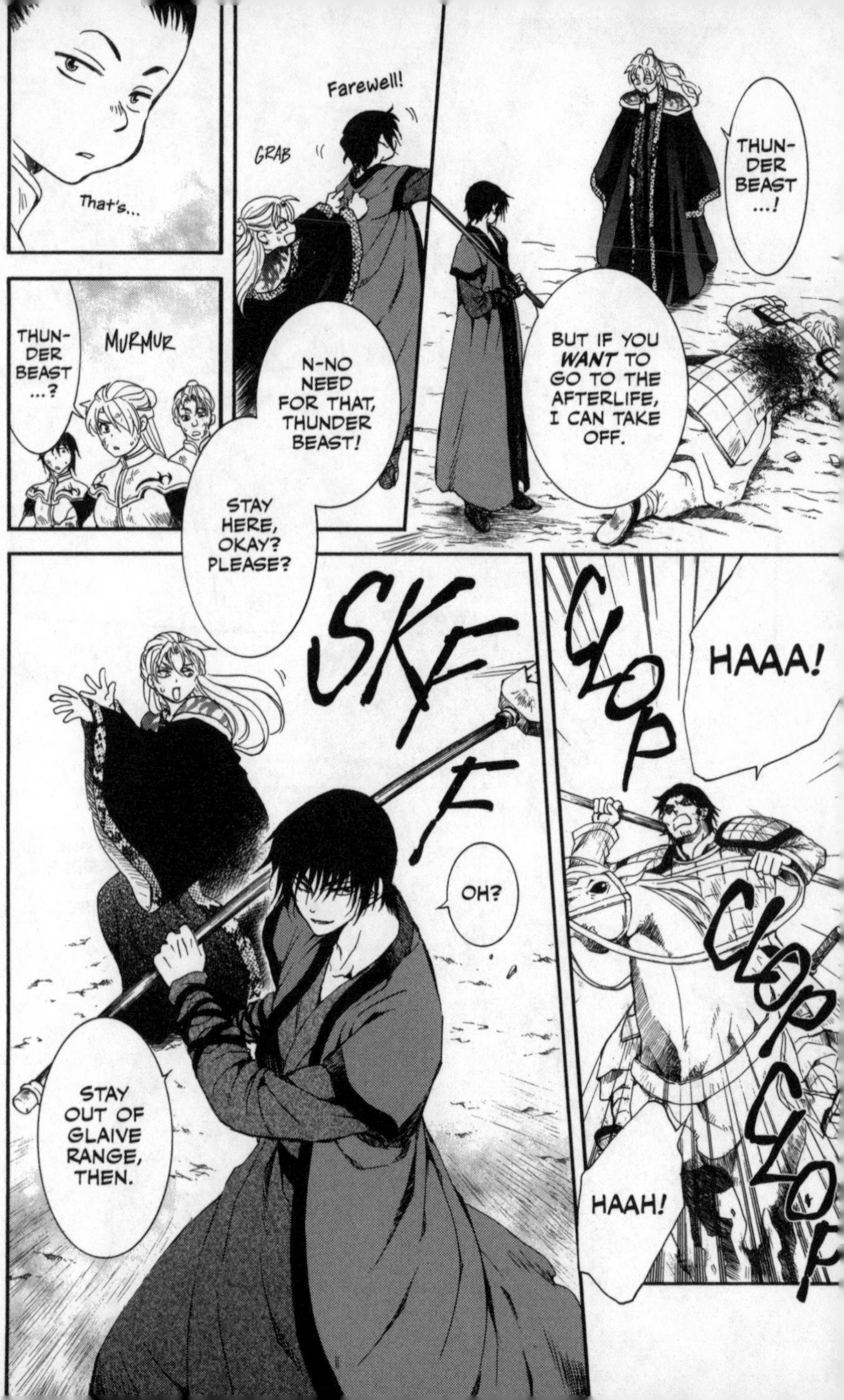
THUNDER-BEAST ...!
Farewell!
GRAB
BUT IF YOU WANT TO GO TO THE AFTERLIFE, I CAN TAKE OFF.
N-NO NEED FOR THAT, THUNDER BEAST!
STAY HERE, OKAY? PLEASE?
That's...
THUNDER-BEAST ...?
MURMUR
HAAA!
CLOP
CLOP CLOP
HAAH!
SKFF
OH?
STAY OUT OF GLAIVE RANGE, THEN.

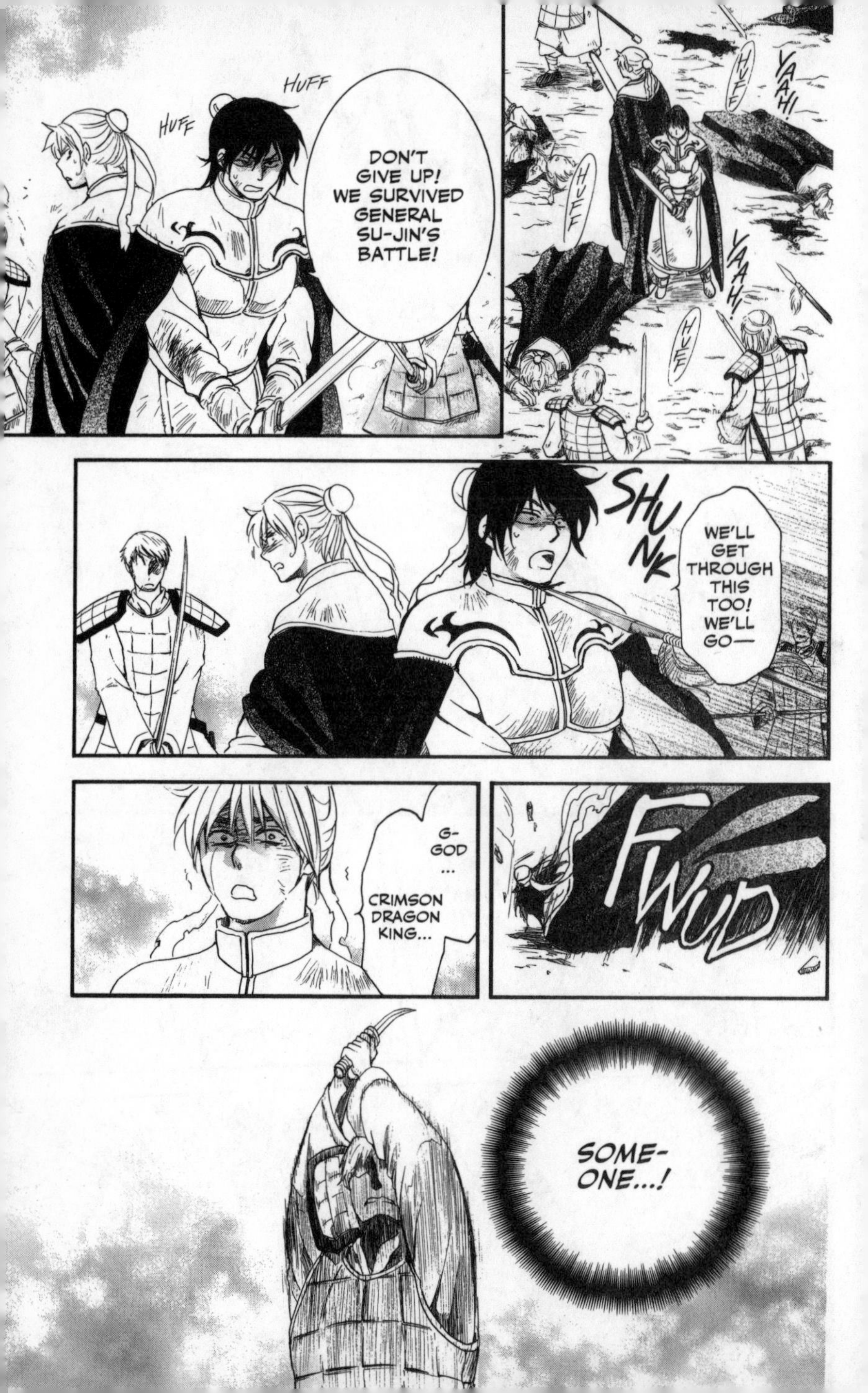
YAAH!
HUFF
HUFF
YAAH!
HUFF
HUFF
HUFF
DON'T GIVE UP! WE SURVIVED GENERAL SU-JIN'S BATTLE!
SHUNK
WE'LL GET THROUGH THIS TOO! WE'LL GO—
FWUD
G-GOD ... CRIMSON DRAGON KING...
SOME-ONE...!

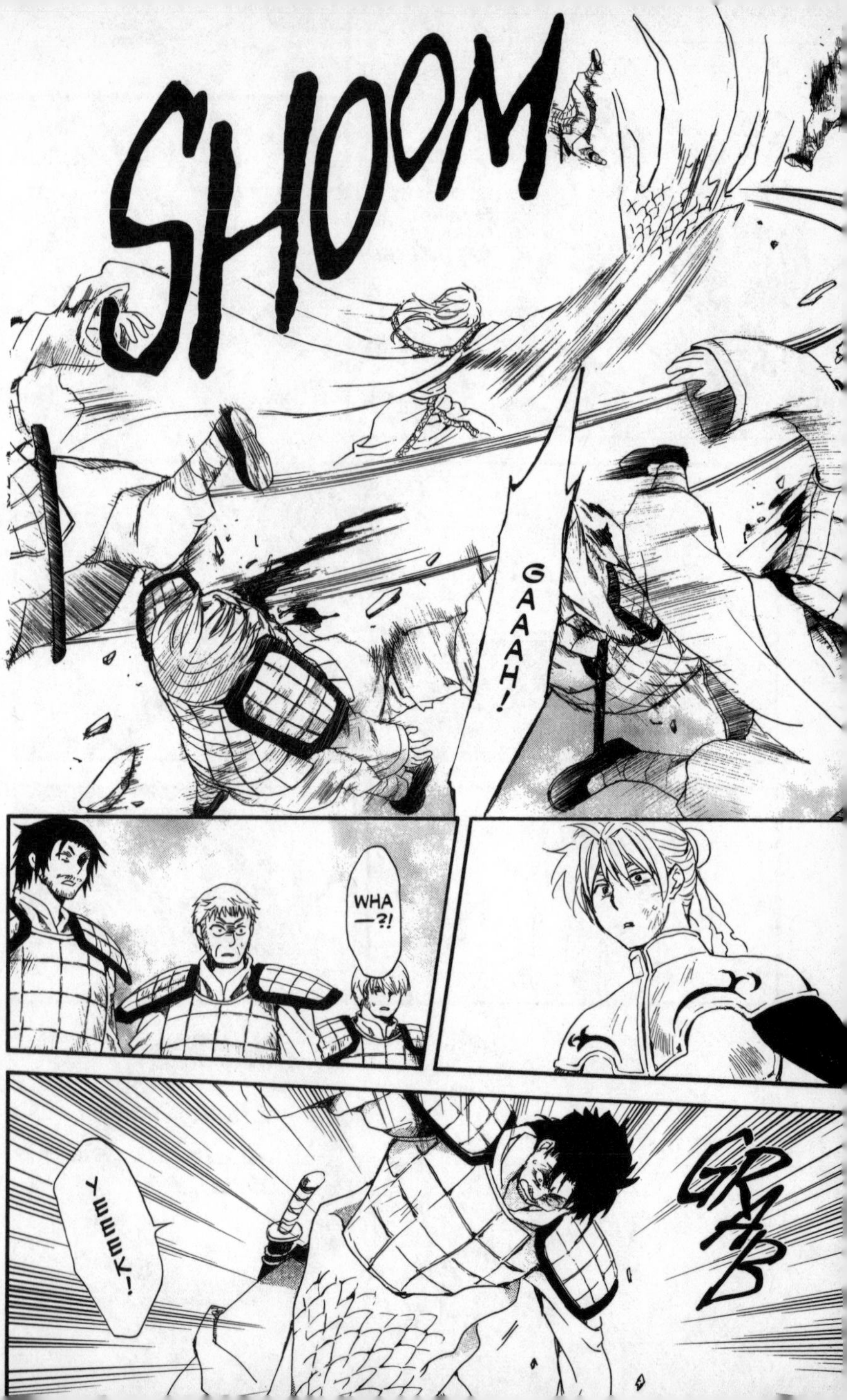
SHOOM
GAAAAH!
WHA—?!
GRAB
YEEEK!

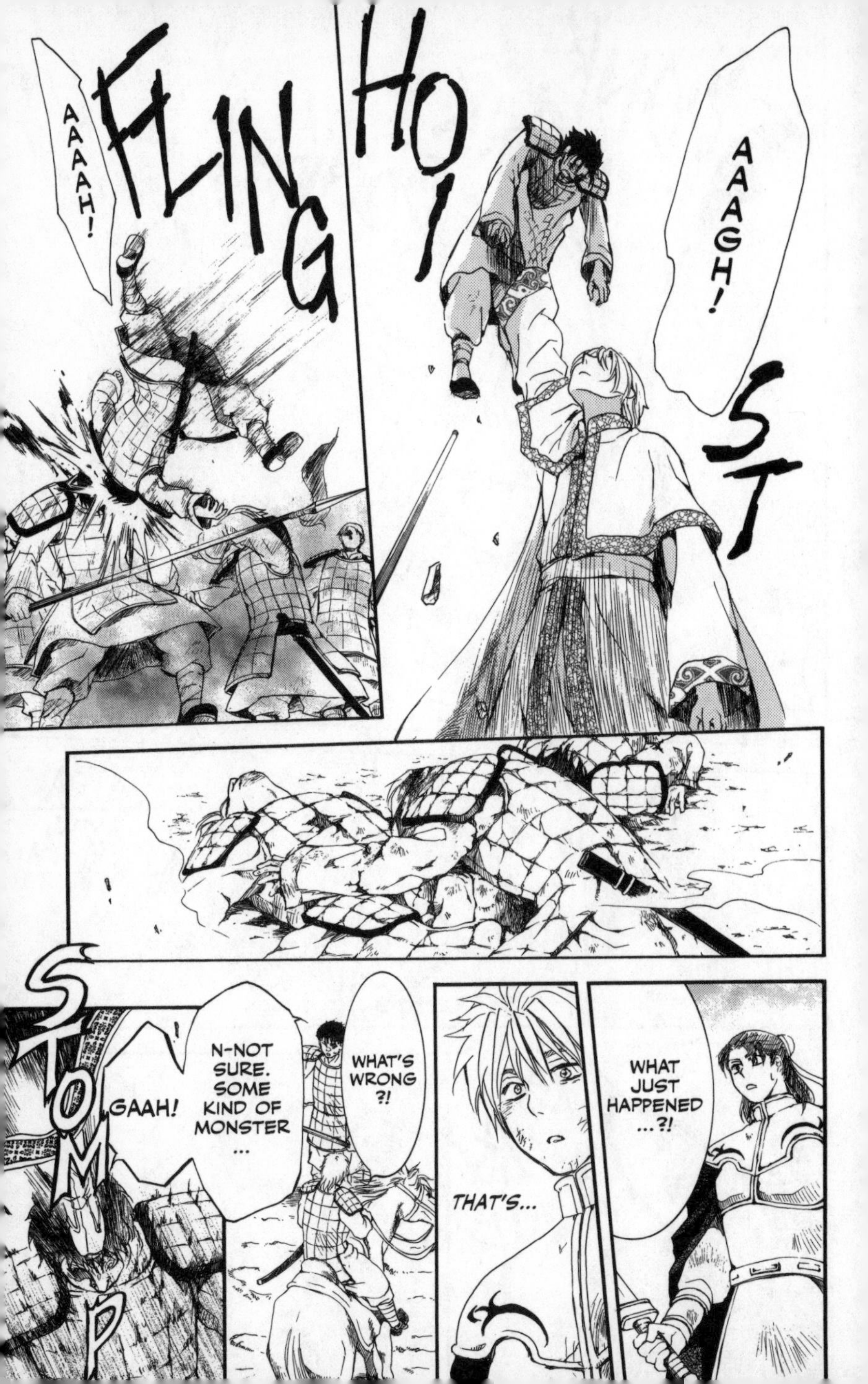
AAAGH!
HOI!
ST
AAAAH!
FLING
WHAT JUST HAPPENED ...?!
THAT'S...
WHAT'S WRONG ?!
N-NOT SURE. SOME KIND OF MONSTER ...
GAAH!
STOMP

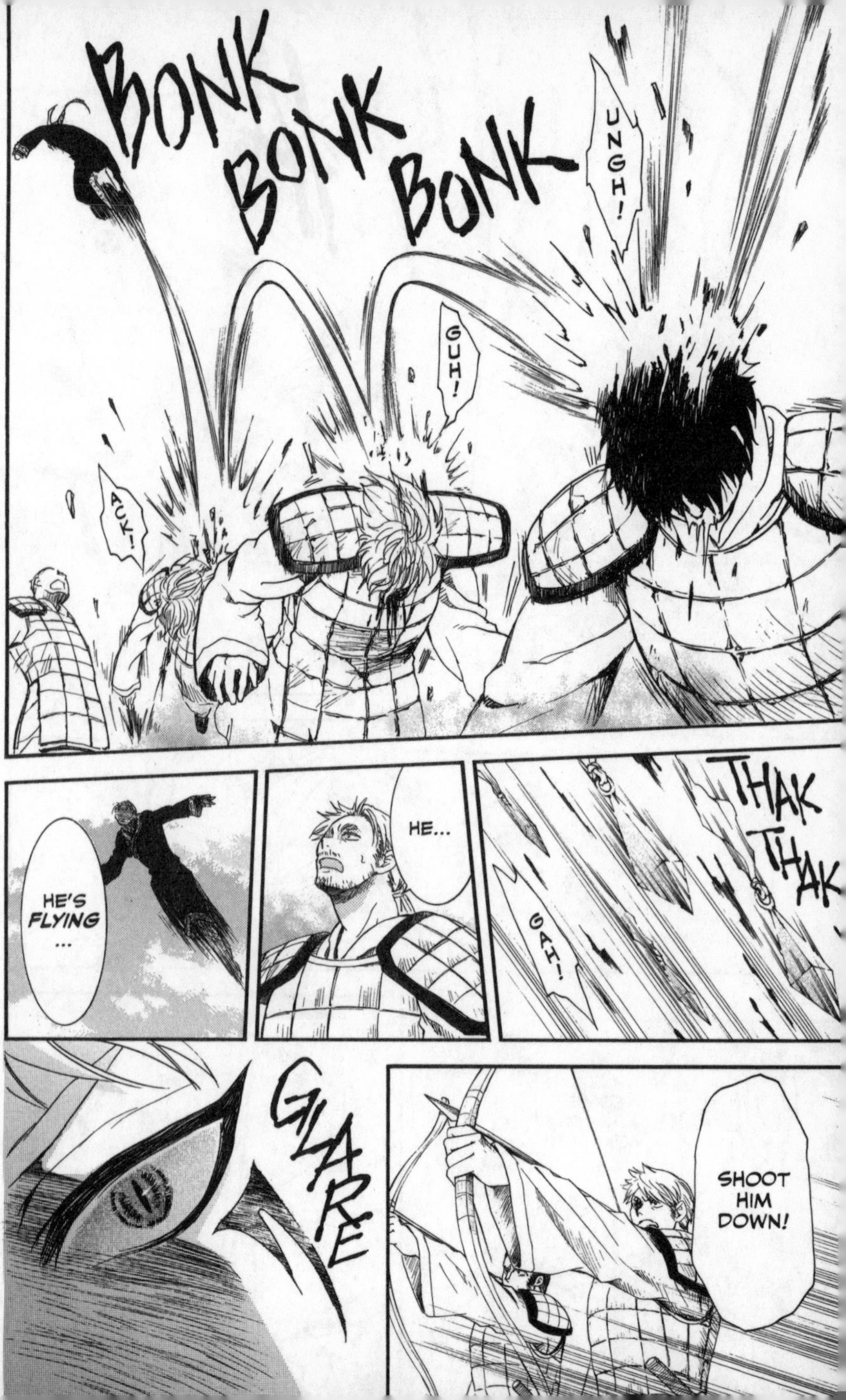
UNGH!
BONK BONK BONK
GUH!
ACK!
THAK THAK
GAH!
HE...
HE'S FLYING ...
SHOOT HIM DOWN!
GLARE

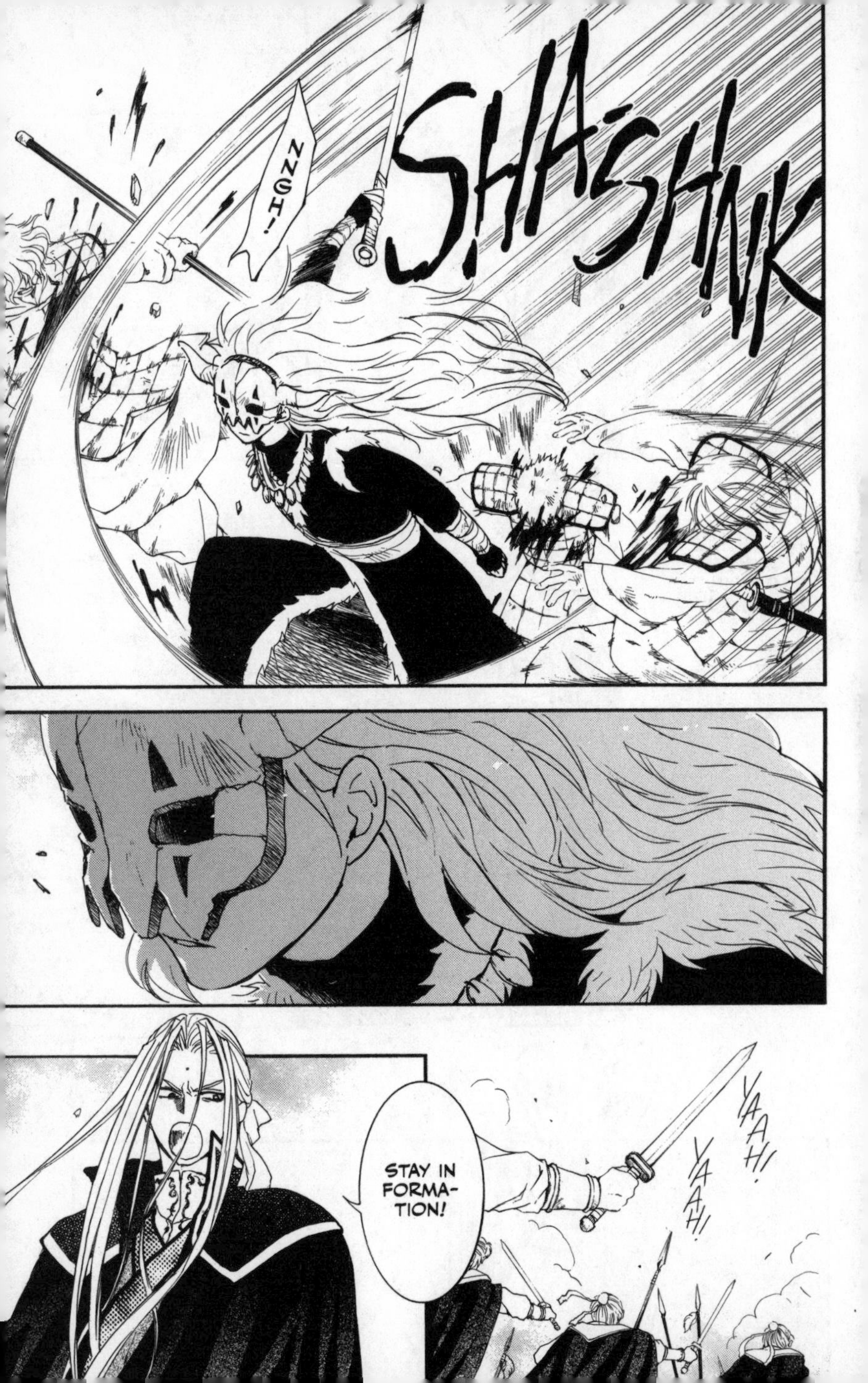
SHASHNK
NNGH!
YAAH! YAAH!
STAY IN FORMATION!

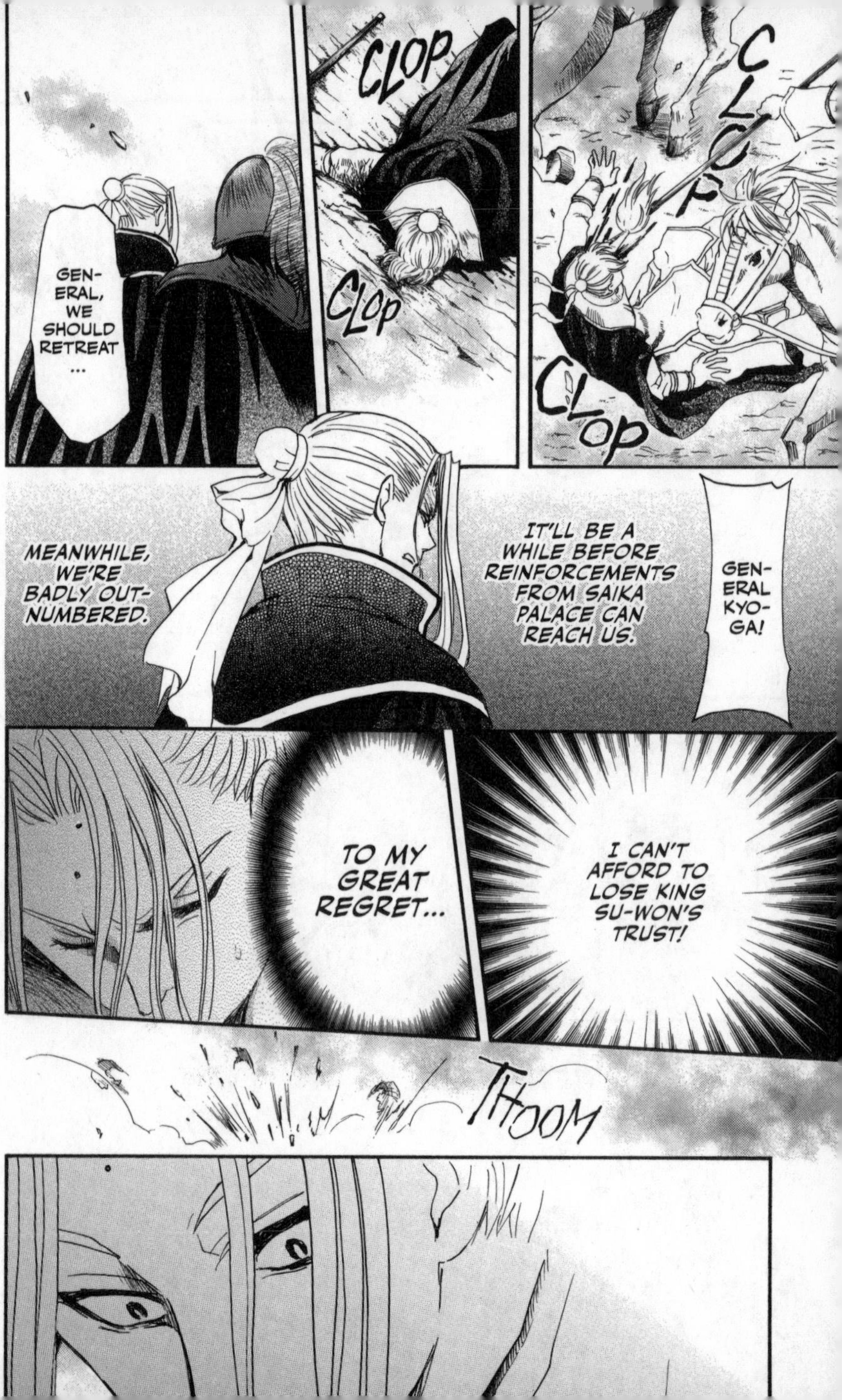
CLOP
CLOP
CLOP
CLOP
CLOP
GEN-ERAL, WE SHOULD RETREAT ...
GEN-ERAL KYO-GA!
IT'LL BE A WHILE BEFORE REINFORCEMENTS FROM SAIKA PALACE CAN REACH US.
MEANWHILE, WE'RE BADLY OUT-NUMBERED.
I CAN'T AFFORD TO LOSE KING SU-WON'S TRUST!
TO MY GREAT REGRET...
THOOM

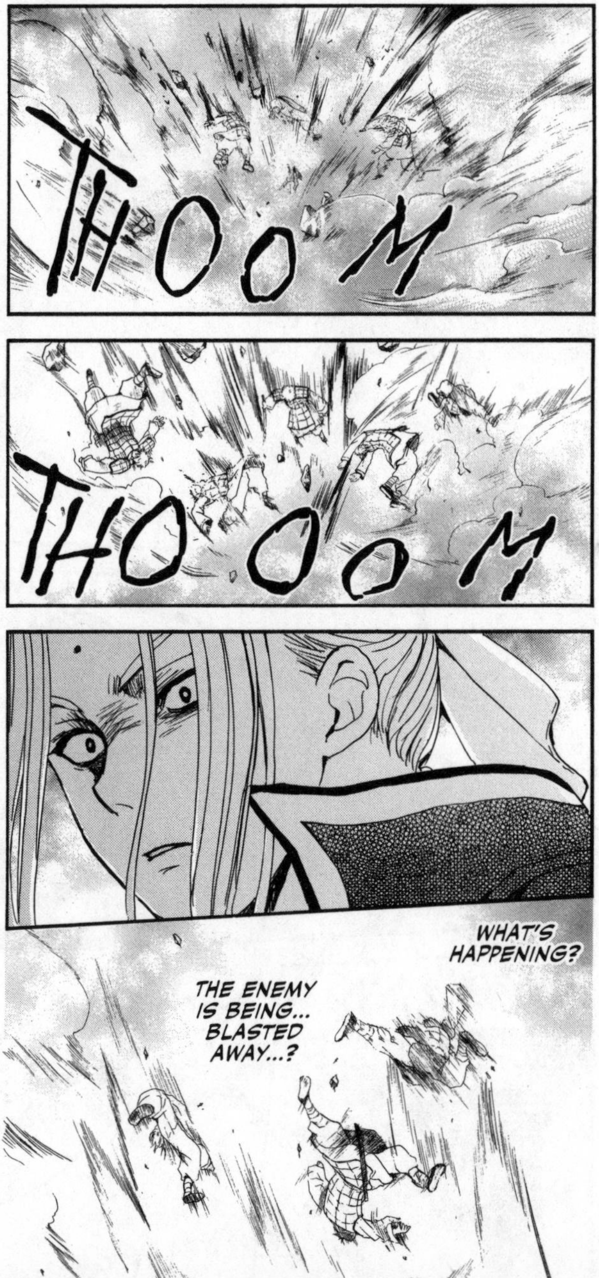
THOOM
THOOOM
WHAT'S HAPPENING?
THE ENEMY IS BEING... BLASTED AWAY...?

I touched on this in another column (meaning in this space) in volume 16, but when the manga gets compiled into volumes, if I have time, I make fixes to things where I had to rush to make it in time for the magazine.

Those who pay close attention to *Hana to Yume* magazine may notice details that weren't published there.

Even so, I still miss some things. Bandages or injuries might appear or disappear... Hair might get longer or shorter... Even Pu-kyu might get longer or shorter.

Yup.

So please overlook those moments and assume that it's part of the confusion of battle.

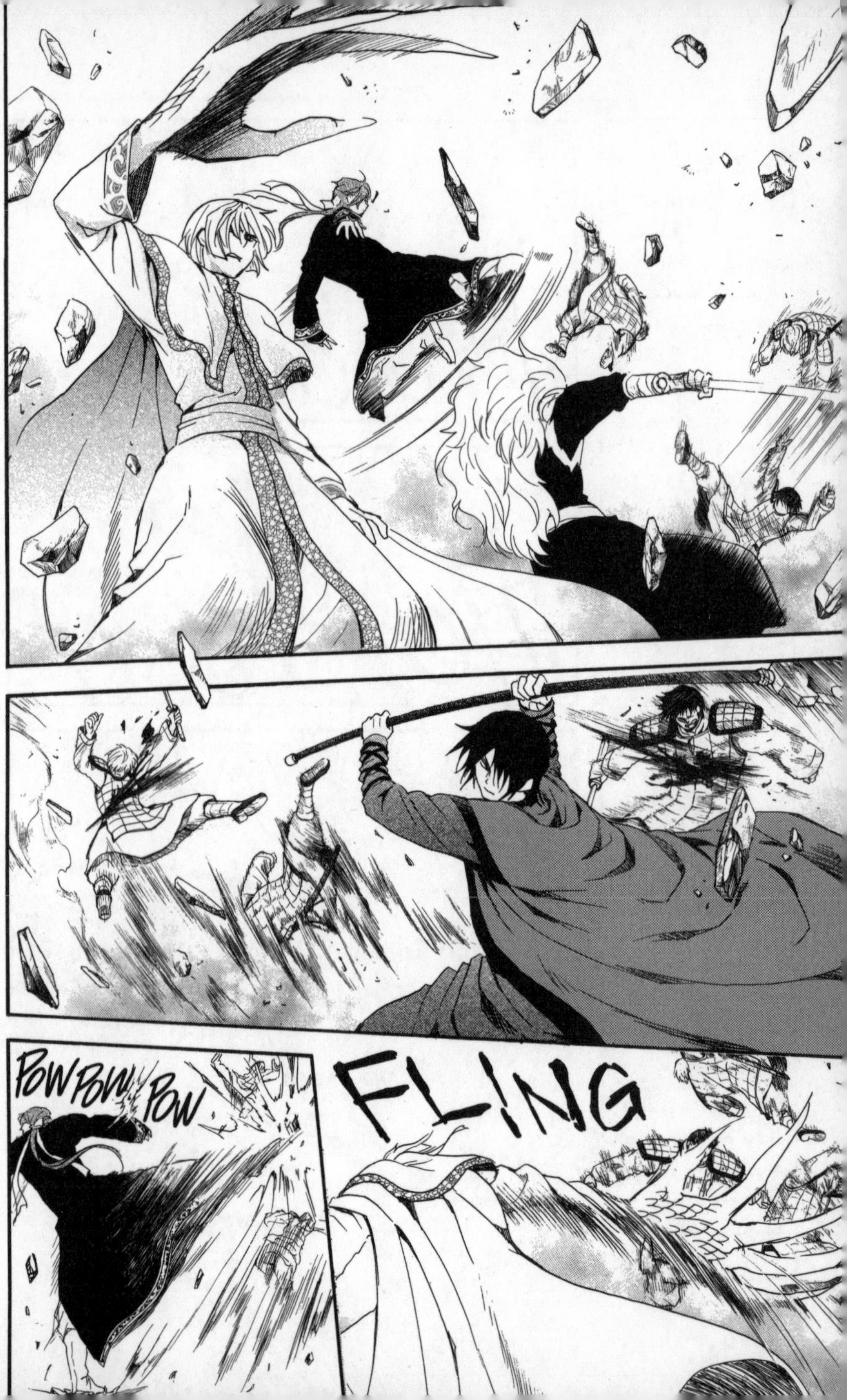
FLING
POW POW POW

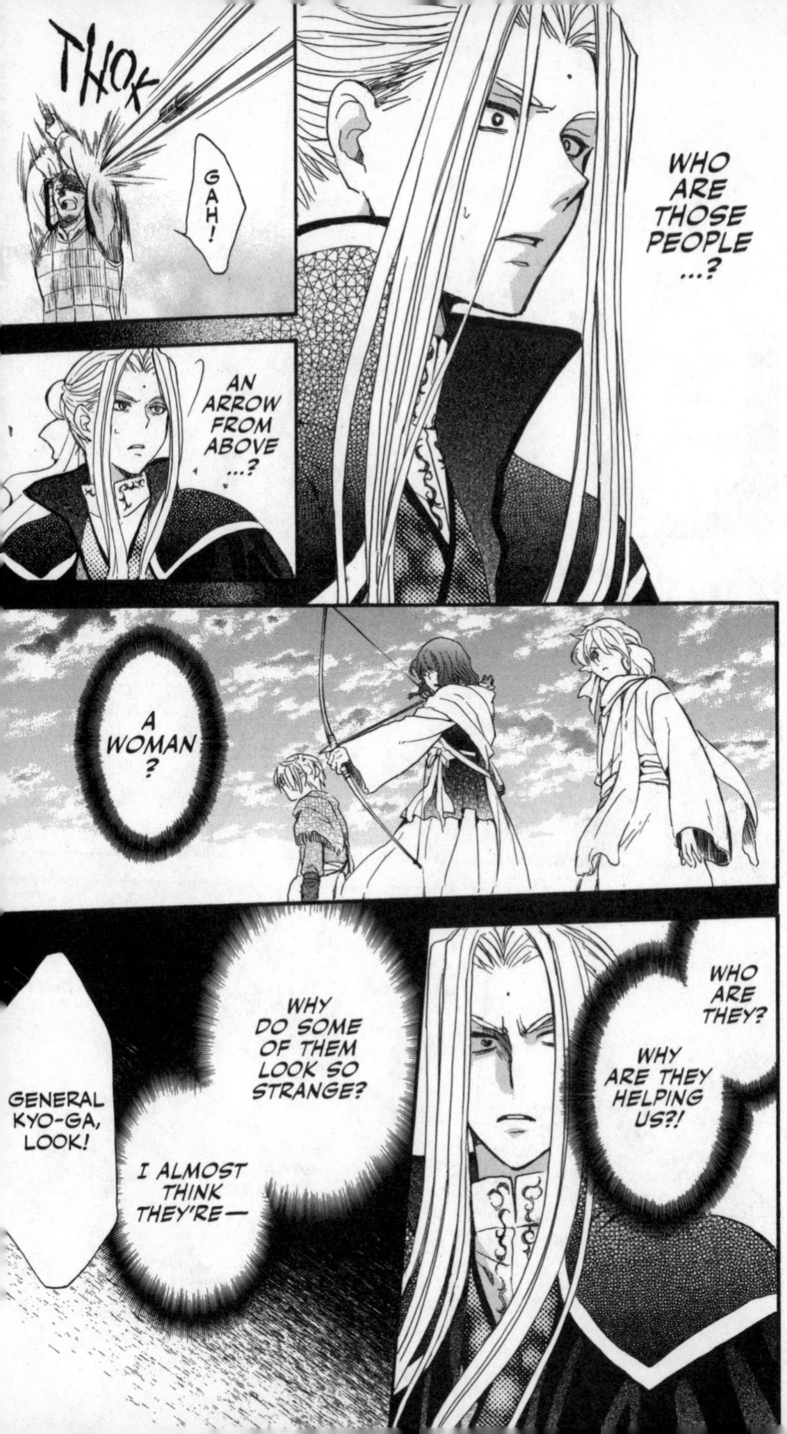
WHO ARE THOSE PEOPLE ...?
THOK
GAH!
AN ARROW FROM ABOVE ...?
A WOMAN?
WHO ARE THEY?
WHY ARE THEY HELPING US?!
WHY DO SOME OF THEM LOOK SO STRANGE?
I ALMOST THINK THEY'RE—
GENERAL KYO-GA, LOOK!

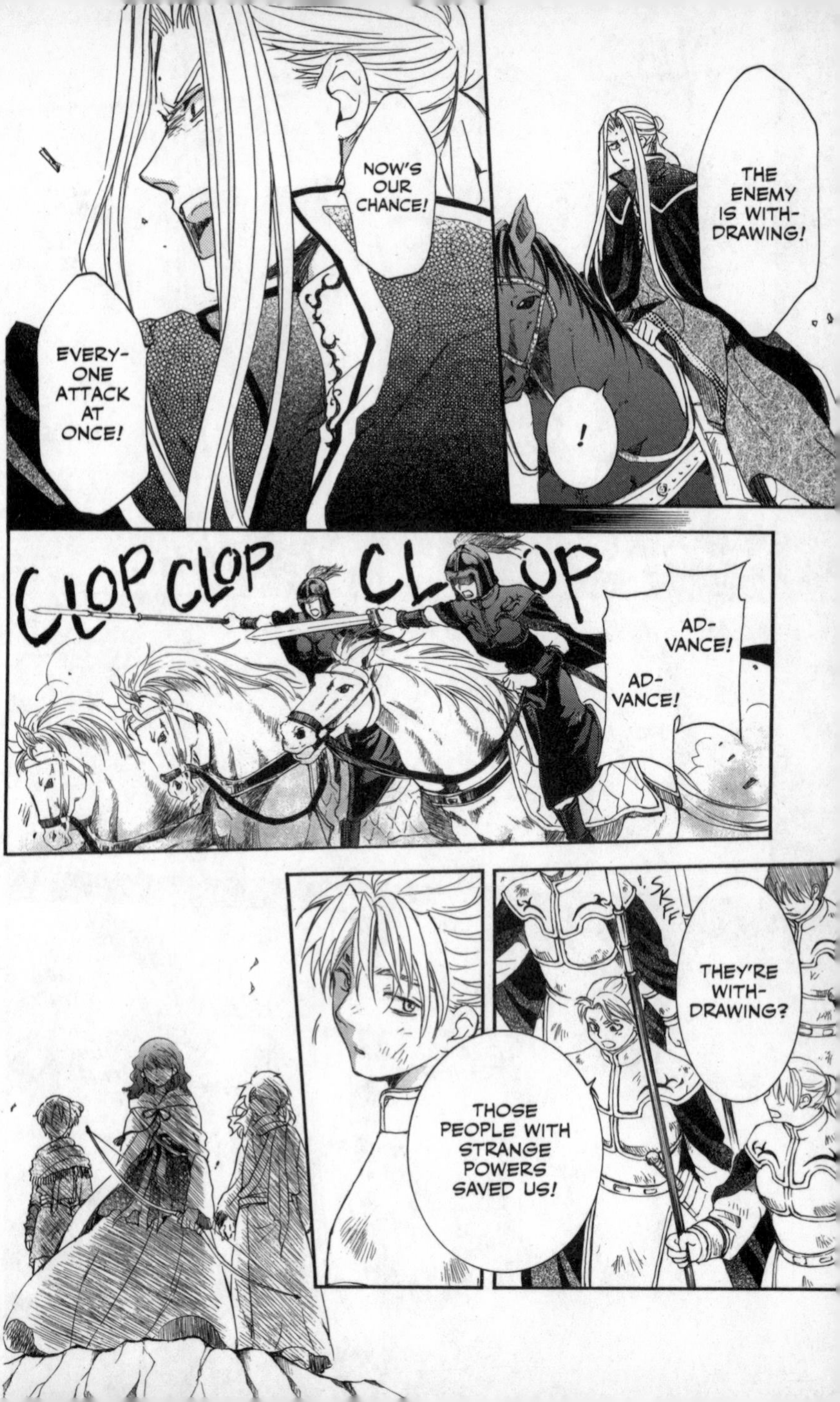
THE ENEMY IS WITH-DRAWING!
!
NOW'S OUR CHANCE!
EVERY-ONE ATTACK AT ONCE!
AD-VANCE!
AD-VANCE!
CLOP CLOP CLOP
SKFF
THEY'RE WITH-DRAWING?
THOSE PEOPLE WITH STRANGE POWERS SAVED US!

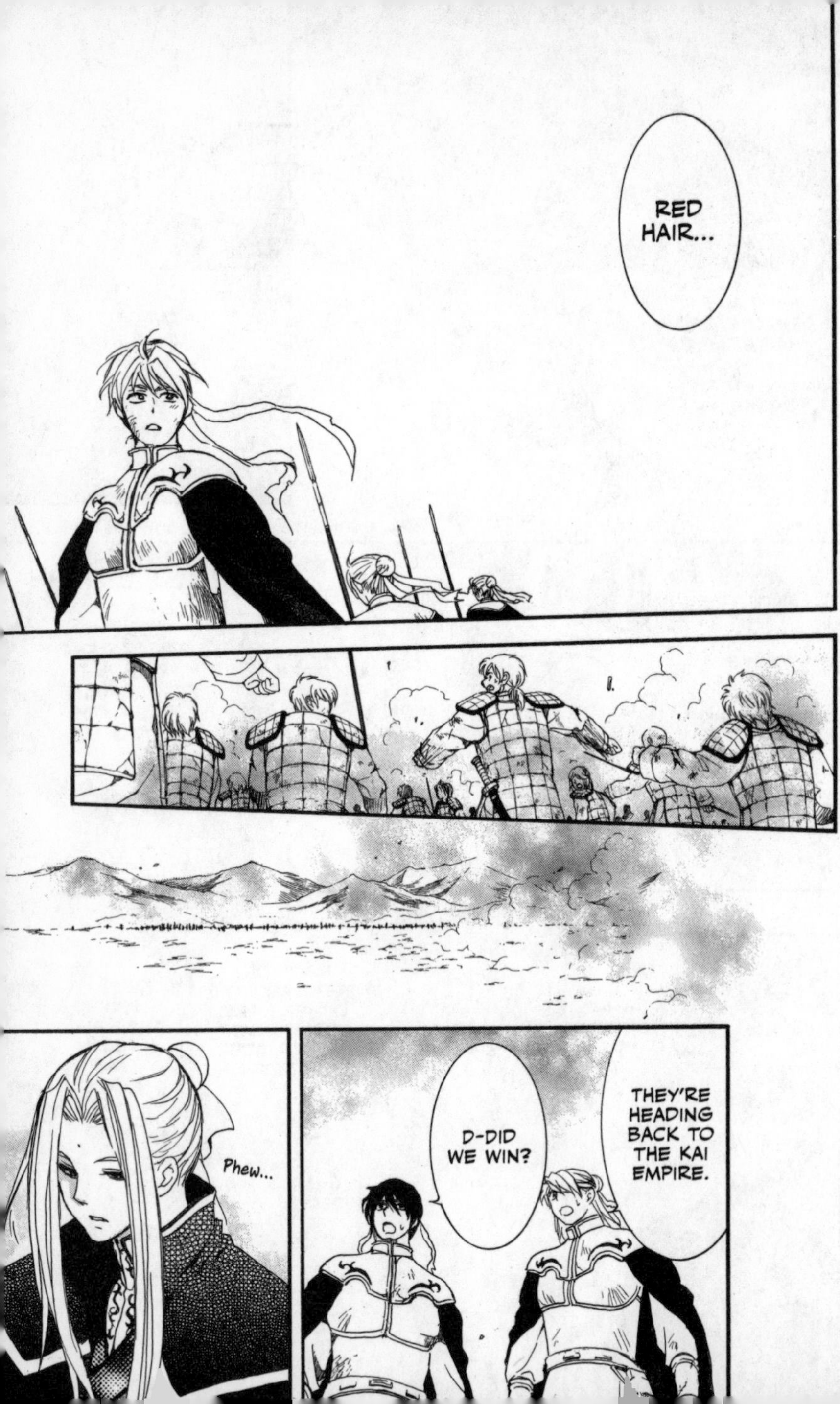
RED HAIR...
THEY'RE HEADING BACK TO THE KAI EMPIRE.
D-DID WE WIN?
Phew...

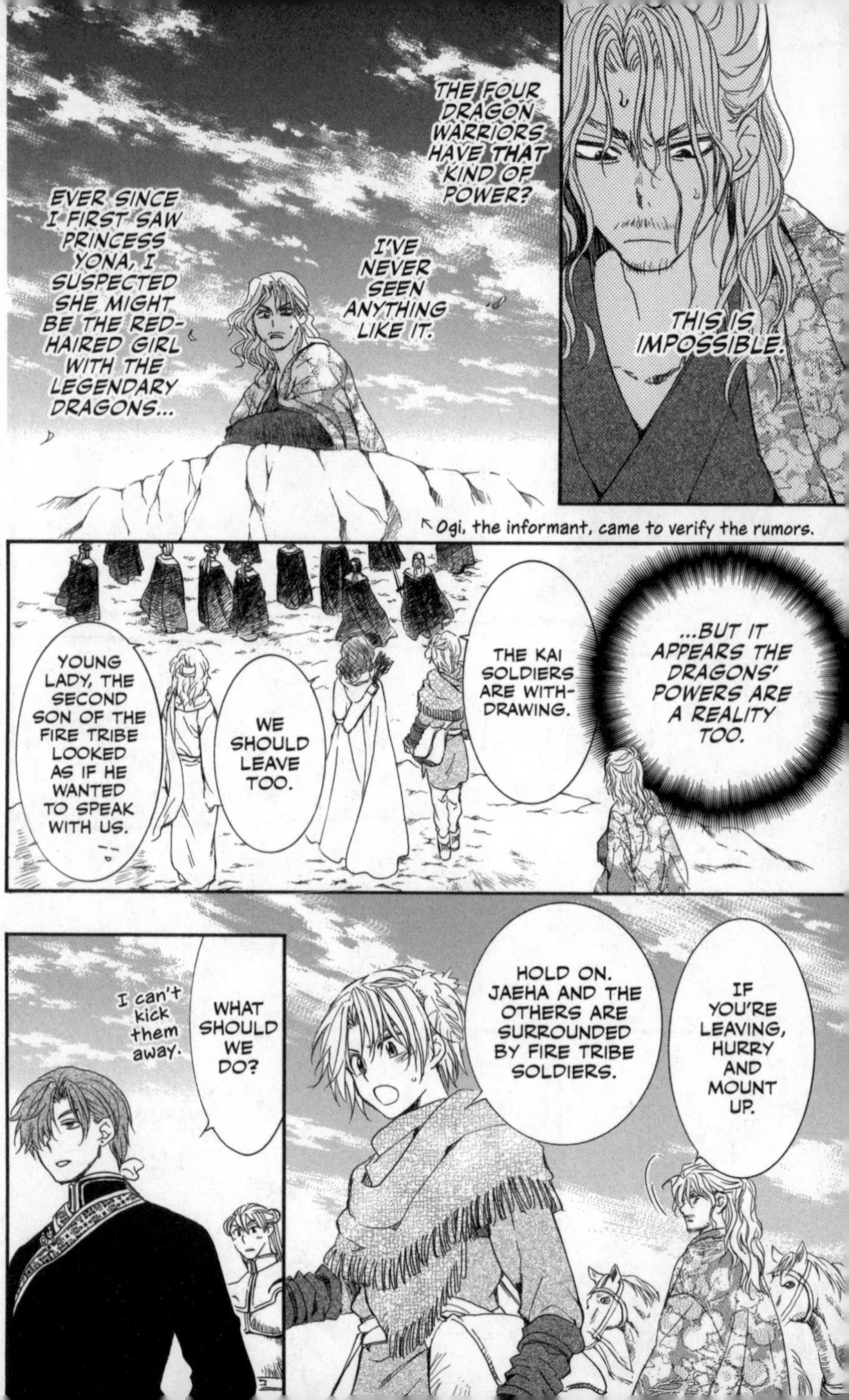
THE FOUR DRAGON WARRIORS HAVE THAT KIND OF POWER?
THIS IS IMPOSSIBLE.
I'VE NEVER SEEN ANYTHING LIKE IT.
EVER SINCE I FIRST SAW PRINCESS YONA, I SUSPECTED SHE MIGHT BE THE RED-HAIRED GIRL WITH THE LEGENDARY DRAGONS...
Ogi, the informant, came to verify the rumors.
...BUT IT APPEARS THE DRAGONS' POWERS ARE A REALITY TOO.
THE KAI SOLDIERS ARE WITH-DRAWING.
WE SHOULD LEAVE TOO.
YOUNG LADY, THE SECOND SON OF THE FIRE TRIBE LOOKED AS IF HE WANTED TO SPEAK WITH US.
IF YOU'RE LEAVING, HURRY AND MOUNT UP.
HOLD ON. JAEHA AND THE OTHERS ARE SURROUNDED BY FIRE TRIBE SOLDIERS.
WHAT SHOULD WE DO?
I can't kick them away.

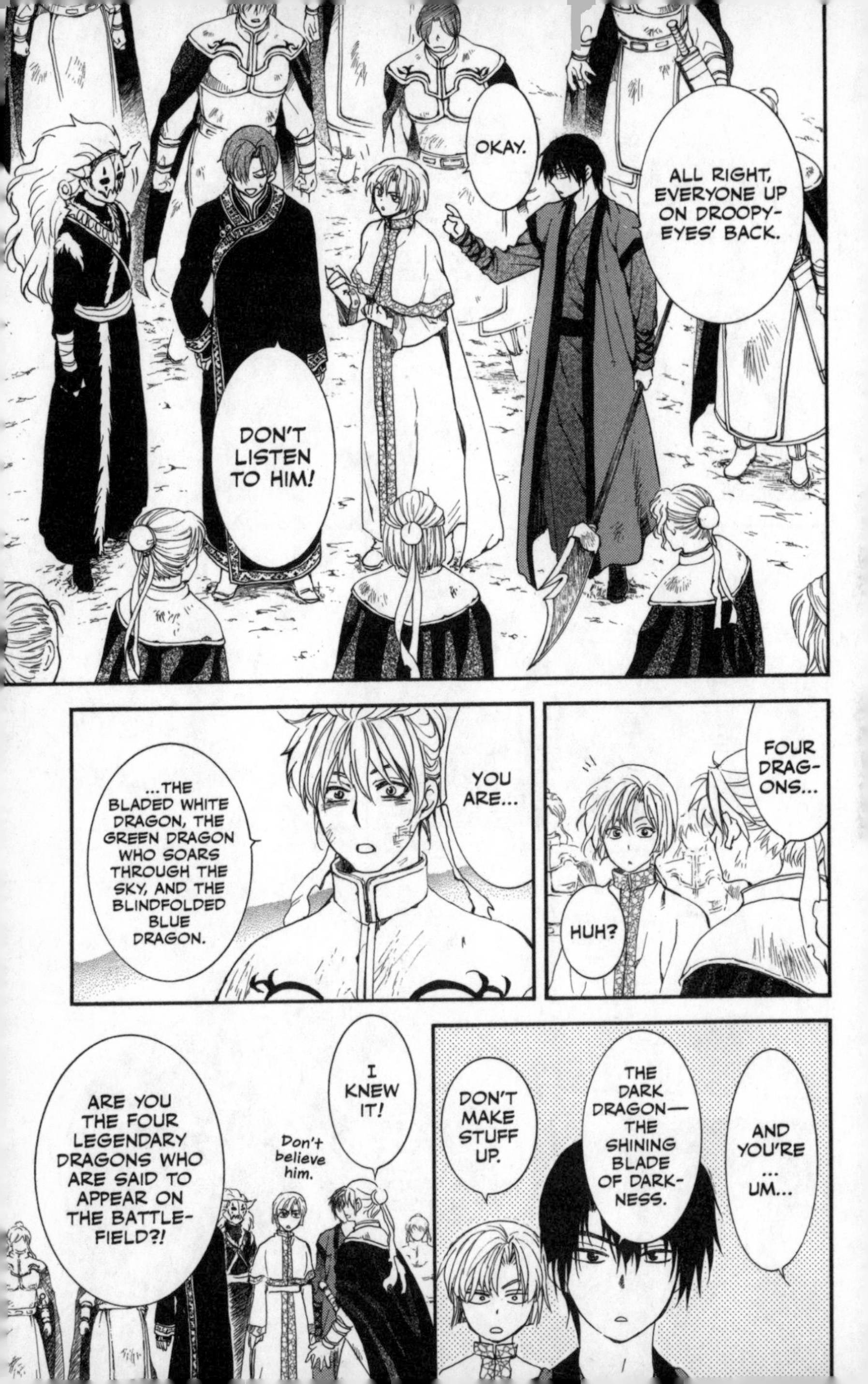
ALL RIGHT, EVERYONE UP ON DROOPY-EYES' BACK.
OKAY.
DON'T LISTEN TO HIM!
FOUR DRAGONS...
HUH?
YOU ARE...
...THE BLADED WHITE DRAGON, THE GREEN DRAGON WHO SOARS THROUGH THE SKY, AND THE BLINDFOLDED BLUE DRAGON.
AND YOU'RE ... UM...
THE DARK DRAGON—THE SHINING BLADE OF DARKNESS.
DON'T MAKE STUFF UP.
I KNEW IT!
Don't believe him.
ARE YOU THE FOUR LEGENDARY DRAGONS WHO ARE SAID TO APPEAR ON THE BATTLEFIELD?!

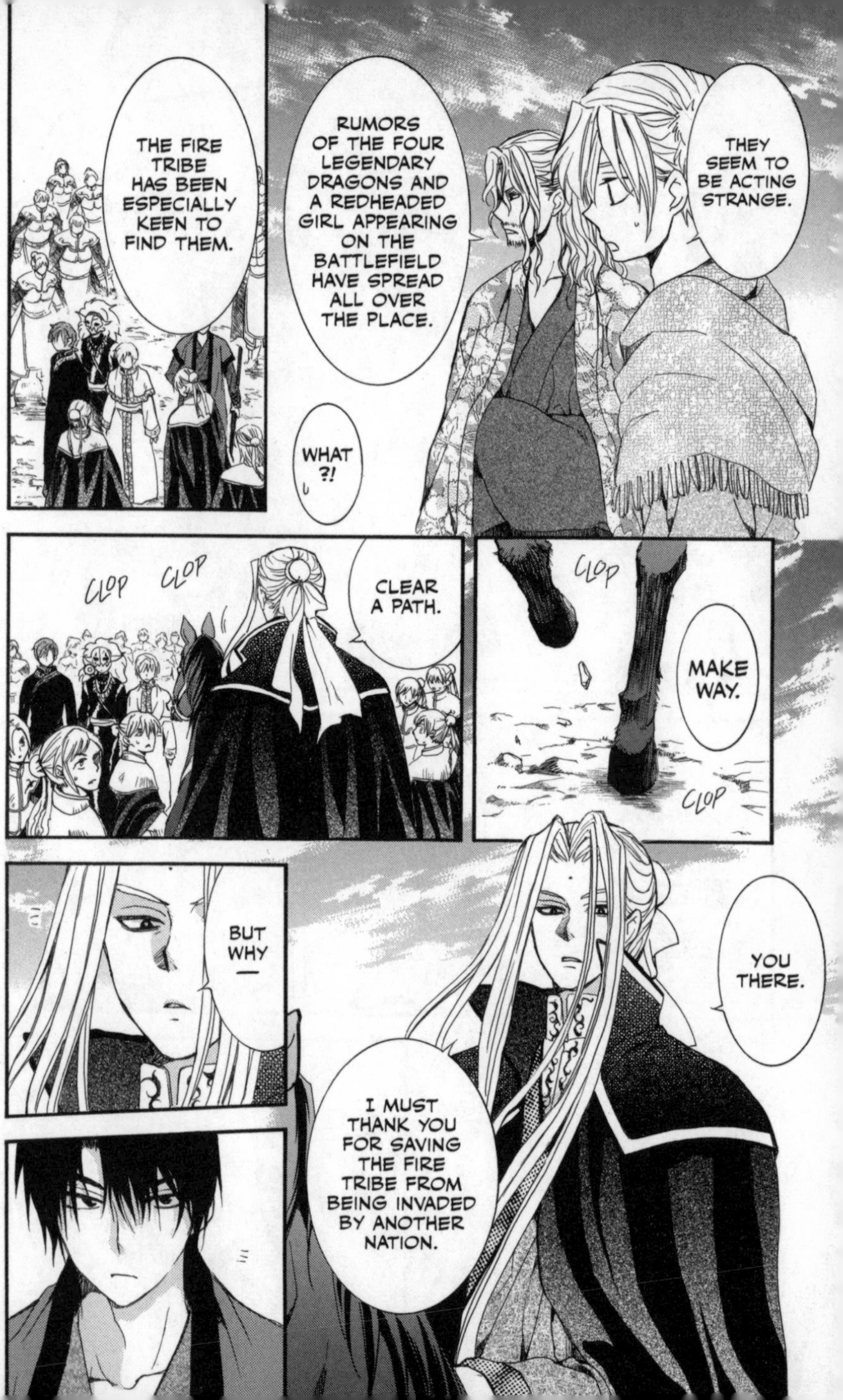
THEY SEEM TO BE ACTING STRANGE.
RUMORS OF THE FOUR LEGENDARY DRAGONS AND A REDHEADED GIRL APPEARING ON THE BATTLEFIELD HAVE SPREAD ALL OVER THE PLACE.
WHAT?!
THE FIRE TRIBE HAS BEEN ESPECIALLY KEEN TO FIND THEM.
CLOP
MAKE WAY.
CLOP
CLEAR A PATH.
CLOP CLOP
YOU THERE.
I MUST THANK YOU FOR SAVING THE FIRE TRIBE FROM BEING INVADED BY ANOTHER NATION.
BUT WHY —

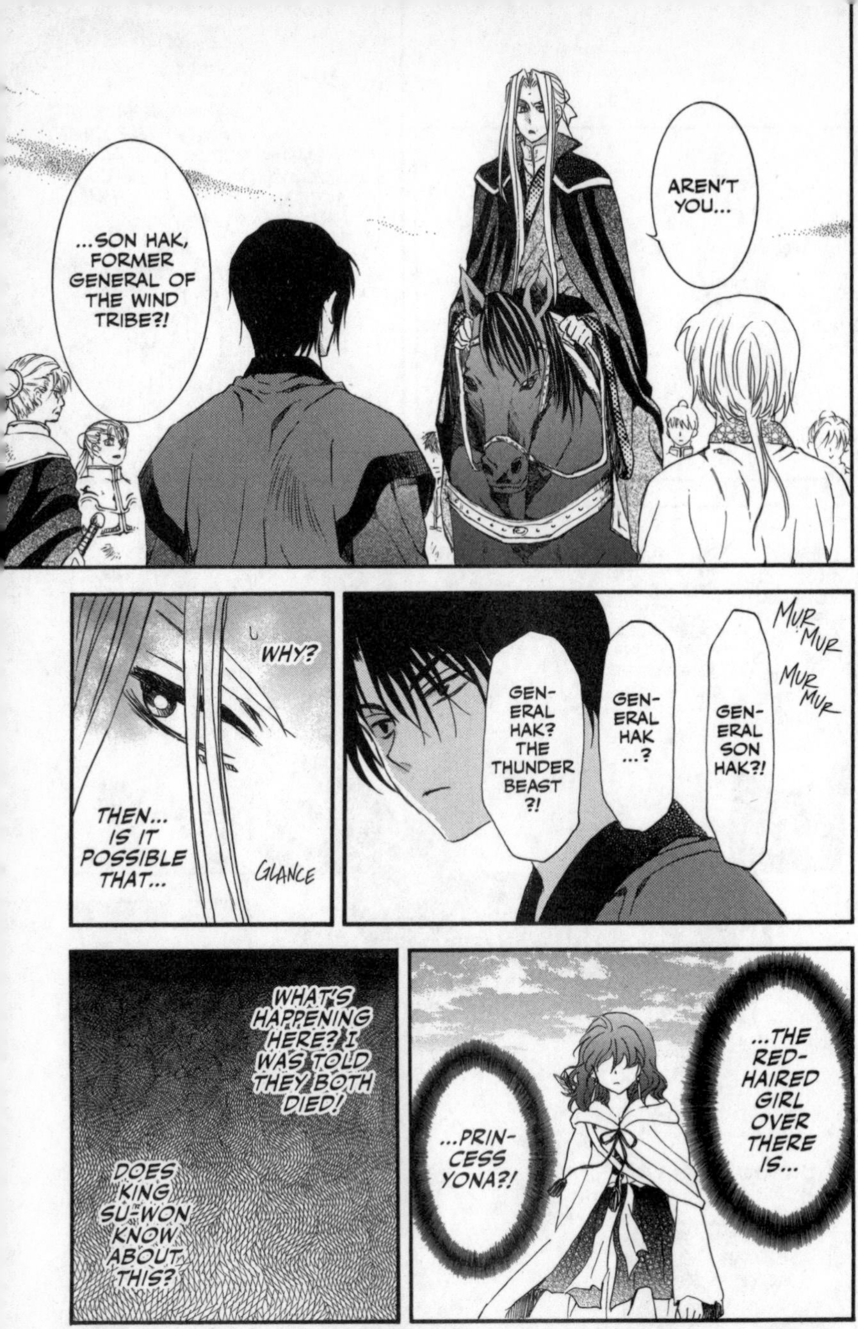
AREN'T YOU...
...SON HAK, FORMER GENERAL OF THE WIND TRIBE?!
MUR MUR
MUR MUR
GENERAL SON HAK?!
GENERAL HAK...?
GENERAL HAK? THE THUNDER BEAST?!
WHY?
THEN... IS IT POSSIBLE THAT...
GLANCE
...THE RED-HAIRED GIRL OVER THERE IS...
...PRINCESS YONA?!
WHAT'S HAPPENING HERE? I WAS TOLD THEY BOTH DIED!
DOES KING SU-WON KNOW ABOUT THIS?

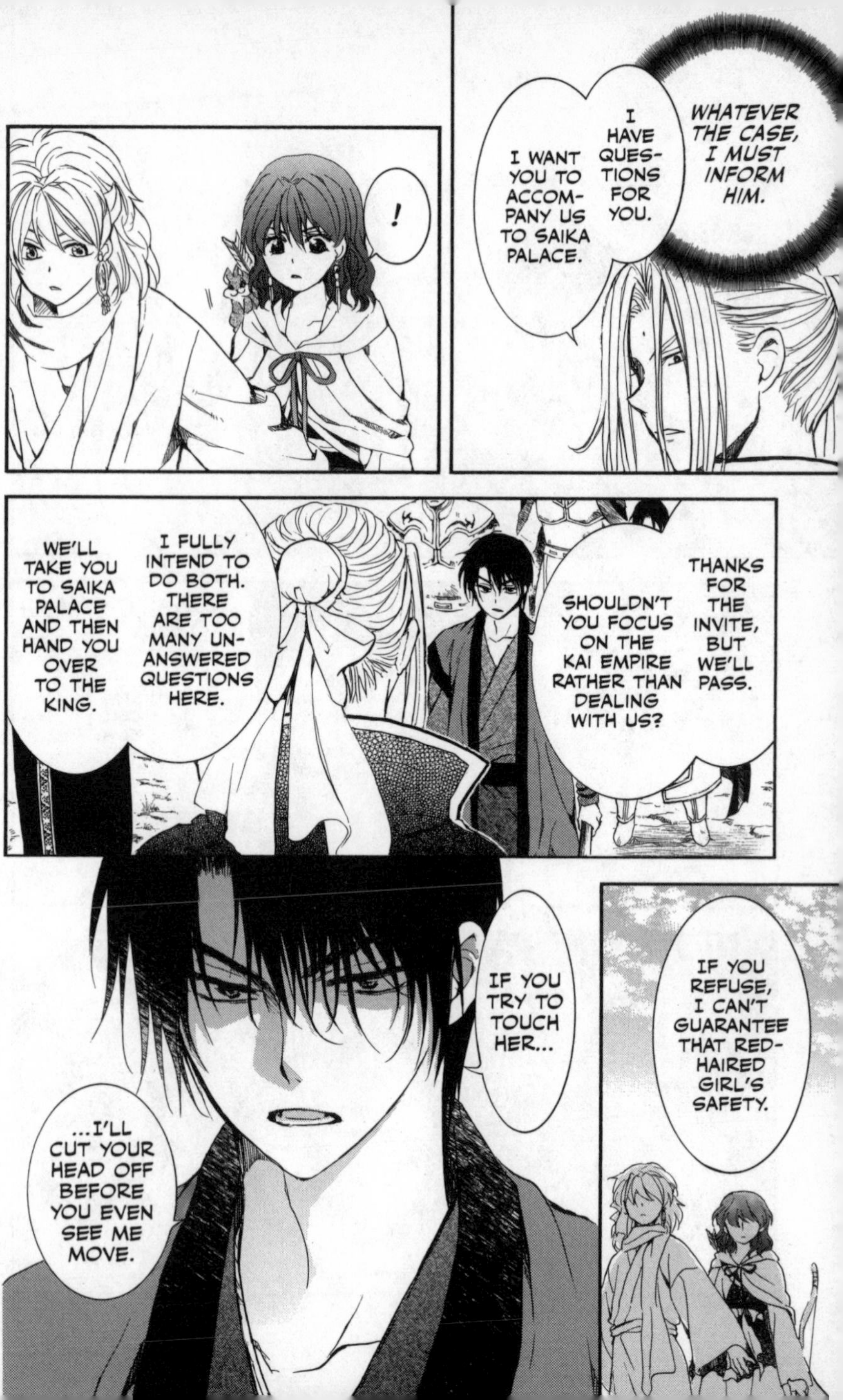
WHATEVER THE CASE, I MUST INFORM HIM.
I HAVE QUESTIONS FOR YOU.
I WANT YOU TO ACCOMPANY US TO SAIKA PALACE.
!
THANKS FOR THE INVITE, BUT WE'LL PASS.
SHOULDN'T YOU FOCUS ON THE KAI EMPIRE RATHER THAN DEALING WITH US?
I FULLY INTEND TO DO BOTH. THERE ARE TOO MANY UNANSWERED QUESTIONS HERE.
WE'LL TAKE YOU TO SAIKA PALACE AND THEN HAND YOU OVER TO THE KING.
IF YOU REFUSE, I CAN'T GUARANTEE THAT RED-HAIRED GIRL'S SAFETY.
IF YOU TRY TO TOUCH HER...
...I'LL CUT YOUR HEAD OFF BEFORE YOU EVEN SEE ME MOVE.

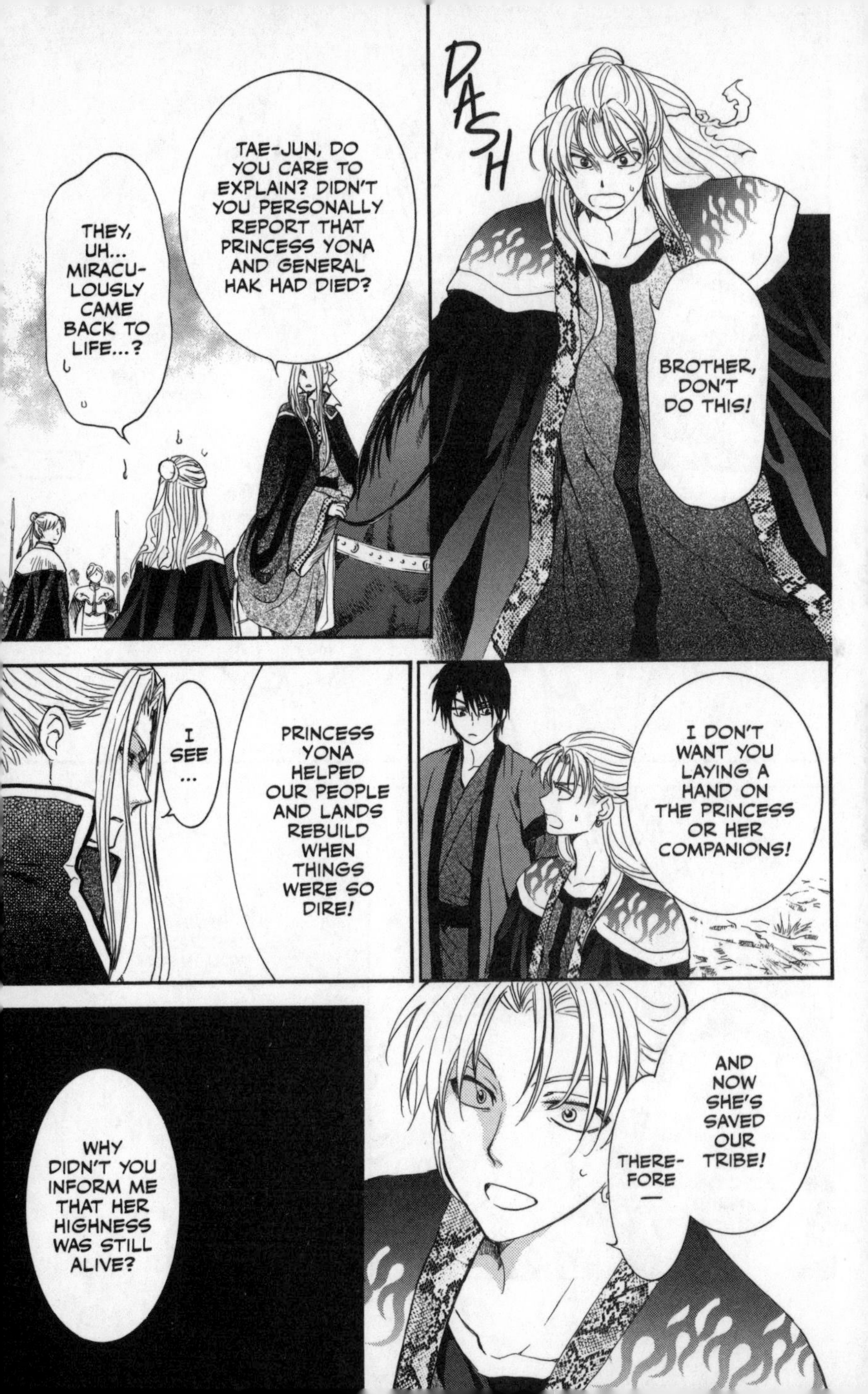
DASH
BROTHER, DON'T DO THIS!
TAE-JUN, DO YOU CARE TO EXPLAIN? DIDN'T YOU PERSONALLY REPORT THAT PRINCESS YONA AND GENERAL HAK HAD DIED?
THEY, UH... MIRACULOUSLY CAME BACK TO LIFE...?
I DON'T WANT YOU LAYING A HAND ON THE PRINCESS OR HER COMPANIONS!
PRINCESS YONA HELPED OUR PEOPLE AND LANDS REBUILD WHEN THINGS WERE SO DIRE!
I SEE...
AND NOW SHE'S SAVED OUR TRIBE!
THEREFORE—
WHY DIDN'T YOU INFORM ME THAT HER HIGHNESS WAS STILL ALIVE?

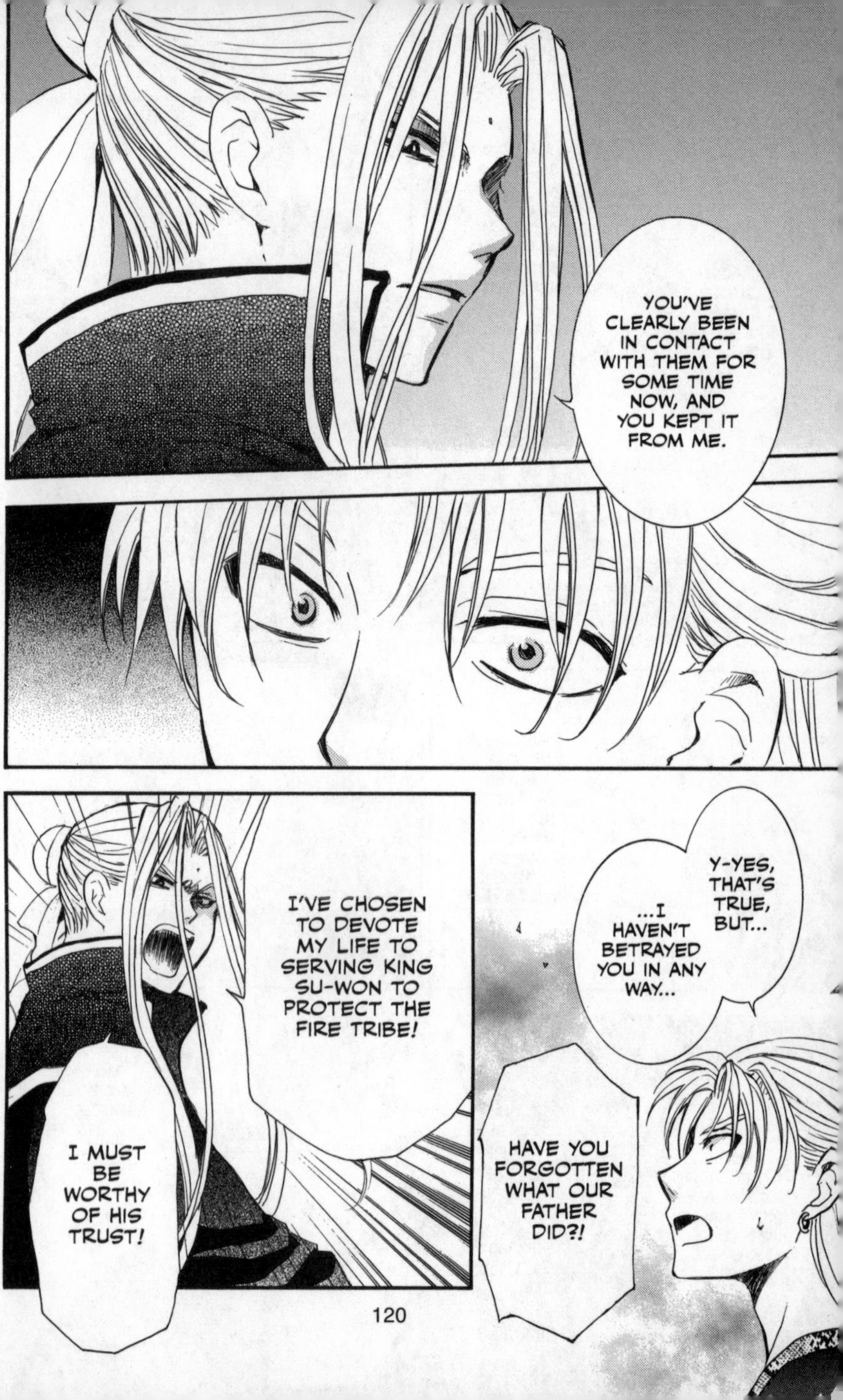
YOU'VE CLEARLY BEEN IN CONTACT WITH THEM FOR SOME TIME NOW, AND YOU KEPT IT FROM ME.
Y-YES, THAT'S TRUE, BUT...
...I HAVEN'T BETRAYED YOU IN ANY WAY...
HAVE YOU FORGOTTEN WHAT OUR FATHER DID?!
I'VE CHOSEN TO DEVOTE MY LIFE TO SERVING KING SU-WON TO PROTECT THE FIRE TRIBE!
I MUST BE WORTHY OF HIS TRUST!

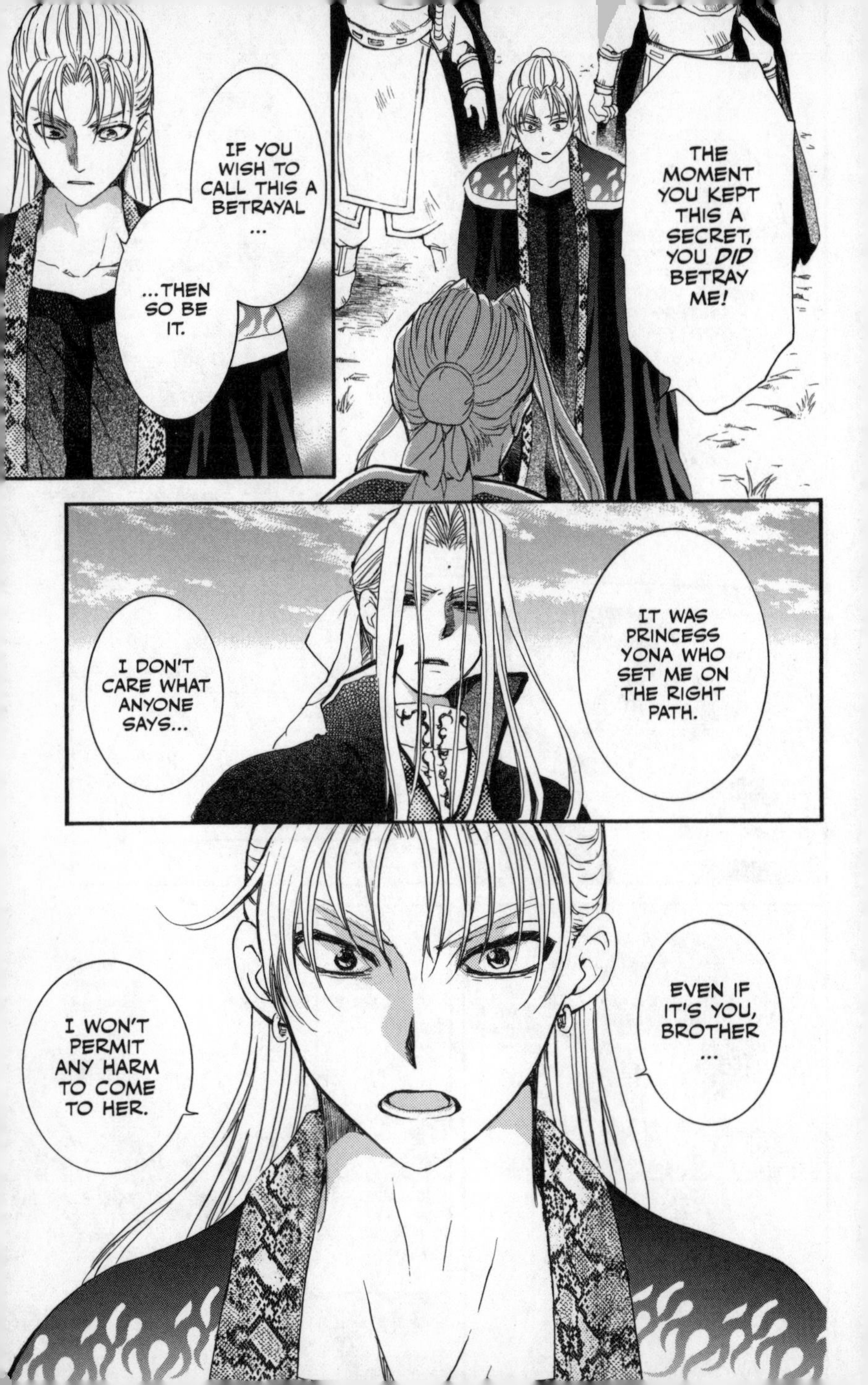
THE MOMENT YOU KEPT THIS A SECRET, YOU *DID* BETRAY ME!
IF YOU WISH TO CALL THIS A BETRAYAL ...
...THEN SO BE IT.
IT WAS PRINCESS YONA WHO SET ME ON THE RIGHT PATH.
I DON'T CARE WHAT ANYONE SAYS...
EVEN IF IT'S YOU, BROTHER ...
I WON'T PERMIT ANY HARM TO COME TO HER.

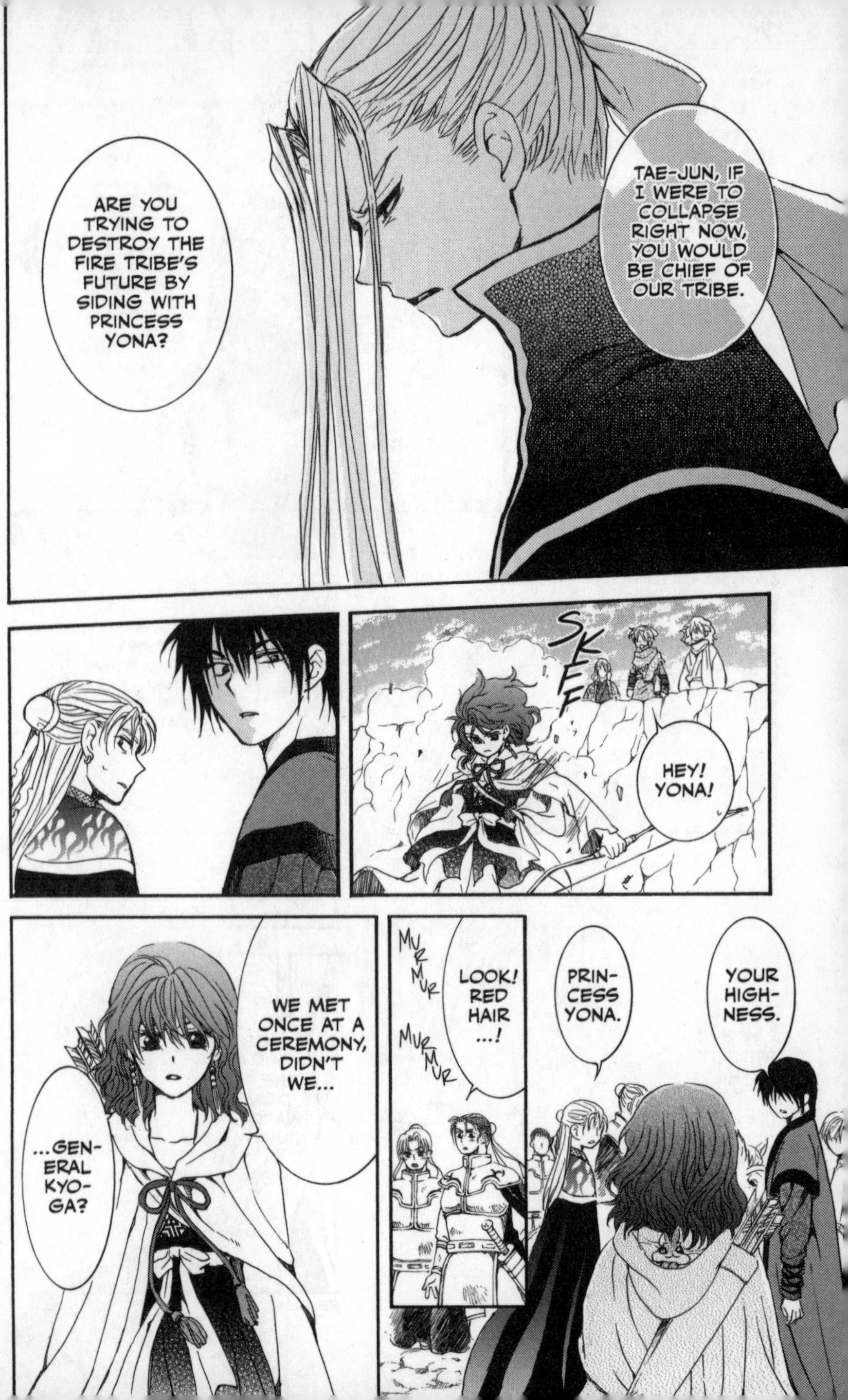
TAE-JUN, IF I WERE TO COLLAPSE RIGHT NOW, YOU WOULD BE CHIEF OF OUR TRIBE.
ARE YOU TRYING TO DESTROY THE FIRE TRIBE'S FUTURE BY SIDING WITH PRINCESS YONA?
SKFF
HEY! YONA!
YOUR HIGH-NESS.
PRIN-CESS YONA.
LOOK! RED HAIR ...!
MURMUR
MURMUR
WE MET ONCE AT A CEREMONY, DIDN'T WE...
...GEN-ERAL KYO-GA?

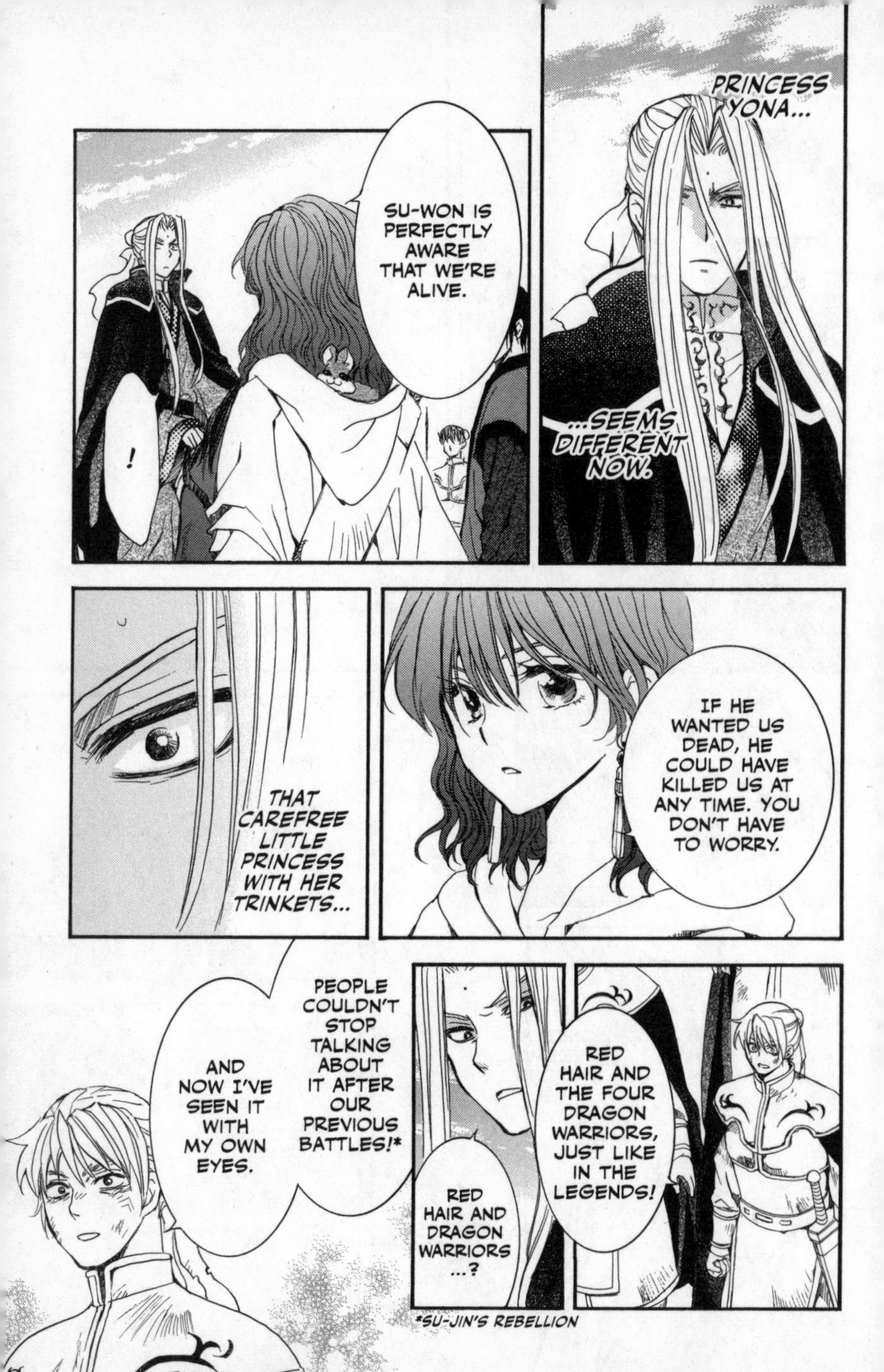
PRINCESS YONA...
...SEEMS DIFFERENT NOW.
SU-WON IS PERFECTLY AWARE THAT WE'RE ALIVE.
!
IF HE WANTED US DEAD, HE COULD HAVE KILLED US AT ANY TIME. YOU DON'T HAVE TO WORRY.
THAT CAREFREE LITTLE PRINCESS WITH HER TRINKETS...
RED HAIR AND THE FOUR DRAGON WARRIORS, JUST LIKE IN THE LEGENDS!
RED HAIR AND DRAGON WARRIORS ...?
PEOPLE COULDN'T STOP TALKING ABOUT IT AFTER OUR PREVIOUS BATTLES!*
AND NOW I'VE SEEN IT WITH MY OWN EYES.

*SU-JIN'S REBELLION

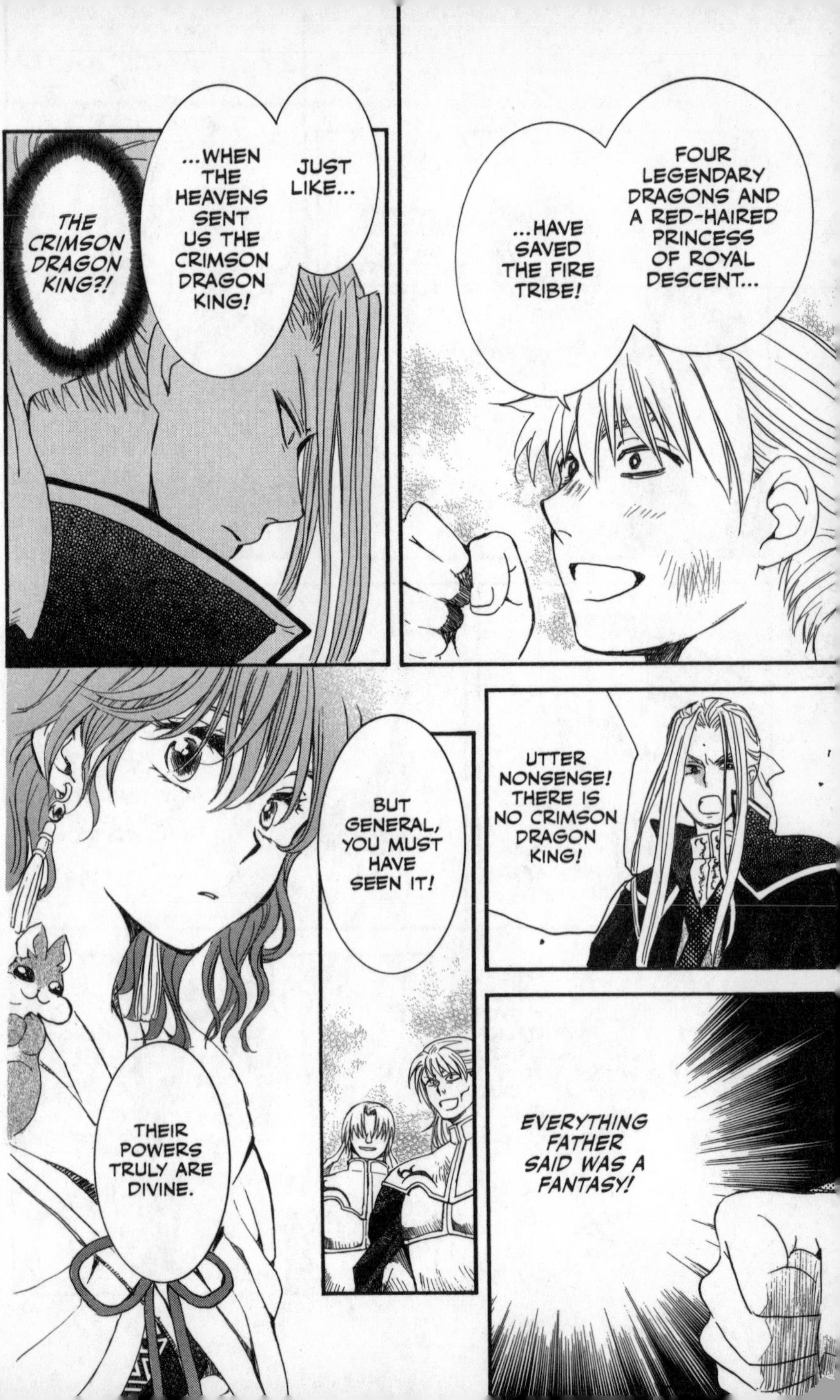
FOUR LEGENDARY DRAGONS AND A RED-HAIRED PRINCESS OF ROYAL DESCENT...
...HAVE SAVED THE FIRE TRIBE!
JUST LIKE...
...WHEN THE HEAVENS SENT US THE CRIMSON DRAGON KING!
THE CRIMSON DRAGON KING?!
UTTER NONSENSE! THERE IS NO CRIMSON DRAGON KING!
EVERYTHING FATHER SAID WAS A FANTASY!
BUT GENERAL, YOU MUST HAVE SEEN IT!
THEIR POWERS TRULY ARE DIVINE.

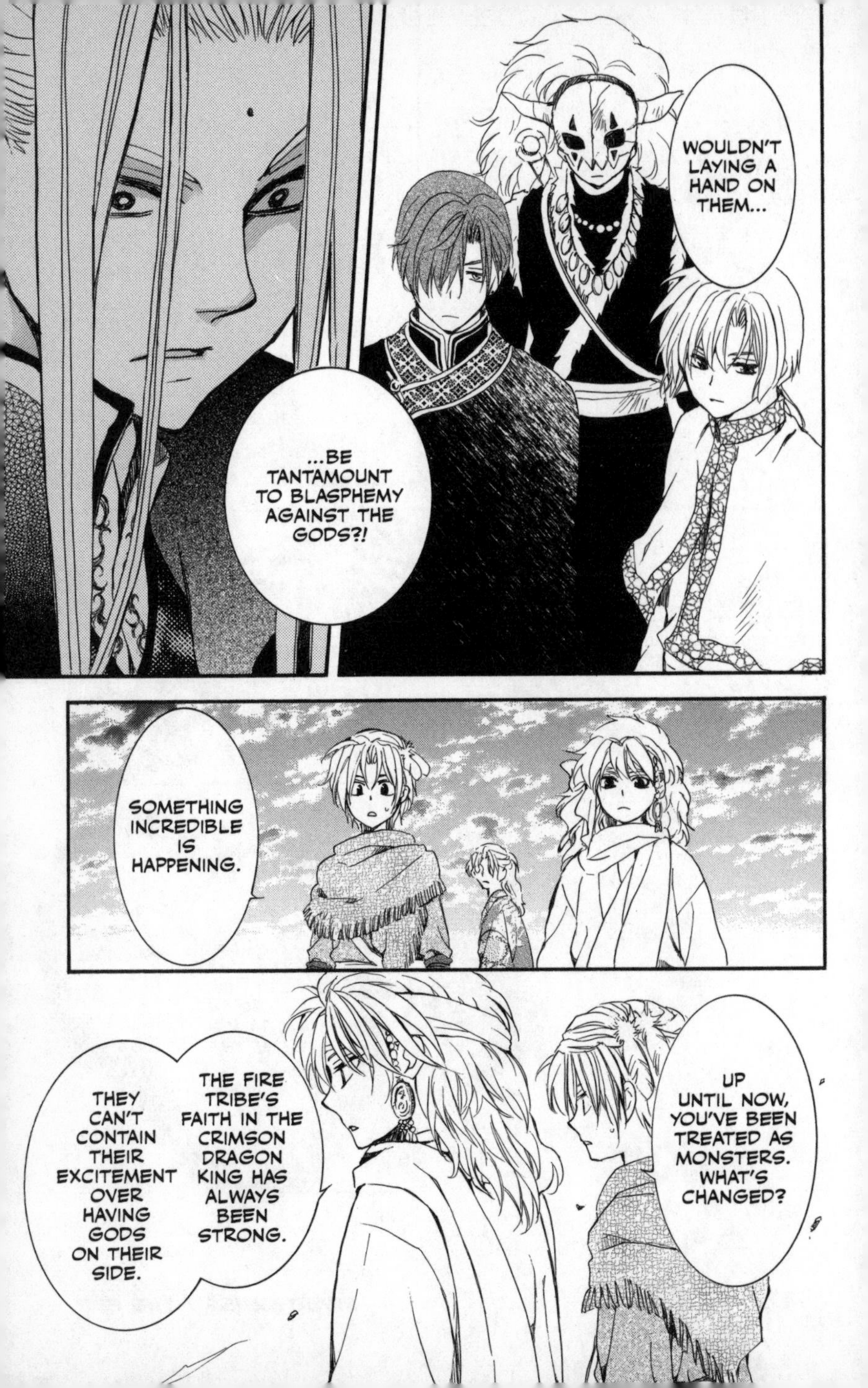
WOULDN'T LAYING A HAND ON THEM...
...BE TANTAMOUNT TO BLASPHEMY AGAINST THE GODS?!
SOMETHING INCREDIBLE IS HAPPENING.
UP UNTIL NOW, YOU'VE BEEN TREATED AS MONSTERS. WHAT'S CHANGED?
THE FIRE TRIBE'S FAITH IN THE CRIMSON DRAGON KING HAS ALWAYS BEEN STRONG.
THEY CAN'T CONTAIN THEIR EXCITEMENT OVER HAVING GODS ON THEIR SIDE.

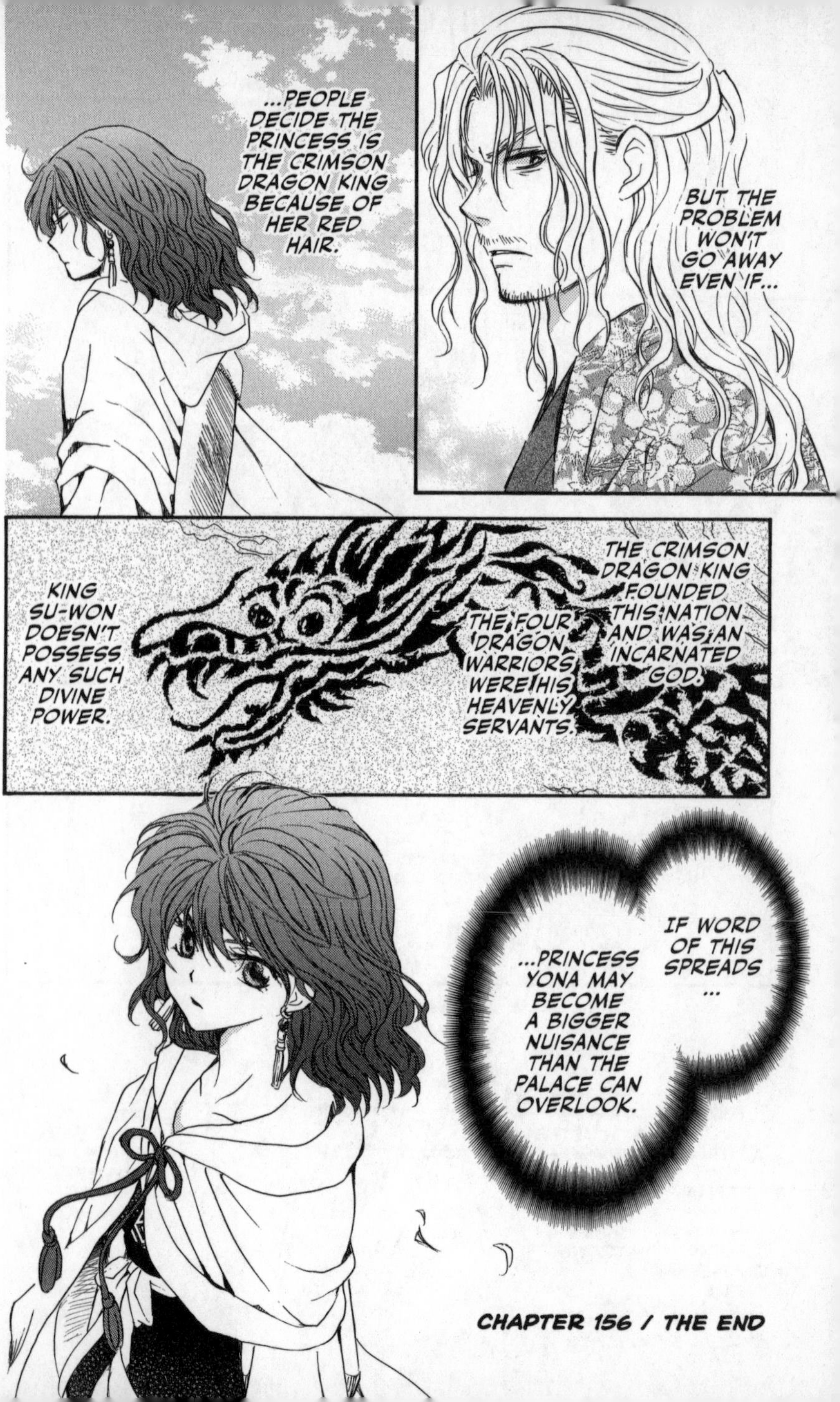
BUT THE PROBLEM WON'T GO AWAY EVEN IF...
...PEOPLE DECIDE THE PRINCESS IS THE CRIMSON DRAGON KING BECAUSE OF HER RED HAIR.
THE CRIMSON DRAGON KING FOUNDED THIS NATION AND WAS AN INCARNATED GOD.
THE FOUR DRAGON WARRIORS WERE HIS HEAVENLY SERVANTS.
KING SU-WON DOESN'T POSSESS ANY SUCH DIVINE POWER.
IF WORD OF THIS SPREADS ...
...PRINCESS YONA MAY BECOME A BIGGER NUISANCE THAN THE PALACE CAN OVERLOOK.
CHAPTER 156 / THE END

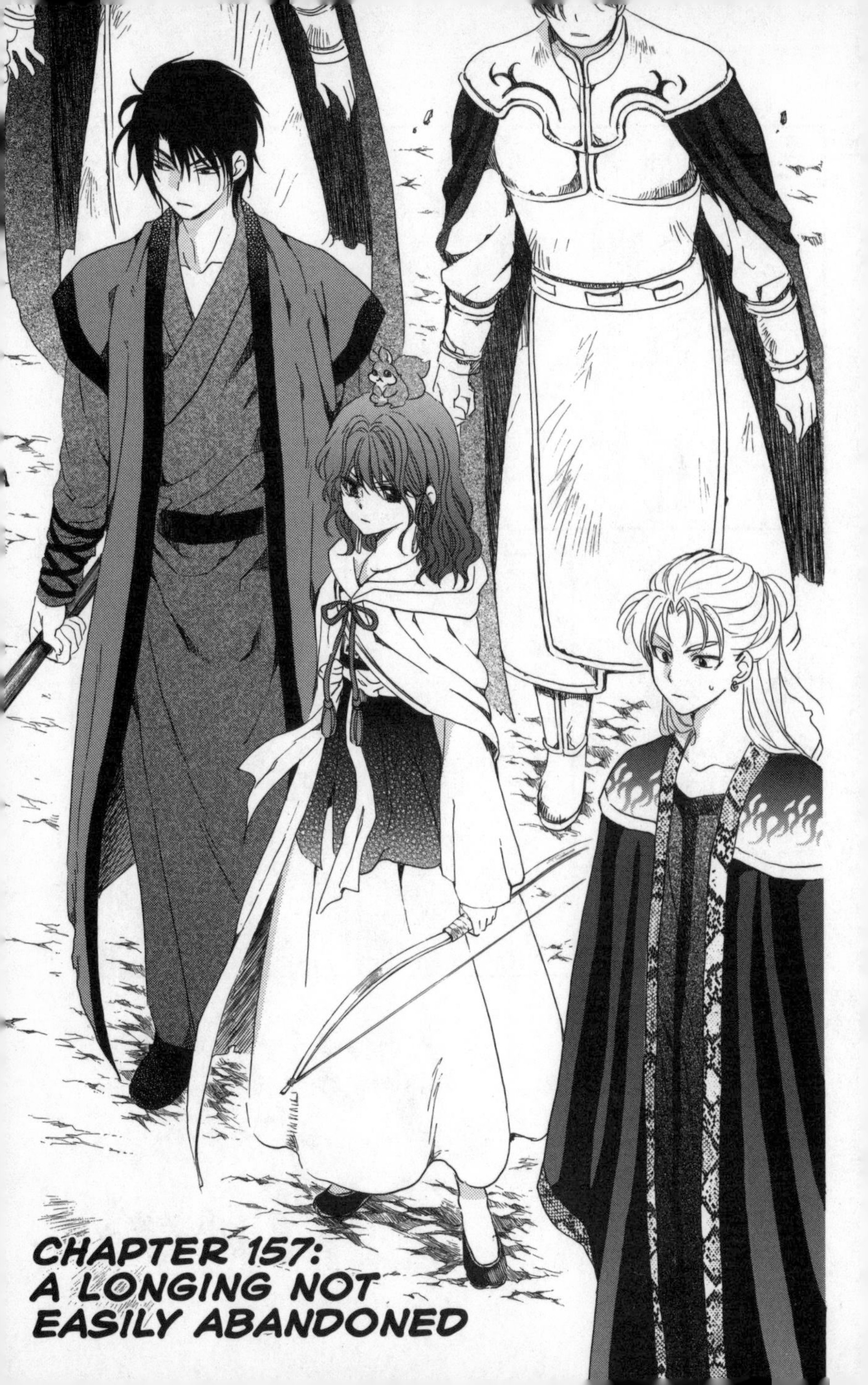
CHAPTER 157:
A LONGING NOT
EASILY ABANDONED

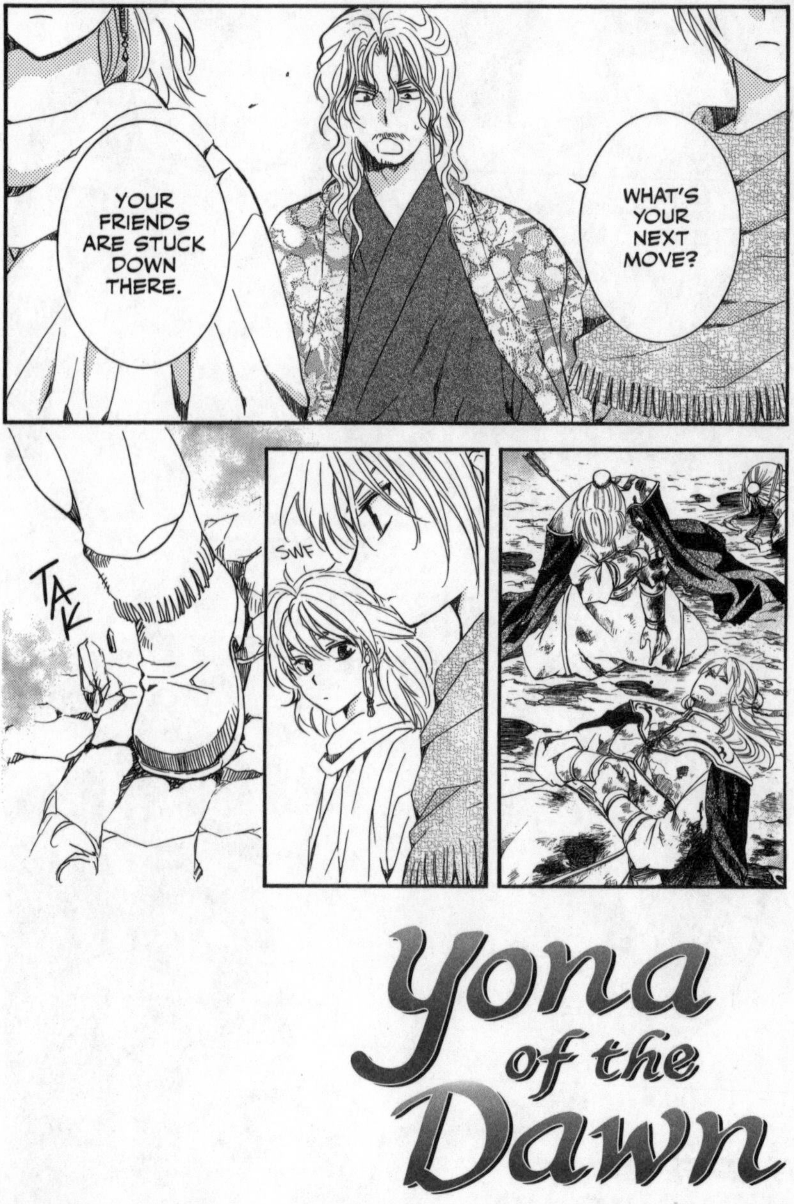
WHAT'S YOUR NEXT MOVE?
YOUR FRIENDS ARE STUCK DOWN THERE.
SWF
TAK

Yona of the Dawn

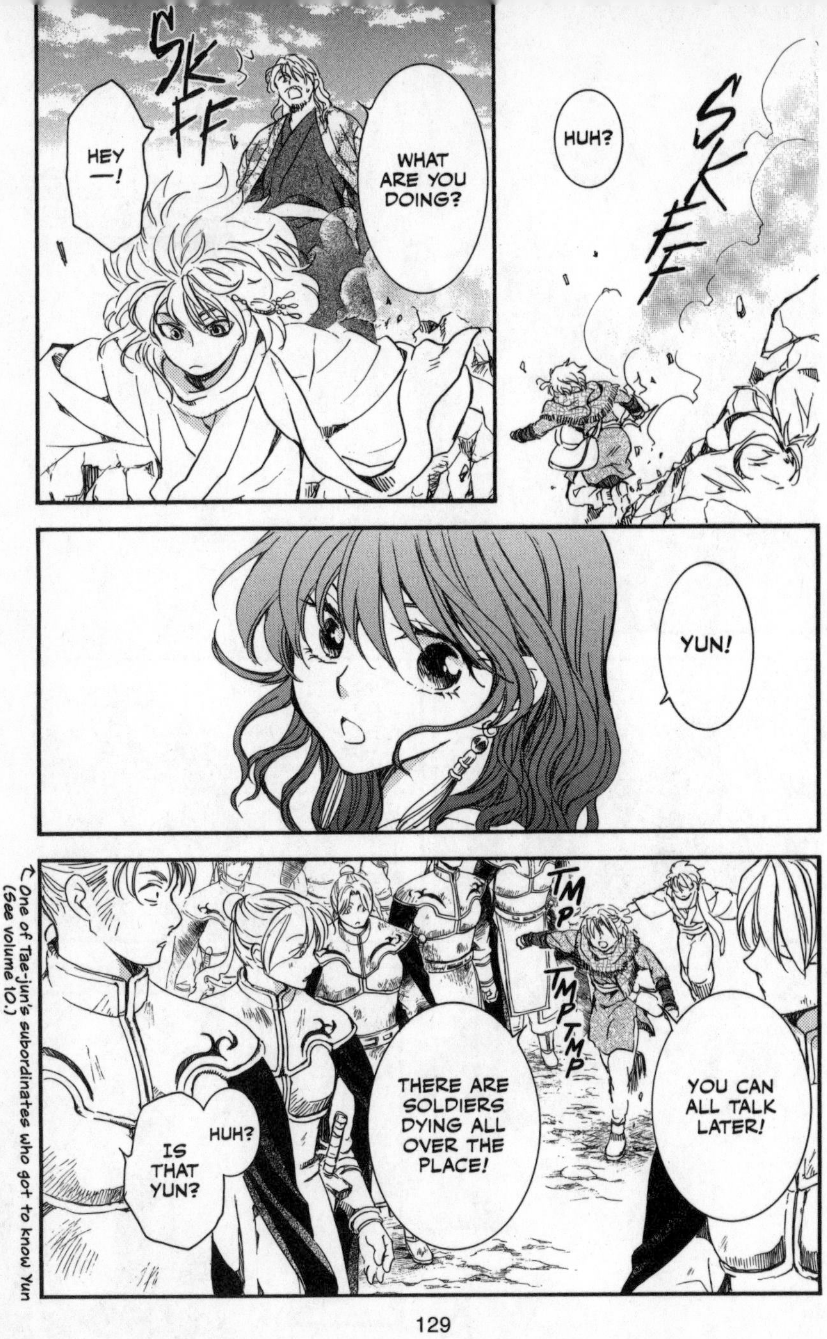
HUH?
SKFF
WHAT ARE YOU DOING?
SKFF
HEY —!
YUN!
YOU CAN ALL TALK LATER!
TMP TMP TMP TMP
THERE ARE SOLDIERS DYING ALL OVER THE PLACE!
HUH? IS THAT YUN?

↑ One of Tae-jun's subordinates who got to know Yun (See volume 10.)

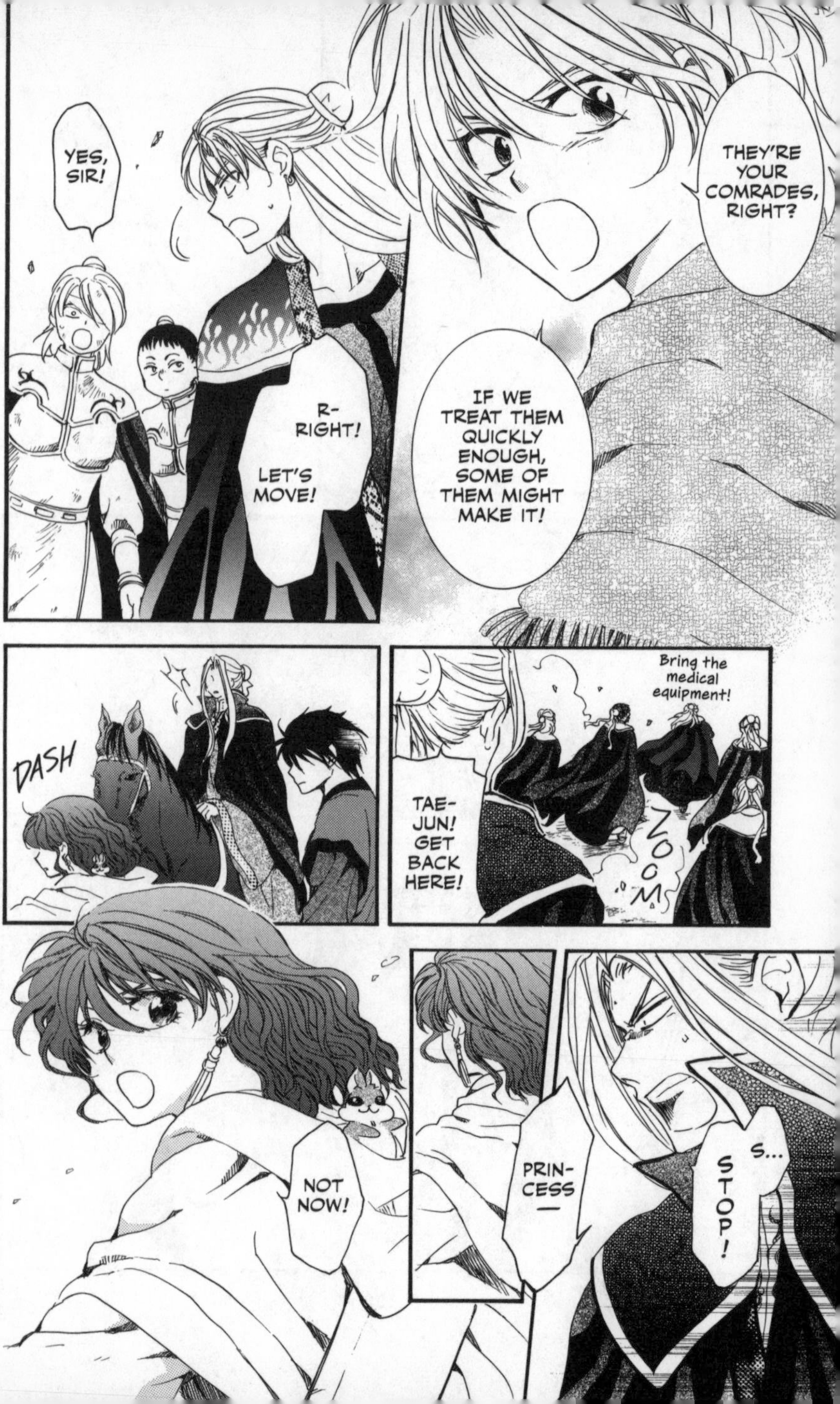
THEY'RE YOUR COMRADES, RIGHT?
IF WE TREAT THEM QUICKLY ENOUGH, SOME OF THEM MIGHT MAKE IT!
R-RIGHT!
LET'S MOVE!
YES, SIR!
Bring the medical equipment!
TAE-JUN! GET BACK HERE!
ZOOM
DASH
S... STOP!
PRIN-CESS—
NOT NOW!

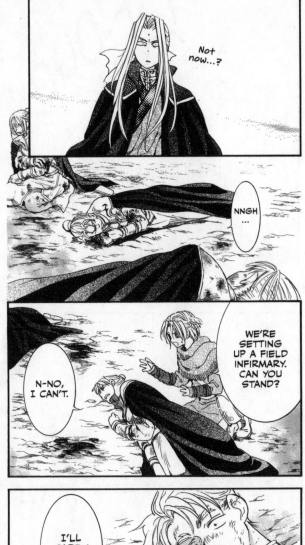

Not now...?
NNGH ...
WE'RE SETTING UP A FIELD INFIRMARY. CAN YOU STAND?
N-NO, I CAN'T.
I'LL CARRY YOU.

In chapter 153, Hak said, "I stopped wanting her to see me that way or imagining us being together," but I think the window of time when he wanted her to see him that way was pretty brief. It wasn't just that he didn't want to get between Su-won and Yona. The fact that he was so far removed from the royal family was a bigger factor. He'd already refused the position of general, so his feelings never took precedence.

It wasn't that being a general would have made him a poor match for a princess, but it would have been very uncharacteristic for him to interfere with her unrequited love. And then, once he finally did become his tribe's general, what mattered most to him was serving Su-won, Yona and Il.

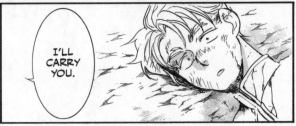

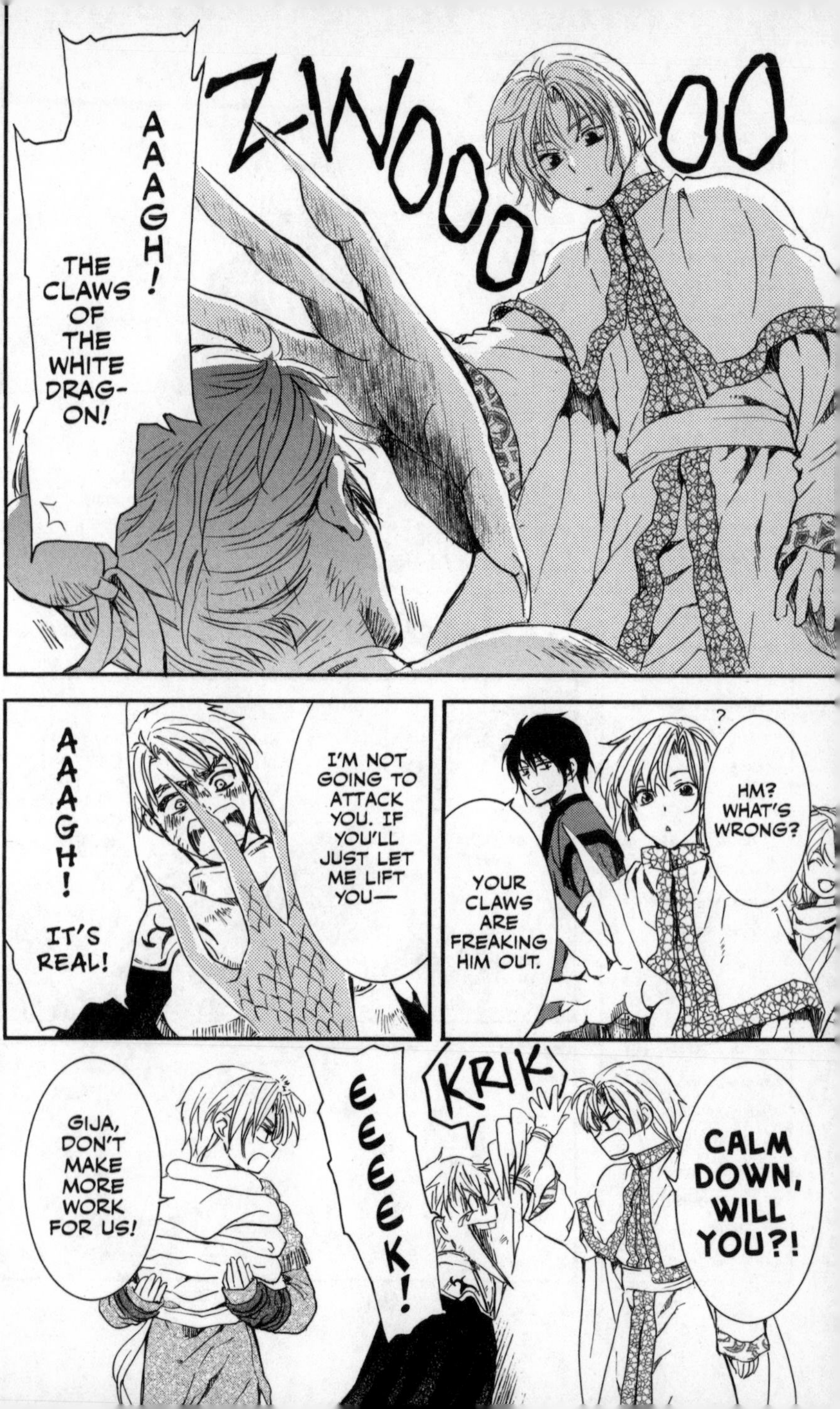
Z-WOOOOOOO
AAAGH! THE CLAWS OF THE WHITE DRAGON!
?
HM? WHAT'S WRONG?
YOUR CLAWS ARE FREAKING HIM OUT.
I'M NOT GOING TO ATTACK YOU. IF YOU'LL JUST LET ME LIFT YOU—
AAAGH! IT'S REAL!
CALM DOWN, WILL YOU?!
KRIK
EEEEK!
GIJA, DON'T MAKE MORE WORK FOR US!

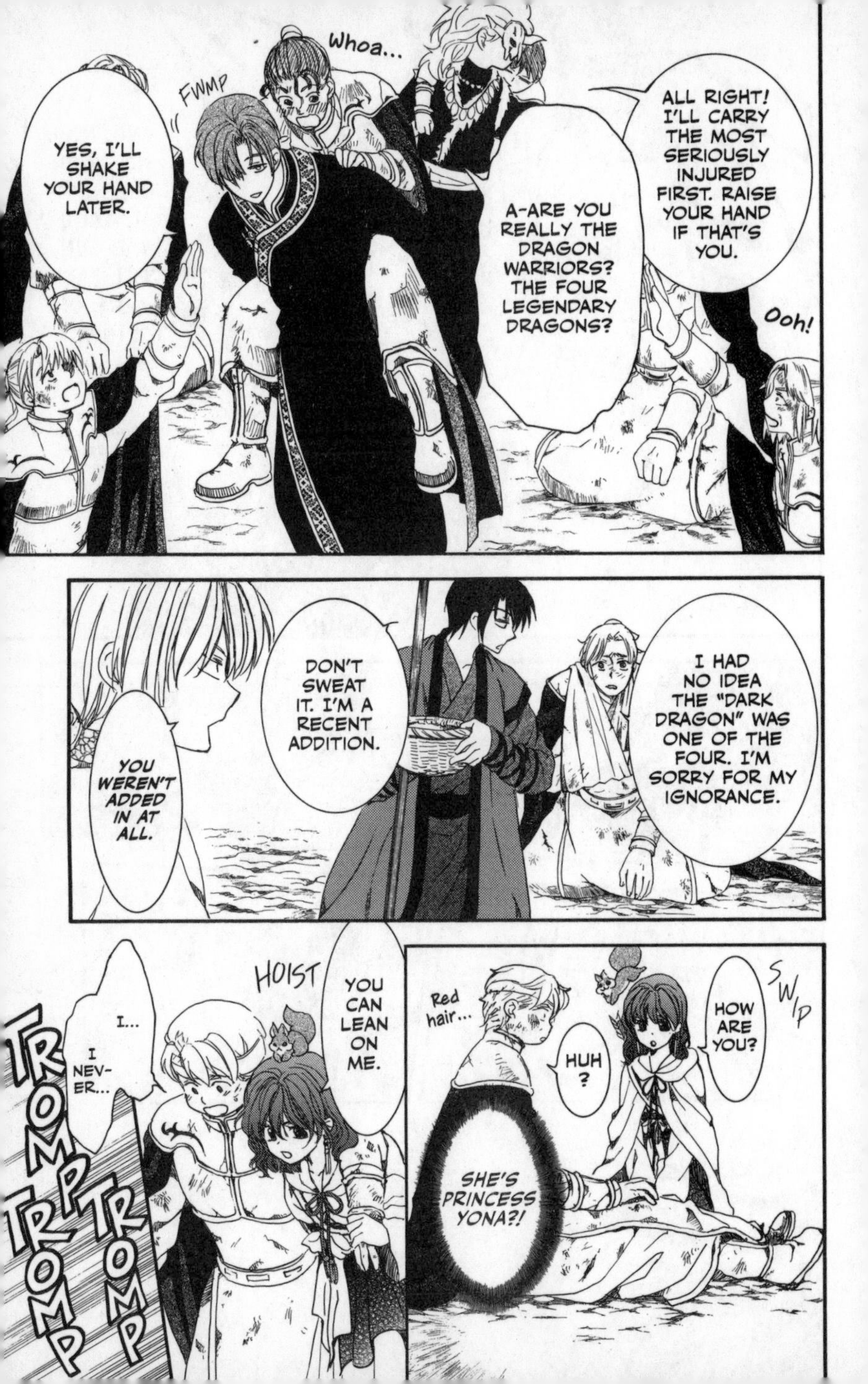
ALL RIGHT! I'LL CARRY THE MOST SERIOUSLY INJURED FIRST. RAISE YOUR HAND IF THAT'S YOU.
Ooh!
Whoa...
A-ARE YOU REALLY THE DRAGON WARRIORS? THE FOUR LEGENDARY DRAGONS?
FWMP
YES, I'LL SHAKE YOUR HAND LATER.
I HAD NO IDEA THE "DARK DRAGON" WAS ONE OF THE FOUR. I'M SORRY FOR MY IGNORANCE.
DON'T SWEAT IT. I'M A RECENT ADDITION.
YOU WEREN'T ADDED IN AT ALL.
SWIP
HOW ARE YOU?
Red hair...
HUH?
SHE'S PRINCESS YONA?!
YOU CAN LEAN ON ME.
HOIST
I...
I NEVER...
TROMP TROMP
TROMP TROMP

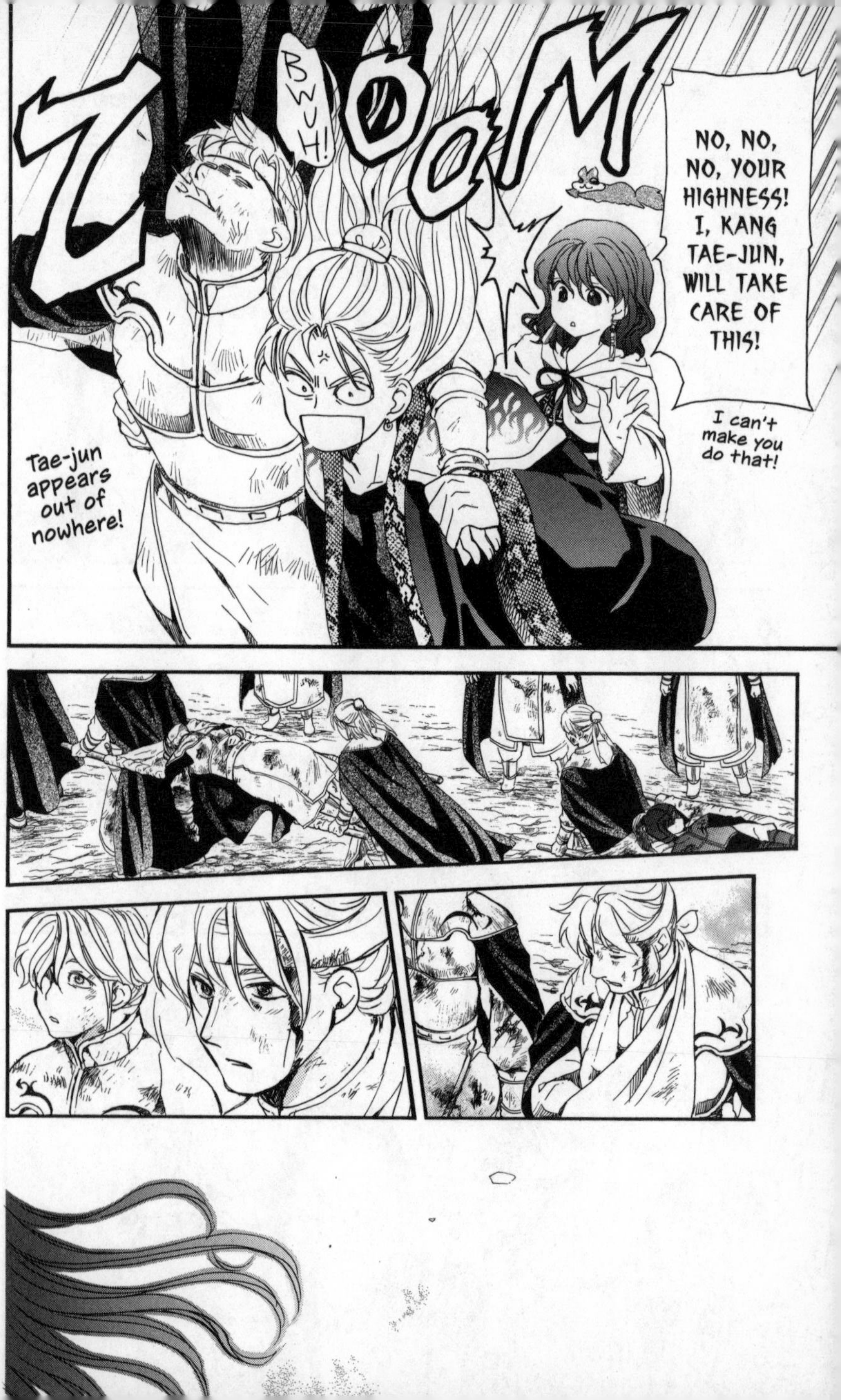
NO, NO, NO, YOUR HIGHNESS! I, KANG TAE-JUN, WILL TAKE CARE OF THIS!
I can't make you do that!
ZOOM
BWUH!
Tae-jun appears out of nowhere!

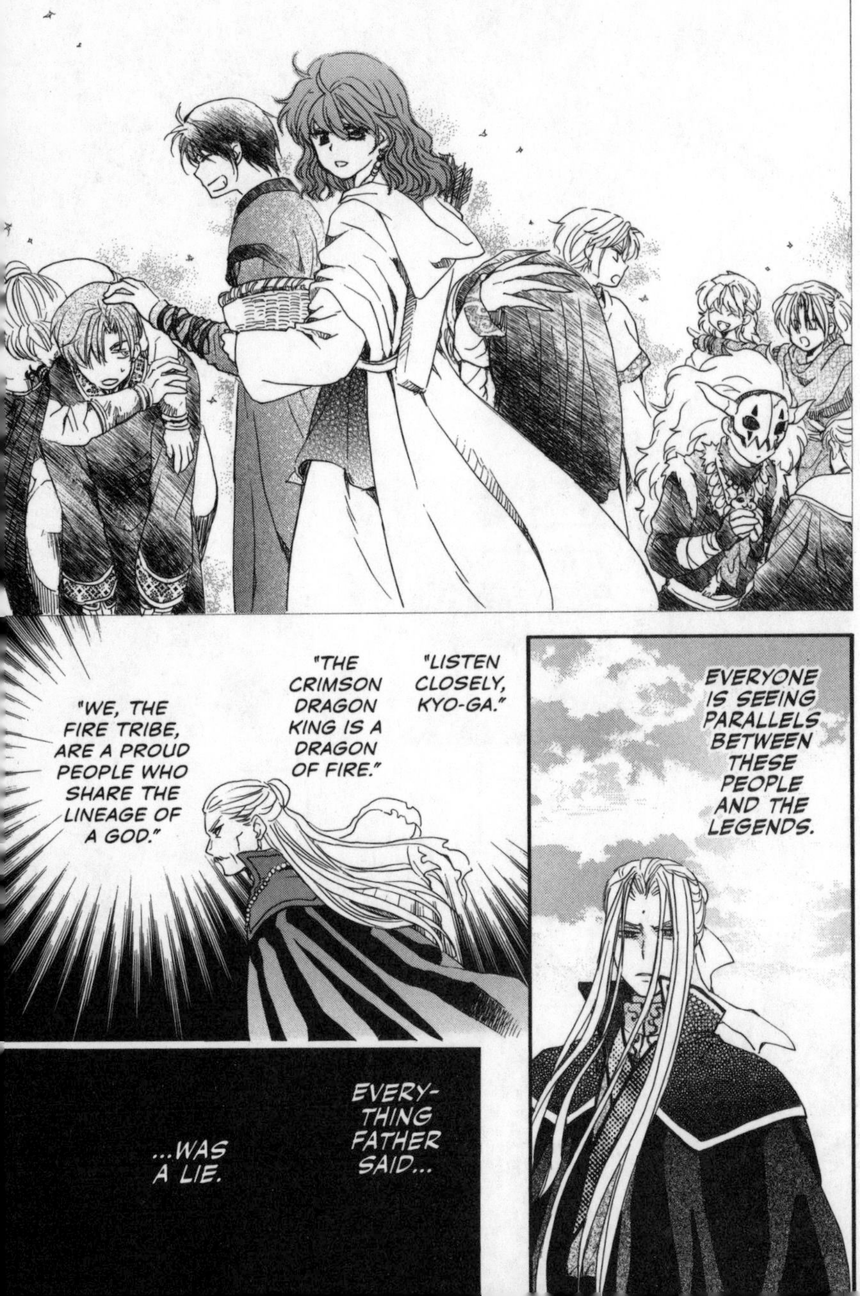
EVERYONE IS SEEING PARALLELS BETWEEN THESE PEOPLE AND THE LEGENDS.
"LISTEN CLOSELY, KYO-GA."
"THE CRIMSON DRAGON KING IS A DRAGON OF FIRE."
"WE, THE FIRE TRIBE, ARE A PROUD PEOPLE WHO SHARE THE LINEAGE OF A GOD."
EVERY-THING FATHER SAID...
...WAS A LIE.

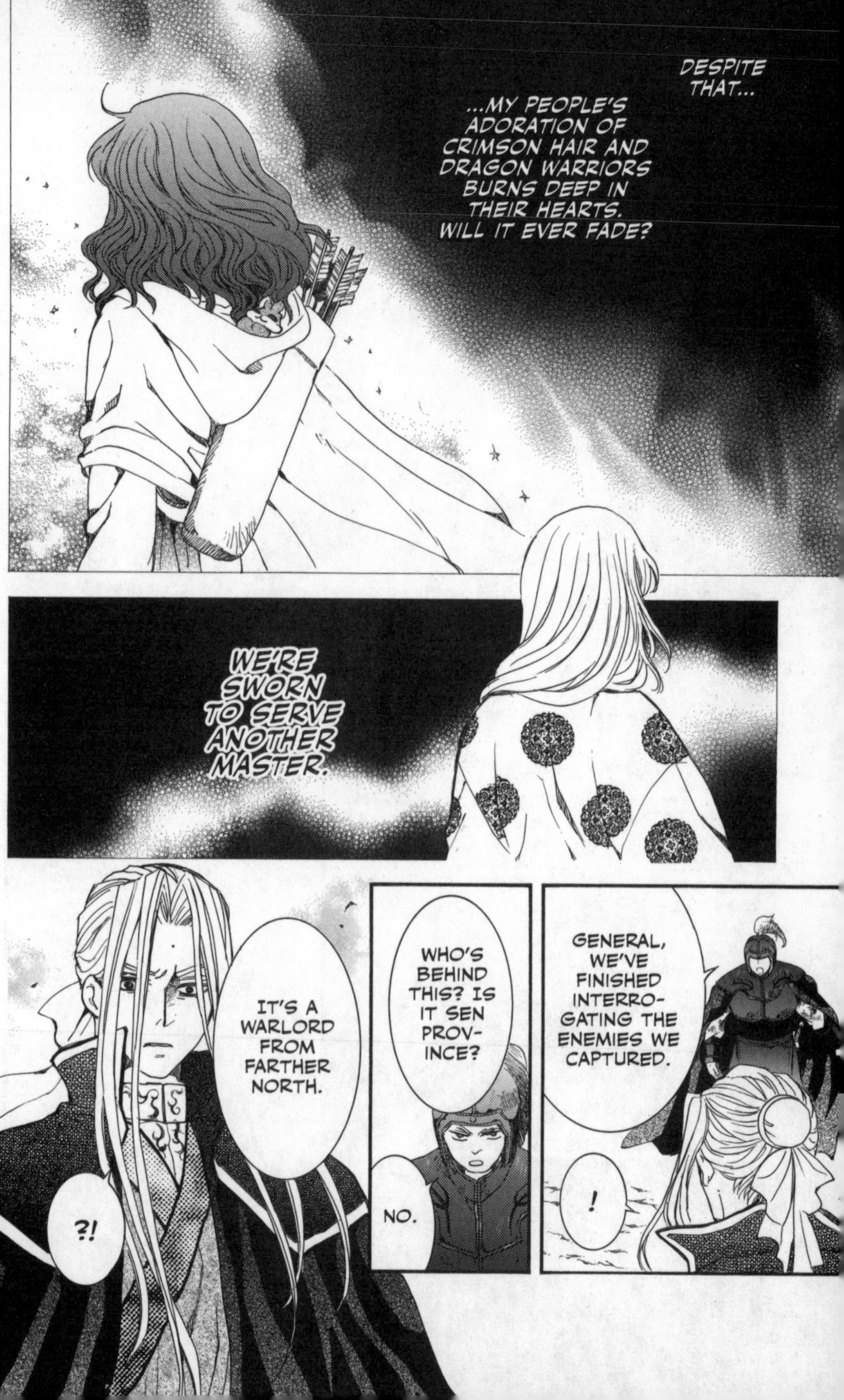
DESPITE THAT...
...MY PEOPLE'S ADORATION OF CRIMSON HAIR AND DRAGON WARRIORS BURNS DEEP IN THEIR HEARTS. WILL IT EVER FADE?
WE'RE SWORN TO SERVE ANOTHER MASTER.
GENERAL, WE'VE FINISHED INTERRO-GATING THE ENEMIES WE CAPTURED.
!
WHO'S BEHIND THIS? IS IT SEN PROV-INCE?
NO.
IT'S A WARLORD FROM FARTHER NORTH.
?!

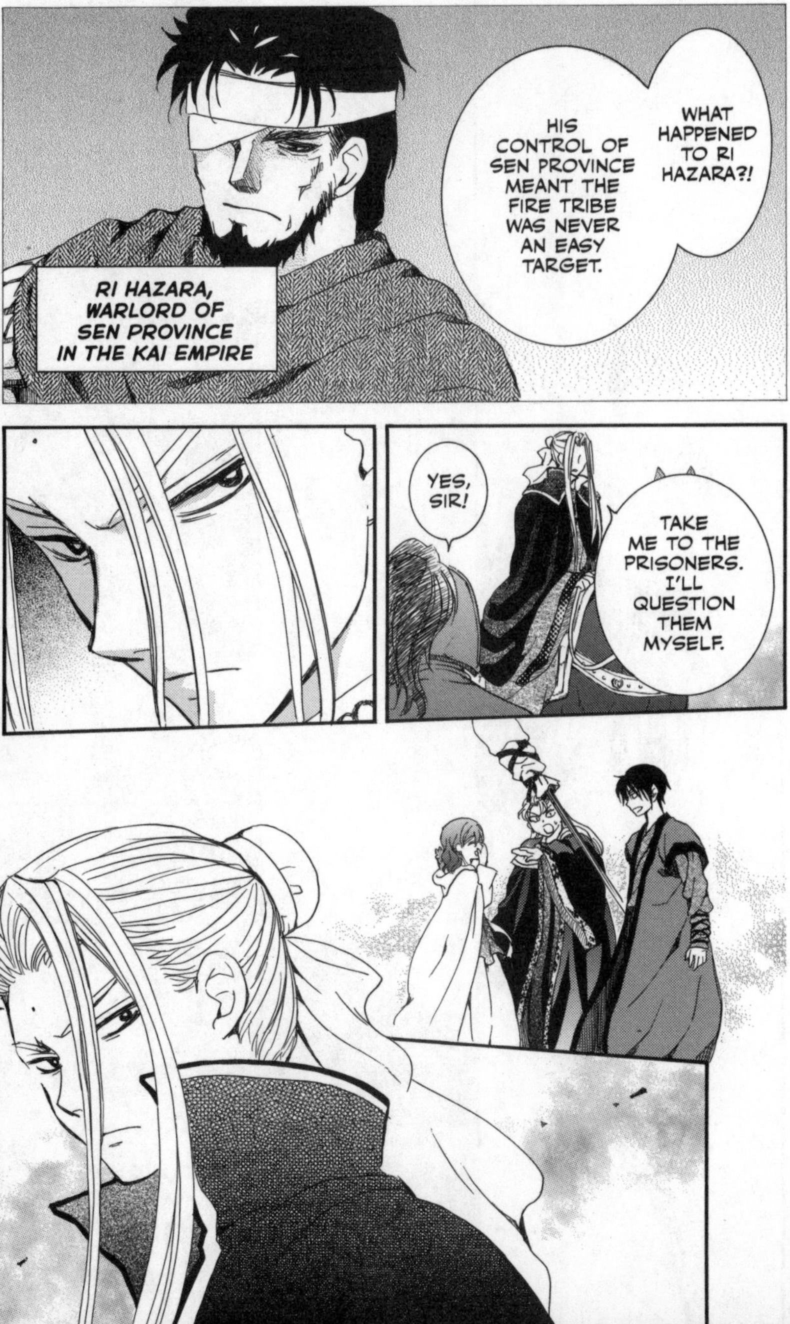
WHAT HAPPENED TO RI HAZARA?!
HIS CONTROL OF SEN PROVINCE MEANT THE FIRE TRIBE WAS NEVER AN EASY TARGET.
RI HAZARA, WARLORD OF SEN PROVINCE IN THE KAI EMPIRE
TAKE ME TO THE PRISONERS. I'LL QUESTION THEM MYSELF.
YES, SIR!

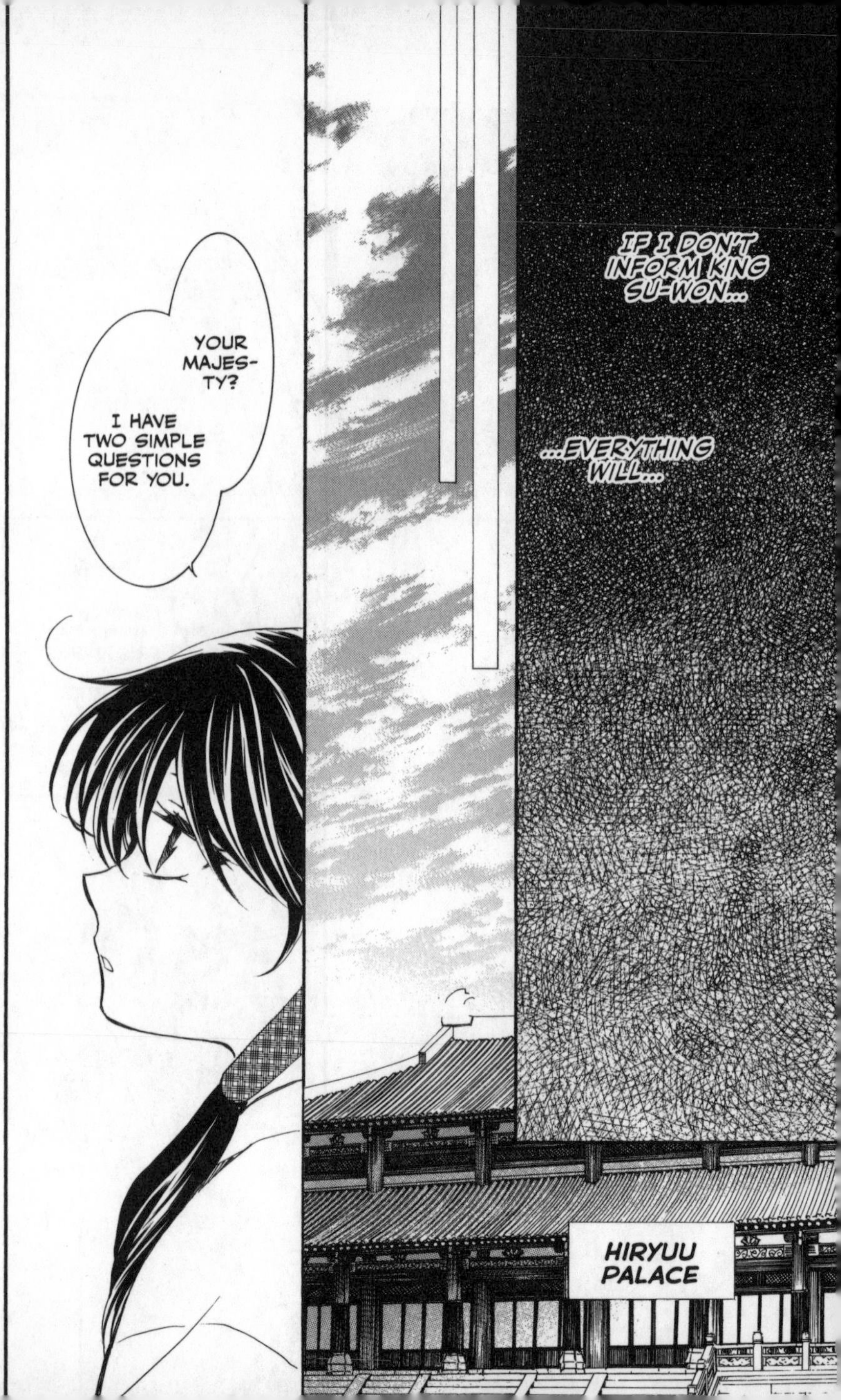
IF I DON'T INFORM KING SU-WON...
...EVERYTHING WILL...
HIRYUU PALACE
YOUR MAJES-TY?
I HAVE TWO SIMPLE QUESTIONS FOR YOU.

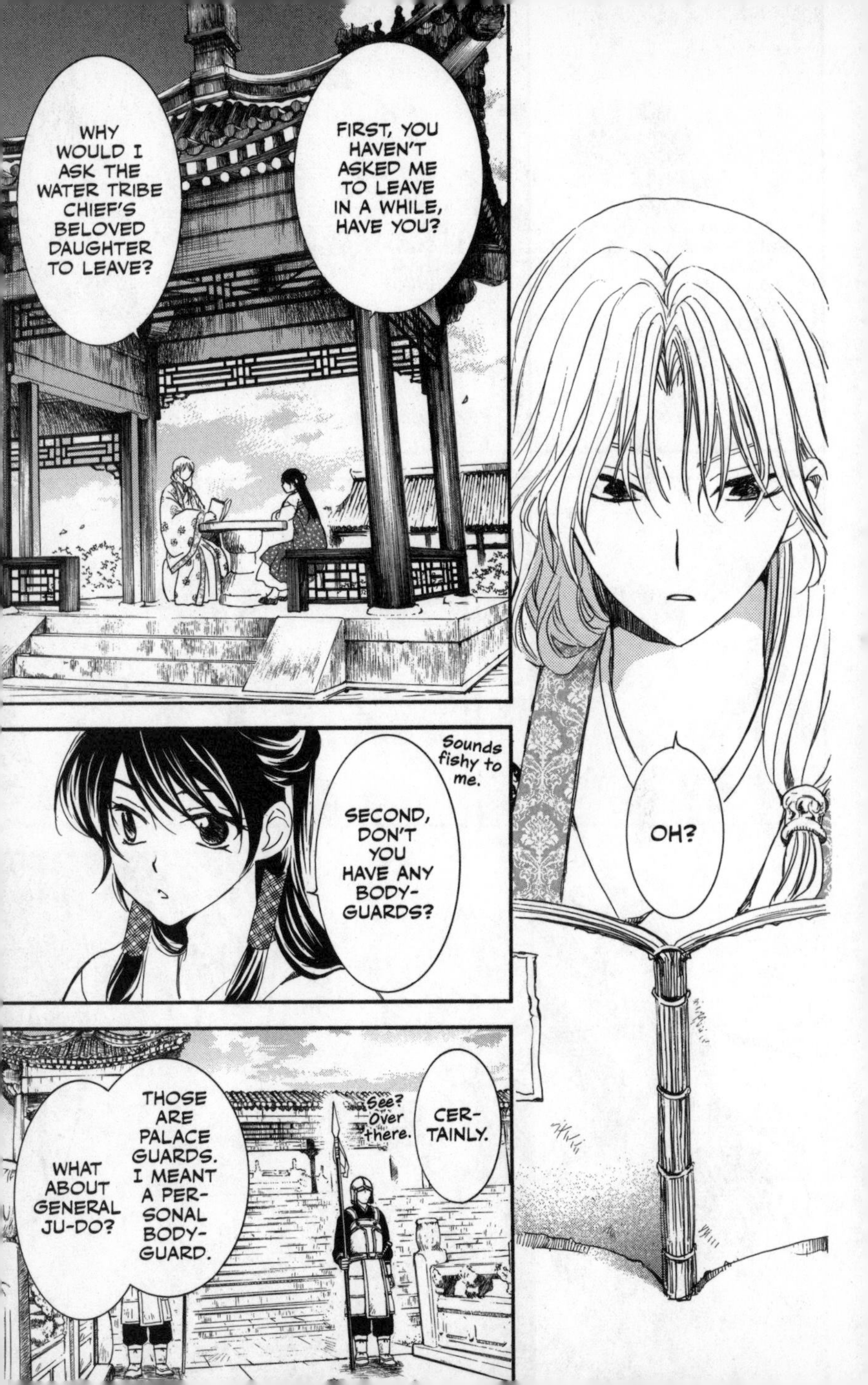
OH?
FIRST, YOU HAVEN'T ASKED ME TO LEAVE IN A WHILE, HAVE YOU?
WHY WOULD I ASK THE WATER TRIBE CHIEF'S BELOVED DAUGHTER TO LEAVE?
Sounds fishy to me.
SECOND, DON'T YOU HAVE ANY BODY-GUARDS?
CER-TAINLY.
See? Over there.
THOSE ARE PALACE GUARDS. I MEANT A PER-SONAL BODY-GUARD.
WHAT ABOUT GENERAL JU-DO?

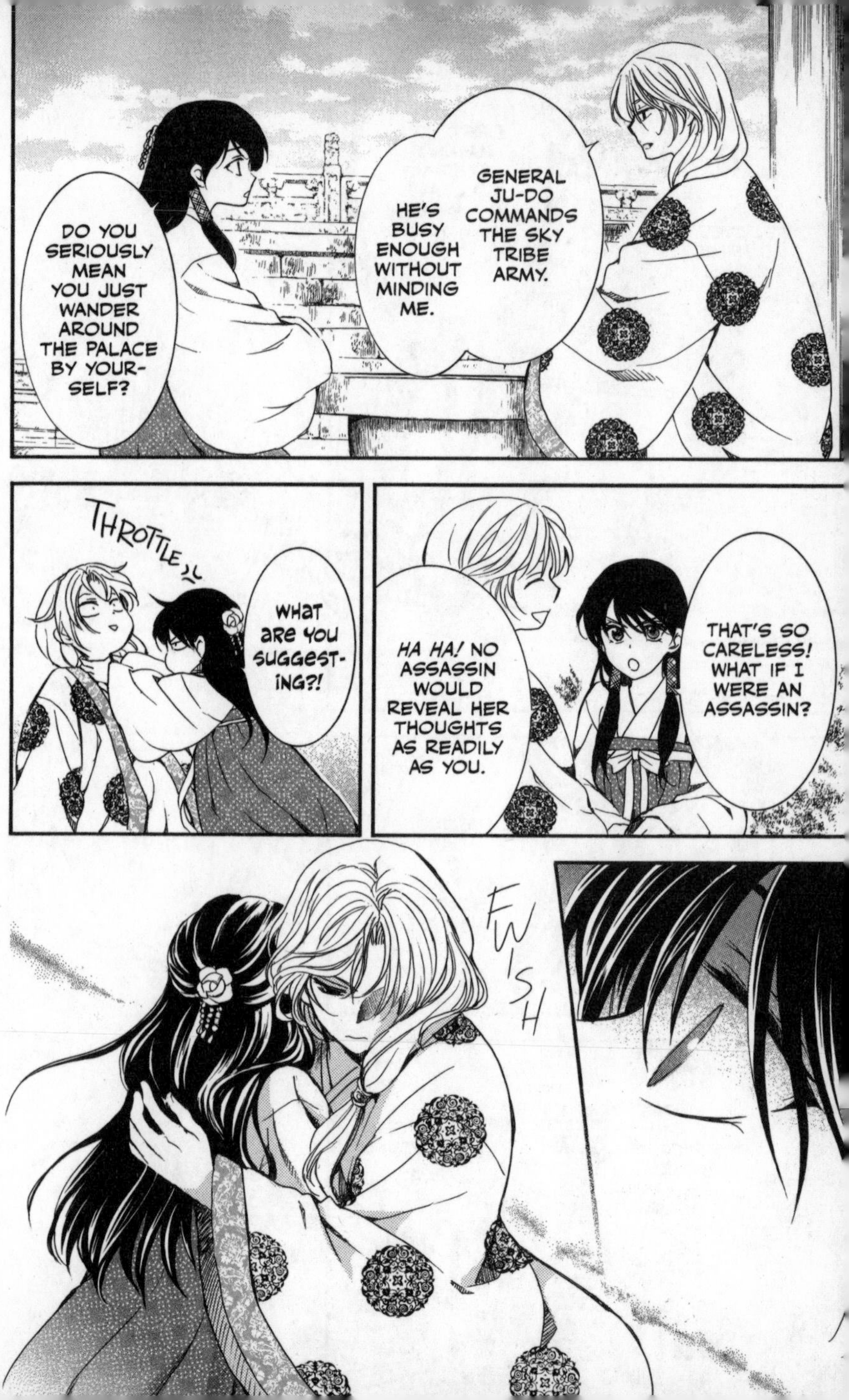
GENERAL JU-DO COMMANDS THE SKY TRIBE ARMY.
HE'S BUSY ENOUGH WITHOUT MINDING ME.
DO YOU SERIOUSLY MEAN YOU JUST WANDER AROUND THE PALACE BY YOUR-SELF?
THAT'S SO CARELESS! WHAT IF I WERE AN ASSASSIN?
HA HA! NO ASSASSIN WOULD REVEAL HER THOUGHTS AS READILY AS YOU.
THROTTLE
WHAT are YOU SUGGEST-ING?!
FWISH

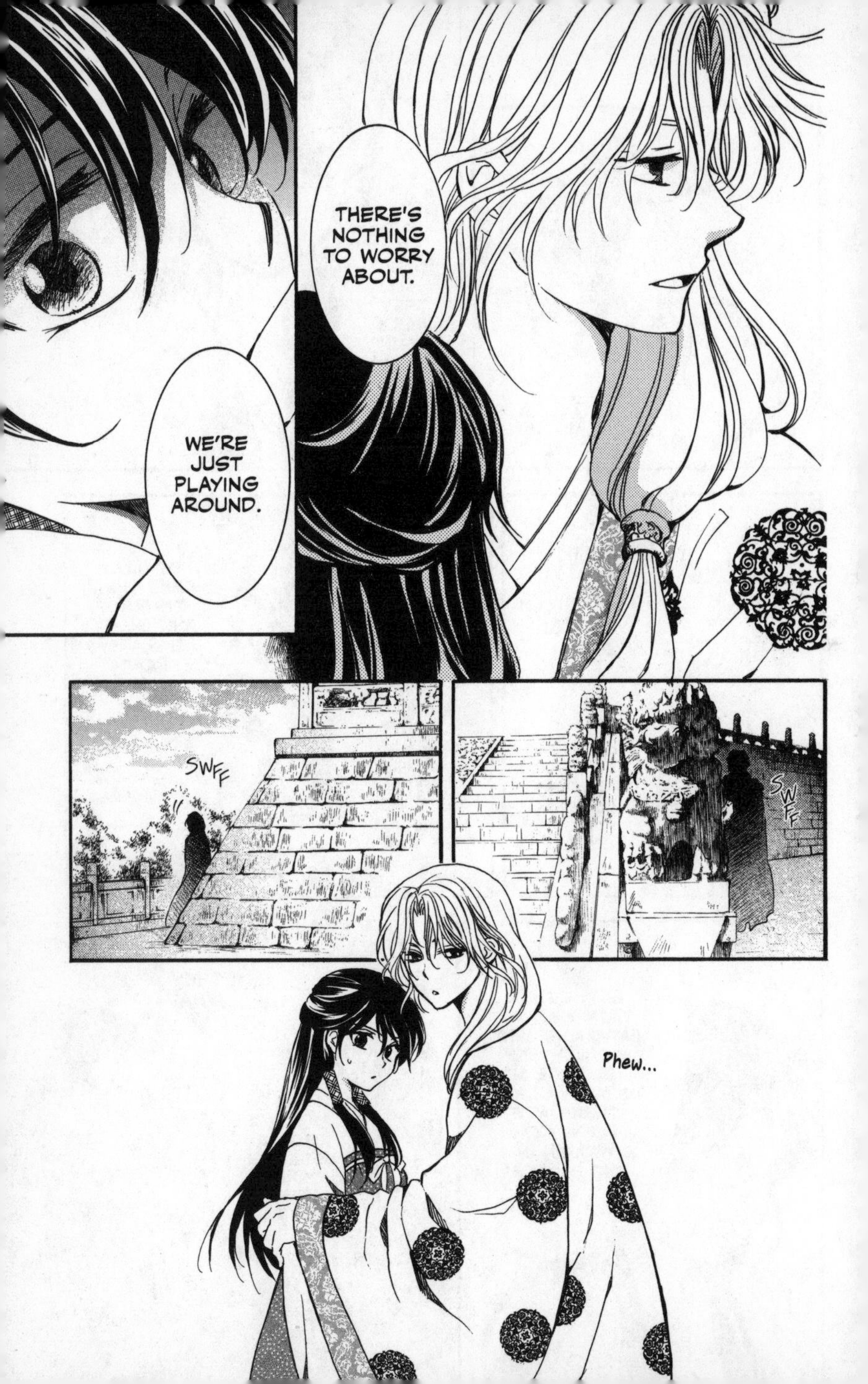
THERE'S NOTHING TO WORRY ABOUT.
WE'RE JUST PLAYING AROUND.
SWFF
SWFF
Phew...

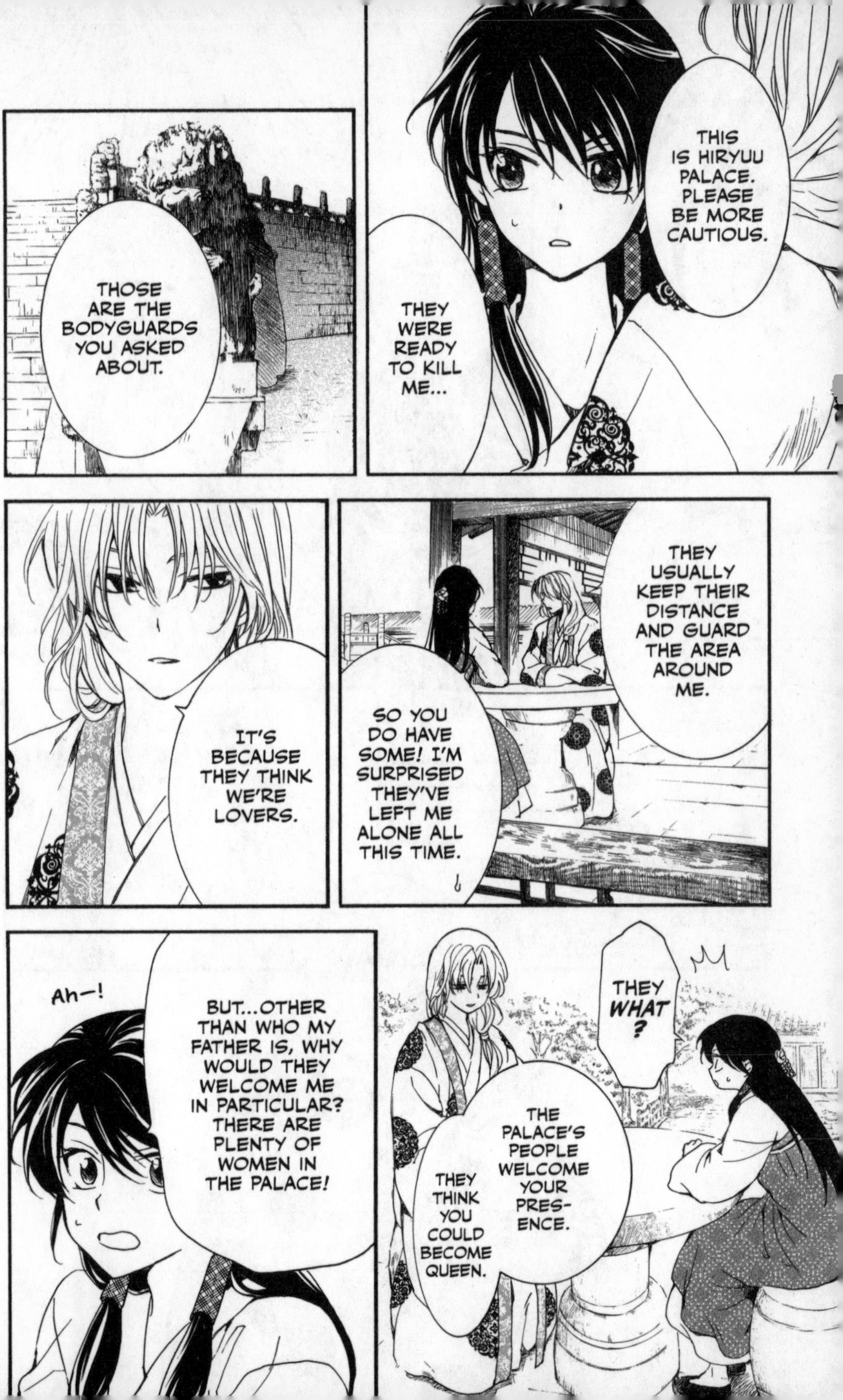
THIS IS HIRYUU PALACE. PLEASE BE MORE CAUTIOUS.
THEY WERE READY TO KILL ME...
THOSE ARE THE BODYGUARDS YOU ASKED ABOUT.
THEY USUALLY KEEP THEIR DISTANCE AND GUARD THE AREA AROUND ME.
SO YOU DO HAVE SOME! I'M SURPRISED THEY'VE LEFT ME ALONE ALL THIS TIME.
IT'S BECAUSE THEY THINK WE'RE LOVERS.
THEY *WHAT*?
THE PALACE'S PEOPLE WELCOME YOUR PRES-ENCE.
THEY THINK YOU COULD BECOME QUEEN.
Ah—!
BUT...OTHER THAN WHO MY FATHER IS, WHY WOULD THEY WELCOME ME IN PARTICULAR? THERE ARE PLENTY OF WOMEN IN THE PALACE!

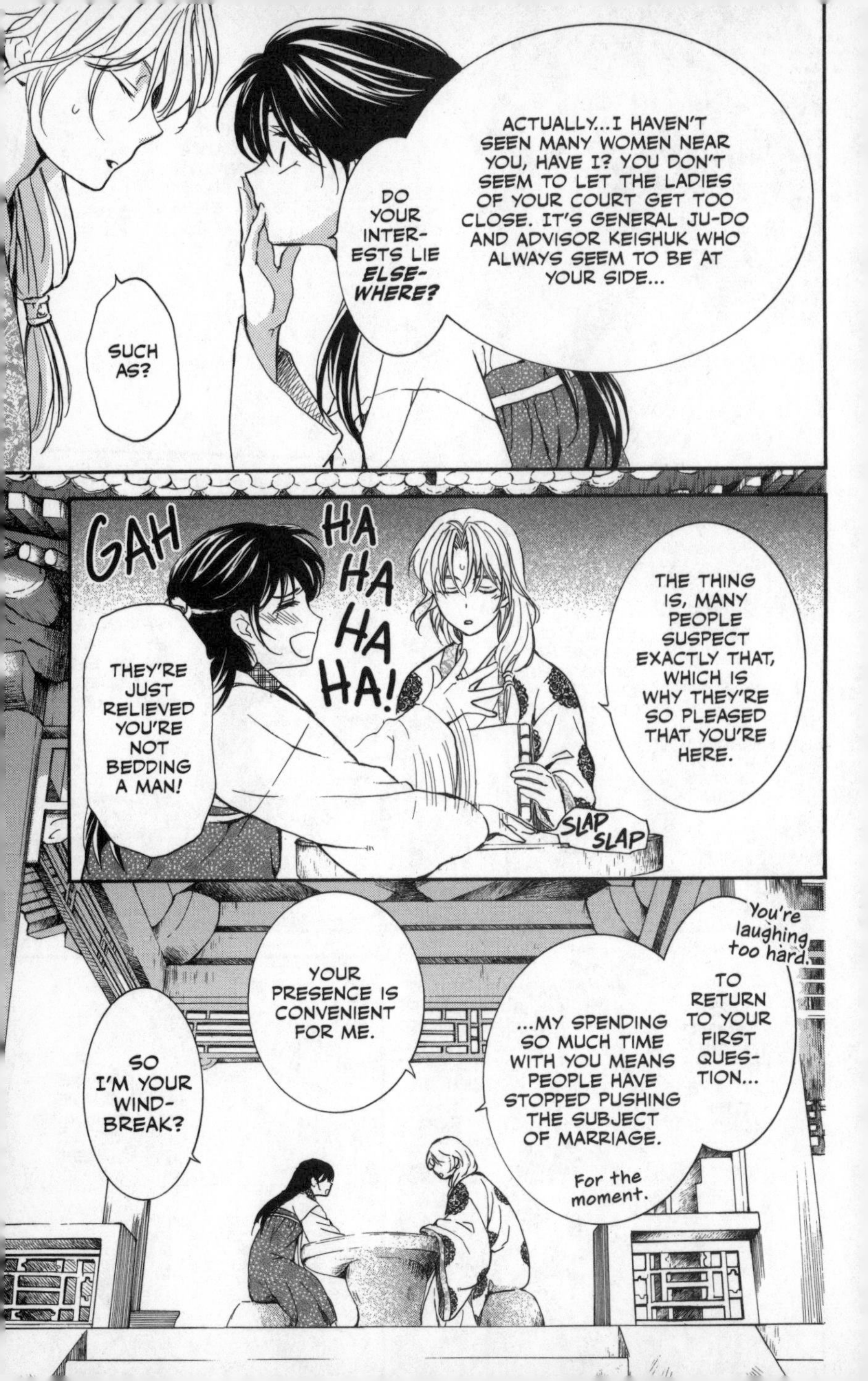
ACTUALLY...I HAVEN'T SEEN MANY WOMEN NEAR YOU, HAVE I? YOU DON'T SEEM TO LET THE LADIES OF YOUR COURT GET TOO CLOSE. IT'S GENERAL JU-DO AND ADVISOR KEISHUK WHO ALWAYS SEEM TO BE AT YOUR SIDE...
DO YOUR INTERESTS LIE *ELSEWHERE?*
SUCH AS?
THE THING IS, MANY PEOPLE SUSPECT EXACTLY THAT, WHICH IS WHY THEY'RE SO PLEASED THAT YOU'RE HERE.
HA HA HA HA!
GAH
THEY'RE JUST RELIEVED YOU'RE NOT BEDDING A MAN!
SLAP SLAP
You're laughing too hard.
TO RETURN TO YOUR FIRST QUESTION...
...MY SPENDING SO MUCH TIME WITH YOU MEANS PEOPLE HAVE STOPPED PUSHING THE SUBJECT OF MARRIAGE.
For the moment.
YOUR PRESENCE IS CONVENIENT FOR ME.
SO I'M YOUR WINDBREAK?

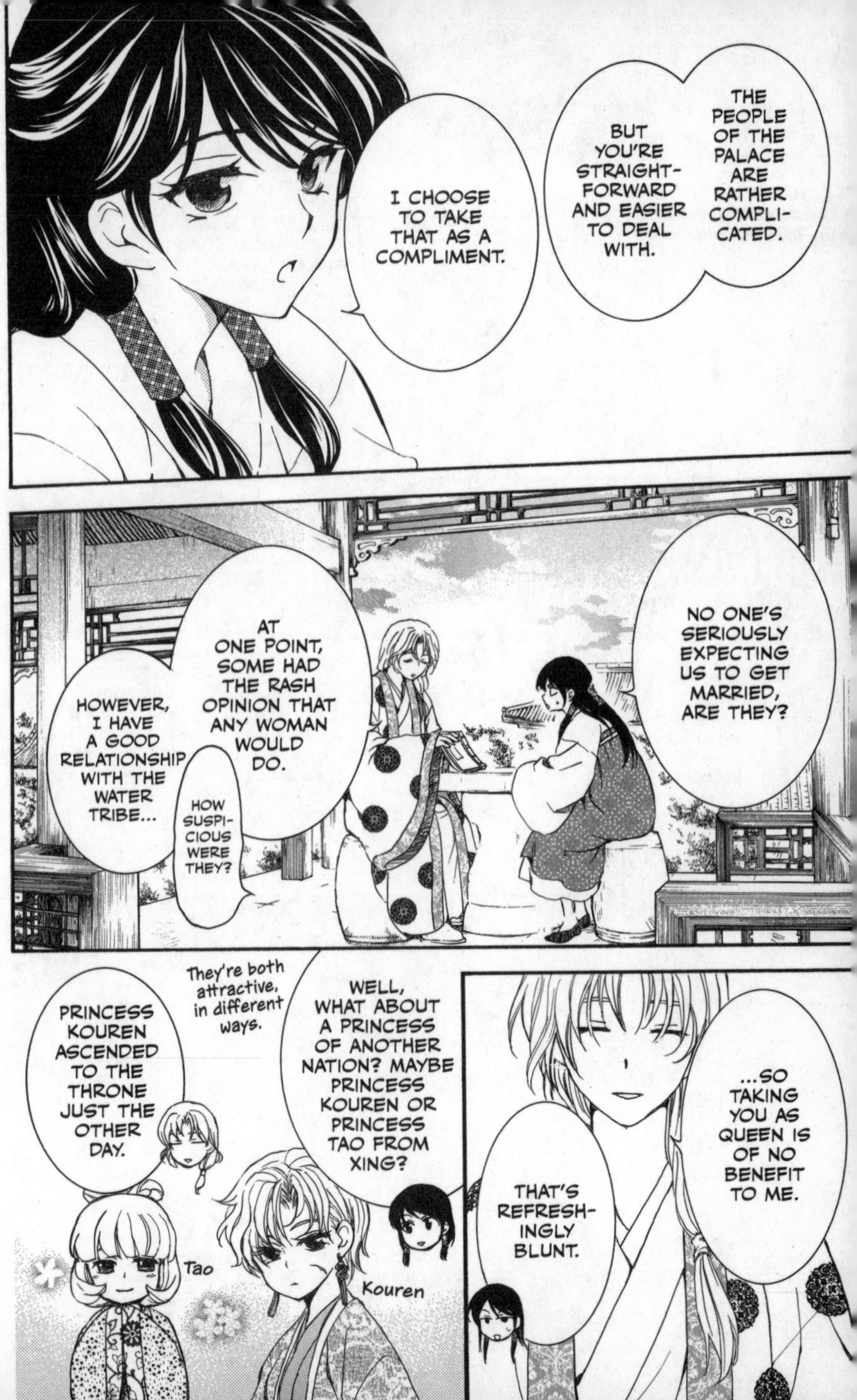
THE PEOPLE OF THE PALACE ARE RATHER COMPLICATED.
BUT YOU'RE STRAIGHT-FORWARD AND EASIER TO DEAL WITH.
I CHOOSE TO TAKE THAT AS A COMPLIMENT.
NO ONE'S SERIOUSLY EXPECTING US TO GET MARRIED, ARE THEY?
AT ONE POINT, SOME HAD THE RASH OPINION THAT ANY WOMAN WOULD DO.
HOWEVER, I HAVE A GOOD RELATIONSHIP WITH THE WATER TRIBE...
HOW SUSPICIOUS WERE THEY?
...SO TAKING YOU AS QUEEN IS OF NO BENEFIT TO ME.
THAT'S REFRESH-INGLY BLUNT.
WELL, WHAT ABOUT A PRINCESS OF ANOTHER NATION? MAYBE PRINCESS KOUREN OR PRINCESS TAO FROM XING?
They're both attractive, in different ways.
PRINCESS KOUREN ASCENDED TO THE THRONE JUST THE OTHER DAY.
Kouren
Tao

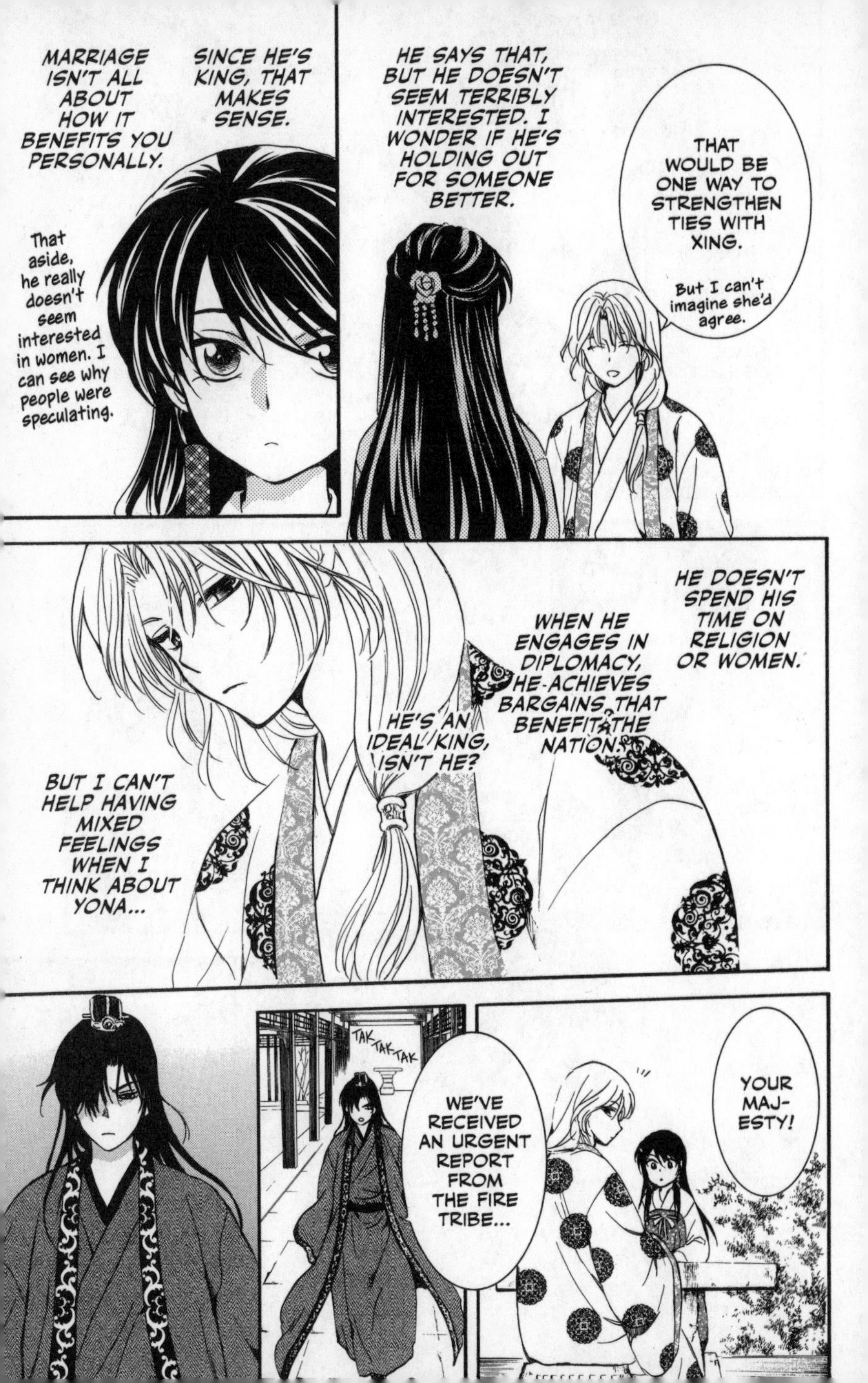
THAT WOULD BE ONE WAY TO STRENGTHEN TIES WITH XING.
But I can't imagine she'd agree.
HE SAYS THAT, BUT HE DOESN'T SEEM TERRIBLY INTERESTED. I WONDER IF HE'S HOLDING OUT FOR SOMEONE BETTER.
SINCE HE'S KING, THAT MAKES SENSE.
MARRIAGE ISN'T ALL ABOUT HOW IT BENEFITS YOU PERSONALLY.
That aside, he really doesn't seem interested in women. I can see why people were speculating.
HE DOESN'T SPEND HIS TIME ON RELIGION OR WOMEN.
WHEN HE ENGAGES IN DIPLOMACY, HE ACHIEVES BARGAINS THAT BENEFIT THE NATION.
HE'S AN IDEAL KING, ISN'T HE?
BUT I CAN'T HELP HAVING MIXED FEELINGS WHEN I THINK ABOUT YONA...
YOUR MAJESTY!
TAK TAK TAK
WE'VE RECEIVED AN URGENT REPORT FROM THE FIRE TRIBE...

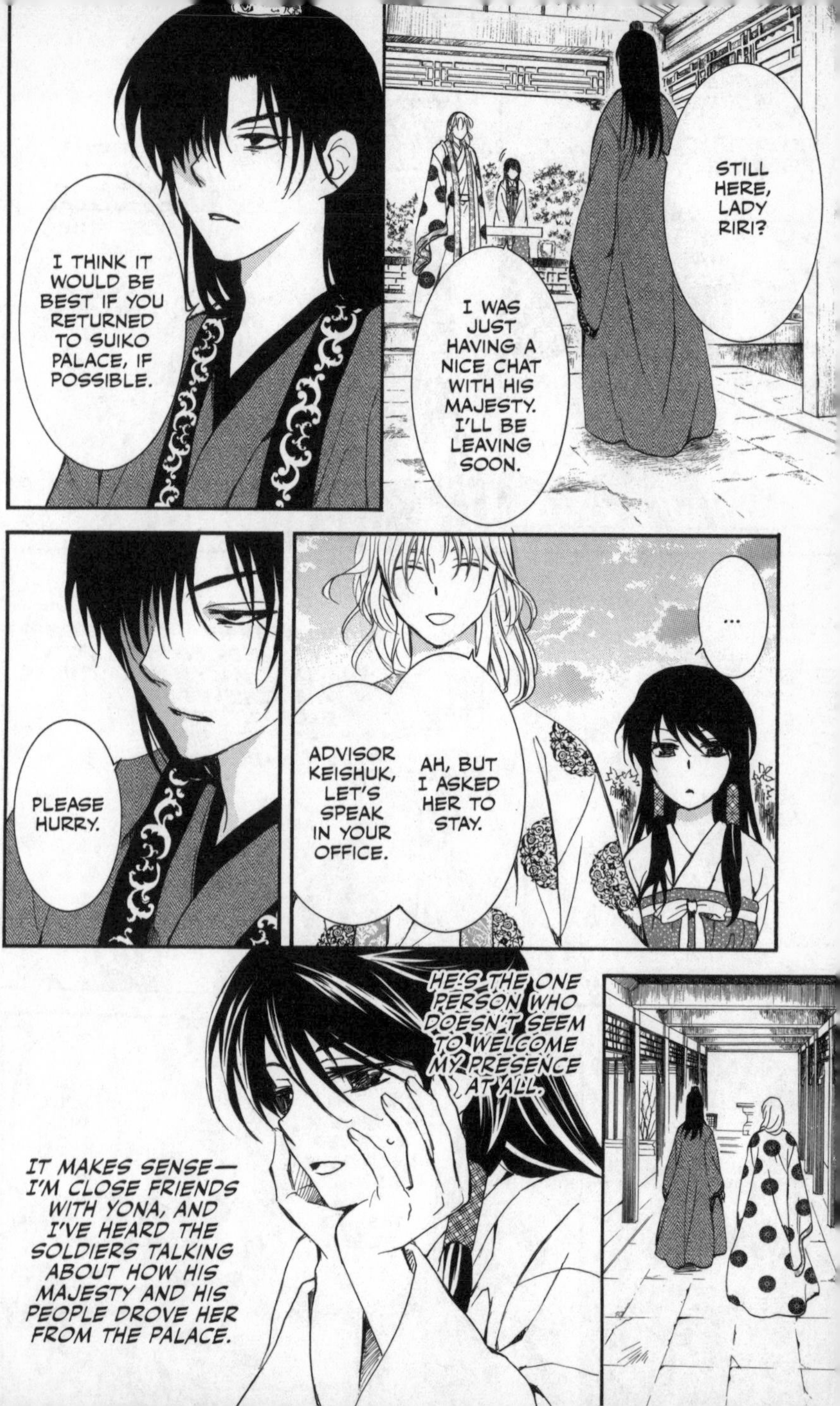
STILL HERE, LADY RIRI?
I WAS JUST HAVING A NICE CHAT WITH HIS MAJESTY. I'LL BE LEAVING SOON.
I THINK IT WOULD BE BEST IF YOU RETURNED TO SUIKO PALACE, IF POSSIBLE.
...
AH, BUT I ASKED HER TO STAY.
ADVISOR KEISHUK, LET'S SPEAK IN YOUR OFFICE.
PLEASE HURRY.
HE'S THE ONE PERSON WHO DOESN'T SEEM TO WELCOME MY PRESENCE AT ALL.
IT MAKES SENSE— I'M CLOSE FRIENDS WITH YONA, AND I'VE HEARD THE SOLDIERS TALKING ABOUT HOW HIS MAJESTY AND HIS PEOPLE DROVE HER FROM THE PALACE.

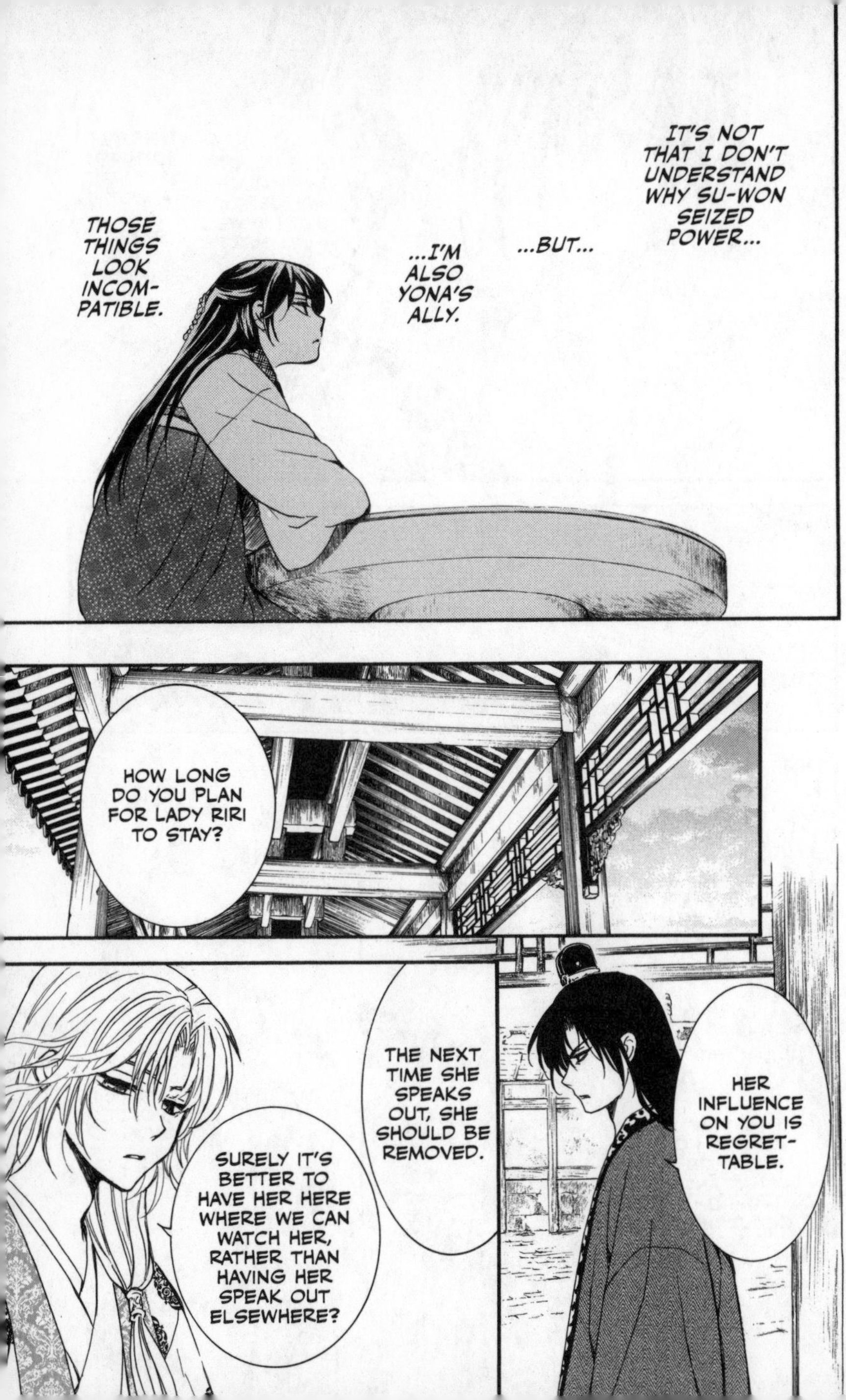
IT'S NOT THAT I DON'T UNDERSTAND WHY SU-WON SEIZED POWER...
...BUT...
...I'M ALSO YONA'S ALLY.
THOSE THINGS LOOK INCOMPATIBLE.
HOW LONG DO YOU PLAN FOR LADY RIRI TO STAY?
HER INFLUENCE ON YOU IS REGRETTABLE.
THE NEXT TIME SHE SPEAKS OUT, SHE SHOULD BE REMOVED.
SURELY IT'S BETTER TO HAVE HER HERE WHERE WE CAN WATCH HER, RATHER THAN HAVING HER SPEAK OUT ELSEWHERE?

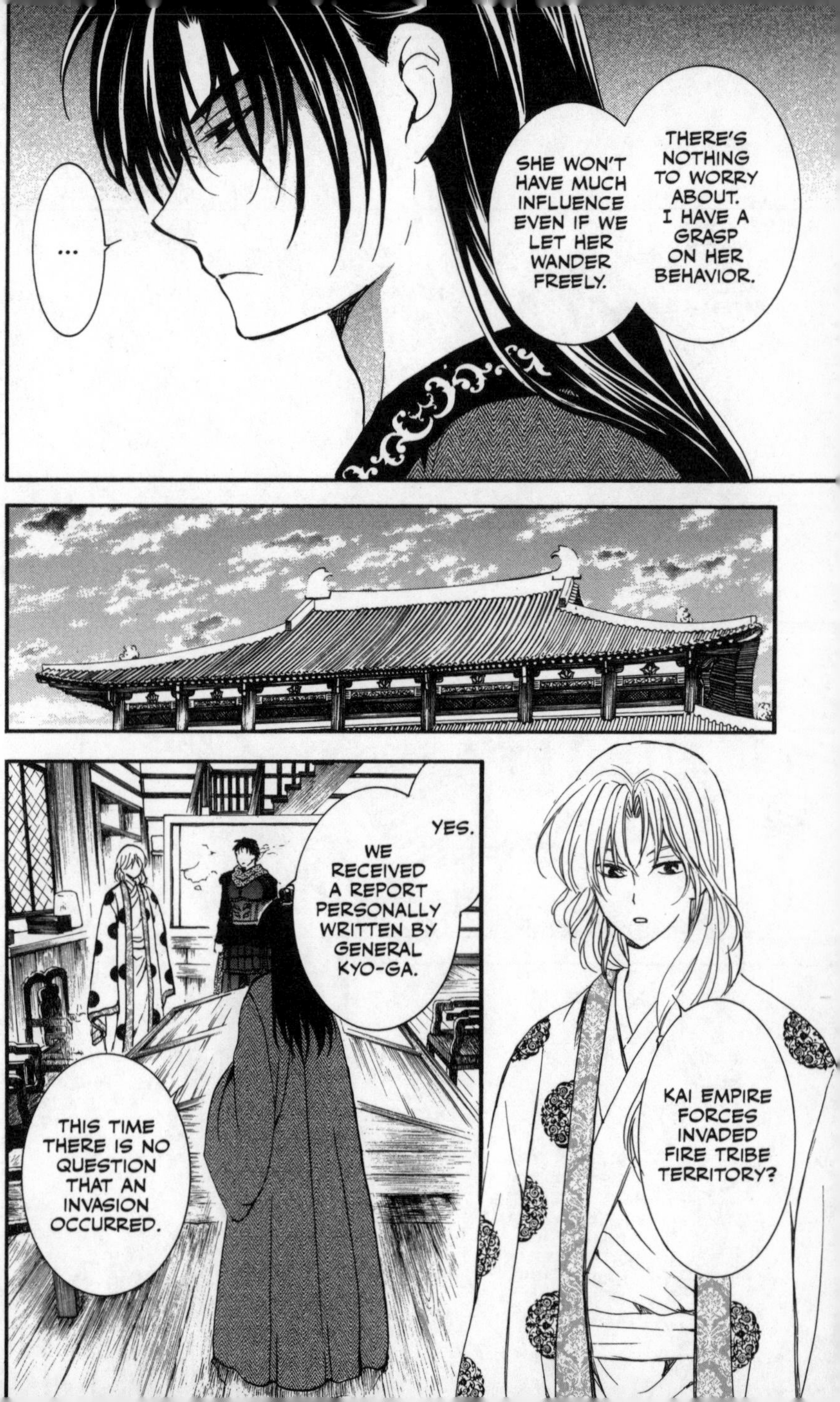
THERE'S NOTHING TO WORRY ABOUT. I HAVE A GRASP ON HER BEHAVIOR.
SHE WON'T HAVE MUCH INFLUENCE EVEN IF WE LET HER WANDER FREELY.
...
KAI EMPIRE FORCES INVADED FIRE TRIBE TERRITORY?
YES.
WE RECEIVED A REPORT PERSONALLY WRITTEN BY GENERAL KYO-GA.
THIS TIME THERE IS NO QUESTION THAT AN INVASION OCCURRED.

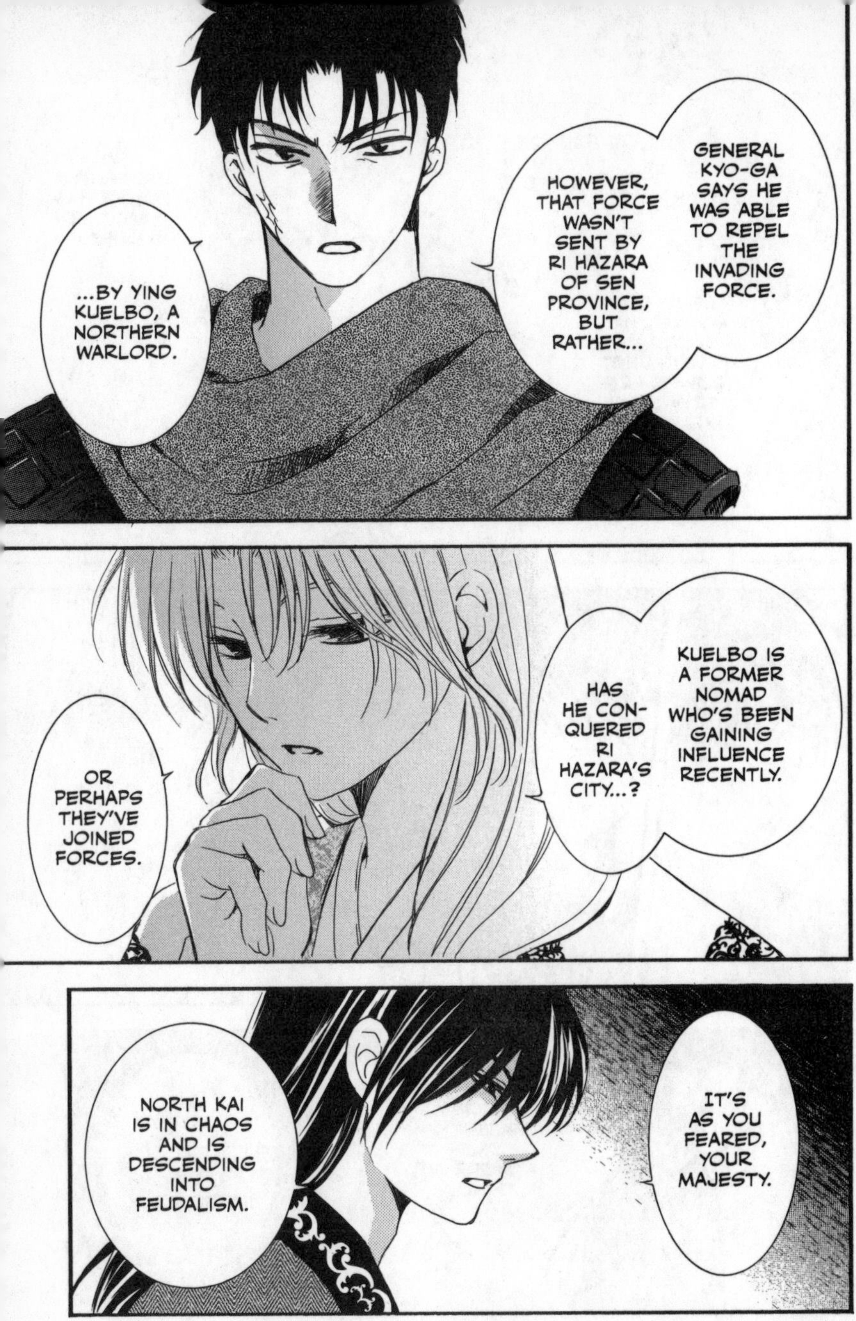
GENERAL KYO-GA SAYS HE WAS ABLE TO REPEL THE INVADING FORCE.
HOWEVER, THAT FORCE WASN'T SENT BY RI HAZARA OF SEN PROVINCE, BUT RATHER...
...BY YING KUELBO, A NORTHERN WARLORD.
KUELBO IS A FORMER NOMAD WHO'S BEEN GAINING INFLUENCE RECENTLY.
HAS HE CONQUERED RI HAZARA'S CITY...?
OR PERHAPS THEY'VE JOINED FORCES.
IT'S AS YOU FEARED, YOUR MAJESTY.
NORTH KAI IS IN CHAOS AND IS DESCENDING INTO FEUDALISM.

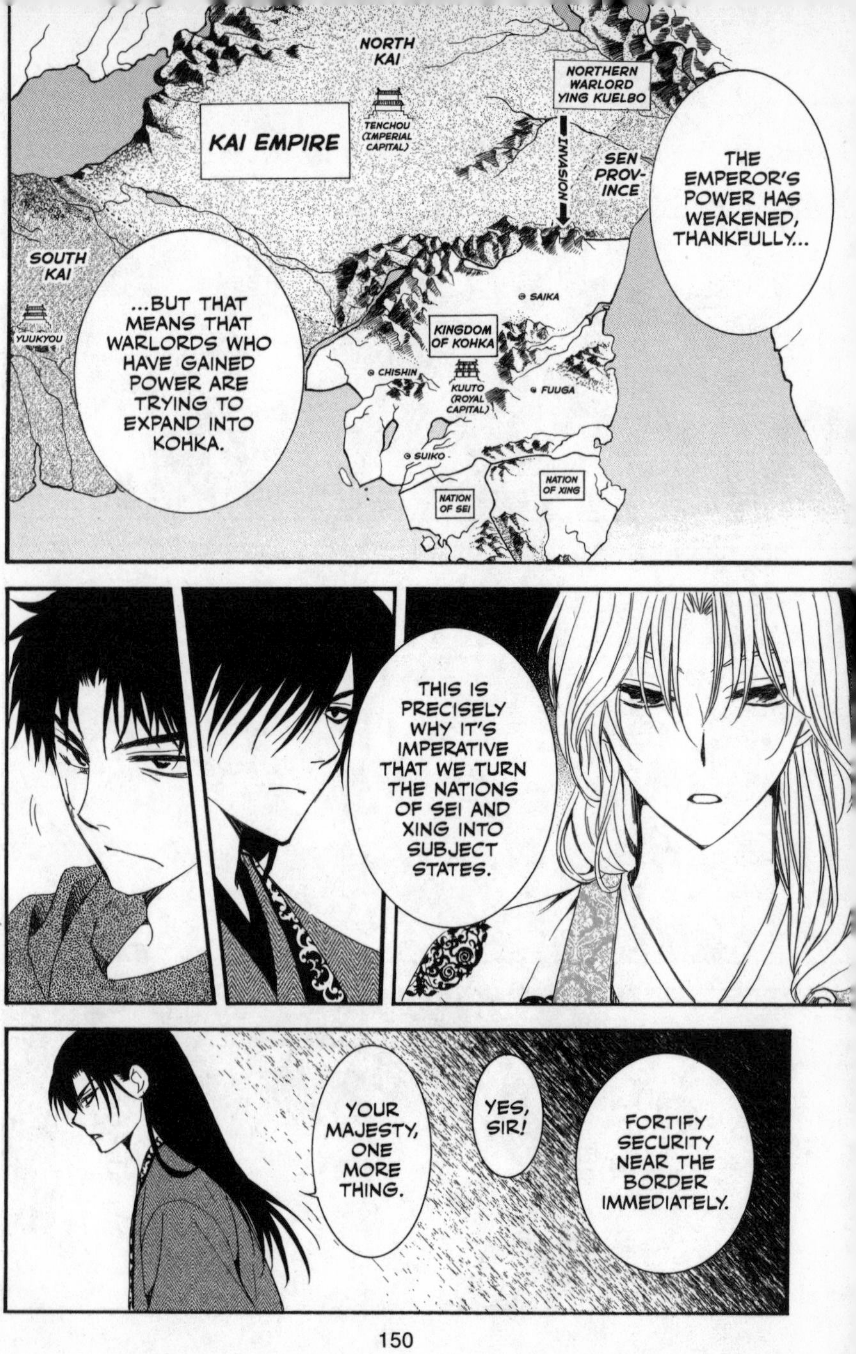
NORTH KAI
NORTHERN WARLORD YING KUELBO
KAI EMPIRE
TENCHOU (IMPERIAL CAPITAL)
INVASION
SEN PROVINCE
THE EMPEROR'S POWER HAS WEAKENED, THANKFULLY...
SOUTH KAI
YUUKYOU
...BUT THAT MEANS THAT WARLORDS WHO HAVE GAINED POWER ARE TRYING TO EXPAND INTO KOHKA.
SAIKA
KINGDOM OF KOHKA
CHISHIN
KUUTO (ROYAL CAPITAL)
FUUGA
SUIKO
NATION OF XING
NATION OF SEI
THIS IS PRECISELY WHY IT'S IMPERATIVE THAT WE TURN THE NATIONS OF SEI AND XING INTO SUBJECT STATES.
FORTIFY SECURITY NEAR THE BORDER IMMEDIATELY.
YES, SIR!
YOUR MAJESTY, ONE MORE THING.

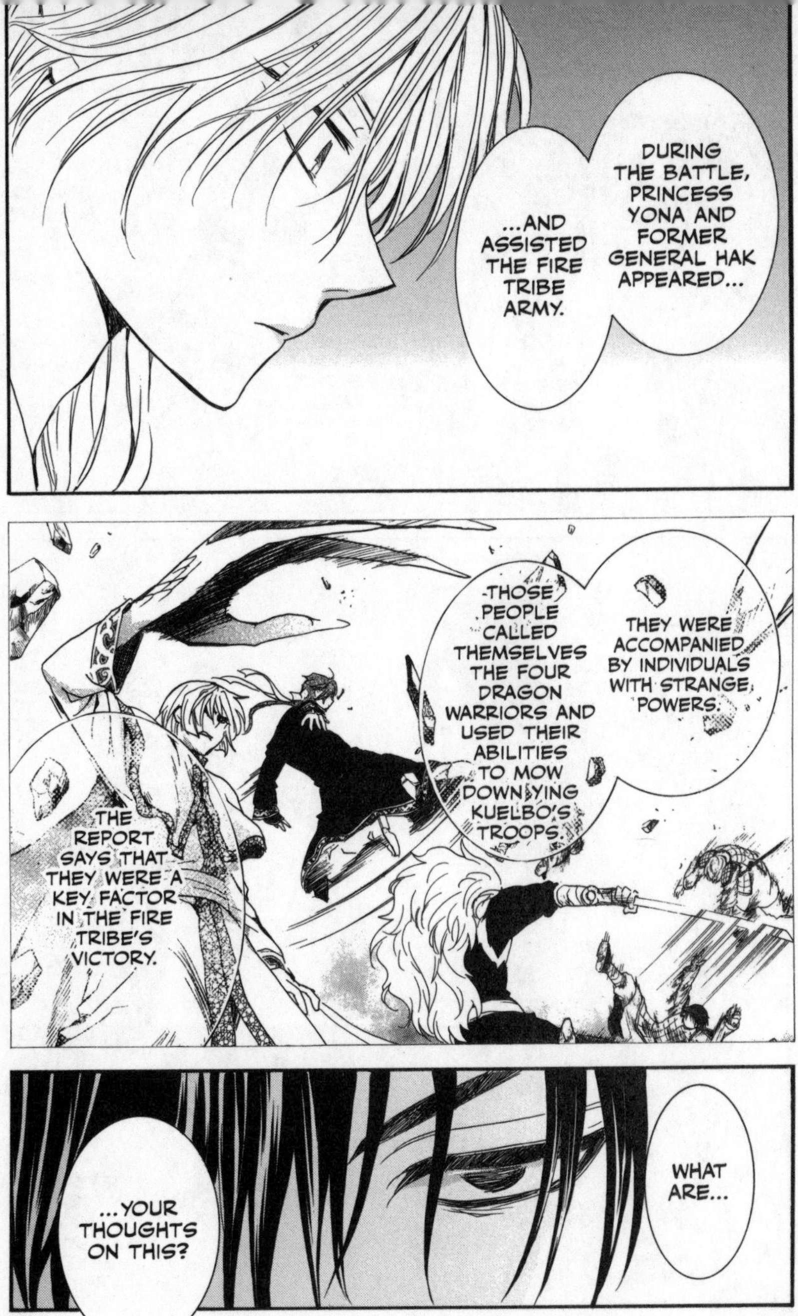
DURING THE BATTLE, PRINCESS YONA AND FORMER GENERAL HAK APPEARED...
...AND ASSISTED THE FIRE TRIBE ARMY.
THEY WERE ACCOMPANIED BY INDIVIDUALS WITH STRANGE POWERS.
THOSE PEOPLE CALLED THEMSELVES THE FOUR DRAGON WARRIORS AND USED THEIR ABILITIES TO MOW DOWN YING KUELBO'S TROOPS.
THE REPORT SAYS THAT THEY WERE A KEY FACTOR IN THE FIRE TRIBE'S VICTORY.
WHAT ARE...
...YOUR THOUGHTS ON THIS?

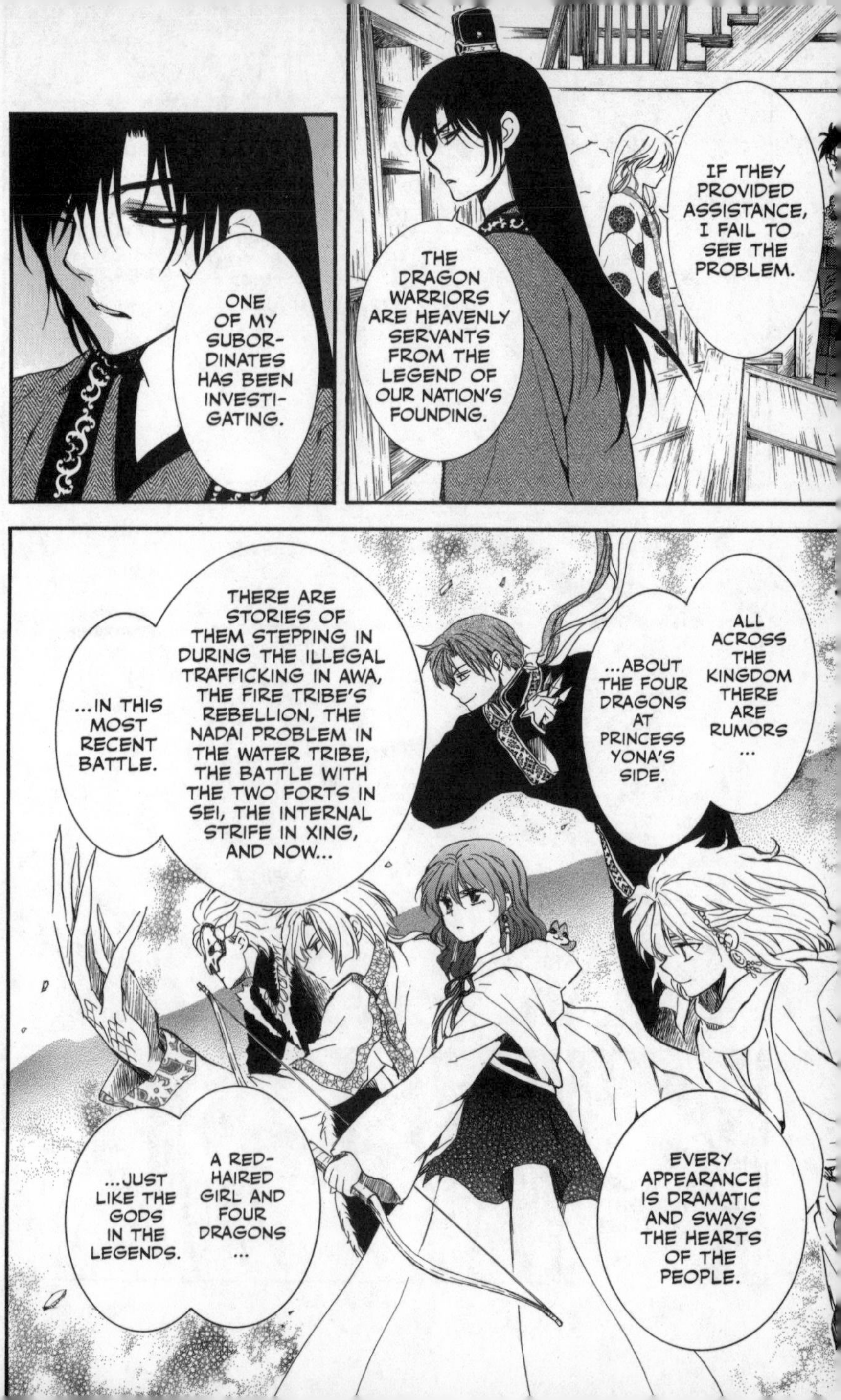
IF THEY PROVIDED ASSISTANCE, I FAIL TO SEE THE PROBLEM.
THE DRAGON WARRIORS ARE HEAVENLY SERVANTS FROM THE LEGEND OF OUR NATION'S FOUNDING.
ONE OF MY SUBOR-DINATES HAS BEEN INVESTI-GATING.
ALL ACROSS THE KINGDOM THERE ARE RUMORS...
...ABOUT THE FOUR DRAGONS AT PRINCESS YONA'S SIDE.
THERE ARE STORIES OF THEM STEPPING IN DURING THE ILLEGAL TRAFFICKING IN AWA, THE FIRE TRIBE'S REBELLION, THE NADAI PROBLEM IN THE WATER TRIBE, THE BATTLE WITH THE TWO FORTS IN SEI, THE INTERNAL STRIFE IN XING, AND NOW...
...IN THIS MOST RECENT BATTLE.
EVERY APPEARANCE IS DRAMATIC AND SWAYS THE HEARTS OF THE PEOPLE.
A RED-HAIRED GIRL AND FOUR DRAGONS...
...JUST LIKE THE GODS IN THE LEGENDS.

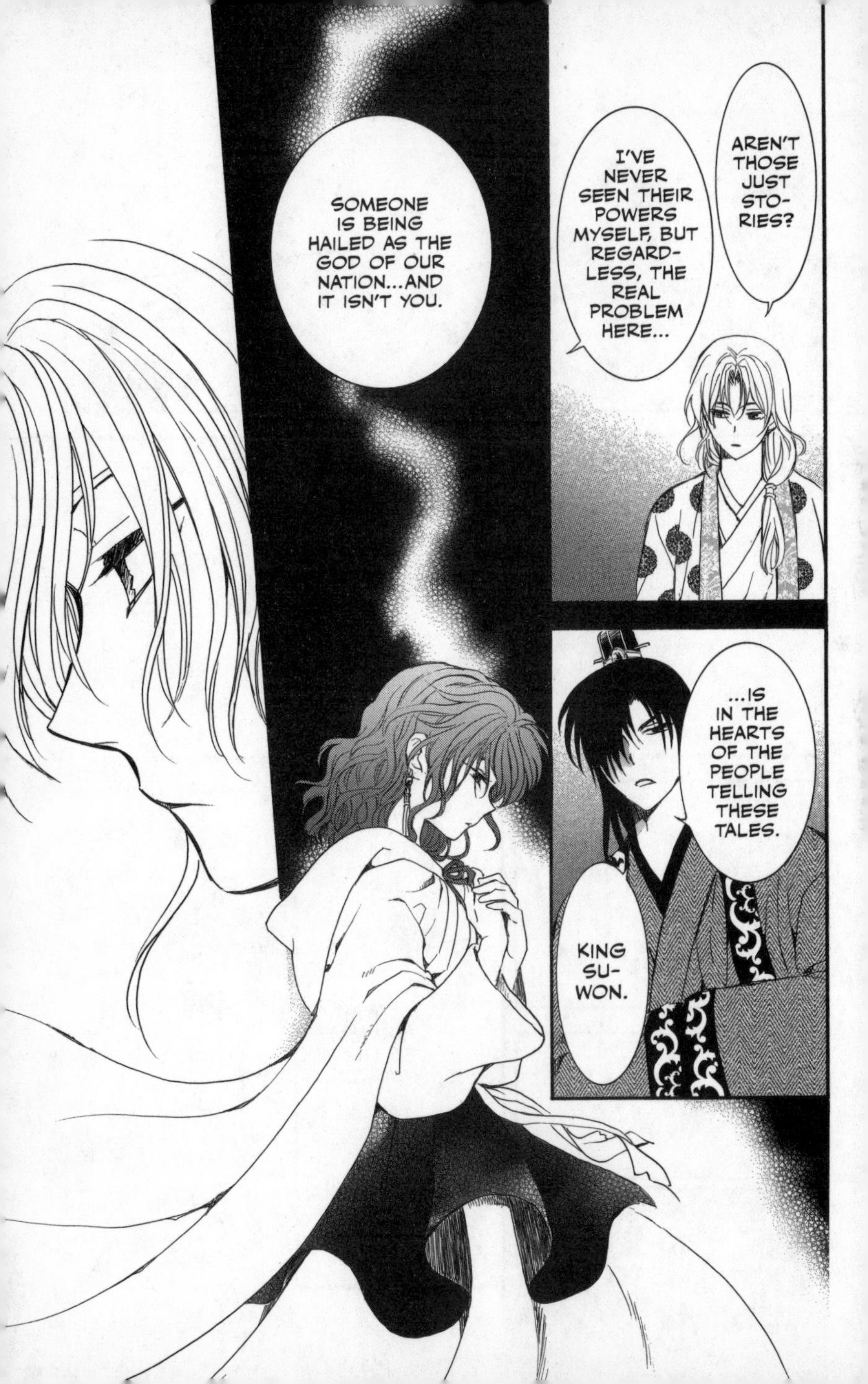
AREN'T THOSE JUST STO-RIES?
I'VE NEVER SEEN THEIR POWERS MYSELF, BUT REGARD-LESS, THE REAL PROBLEM HERE...
...IS IN THE HEARTS OF THE PEOPLE TELLING THESE TALES.
KING SU-WON.
SOMEONE IS BEING HAILED AS THE GOD OF OUR NATION...AND IT ISN'T YOU.

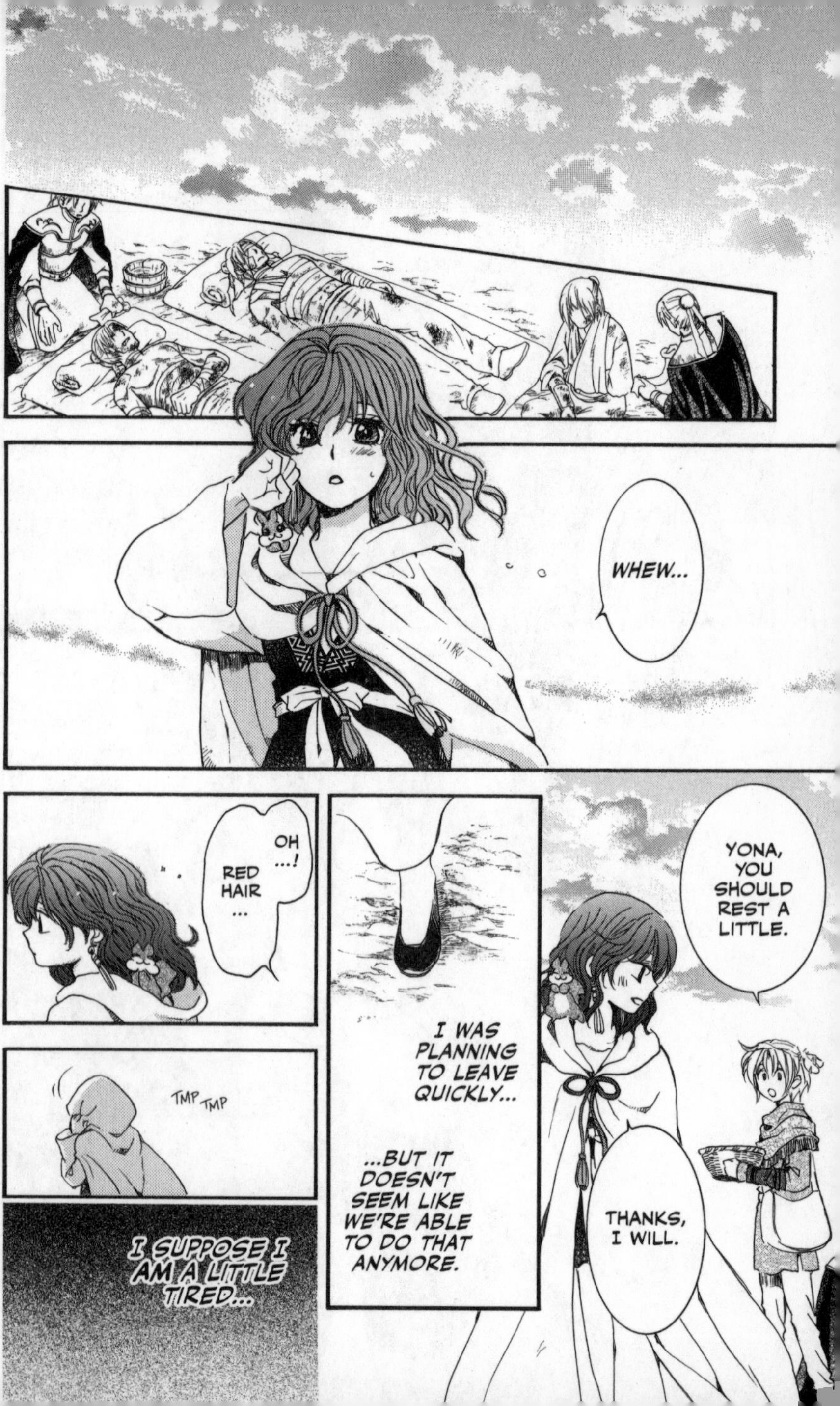
WHEW...
YONA, YOU SHOULD REST A LITTLE.
THANKS, I WILL.
I WAS PLANNING TO LEAVE QUICKLY...
...BUT IT DOESN'T SEEM LIKE WE'RE ABLE TO DO THAT ANYMORE.
OH ...! RED HAIR ...
TMP TMP
I SUPPOSE I AM A LITTLE TIRED...

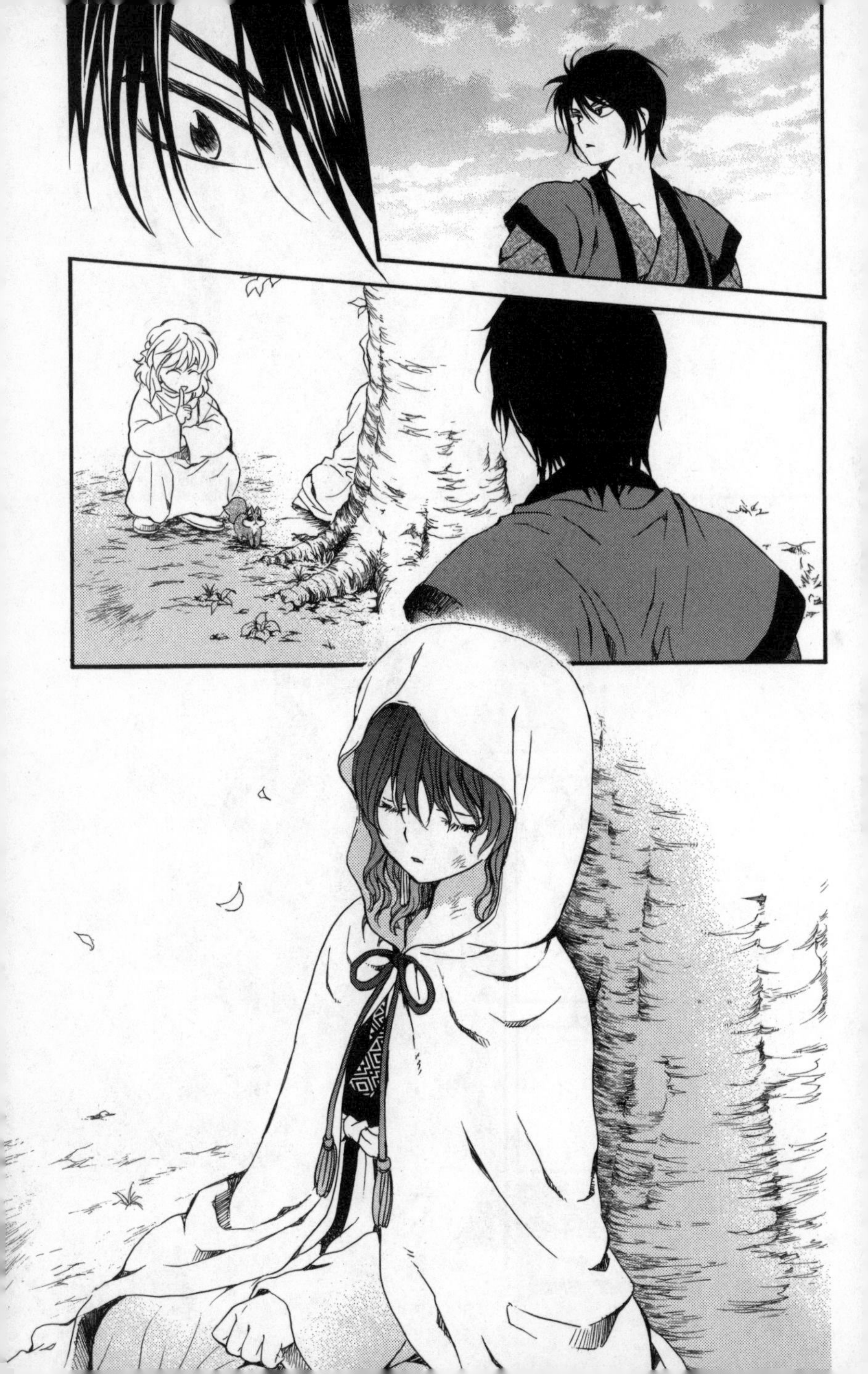

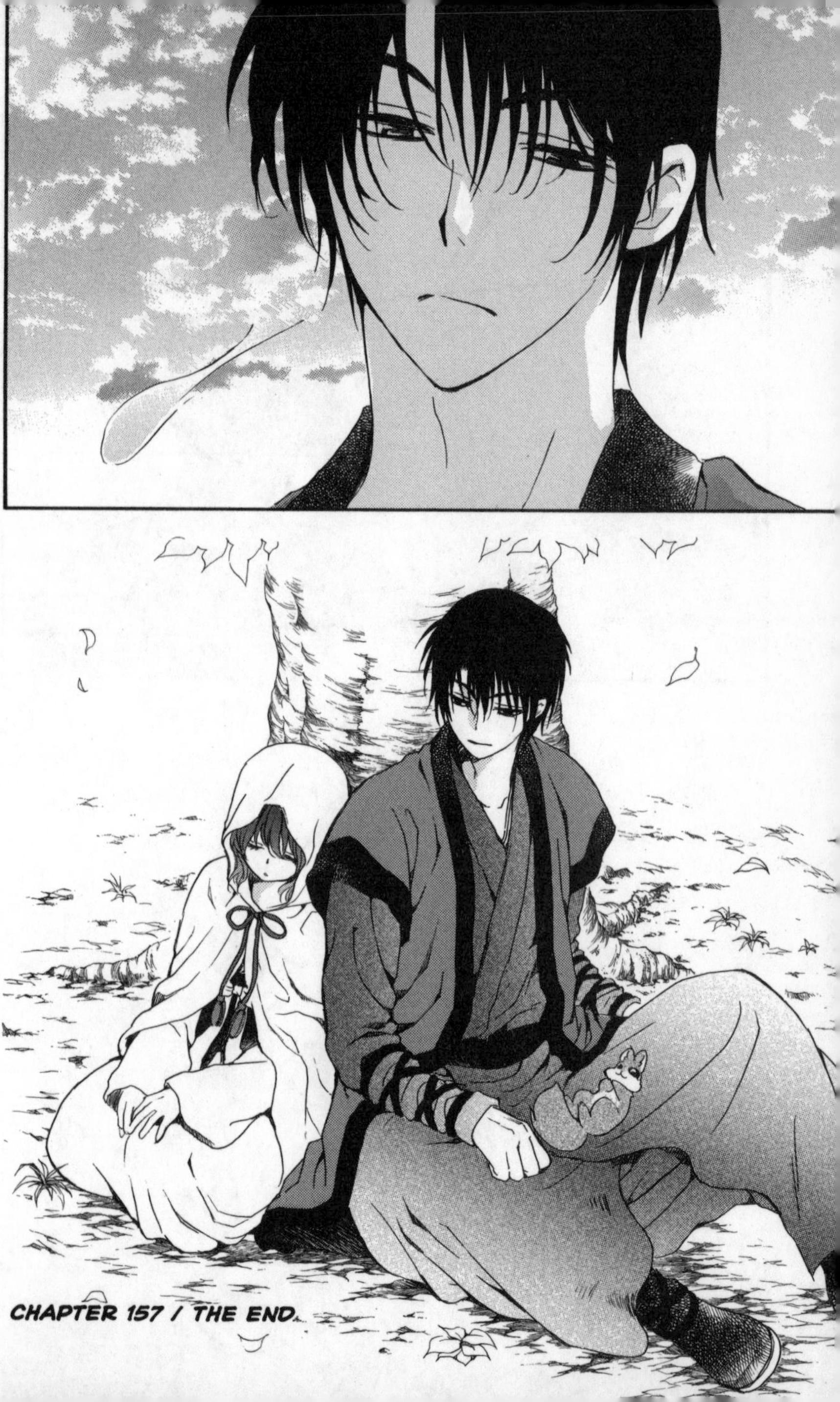
CHAPTER 157 / THE END

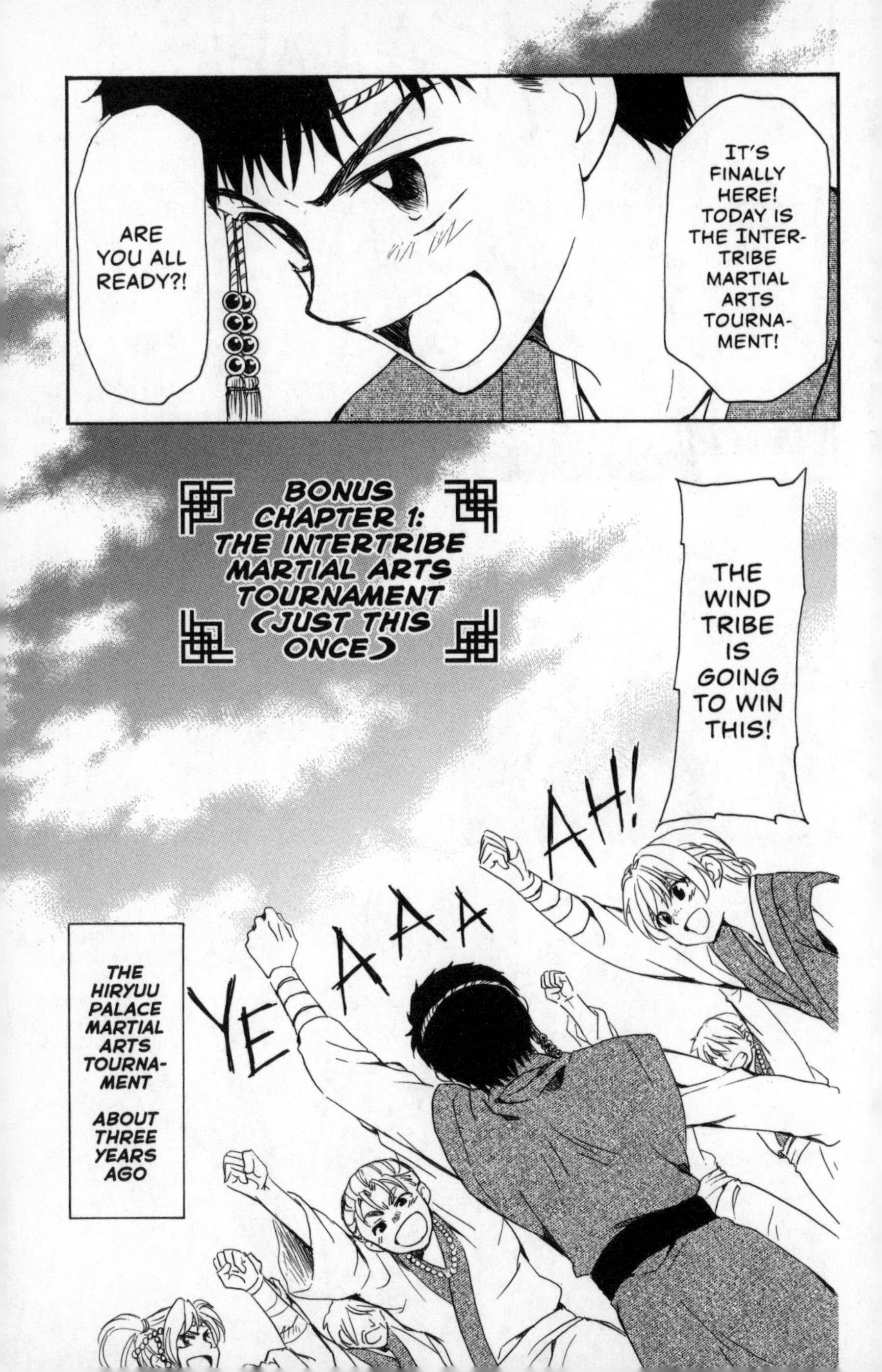

IT'S FINALLY HERE! TODAY IS THE INTER-TRIBE MARTIAL ARTS TOURNA-MENT!
ARE YOU ALL READY?!
THE WIND TRIBE IS GOING TO WIN THIS!
BONUS CHAPTER 1: THE INTERTRIBE MARTIAL ARTS TOURNAMENT (JUST THIS ONCE)
YEAAAAH!
THE HIRYUU PALACE MARTIAL ARTS TOURNA-MENT
ABOUT THREE YEARS AGO

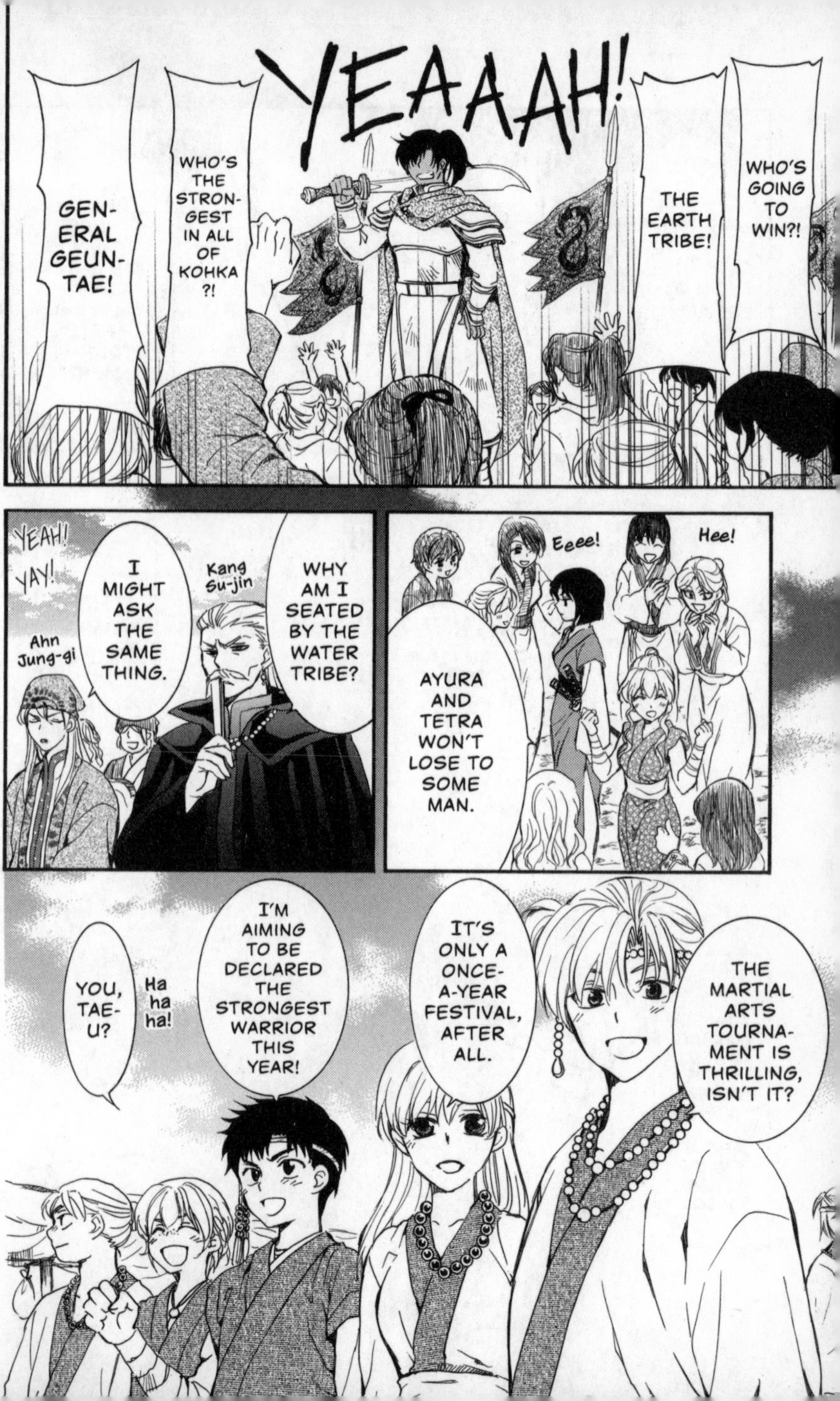
WHO'S GOING TO WIN?!
THE EARTH TRIBE!
YEAAAH!
WHO'S THE STRONGEST IN ALL OF KOHKA?!
GENERAL GEUNTAE!
Hee!
Eeee!
AYURA AND TETRA WON'T LOSE TO SOME MAN.
WHY AM I SEATED BY THE WATER TRIBE?
Kang Su-jin
I MIGHT ASK THE SAME THING.
Ahn Jung-gi
YEAH!
YAY!
THE MARTIAL ARTS TOURNAMENT IS THRILLING, ISN'T IT?
IT'S ONLY A ONCE-A-YEAR FESTIVAL, AFTER ALL.
I'M AIMING TO BE DECLARED THE STRONGEST WARRIOR THIS YEAR!
Ha ha ha!
YOU, TAE-U?

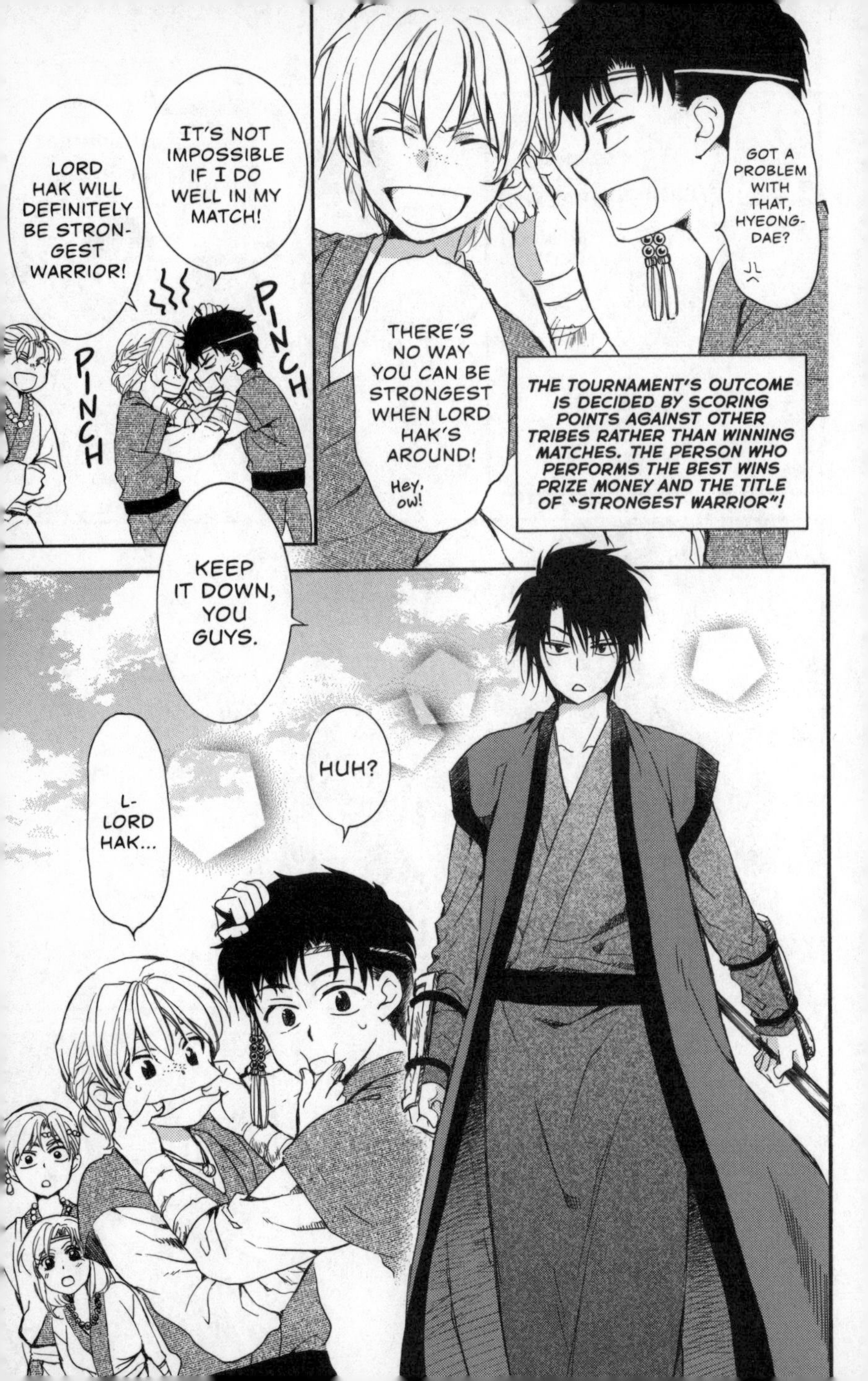
GOT A PROBLEM WITH THAT, HYEONG-DAE?
THERE'S NO WAY YOU CAN BE STRONGEST WHEN LORD HAK'S AROUND!
Hey, ow!
THE TOURNAMENT'S OUTCOME IS DECIDED BY SCORING POINTS AGAINST OTHER TRIBES RATHER THAN WINNING MATCHES. THE PERSON WHO PERFORMS THE BEST WINS PRIZE MONEY AND THE TITLE OF "STRONGEST WARRIOR"!
IT'S NOT IMPOSSIBLE IF I DO WELL IN MY MATCH!
PINCH
PINCH
LORD HAK WILL DEFINITELY BE STRONGEST WARRIOR!
KEEP IT DOWN, YOU GUYS.
HUH?
L-LORD HAK...

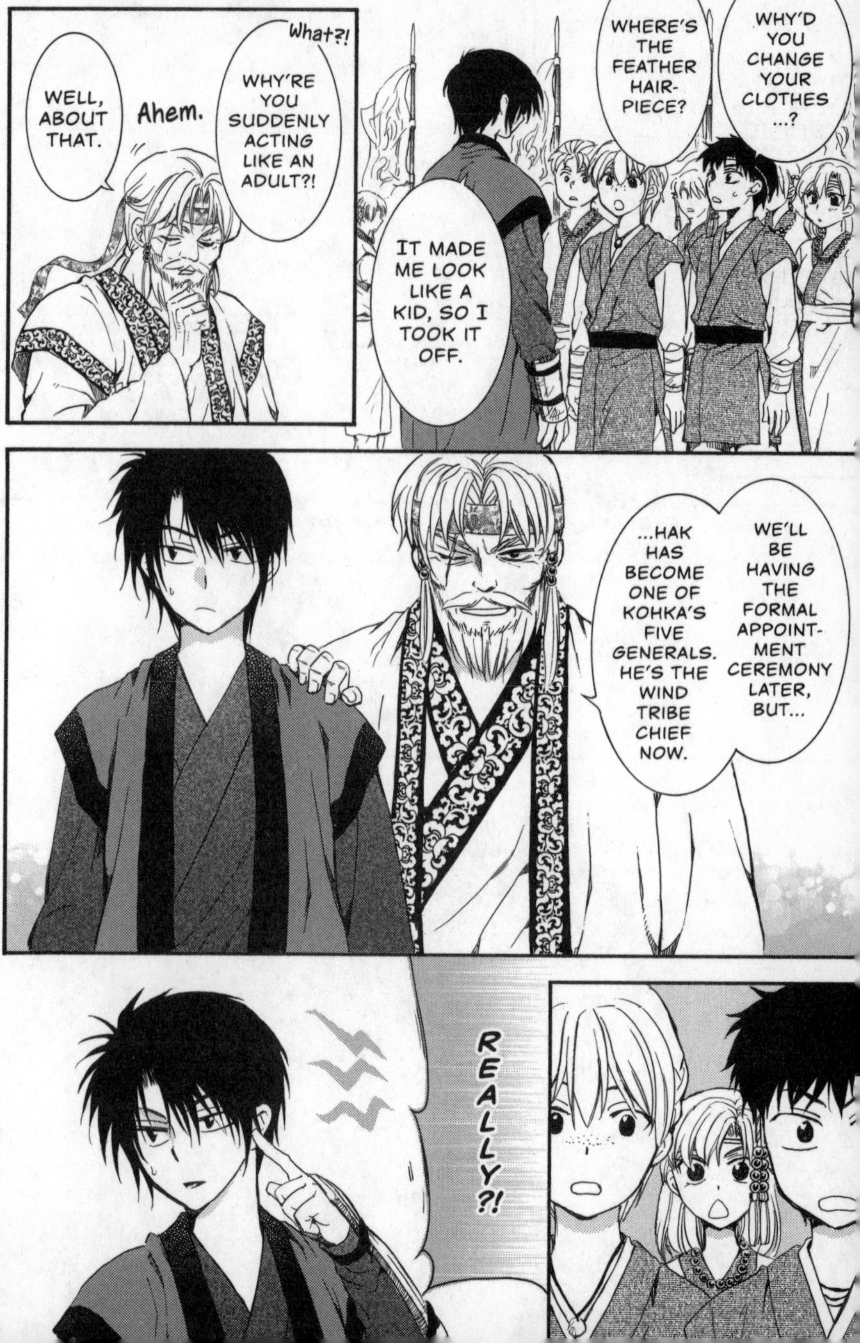
WHY'D YOU CHANGE YOUR CLOTHES ...?
WHERE'S THE FEATHER HAIR-PIECE?
IT MADE ME LOOK LIKE A KID, SO I TOOK IT OFF.
What?!
WHY'RE YOU SUDDENLY ACTING LIKE AN ADULT?!
Ahem.
WELL, ABOUT THAT.
WE'LL BE HAVING THE FORMAL APPOINT-MENT CEREMONY LATER, BUT...
...HAK HAS BECOME ONE OF KOHKA'S FIVE GENERALS. HE'S THE WIND TRIBE CHIEF NOW.
REALLY?!

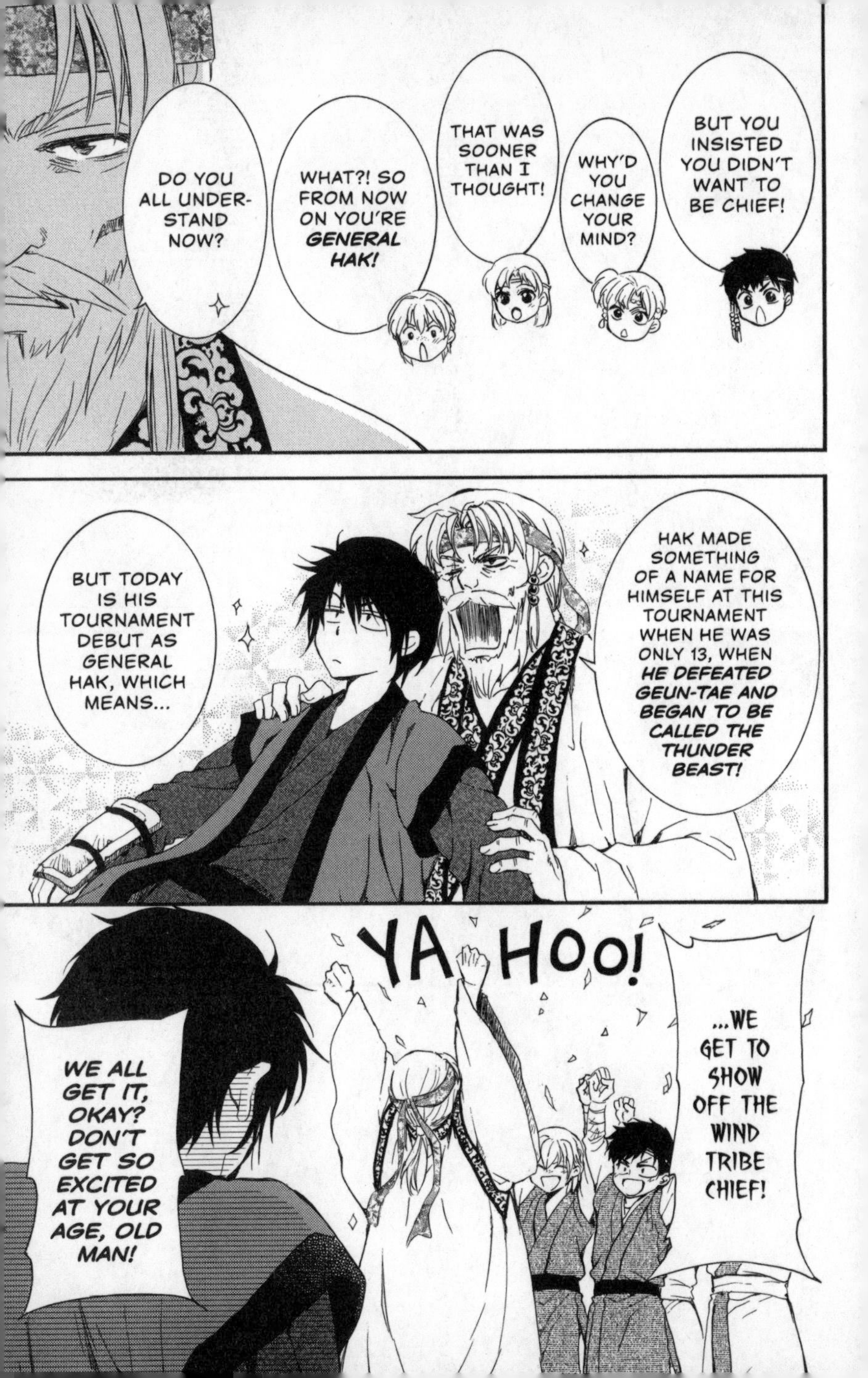
BUT YOU INSISTED YOU DIDN'T WANT TO BE CHIEF!
WHY'D YOU CHANGE YOUR MIND?
THAT WAS SOONER THAN I THOUGHT!
WHAT?! SO FROM NOW ON YOU'RE **GENERAL HAK!**
DO YOU ALL UNDER-STAND NOW?
HAK MADE SOMETHING OF A NAME FOR HIMSELF AT THIS TOURNAMENT WHEN HE WAS ONLY 13, WHEN **HE DEFEATED GEUN-TAE AND BEGAN TO BE CALLED THE THUNDER BEAST!**
BUT TODAY IS HIS TOURNAMENT DEBUT AS GENERAL HAK, WHICH MEANS...
...WE GET TO SHOW OFF THE WIND TRIBE CHIEF!
YA HOO!
WE ALL GET IT, OKAY? DON'T GET SO EXCITED AT YOUR AGE, OLD MAN!

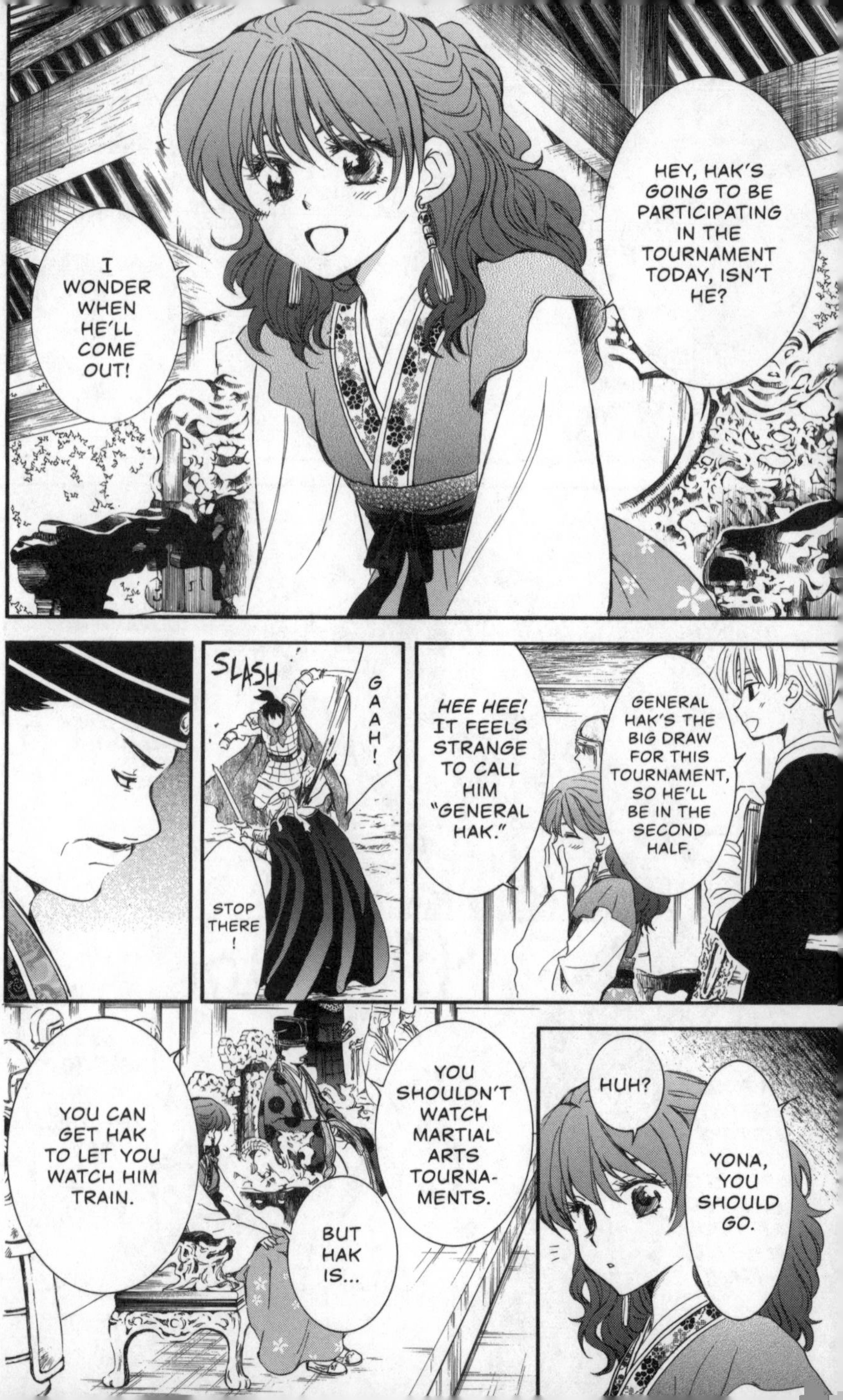
HEY, HAK'S GOING TO BE PARTICIPATING IN THE TOURNAMENT TODAY, ISN'T HE?
I WONDER WHEN HE'LL COME OUT!
GENERAL HAK'S THE BIG DRAW FOR THIS TOURNAMENT, SO HE'LL BE IN THE SECOND HALF.
HEE HEE! IT FEELS STRANGE TO CALL HIM "GENERAL HAK."
SLASH
GAAH!
STOP THERE!
HUH?
YONA, YOU SHOULD GO.
YOU SHOULDN'T WATCH MARTIAL ARTS TOURNA-MENTS.
BUT HAK IS...
YOU CAN GET HAK TO LET YOU WATCH HIM TRAIN.

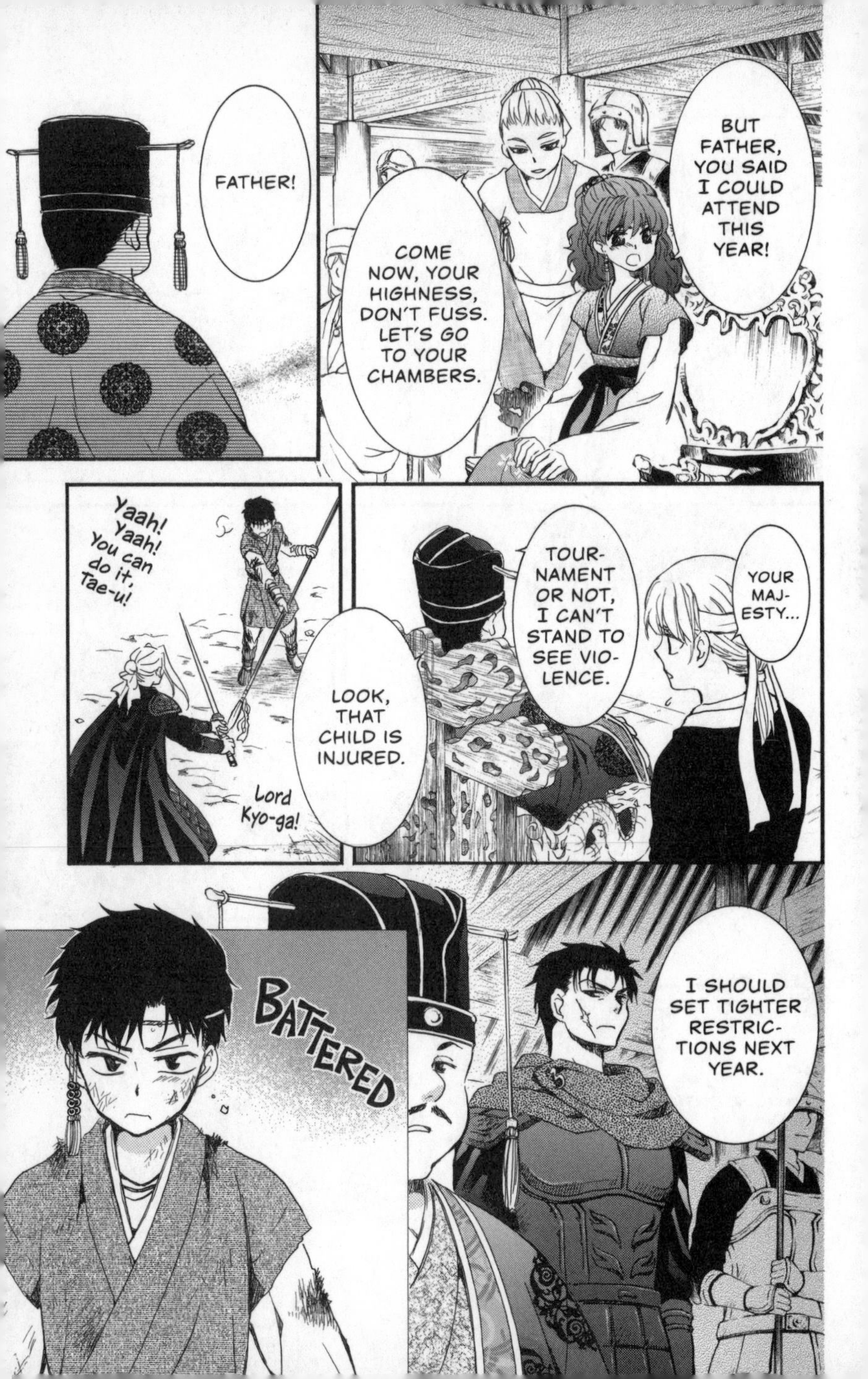
BUT FATHER, YOU SAID I COULD ATTEND THIS YEAR!
COME NOW, YOUR HIGHNESS, DON'T FUSS. LET'S GO TO YOUR CHAMBERS.
FATHER!
YOUR MAJ-ESTY...
TOUR-NAMENT OR NOT, I CAN'T STAND TO SEE VIO-LENCE.
LOOK, THAT CHILD IS INJURED.
Yaah! Yaah! You can do it, Tae-u!
Lord Kyo-ga!
I SHOULD SET TIGHTER RESTRIC-TIONS NEXT YEAR.
BATTERED

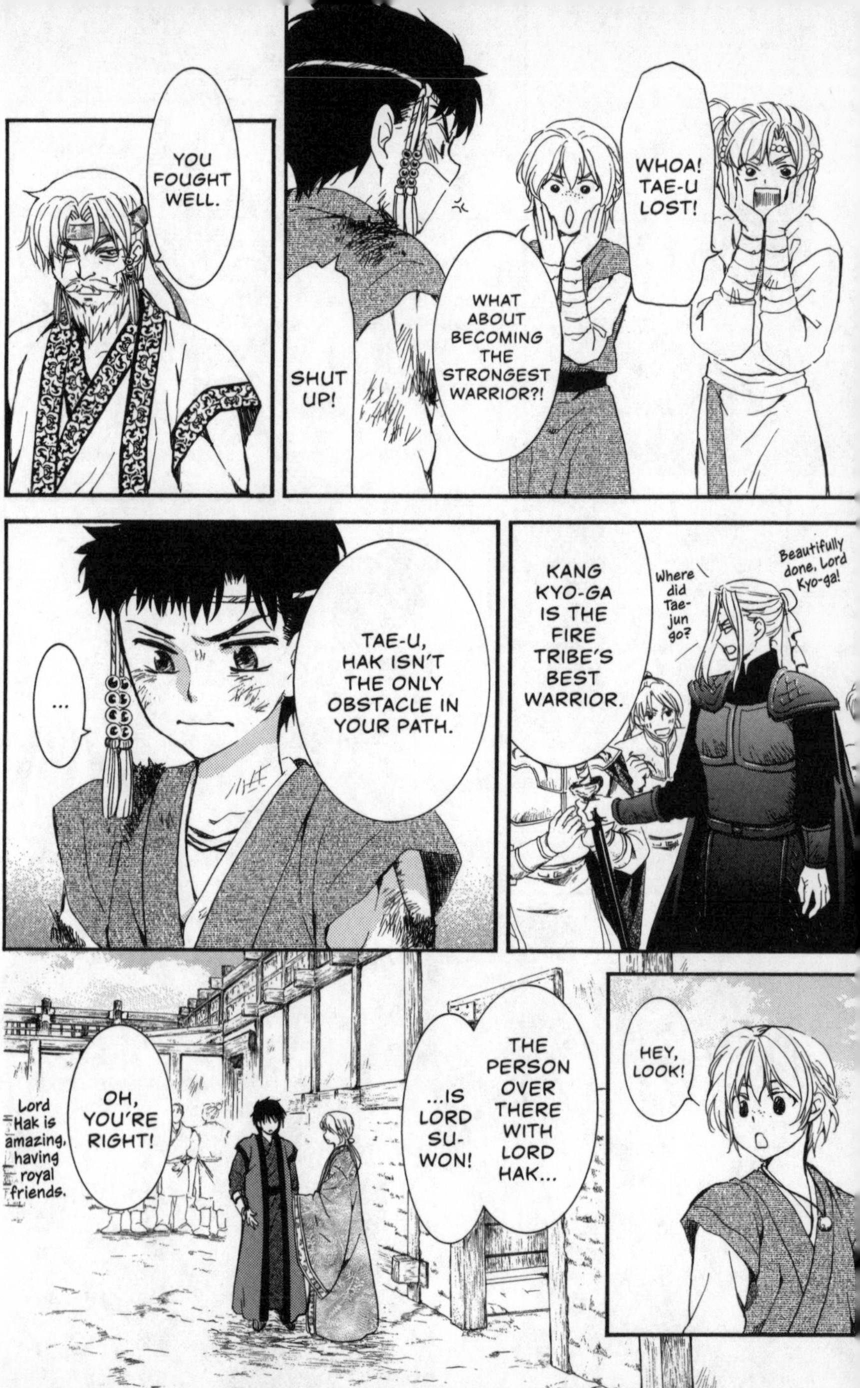
WHOA! TAE-U LOST!
WHAT ABOUT BECOMING THE STRONGEST WARRIOR?!
SHUT UP!
YOU FOUGHT WELL.
Beautifully done, Lord Kyo-ga!
Where did Tae-jun go?
KANG KYO-GA IS THE FIRE TRIBE'S BEST WARRIOR.
TAE-U, HAK ISN'T THE ONLY OBSTACLE IN YOUR PATH.
...
HEY, LOOK!
THE PERSON OVER THERE WITH LORD HAK...
...IS LORD SU-WON!
OH, YOU'RE RIGHT!
Lord Hak is amazing, having royal friends.

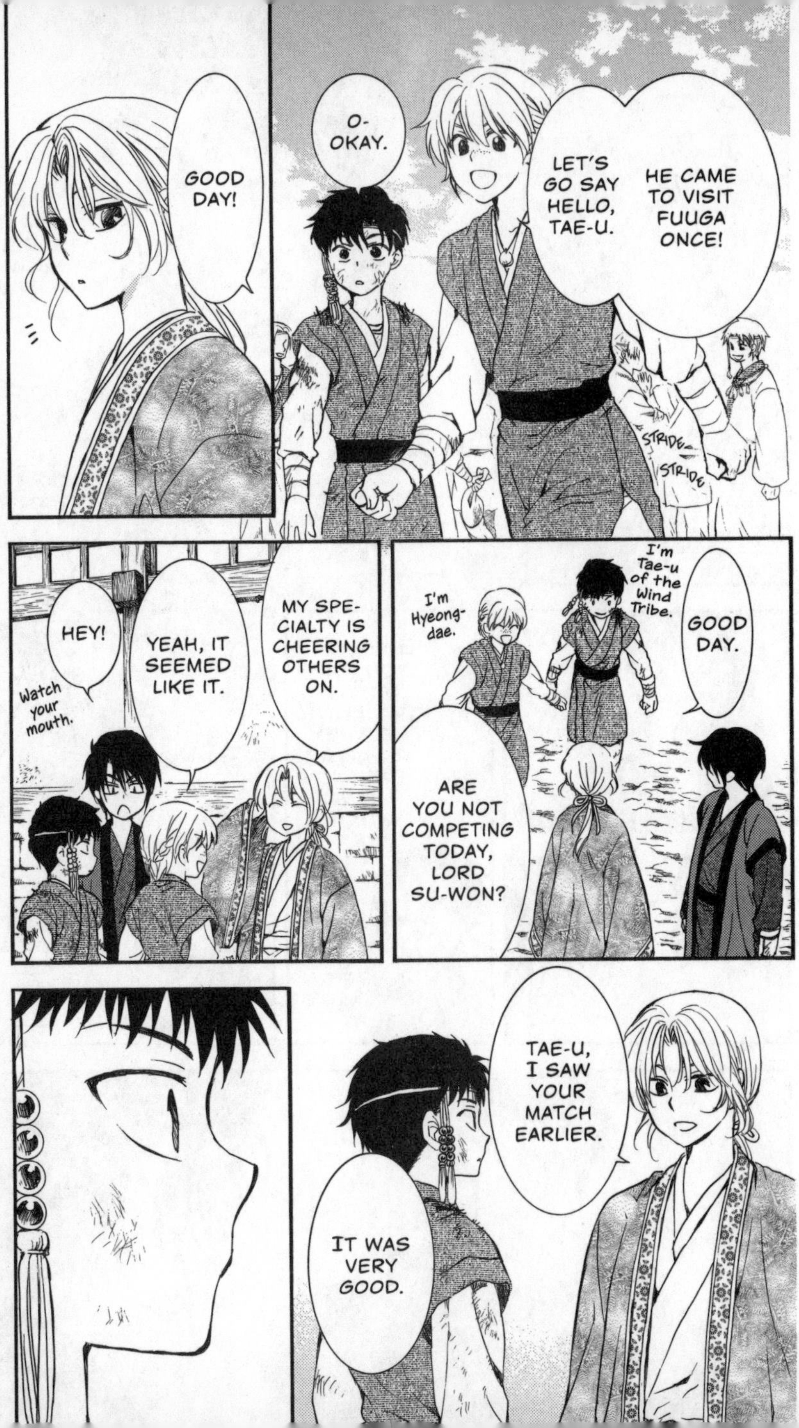
HE CAME TO VISIT FUUGA ONCE!
LET'S GO SAY HELLO, TAE-U.
O-OKAY.
STRIDE
STRIDE
GOOD DAY!
GOOD DAY.
I'm Tae-u of the Wind Tribe.
I'm Hyeong-dae.
ARE YOU NOT COMPETING TODAY, LORD SU-WON?
MY SPECIALTY IS CHEERING OTHERS ON.
YEAH, IT SEEMED LIKE IT.
HEY!
Watch your mouth.
TAE-U, I SAW YOUR MATCH EARLIER.
IT WAS VERY GOOD.

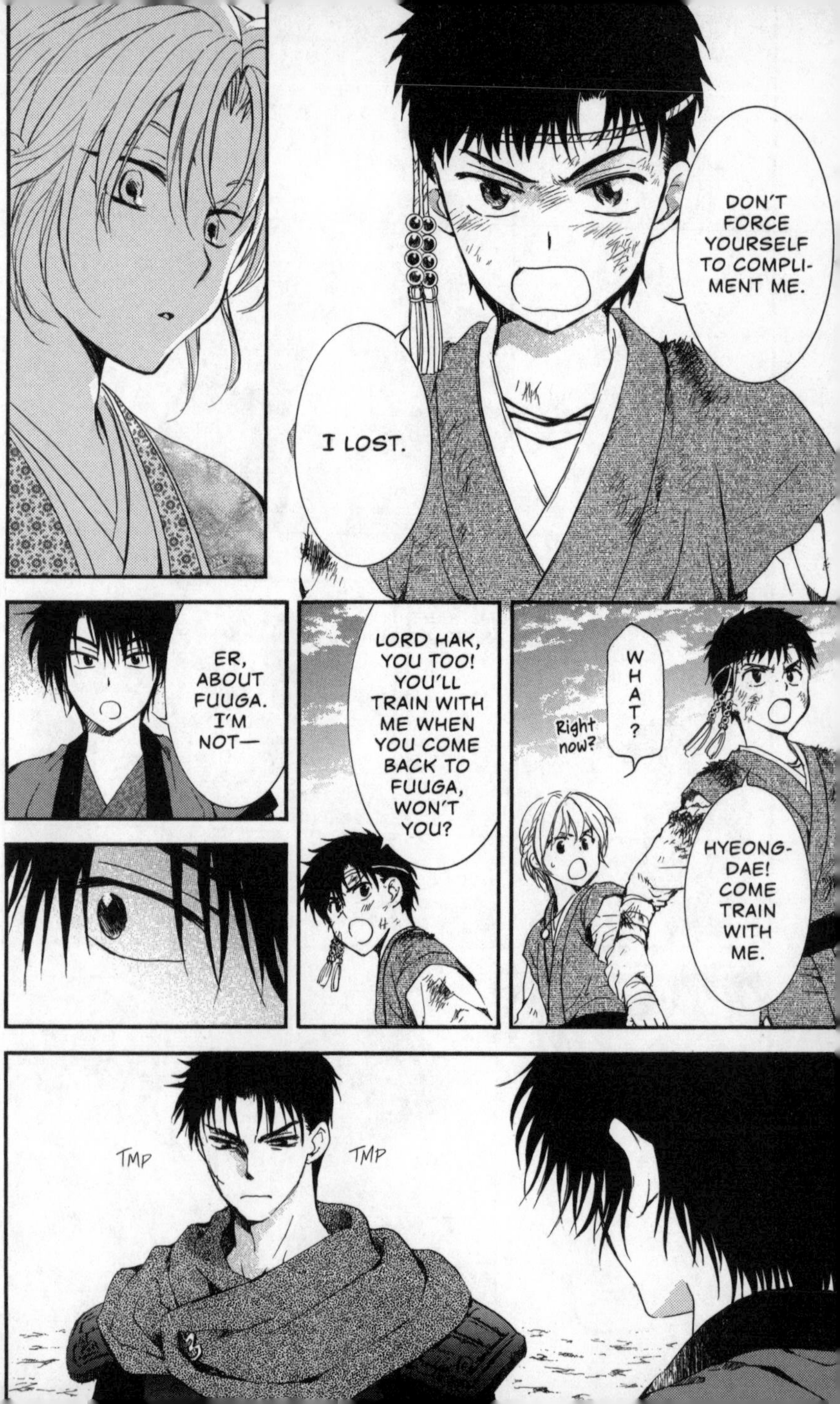

DON'T FORCE YOURSELF TO COMPLIMENT ME.
I LOST.
HYEONG-DAE! COME TRAIN WITH ME.
WHAT?
Right now?
LORD HAK, YOU TOO! YOU'LL TRAIN WITH ME WHEN YOU COME BACK TO FUUGA, WON'T YOU?
ER, ABOUT FUUGA. I'M NOT—
TMP
TMP

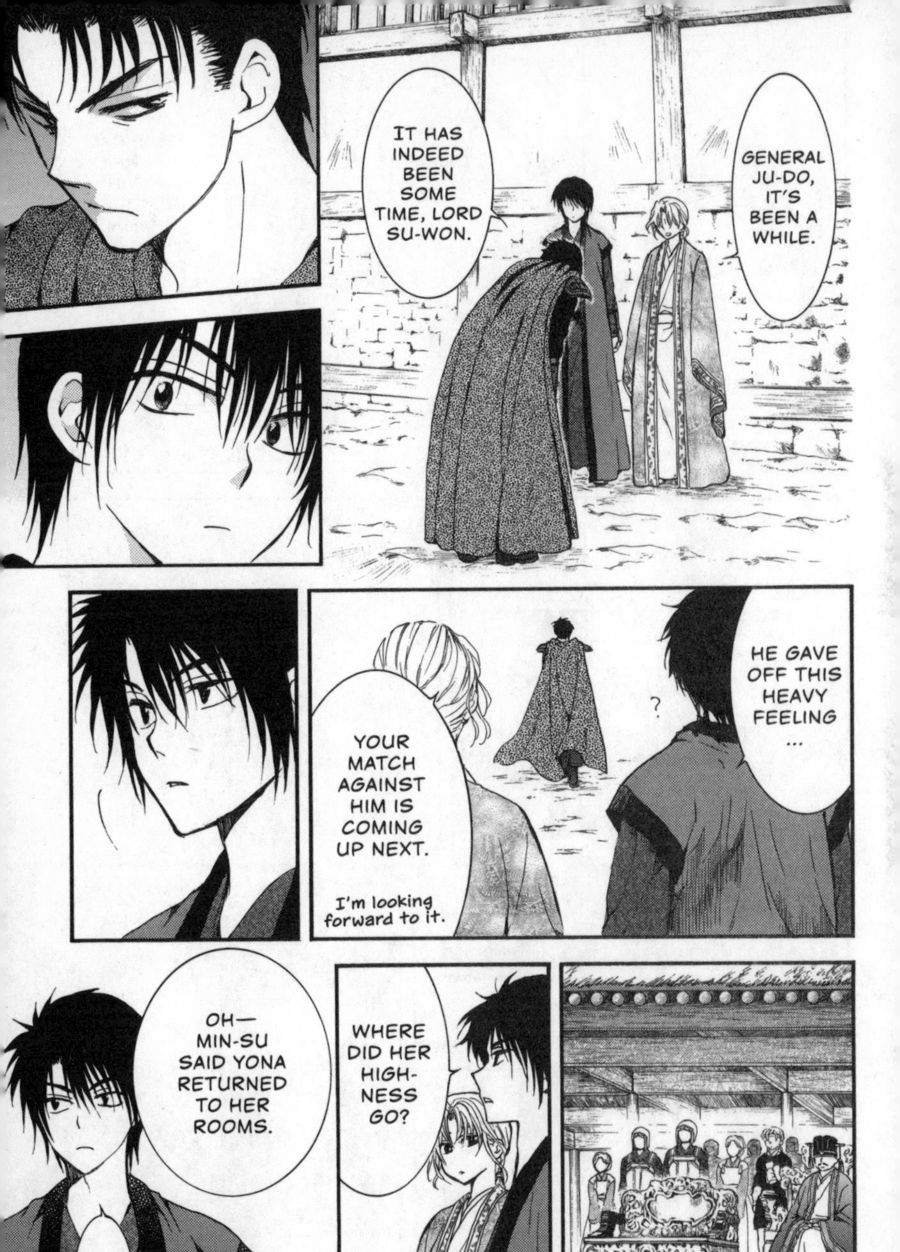
GENERAL JU-DO, IT'S BEEN A WHILE.
IT HAS INDEED BEEN SOME TIME, LORD SU-WON.
HE GAVE OFF THIS HEAVY FEELING ...
?
YOUR MATCH AGAINST HIM IS COMING UP NEXT.
I'm looking forward to it.
WHERE DID HER HIGHNESS GO?
OH— MIN-SU SAID YONA RETURNED TO HER ROOMS.
HMM ...

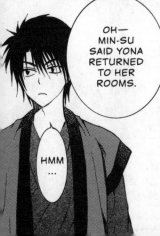

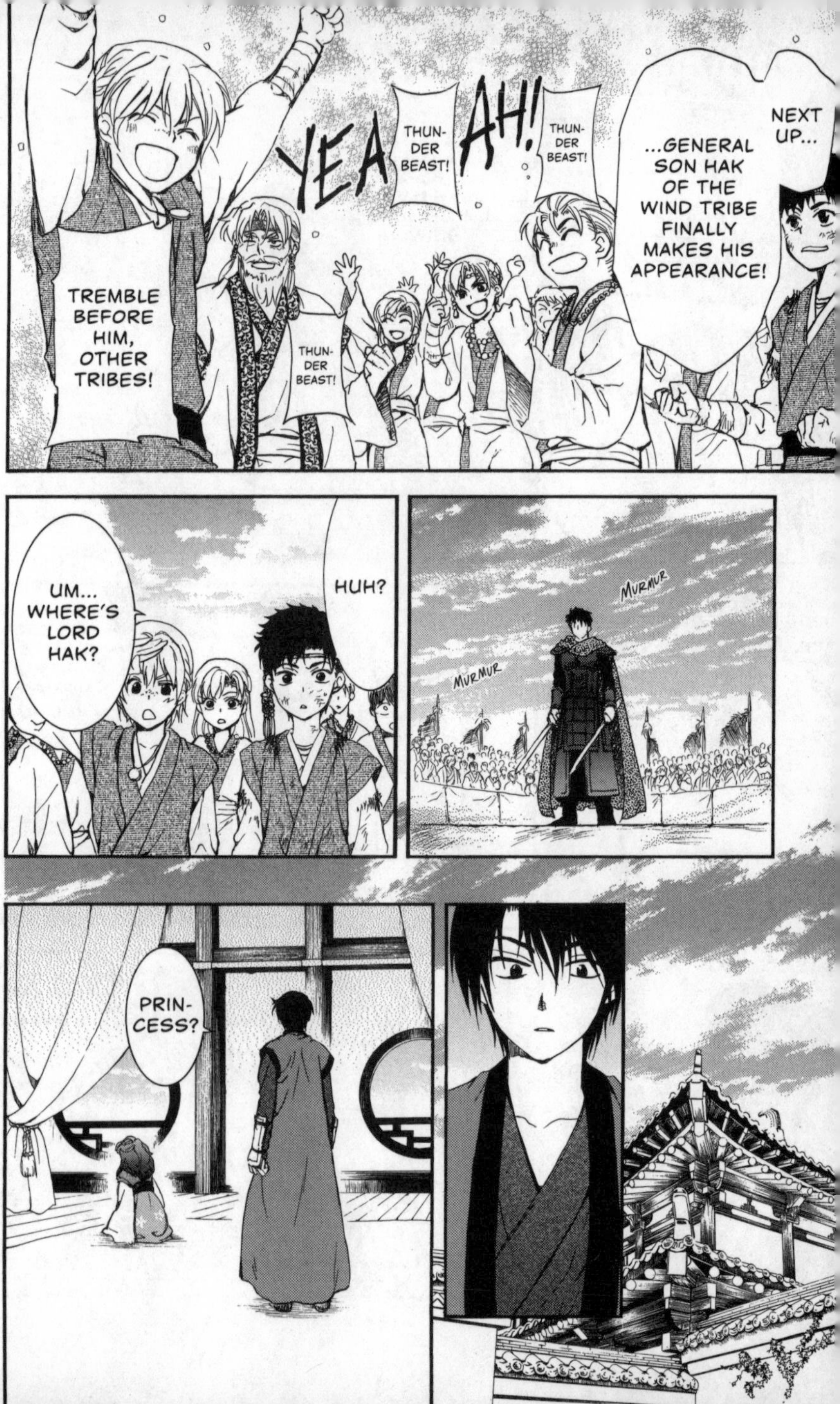
NEXT UP...
...GENERAL SON HAK OF THE WIND TRIBE FINALLY MAKES HIS APPEARANCE!
THUN-DER BEAST!
YEA AH!
THUN-DER BEAST!
THUN-DER BEAST!
TREMBLE BEFORE HIM, OTHER TRIBES!
MURMUR
MURMUR
HUH?
UM... WHERE'S LORD HAK?
PRIN-CESS?

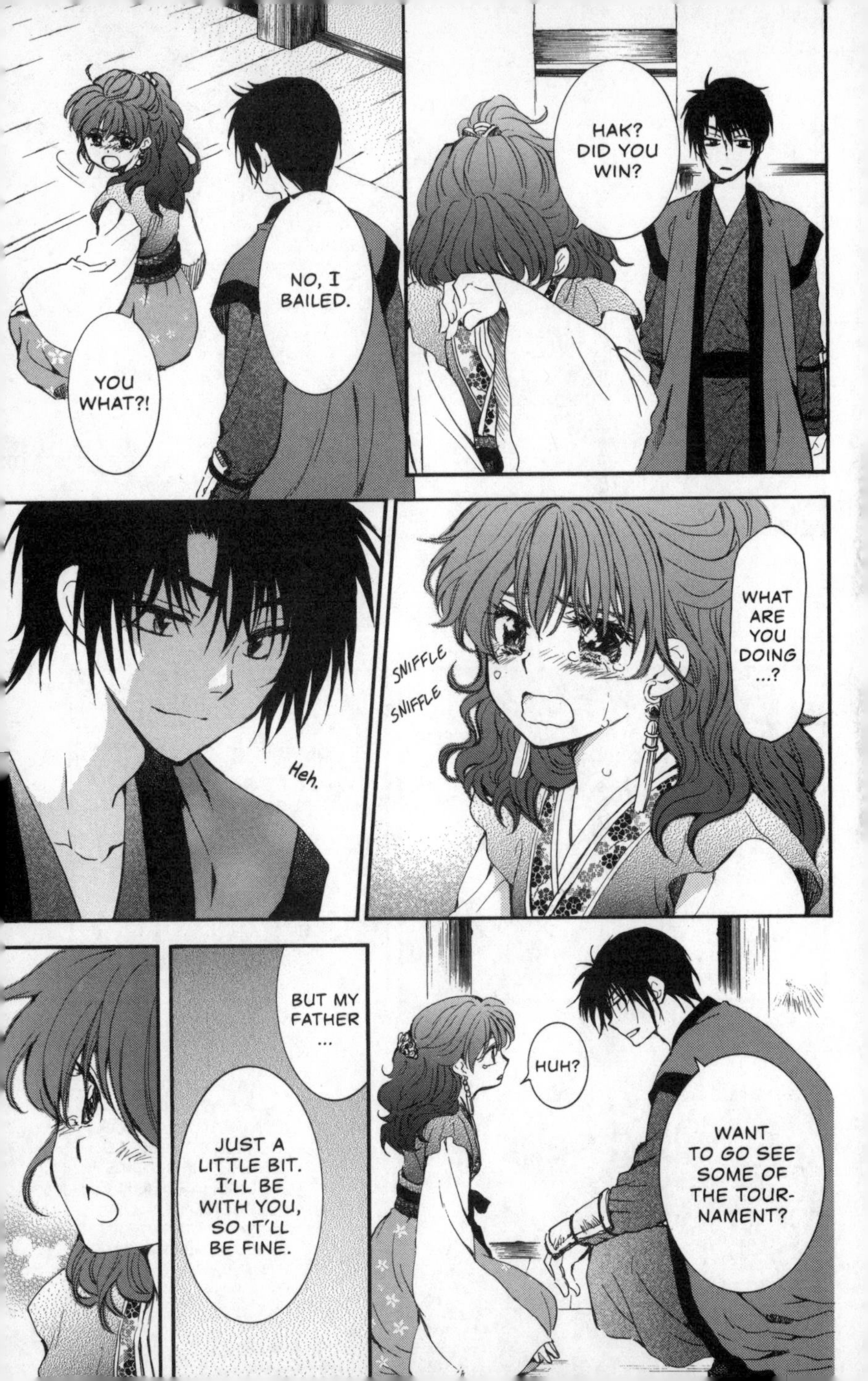
HAK? DID YOU WIN?
NO, I BAILED.
YOU WHAT?!
WHAT ARE YOU DOING ...?
SNIFFLE SNIFFLE
Heh.
WANT TO GO SEE SOME OF THE TOUR-NAMENT?
HUH?
BUT MY FATHER ...
JUST A LITTLE BIT. I'LL BE WITH YOU, SO IT'LL BE FINE.

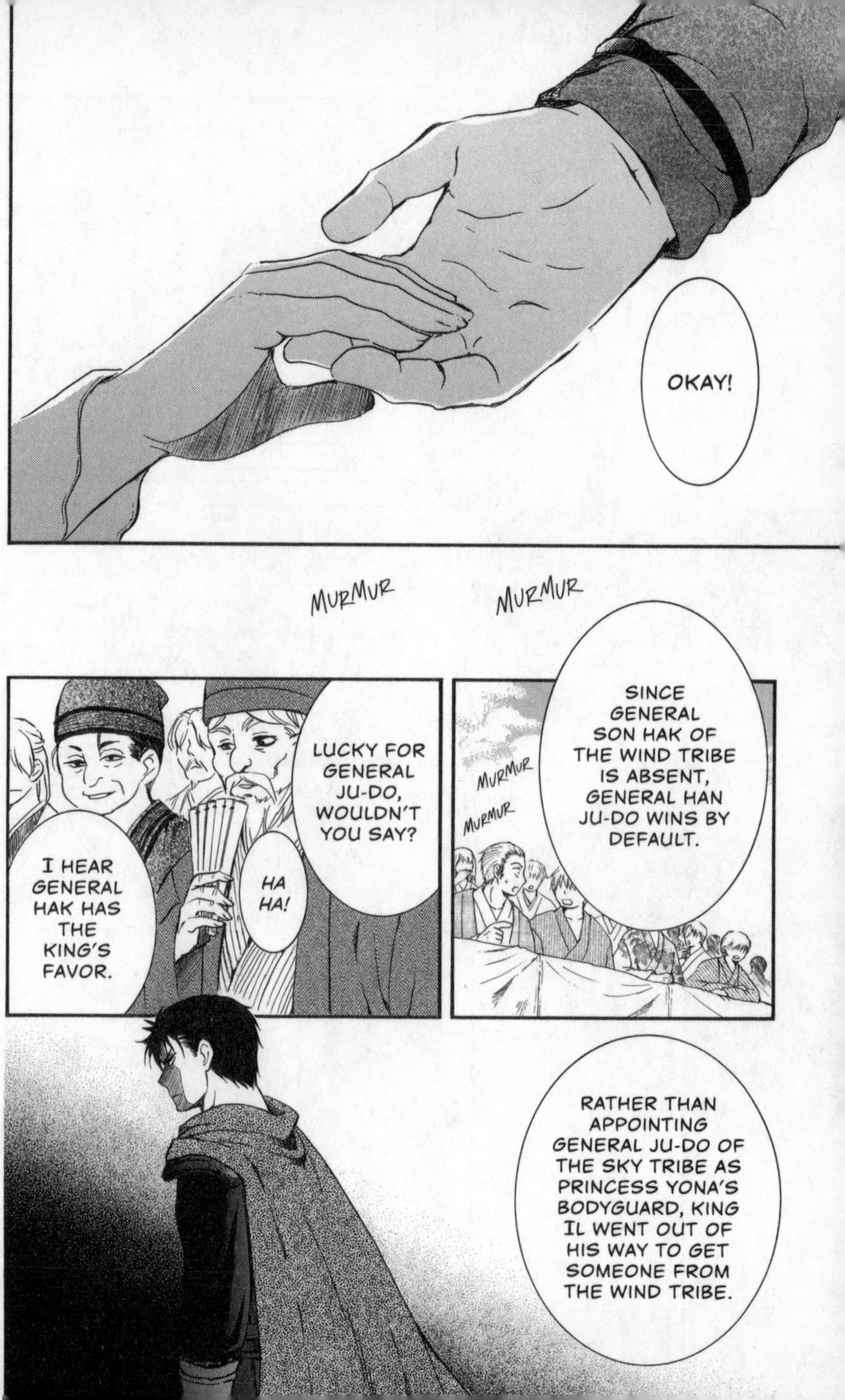
OKAY!
MURMUR
MURMUR
SINCE GENERAL SON HAK OF THE WIND TRIBE IS ABSENT, GENERAL HAN JU-DO WINS BY DEFAULT.
MURMUR
MURMUR
LUCKY FOR GENERAL JU-DO, WOULDN'T YOU SAY?
HA HA!
I HEAR GENERAL HAK HAS THE KING'S FAVOR.
RATHER THAN APPOINTING GENERAL JU-DO OF THE SKY TRIBE AS PRINCESS YONA'S BODYGUARD, KING IL WENT OUT OF HIS WAY TO GET SOMEONE FROM THE WIND TRIBE.

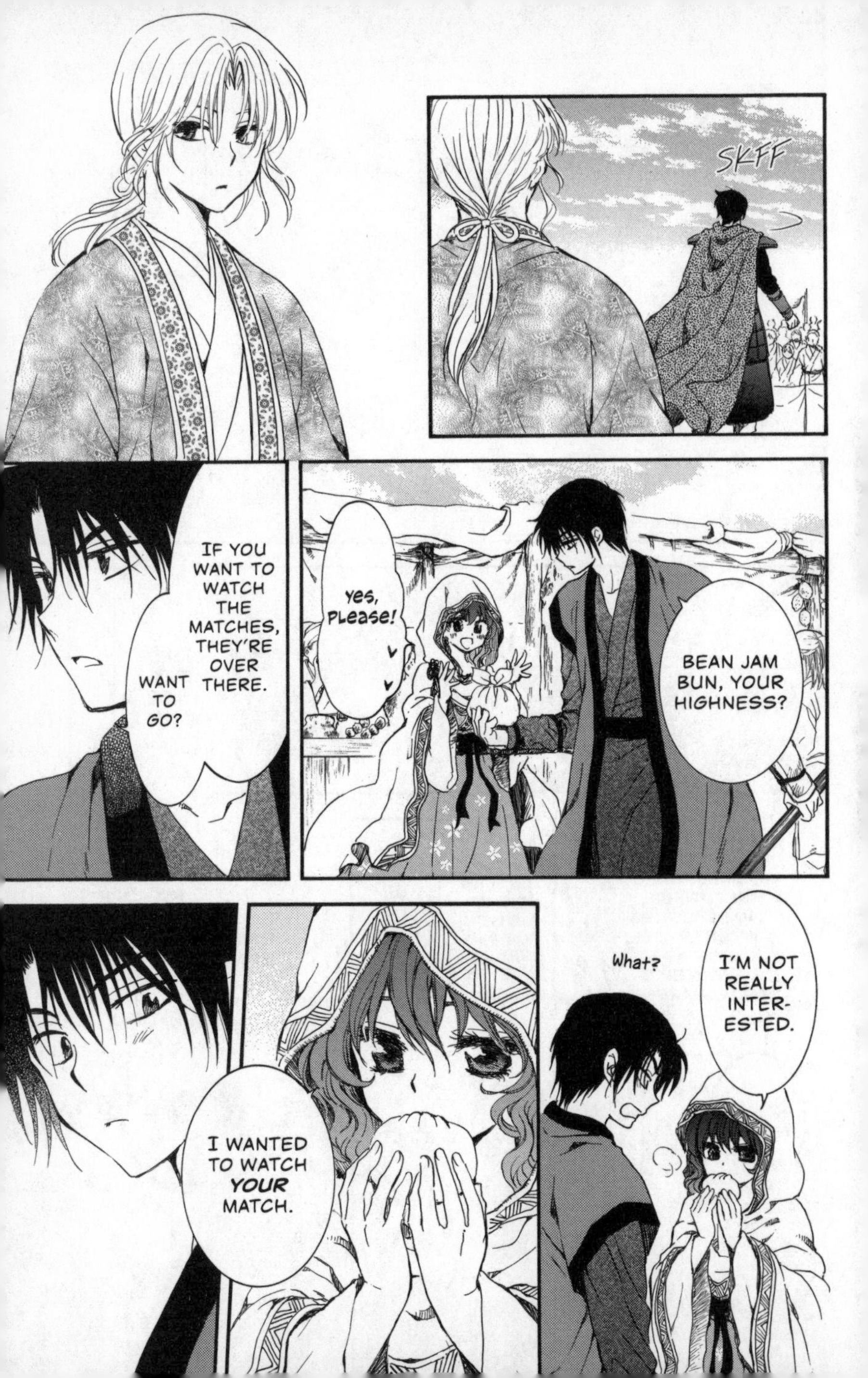
SKFF
BEAN JAM BUN, YOUR HIGHNESS?
Yes, please!
IF YOU WANT TO WATCH THE MATCHES, THEY'RE OVER THERE.
WANT TO GO?
I'M NOT REALLY INTER-ESTED.
What?
I WANTED TO WATCH YOUR MATCH.

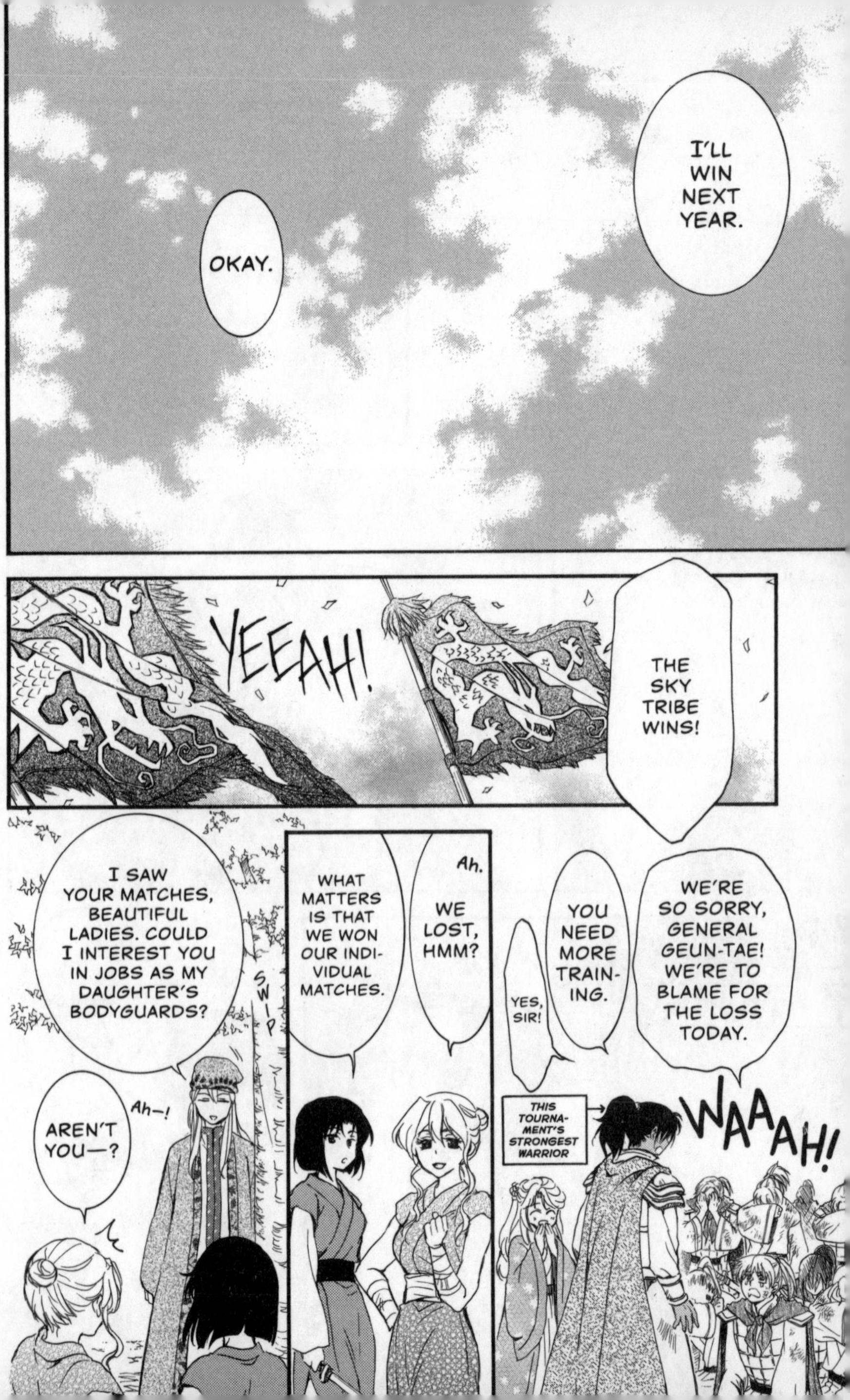
I'LL WIN NEXT YEAR.
OKAY.
THE SKY TRIBE WINS!
YEEAH!
WE'RE SO SORRY, GENERAL GEUN-TAE! WE'RE TO BLAME FOR THE LOSS TODAY.
YOU NEED MORE TRAINING.
YES, SIR!
WAAAH!
THIS TOURNAMENT'S STRONGEST WARRIOR
Ah.
WE LOST, HMM?
WHAT MATTERS IS THAT WE WON OUR INDIVIDUAL MATCHES.
I SAW YOUR MATCHES, BEAUTIFUL LADIES. COULD I INTEREST YOU IN JOBS AS MY DAUGHTER'S BODYGUARDS?
SWIP
Ah—!
AREN'T YOU—?

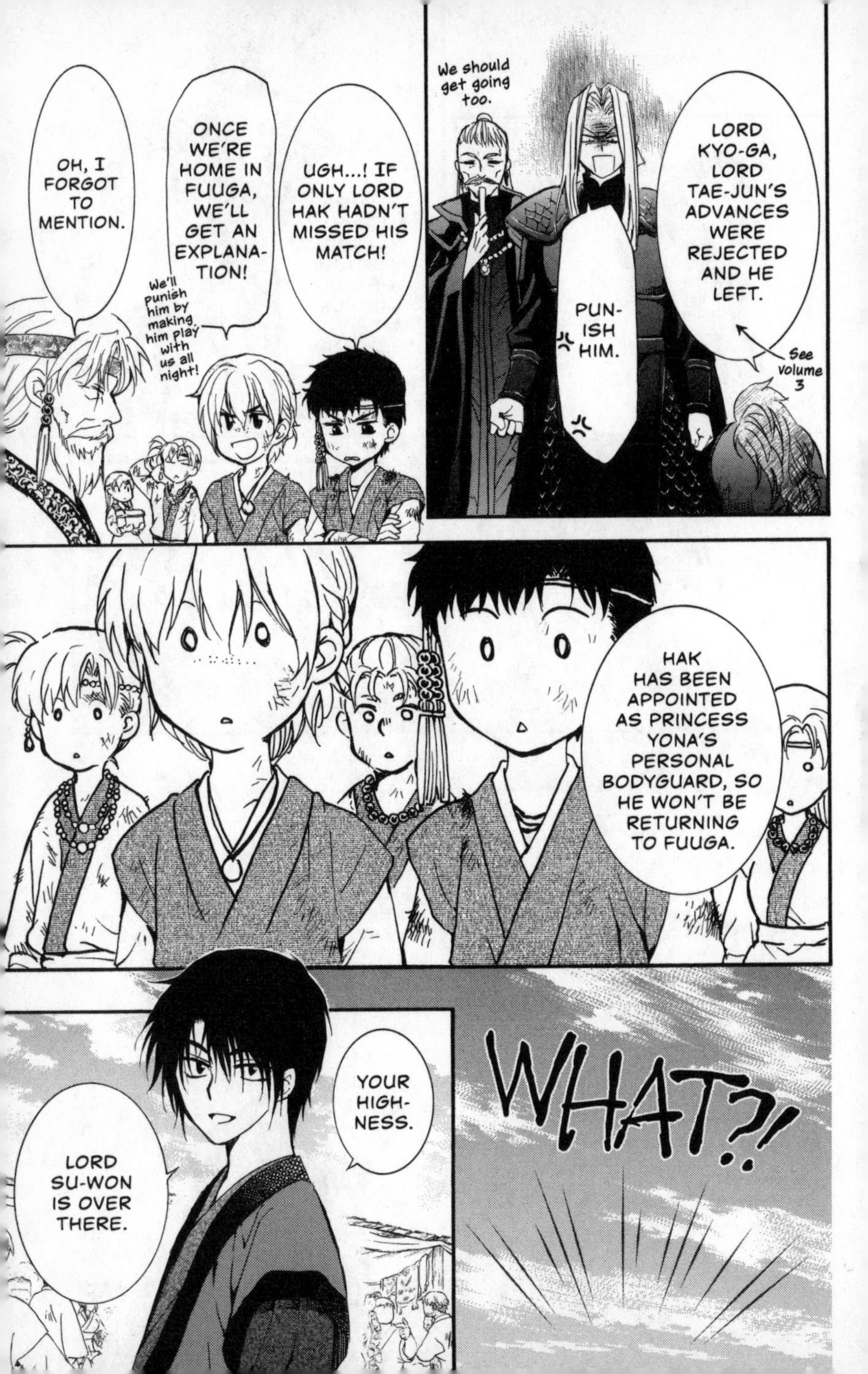
LORD KYO-GA, LORD TAE-JUN'S ADVANCES WERE REJECTED AND HE LEFT.
We should get going too.
PUN-ISH HIM.
See volume 3
UGH...! IF ONLY LORD HAK HADN'T MISSED HIS MATCH!
ONCE WE'RE HOME IN FUUGA, WE'LL GET AN EXPLANATION!
We'll punish him by making him play with us all night!
OH, I FORGOT TO MENTION.
HAK HAS BEEN APPOINTED AS PRINCESS YONA'S PERSONAL BODYGUARD, SO HE WON'T BE RETURNING TO FUUGA.
WHAT?!
YOUR HIGHNESS.
LORD SU-WON IS OVER THERE.

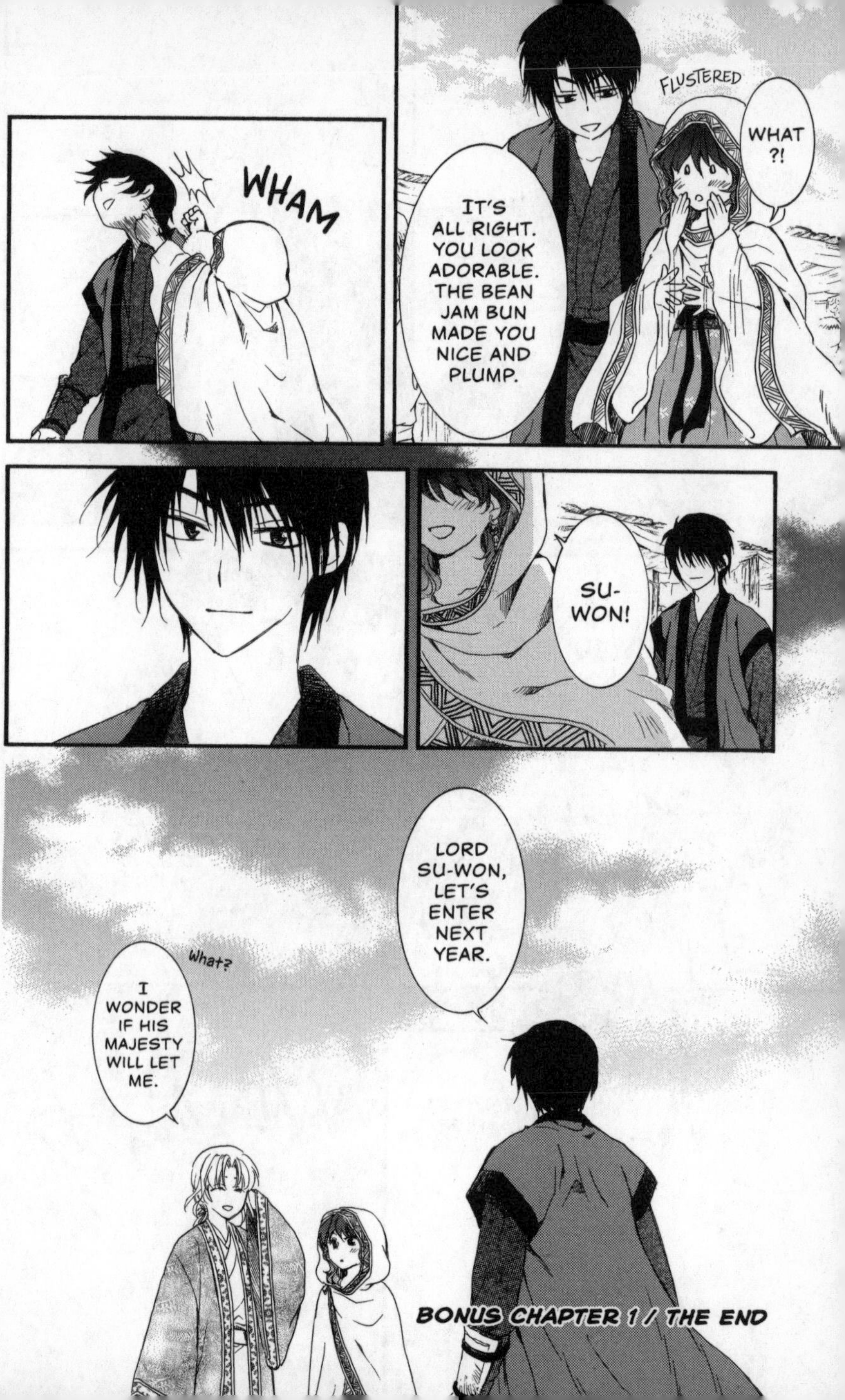
FLUSTERED
WHAT ?!
IT'S ALL RIGHT. YOU LOOK ADORABLE. THE BEAN JAM BUN MADE YOU NICE AND PLUMP.
WHAM
SU-WON!
LORD SU-WON, LET'S ENTER NEXT YEAR.
What?
I WONDER IF HIS MAJESTY WILL LET ME.
BONUS CHAPTER 1 / THE END

BONUS CHAPTER 2: TAKE CARE, PART 3

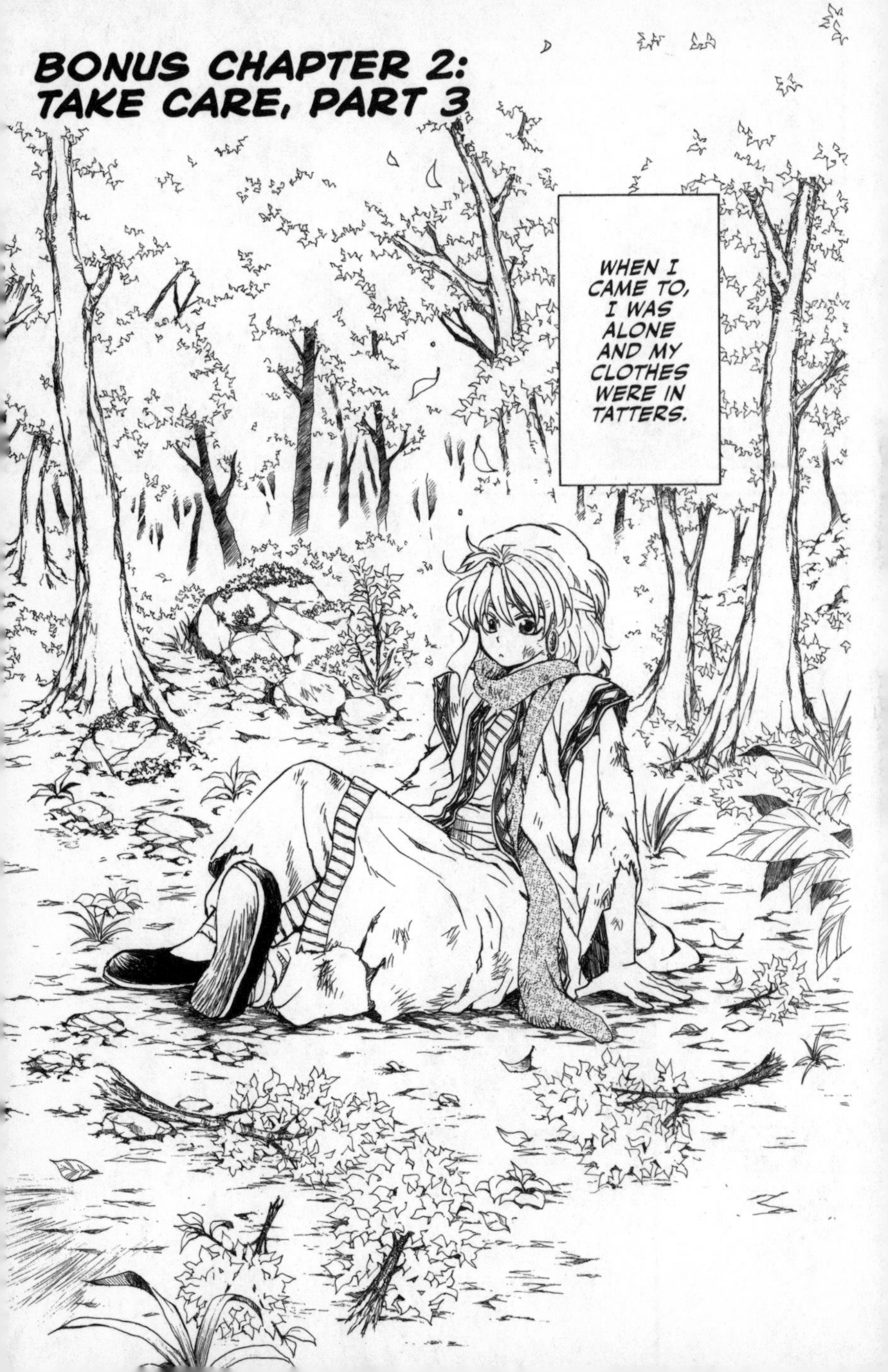
WHEN I CAME TO, I WAS ALONE AND MY CLOTHES WERE IN TATTERS.

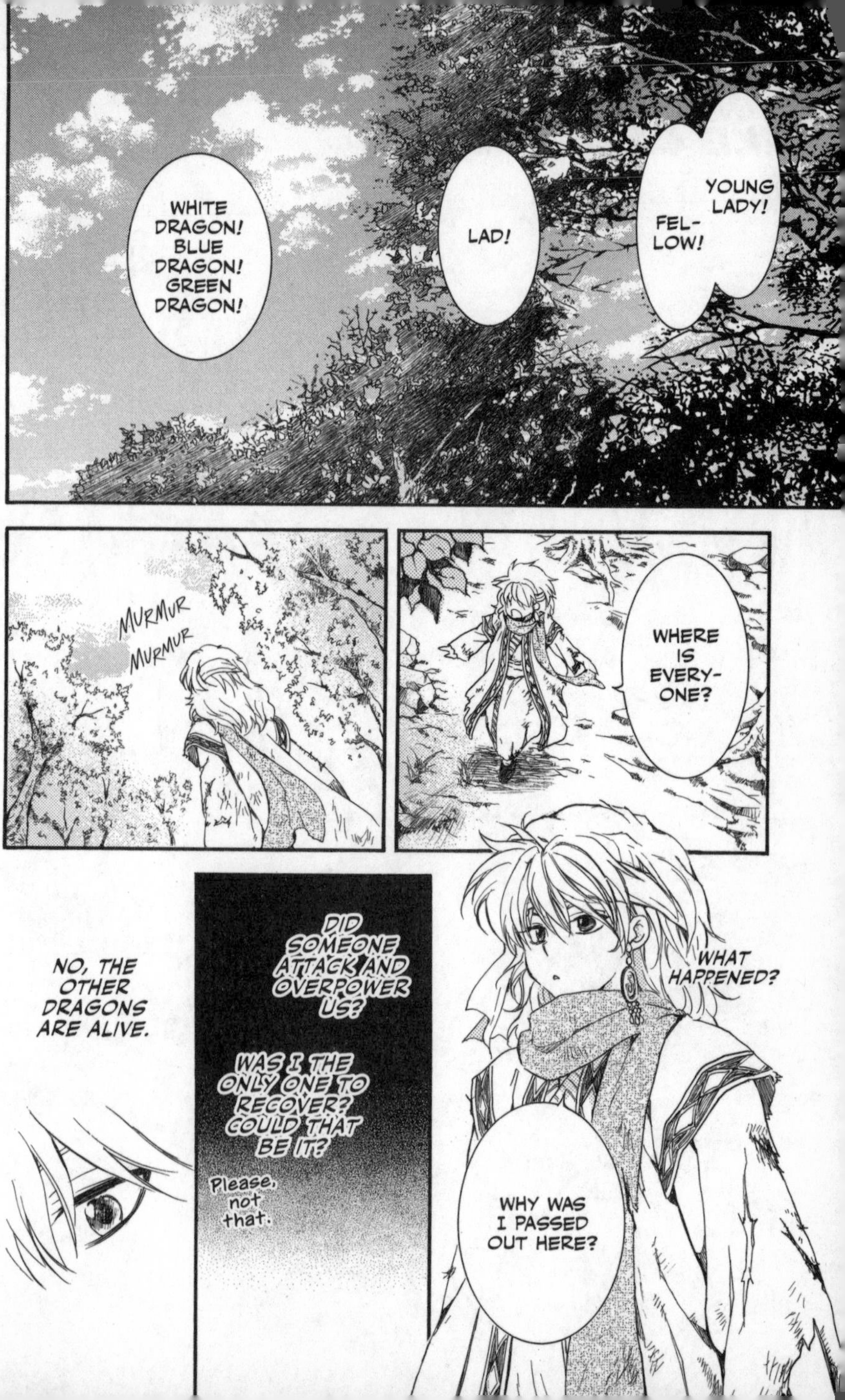
YOUNG LADY!
FEL-LOW!
LAD!
WHITE DRAGON! BLUE DRAGON! GREEN DRAGON!
WHERE IS EVERY-ONE?
MURMUR
MURMUR
WHAT HAPPENED?
WHY WAS I PASSED OUT HERE?
DID SOMEONE ATTACK AND OVERPOWER US?
WAS I THE ONLY ONE TO RECOVER? COULD THAT BE IT?
Please, not that.
NO, THE OTHER DRAGONS ARE ALIVE.

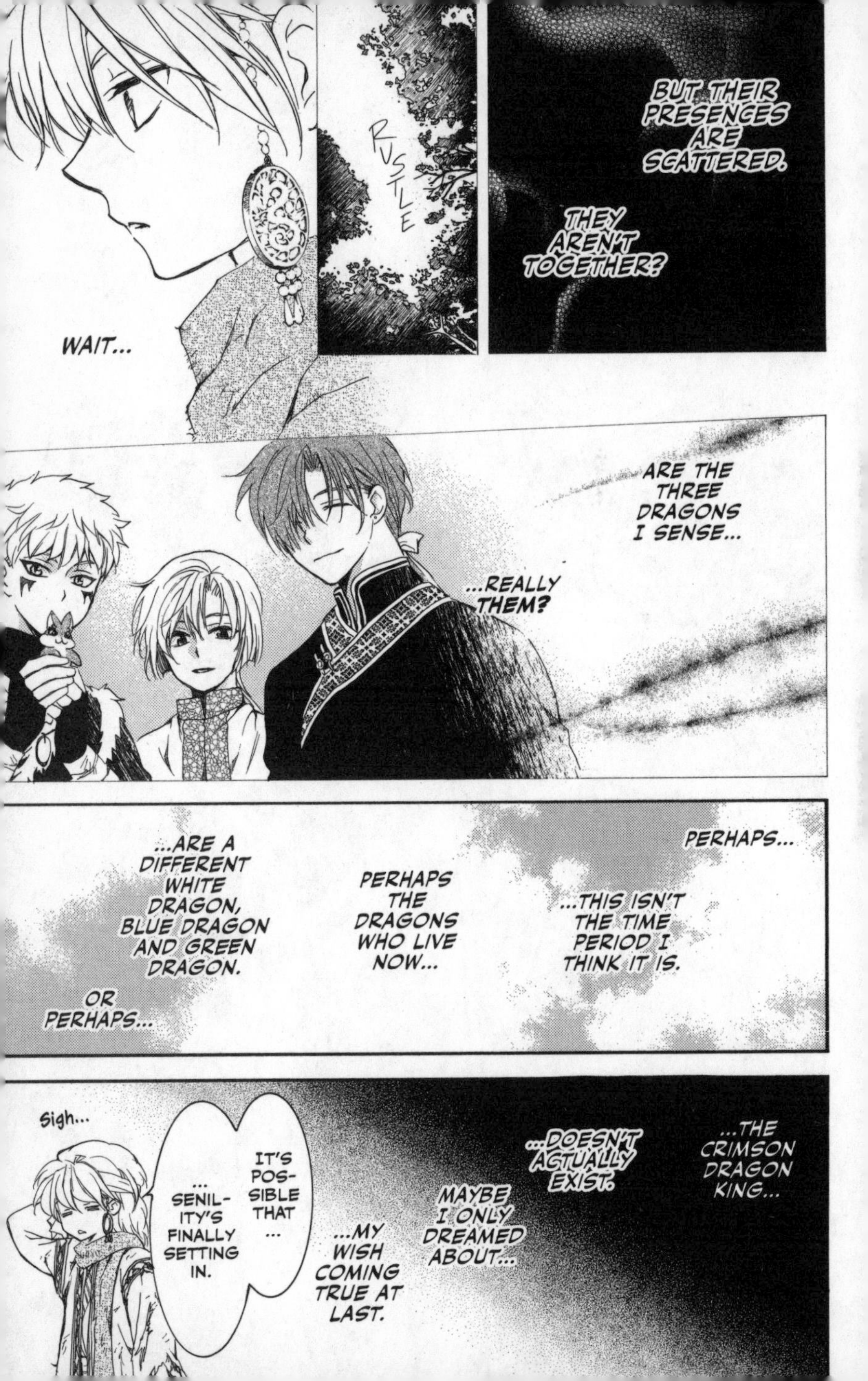
BUT THEIR PRESENCES ARE SCATTERED.
THEY AREN'T TOGETHER?
RUSTLE
WAIT...
ARE THE THREE DRAGONS I SENSE...
...REALLY THEM?
PERHAPS...
...THIS ISN'T THE TIME PERIOD I THINK IT IS.
PERHAPS THE DRAGONS WHO LIVE NOW...
...ARE A DIFFERENT WHITE DRAGON, BLUE DRAGON AND GREEN DRAGON.
OR PERHAPS...
...THE CRIMSON DRAGON KING...
...DOESN'T ACTUALLY EXIST.
MAYBE I ONLY DREAMED ABOUT...
...MY WISH COMING TRUE AT LAST.
IT'S POS-SIBLE THAT ...
... SENIL-ITY'S FINALLY SETTING IN.
Sigh...

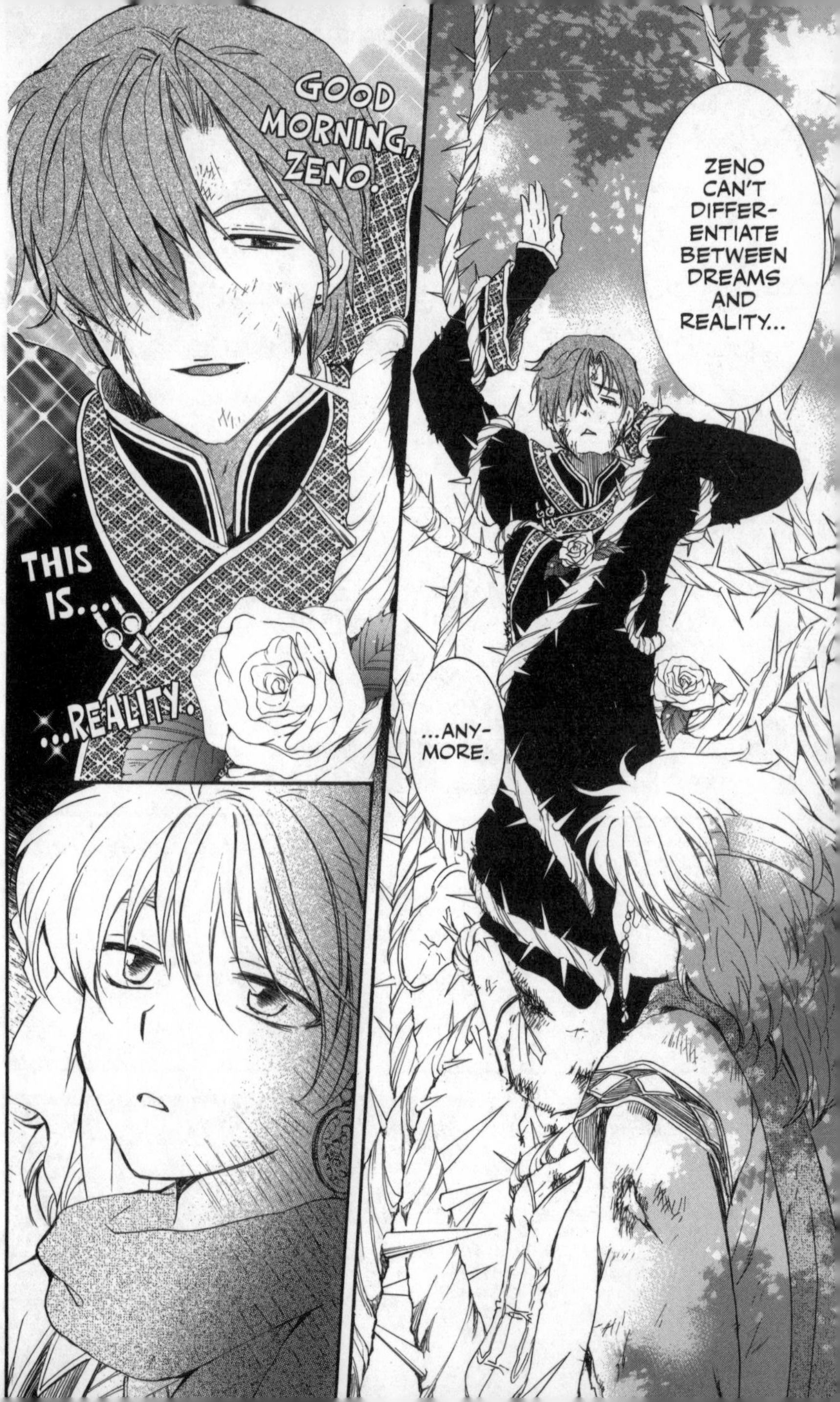
ZENO CAN'T DIFFER-ENTIATE BETWEEN DREAMS AND REALITY...
...ANY-MORE.
GOOD MORNING, ZENO.
THIS IS...
...REALITY.

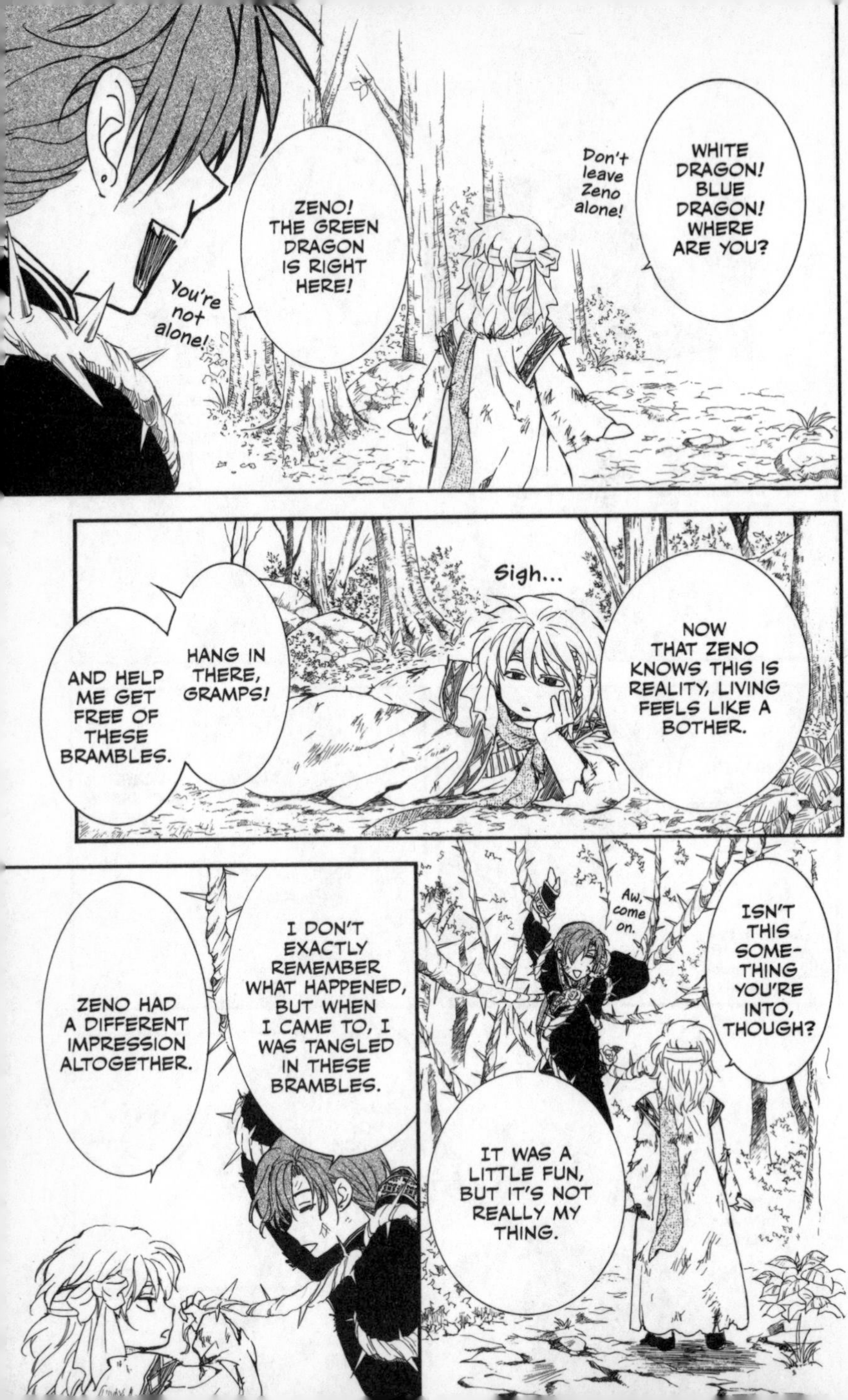
WHITE DRAGON! BLUE DRAGON! WHERE ARE YOU?
Don't leave Zeno alone!
ZENO! THE GREEN DRAGON IS RIGHT HERE!
You're not alone!
NOW THAT ZENO KNOWS THIS IS REALITY, LIVING FEELS LIKE A BOTHER.
Sigh...
HANG IN THERE, GRAMPS!
AND HELP ME GET FREE OF THESE BRAMBLES.
ISN'T THIS SOME-THING YOU'RE INTO, THOUGH?
Aw, come on.
I DON'T EXACTLY REMEMBER WHAT HAPPENED, BUT WHEN I CAME TO, I WAS TANGLED IN THESE BRAMBLES.
IT WAS A LITTLE FUN, BUT IT'S NOT REALLY MY THING.
ZENO HAD A DIFFERENT IMPRESSION ALTOGETHER.

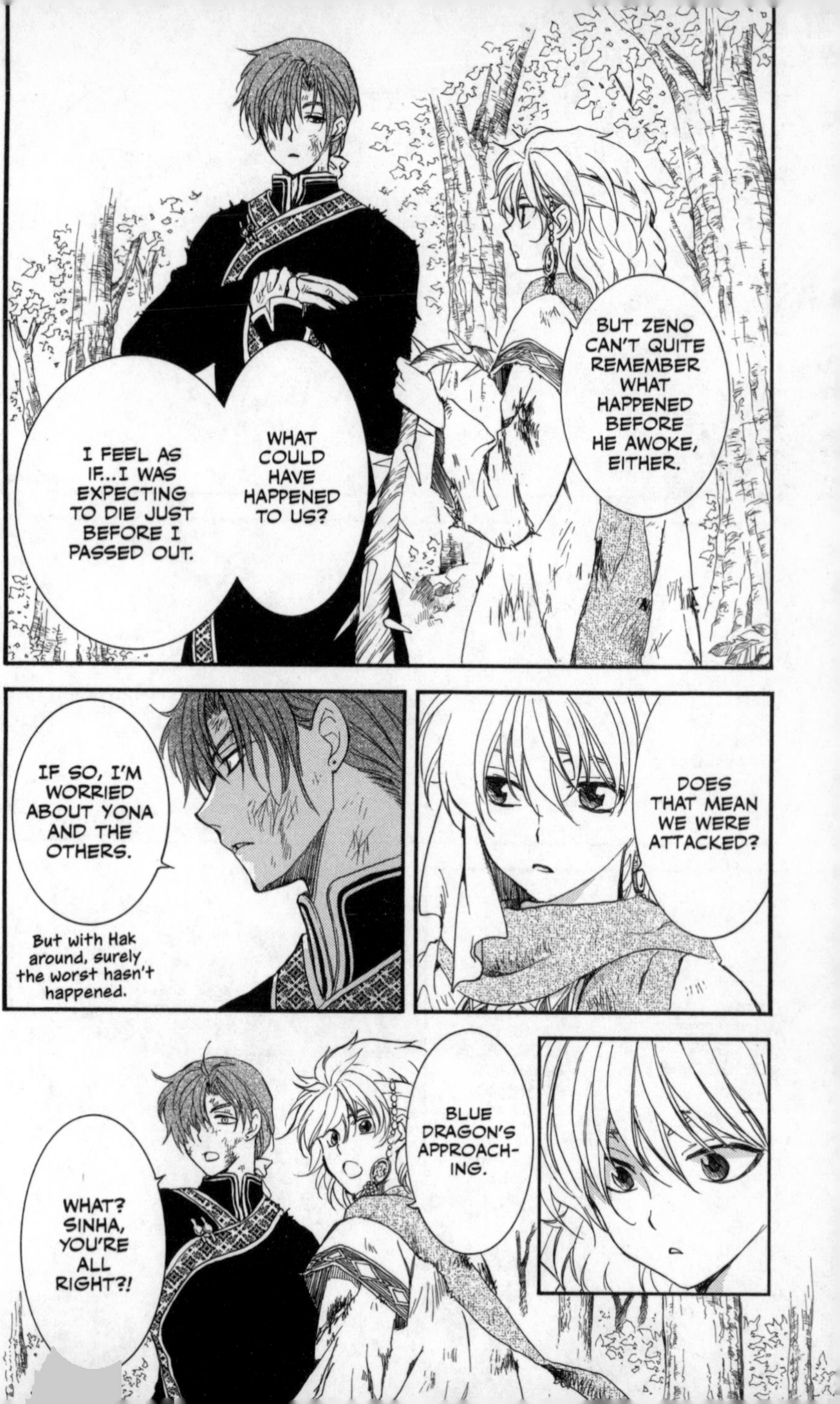
BUT ZENO CAN'T QUITE REMEMBER WHAT HAPPENED BEFORE HE AWOKE, EITHER.
WHAT COULD HAVE HAPPENED TO US?
I FEEL AS IF...I WAS EXPECTING TO DIE JUST BEFORE I PASSED OUT.
DOES THAT MEAN WE WERE ATTACKED?
IF SO, I'M WORRIED ABOUT YONA AND THE OTHERS.
But with Hak around, surely the worst hasn't happened.
BLUE DRAGON'S APPROACH-ING.
WHAT? SINHA, YOU'RE ALL RIGHT?!

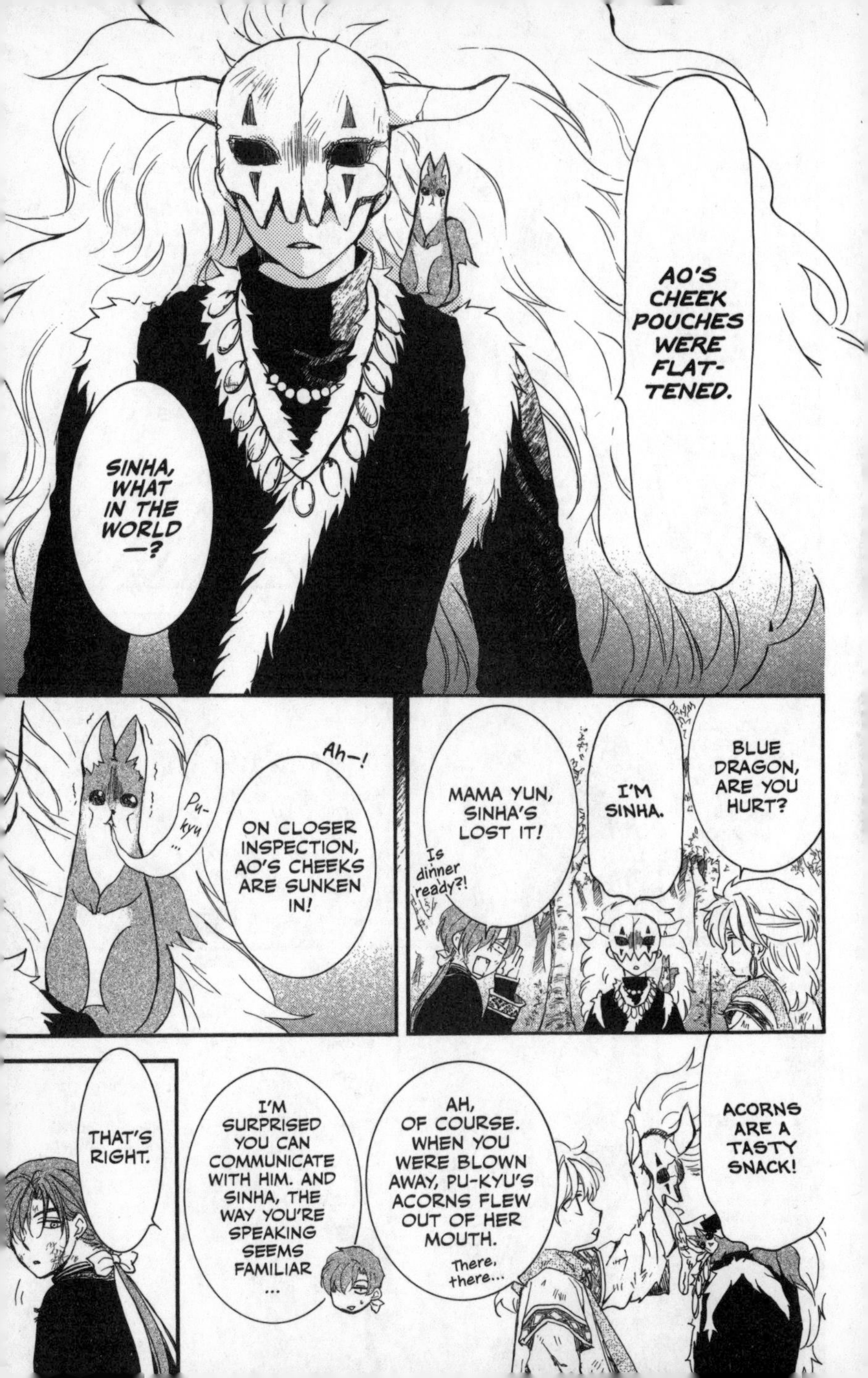
AO'S CHEEK POUCHES WERE FLAT-TENED.
SINHA, WHAT IN THE WORLD—?
BLUE DRAGON, ARE YOU HURT?
I'M SINHA.
MAMA YUN, SINHA'S LOST IT!
Is dinner ready?!
Ah—!
ON CLOSER INSPECTION, AO'S CHEEKS ARE SUNKEN IN!
Pu-kyu...
ACORNS ARE A TASTY SNACK!
AH, OF COURSE. WHEN YOU WERE BLOWN AWAY, PU-KYU'S ACORNS FLEW OUT OF HER MOUTH.
There, there...
I'M SURPRISED YOU CAN COMMUNICATE WITH HIM. AND SINHA, THE WAY YOU'RE SPEAKING SEEMS FAMILIAR...
THAT'S RIGHT.

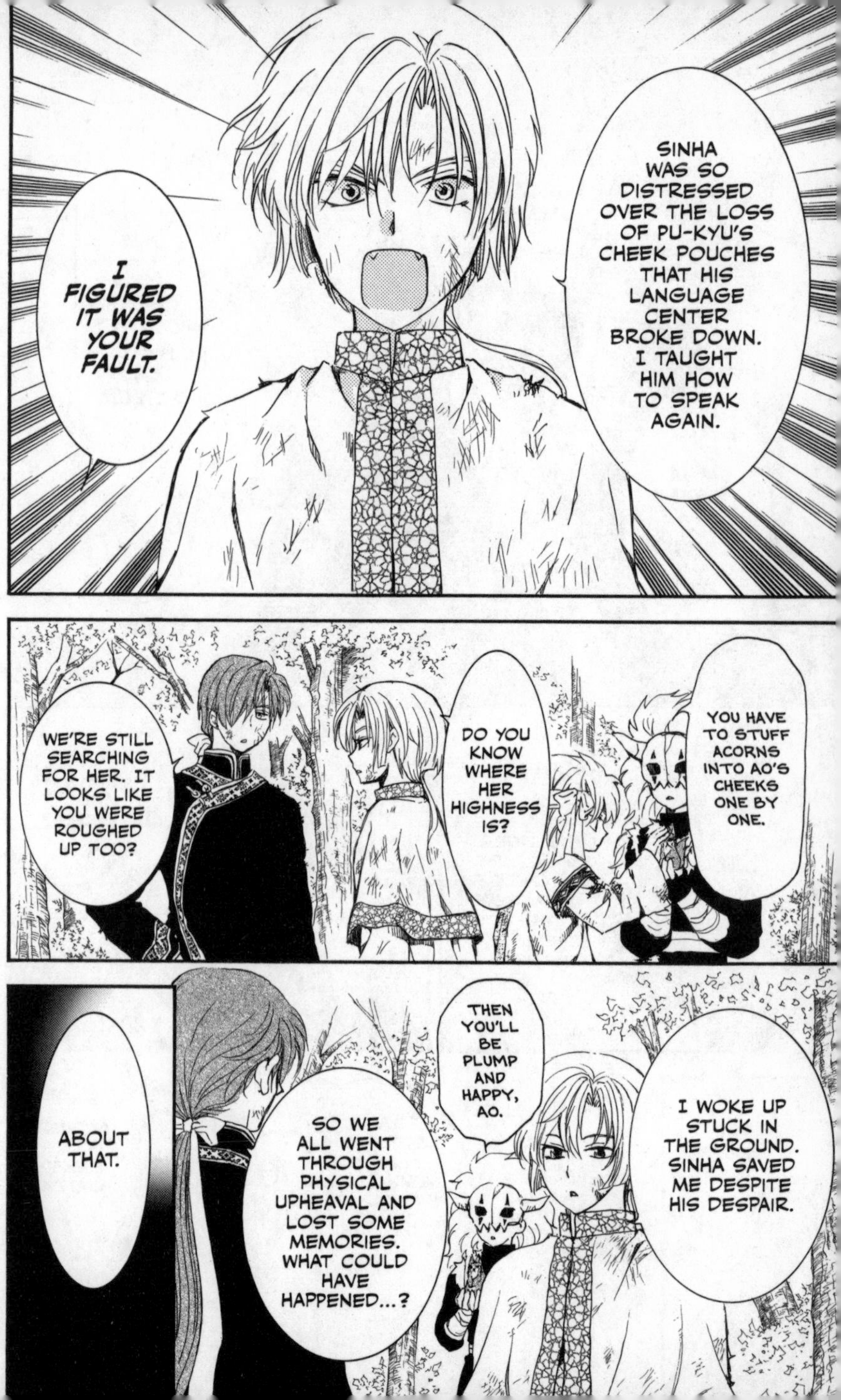
SINHA WAS SO DISTRESSED OVER THE LOSS OF PU-KYU'S CHEEK POUCHES THAT HIS LANGUAGE CENTER BROKE DOWN. I TAUGHT HIM HOW TO SPEAK AGAIN.
I FIGURED IT WAS YOUR FAULT.
YOU HAVE TO STUFF ACORNS INTO AO'S CHEEKS ONE BY ONE.
DO YOU KNOW WHERE HER HIGHNESS IS?
WE'RE STILL SEARCHING FOR HER. IT LOOKS LIKE YOU WERE ROUGHED UP TOO?
I WOKE UP STUCK IN THE GROUND. SINHA SAVED ME DESPITE HIS DESPAIR.
THEN YOU'LL BE PLUMP AND HAPPY, AO.
SO WE ALL WENT THROUGH PHYSICAL UPHEAVAL AND LOST SOME MEMORIES. WHAT COULD HAVE HAPPENED...?
ABOUT THAT.

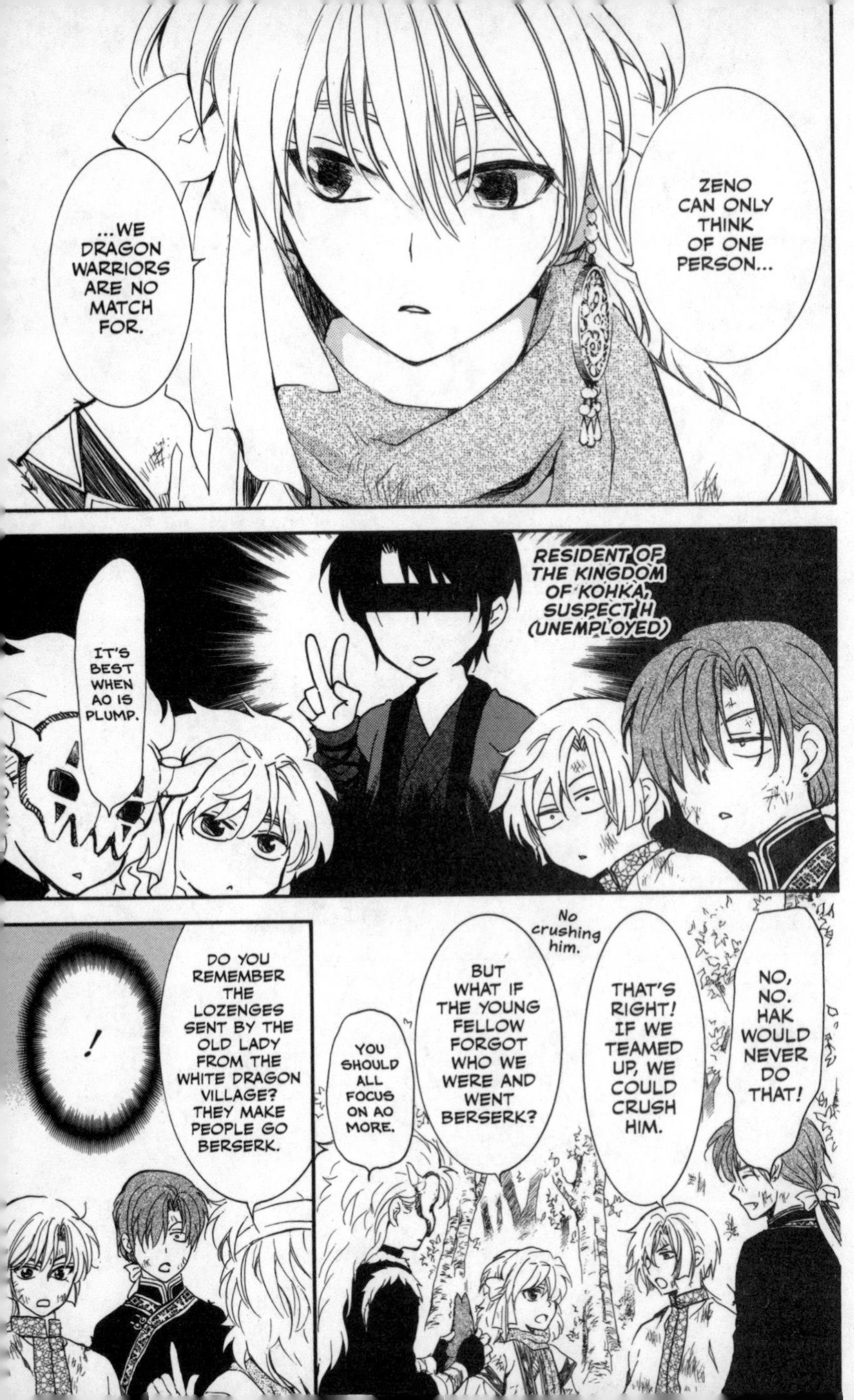
ZENO CAN ONLY THINK OF ONE PERSON...
...WE DRAGON WARRIORS ARE NO MATCH FOR.
RESIDENT OF THE KINGDOM OF KOHKA, SUSPECT H (UNEMPLOYED)
IT'S BEST WHEN AO IS PLUMP.
NO, NO. HAK WOULD NEVER DO THAT!
THAT'S RIGHT! IF WE TEAMED UP, WE COULD CRUSH HIM.
No crushing him.
BUT WHAT IF THE YOUNG FELLOW FORGOT WHO WE WERE AND WENT BERSERK?
YOU SHOULD ALL FOCUS ON AO MORE.
DO YOU REMEMBER THE LOZENGES SENT BY THE OLD LADY FROM THE WHITE DRAGON VILLAGE? THEY MAKE PEOPLE GO BERSERK.
!

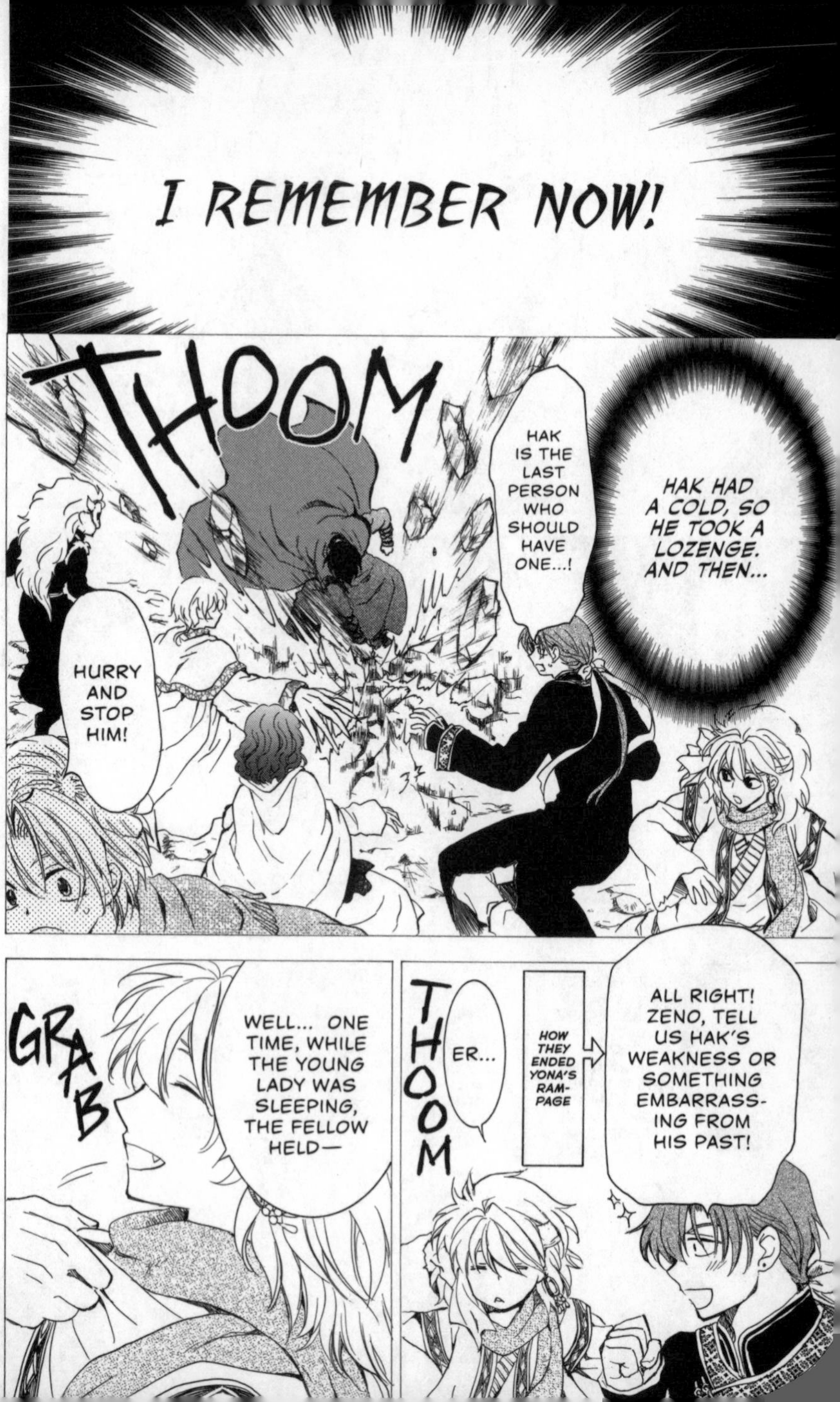
I REMEMBER NOW!
HAK HAD A COLD, SO HE TOOK A LOZENGE. AND THEN...
HAK IS THE LAST PERSON WHO SHOULD HAVE ONE...!
THOOM
HURRY AND STOP HIM!
ALL RIGHT! ZENO, TELL US HAK'S WEAKNESS OR SOMETHING EMBARRASSING FROM HIS PAST!
HOW THEY ENDED YONA'S RAMPAGE
ER...
THOOM
WELL... ONE TIME, WHILE THE YOUNG LADY WAS SLEEPING, THE FELLOW HELD—
GRAB

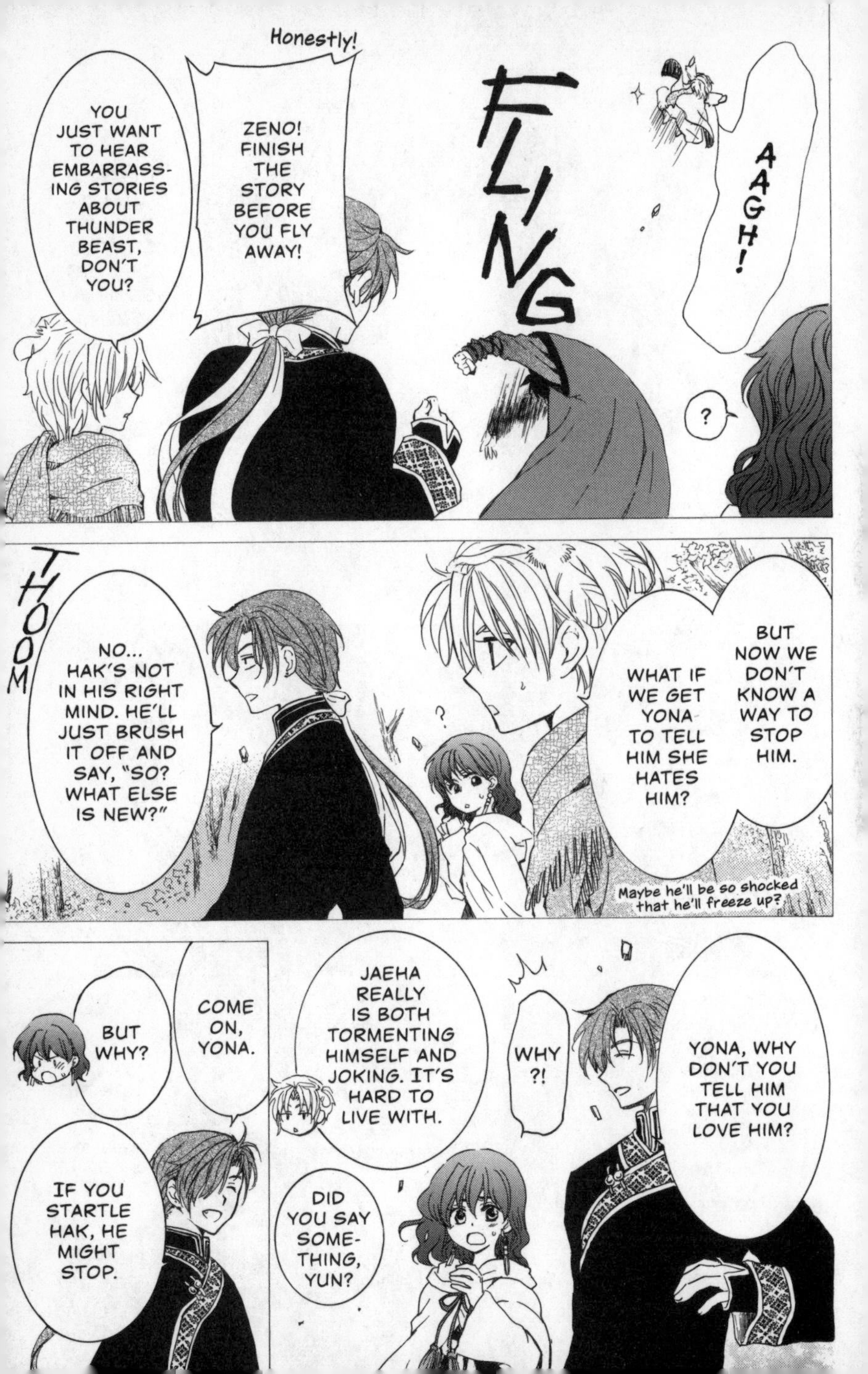
AAGH!
FLING
?
Honestly!
ZENO! FINISH THE STORY BEFORE YOU FLY AWAY!
YOU JUST WANT TO HEAR EMBARRASSING STORIES ABOUT THUNDER BEAST, DON'T YOU?
BUT NOW WE DON'T KNOW A WAY TO STOP HIM.
WHAT IF WE GET YONA TO TELL HIM SHE HATES HIM?
Maybe he'll be so shocked that he'll freeze up?
?
NO... HAK'S NOT IN HIS RIGHT MIND. HE'LL JUST BRUSH IT OFF AND SAY, "SO? WHAT ELSE IS NEW?"
THOOM
YONA, WHY DON'T YOU TELL HIM THAT YOU LOVE HIM?
WHY?!
JAEHA REALLY IS BOTH TORMENTING HIMSELF AND JOKING. IT'S HARD TO LIVE WITH.
DID YOU SAY SOMETHING, YUN?
COME ON, YONA.
BUT WHY?
IF YOU STARTLE HAK, HE MIGHT STOP.

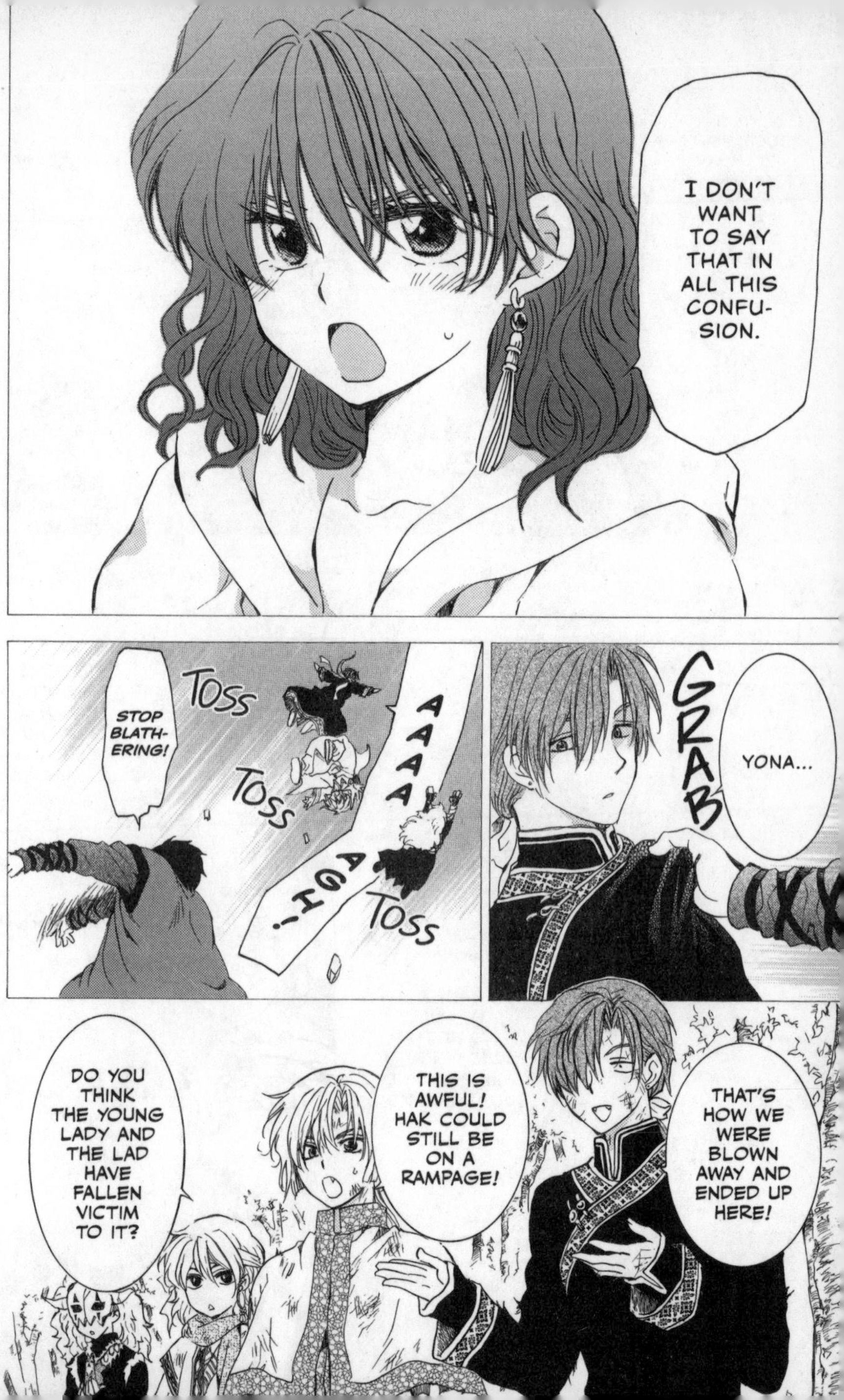
I DON'T WANT TO SAY THAT IN ALL THIS CONFU-SION.
GRAB
YONA...
STOP BLATH-ERING!
TOSS
AAAAAGH!-
TOSS
TOSS
THAT'S HOW WE WERE BLOWN AWAY AND ENDED UP HERE!
THIS IS AWFUL! HAK COULD STILL BE ON A RAMPAGE!
DO YOU THINK THE YOUNG LADY AND THE LAD HAVE FALLEN VICTIM TO IT?

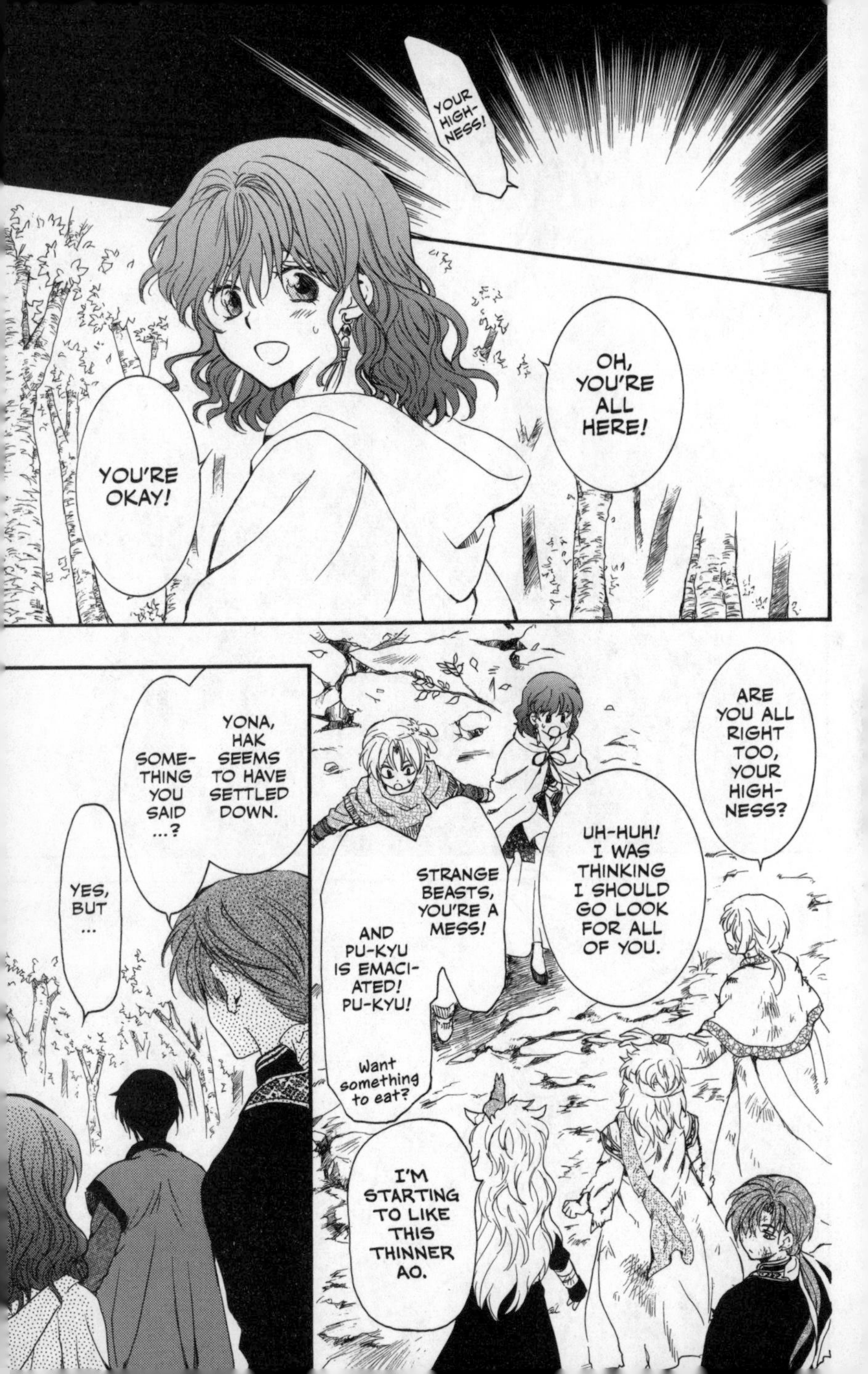
YOUR HIGH-NESS!
OH, YOU'RE ALL HERE!
YOU'RE OKAY!
ARE YOU ALL RIGHT TOO, YOUR HIGH-NESS?
UH-HUH! I WAS THINKING I SHOULD GO LOOK FOR ALL OF YOU.
STRANGE BEASTS, YOU'RE A MESS!
AND PU-KYU IS EMACI-ATED! PU-KYU!
Want something to eat?
I'M STARTING TO LIKE THIS THINNER AO.
YONA, HAK SEEMS TO HAVE SETTLED DOWN.
SOME-THING YOU SAID ...?
YES, BUT ...

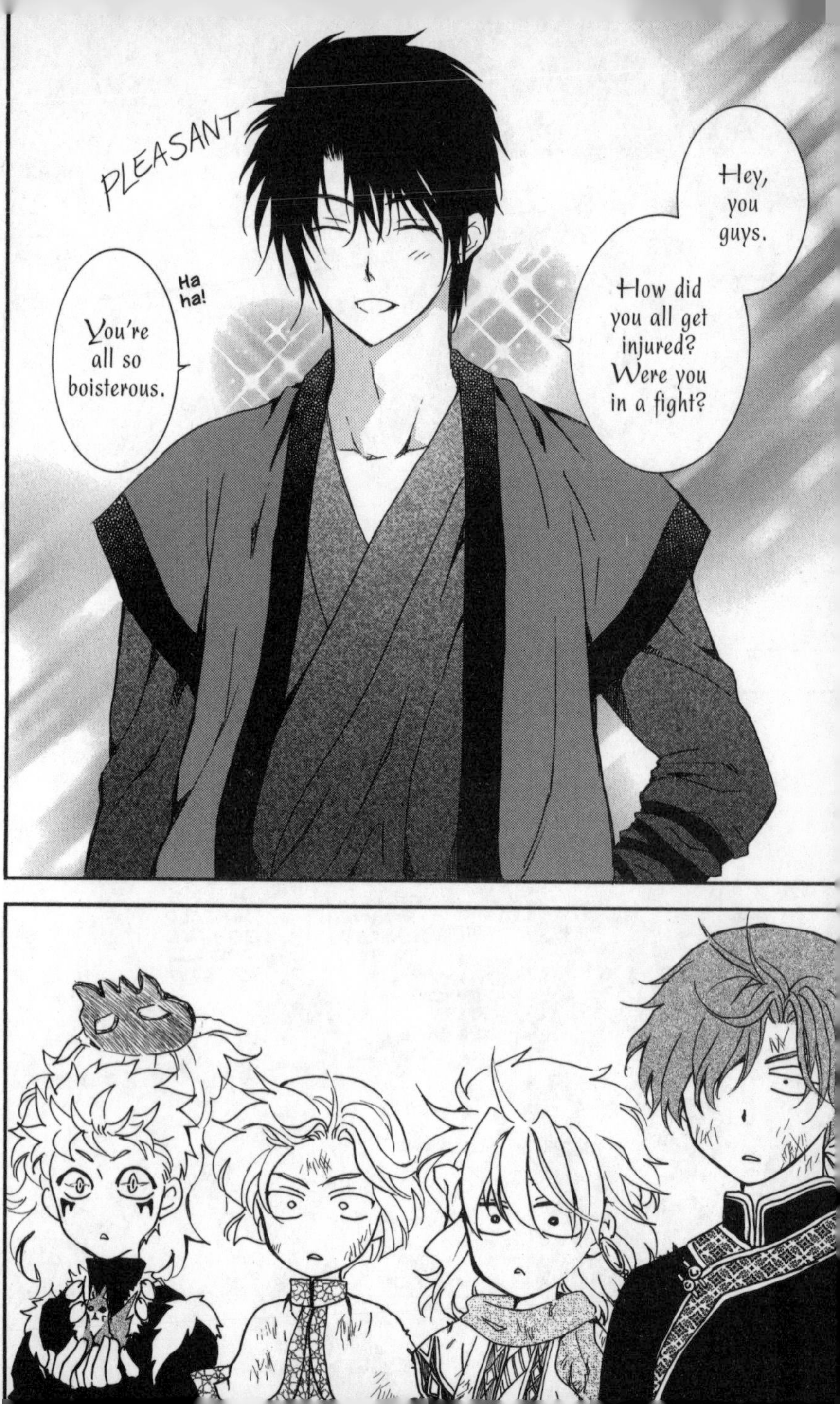
Hey, you guys.
How did you all get injured? Were you in a fight?
PLEASANT
Ha ha!
You're all so boisterous.

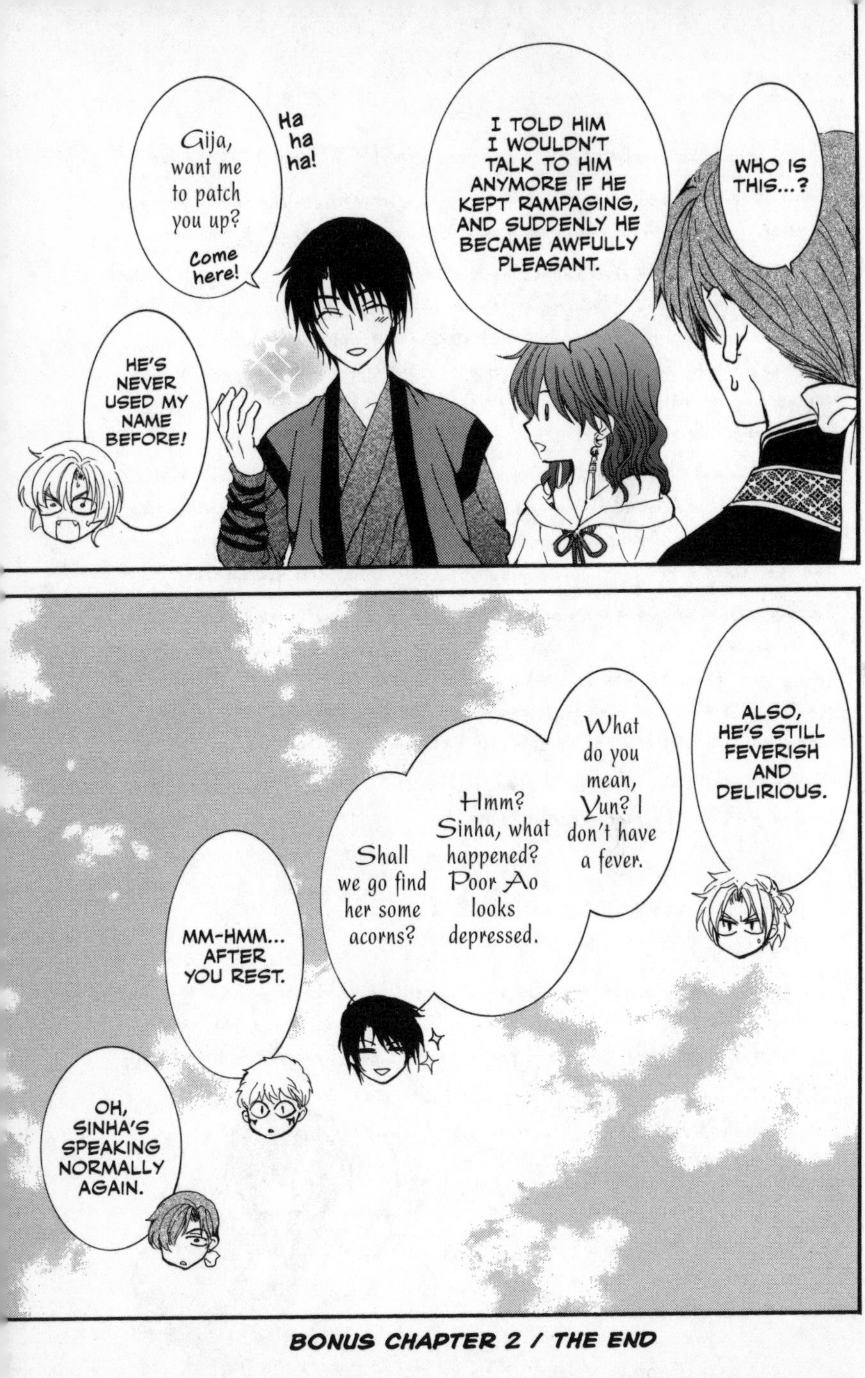
WHO IS THIS...?
I TOLD HIM I WOULDN'T TALK TO HIM ANYMORE IF HE KEPT RAMPAGING, AND SUDDENLY HE BECAME AWFULLY PLEASANT.
Ha ha ha!
Gija, want me to patch you up?
Come here!
HE'S NEVER USED MY NAME BEFORE!
ALSO, HE'S STILL FEVERISH AND DELIRIOUS.
What do you mean, Yun? I don't have a fever.
Hmm? Sinha, what happened? Poor Ao looks depressed.
Shall we go find her some acorns?
MM-HMM... AFTER YOU REST.
OH, SINHA'S SPEAKING NORMALLY AGAIN.

BONUS CHAPTER 2 / THE END

Afterword

"The Intertribe Martial Arts Tournament (Just This Once)" Addendum

I was wondering what to draw for a bonus chapter and decided on this story. However, I didn't have enough pages, so it was tricky to put it all together.

This story takes place several days after chapter 3, "Hidden Strength." In that chapter, Grandpa and Hak come to Hiryuu Palace for the Five-Tribe Council. The other tribe chiefs stay at Hiryuu Palace for a while... → There's some incident involving Tae-jun... → Hak becomes Yona's personal bodyguard as well as a general... → Tae-u and the others come to Hiryuu Palace for the martial arts tournament. Something like that.

The martial arts tournament is held once a year as public entertainment, but Il isn't very enthusiastic about it and frequently makes changes to the rules. An age limit was added and participation became restricted to certain individuals. Tae-u and the others didn't participate in subsequent martial arts tournaments.

If Hak hadn't become Yona's personal bodyguard, I think he would have shown up for his match with Ju-do. Until then, he had distanced himself from the royal family and Yona, but now he'd made up his mind to face them. He thought that staying by Yona's side is what Il would have wanted. When Hak decides to do something, he sticks to it, so he didn't go back to Fuuga for three years.

Overall, it was a fun chapter to draw, but what I liked best was drawing Su-jin, Jung-gi and a younger Ayura and Tetra.

"Take Care, Part 3"

As usual, creating storyboards for such unpredictable stories takes a long time. I pretty much wrote this to get Zeno and Sinha to talk. In the drama CD, the cast was able to re-create it perfectly, so I encourage you to listen to it!

Side note: I finished the storyboard and final art pages at the same time as chapter 157, so it was quite hectic.

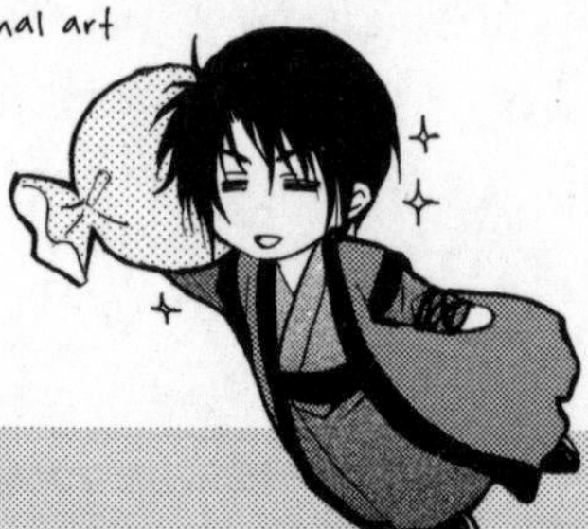

Hak and Jaeha are on the cover. Hak is like an older brother amongst the members of the Wind Tribe. He'll never admit it, but Hak now sees Jaeha and Gija as older brothers around whom he can be a bit vulnerable.

—Mizuho Kusanagi

Born on February 3 in Kumamoto Prefecture in Japan, Mizuho Kusanagi began her professional manga career with *Yoiko no Kokoroe* (The Rules of a Good Child) in 2003. Her other works include *NG Life*, which was serialized in *Hana to Yume* and *The Hana to Yume* magazines and published by Hakusensha in Japan. *Yona of the Dawn* was adapted into an anime in 2014.

YONA OF THE DAWN
VOL.27
Shojo Beat Edition

STORY AND ART BY
MIZUHO KUSANAGI

English Adaptation/Ysabet Reinhardt MacFarlane
Translation/JN Productions
Touch-Up Art & Lettering/Lys Blakeslee
Design/Philana Chen
Editor/Amy Yu

Akatsuki no Yona by Mizuho Kusanagi
© Mizuho Kusanagi 2018
All rights reserved.
First published in Japan in 2018 by HAKUSENSHA, Inc., Tokyo.
English language translation rights arranged with
HAKUSENSHA, Inc., Tokyo.

The stories, characters and incidents mentioned in this publication
are entirely fictional.

Printed in the U.S.A.

Published by VIZ Media, LLC
P.O. Box 77010
San Francisco, CA 94107

10 9 8 7 6 5 4 3 2 1
First printing, December 2020

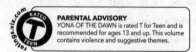

viz.com   shojobeat.com